Britannia Airways

The Story of the United Kingdom's Largest Holiday Airline

Graham M Simons

AIR WORLD

Britannia Airways
The Story of the United Kingdom's Largest Holiday Airline

First published in Great Britain in 2020 by Air World Books,
an imprint of Pen & Sword Books Ltd,
Yorkshire - Philadelphia

Typeset in 9pt Times by GMS Enterprises
Printed and bound in India by Replika Press Pvt Ltd

Pen & Sword Books Ltd incorporates the imprints of Air World Books, Pen & Sword Archaeology, Atlas, Aviation, Battleground, Discovery, Family History, History, Maritime, Military, Naval, Politics, Social History, Transport, True Crime, Claymore Press, Frontline Books, Praetorian Press, Seaforth Publishing and White Owl.

For a complete list of Pen & Sword titles please contact:

PEN & SWORD BOOKS LTD
47 Church Street, Barnsley, South Yorkshire, S70 2AS, UK.
E-mail: enquiries@pen-and-sword.co.uk
Website: www.pen-and-sword.co.uk

Or

PEN AND SWORD BOOKS,
1950 Lawrence Road, Havertown, PA 19083, USA
E-mail: Uspen-and-sword@casematepublishers.com
Website: www.penandswordbooks.com

Contents

Acknowledgements

A book of this nature would not have been possible without the help of many people and organisations. Of primary assistance was Karoly 'Kaz' Ale, who freely opened his huge collection of images and documents to me. Special thanks must also go to Gavin Scott, for all his memories and hilarious e-mails!

My thanks also go out to - in no particular order - Martin Mace, Amy Jordan, Laura Hirst and Charles Hewitt at Pen & Sword, John Hamlin, David Lee, Phil McCrackin, Simon Peters, Ian Frimston, Emma Dayle, Vicky Craner, Matt Black, Judy Pirie, Bernard Newton, Kirk Smeeton, John McMillian, Lynda Poulter (Gamble), Chris Goodwin, Nick White, John Lapwood, Robert Faucett and the many other former Britannia Airways staff that made contact.

I am also indebted to many people and organisations for providing photographs for this story, but in some cases it has not been possible to identify the original photographer and so credits are given in the appropriate places to the immediate supplier. If any of the pictures have not been correctly credited, please accept my apologies.

The late Captain Mike Russell FRAeS of Britannia Airways with two of his loves - De Havilland DH89 Dragon Rapide G-AGTM/NF875 and a company Boeing 767.

It was Mike who first planted the idea of a Britannia Airways book in my mind way back in 1991 during a tour he and I made of Scotland with the Royal Aeronautical Society's Sir Frederick Tymms Memorial Lecture on Captain E E Fresson OBE - an act for which I am eternally grateful. *(author)*

Introduction

Back in the early 1990s, I was privileged to research, write and compile three airline histories: *The Spirit of Dan-Air, Colours in the Sky – the story of Autair International Airways and Court Line Aviation* and *It Was Nice to Fly With Friends – the story of Air Europe*.

During that time I met, interviewed and more importantly gained the trust of many of the major key players in the industry. People like Fred Newman, the chairman of Dan-Air for thirty-seven of the airline's forty-year history, William 'Bill' Armstrong, the founder and chairman of Autair - and so many other airlines he could not remember them all! Ed Posey, the managing director of Court Line Aviation, who took the eventual collapse very personally, Errol Cossey, one of the three founders of Air Europe, who sold out at just the right time before moving on to found Air 2000, selling that and founding Flying Colours, selling that and... David James, then the darling 'Company Doctor' of the City of London who was supposed to look after the banks interests, but fell in love with the smell of the kerosene and roar of the jets. They all saw dealing with me as being fraught with commercial danger – after all, most were still actively involved in the holiday business in one shape or form - but this understandable caution was balanced by their egos that wanted to be of assistance to ensure their story was told! Even so, they all tended to play things very close to their chests.

Since then, I have written other airline stories, but I seem to be continually drawn back to gathering material on 'The Independents'. These research notes, first-hand interviews and audio recordings I had made lay filed away in my loft, gradually being added to as more and more information surfaced. Each book was as accurate as I could make it, but I always had the nagging doubt in the back of my mind that although they were helpful, I was also being humoured and the full story was not being revealed. There were things that were hinted at, and a few things said in confidence that I was asked not to print. Sure, everything day-to-day was told, but the background activities, the business concepts and models I sensed were being held back – like good poker players they revealed little beyond the immediate play!

Since 1970, when I became involved with the creation of the aeronautical collection at Duxford, I had been fascinated by the charter airline industry that went under many names: 'package tours', 'Inclusive Tours', even 'cheapies'. Whatever the name, it all fell under the dismissive concept of 'Buckets and Spades to Benidorm' by those who thought themselves as 'travellers', not tourists. With the brash confidence of youth, I made contact with many of the people and companies - contact that was maintained over many years.

Quickly I realized that many of the owners and operators were what could only be called 'characters'. People like the high-flying Freddie Laker – a supreme publicist with a puckish sense of humour that concealed one of civil aviation's sharpest technical brains and a will of iron. The cocaine snorting Harry Goodman, a cross between an East End barrow-boy and a cavalier salesman who could - and did - sell anything to anyone. Harold Bamberg, the suave, sharp-suited owner of Eagle Airways, who once the airline collapsed and was taken over, virtually disappeared. Tom Gullick, the 'stack-em-high, sell-em-cheap' hard-drinking managing director of Clarksons Holidays, who claimed to be the inventor of 'vertical integration' and the infamous 'seat-back catering'. Vladimir Raitz, the man who many credit with starting it all with his Horizon Holidays. The wonderful Monique Agazarian, who in the 1950s owned Island Air Services and who used to run scheduled services flights across the channel and pleasure flights from London Heathrow – and who later owned and operated a flight simulator complex in the basement of the Piccadilly Hotel just off Piccadilly Circus under the advertising slogan of 'Fly Down Piccadilly'! The dour, secretive and monosyllabic 'Captain' T E D Langton, the tour operator who wanted his own airline, J E D Williams who created the airline that had the old lady in a wheelchair on the tails of their aircraft... They are just a few of the many that had a tale to tell, but for whatever reason were reticent.

The package holiday has undoubtedly changed the way we live. It has influenced what we eat and what we drink. Its brochures changed our dreams and aspirations; indeed, the evolution of the holiday brochure is nothing less than a template for the graphic designers' art!

Despite the occasional outbreak of loutish behaviour by Brits abroad - usually blown up to the extreme by the British media - it is likely that the annual holiday has produced an overall gain in international understanding and a reduction in blinkered nationalism.

From rickety Rapides to draughty Dakotas, through turbo-props to Tangier and turbines to Thessaloniki these travel and aviation entrepreneurs opened up the Mediterranian - and then set their sights on further afield, changing the landscape wherever they landed.

Without a doubt the convenience and perceived security of the inclusive tour holiday - carried to the extreme with the all-inclusive deal - will ensure the survival of those prepared to adapt indeed survive.

The 'package deal' broke the protectionist policies of the state airlines and, through the introduction of seat-only deals, spawned the low-cost airlines offering rock-bottom deals to European destinations.

One airline that always stood out for me was Britannia Airways - even in the early days the company had a certain mystique about it. There was always an air of 'class' there; something that suggested a certain prepossessing 'Britishness' that seemed to click with the aspiring middle classes. It was an airline that I always planned on telling it's story - and now seems a good a time as any since it has disappeared into the corporate conglomerate that is TUI. Those three letters apparently pronounced 'too-ee' - is short for Touristik Union International - an Anglo-German travel and tourism conglomerate headquartered in Hannover, Germany. It is currently the largest leisure, travel and tourism company in the world, and owns travel agencies, hotels, airlines, cruise ships and retail stores. The group owns a number of European airlines that currently make up the largest holiday fleet in Europe - and several Eurpoean tour operators.

To tell the story of Britannia Airways - and its predecessor Euravia - is impossible without telling the story of Universal Sky Tours and Thomson Travel, for theirs was a truly symbiotic relationship. They each needed the other to exist and thrive, despite the cut-throat competition with margins cut to the bone.

Much of the airline's identity came from the Lady Britannia emblem painted large on the tails of their airliner fleet. Britannia was the female personification of the British Isles, who has been a popular figure since the first century when she was first depicted as a warrior goddess. It was seen as a symbol of British unity, liberty and strength, that meant she often resurfaced during particularly challenging times. Like Columbia in the US and Marianne in France, Britannia became more prominent in times of war or when national pride was booming.

Her appearance in the 17th century came not long after James I brought together England, Wales, Scotland and Ireland under one rule, and more recently the Cool Britannia movement heralded a time of renewed optimism.

In the eyes of many, Britannia screamed all that they saw as being good about Great Britain. Here, therefore, was a heritage, image and ideal that the airline could use to its own best advantage - even if many of the staff somewhat disparagingly nicknamed the logo 'the old lady in a wheelchair'. Through the use of the logo, to the red, white and blue colour schemes and the traditional Shepherds - or was it Cottage? - Pie inflight meal that seemed to be served on every return journey that offered an onboard 'welcome home to Blighty', Britannia Airways personified an upbeat, up-market image, that made use of the latest equipment, flying to destinations that were always stretching the realms of the new British Empire of the UK travelling public.

On a practical level, throughout this book are scattered numerous covers of assorted Inflight magazines and some advertising material. Most are not captioned, for they are usually self-explanatory - they are intended to jog the reader's memory into thinking '...oh! I remember seeing that!'

Of the many hundreds of images I have used in this book, I make no apologies for the lack of quality in some. Today, in 2020, we have all been spoiled by the ability to take hundreds of pin-sharp digital images whenever and wherever we want. Some readers, I am sure, are not even old enough to remember the days of 'Instamatic' camera with twelve shot cartridge films that were in use when I first saw Britannia's Brits. These images were often printed up on horrible 'orange-peel' textured paper, that when scanned, often appear out of focus! Even with a thirty-five-millimetre camera, the cost of film, processing and printing meant that images had to be rationed. Many of the pictures used are from personal collections; some are repairs of company promotional material, a few are from newspaper cuttings pasted in albums without credit. All, however, are historic in the sense that they show aspects of the company and its forerunners story.

So, before we get to the meat of the story, we need to go back, way back and discover the origins of not only the airline but the industry it once served...

Graham M Simons
Peterborough
1 January 2020.

Chapter 1

Sky Tramps and Travel Agents

With few exceptions, the trickle of British people who went on holiday abroad before the Second World War were looking for adventure or bettering their minds, not to lie around on beaches. Foreign holidays were almost exclusively for the wealthy, starting when the aristocratic 'grand tour' of Europe became particularly fashionable in the 18th century. The hardships were many, but by the mid-19th century, the coming of the railways made mass travel affordable. In 1841, Thomas Cook organised his first excursion, by train from Leicester to Loughborough. By 1855 he was leading tours to the continent and by 1866 to the United States, with his first round-the-world tour following in 1872. The focus of such excursions was usually on culture, adventure or health.

By the turn of the century, the first commercially organised British ski trips were heading for the Alps. So it remained until the outbreak of the Great War - when of course, everything stopped. In the nineteen twenties and thirties air travel was very much a luxury item, available to either civil servants travelling on government business or the very wealthy. Clearly, this showed that while foreign travel remained an indulgence mainly of the middle classes and upper classes, by the 1930s its magnetism was slowly drawing in entrepreneurs from humbler backgrounds.

In 1934, South Africa-born British entrepreneur William Heygate Edmund Colborne 'Billy' Butlin had the idea for a concept that became synonymous with him - the British holiday camp. Although holiday camps such as Warner's existed in one form or another before Butlin opened his first, it was Butlin who turned holiday camps into a multi-million-pound industry and an essential aspect of British culture.

Billy Butlin was twelve when his mother emigrated to Canada, leaving him in the care of his aunt for two years. Once settled in Toronto, his mother invited him to join her there.

In Canada, Butlin struggled to fit in at school and soon left for a job in Toronto department store Eatons. In World War One he enlisted as a bugler in the Canadian Army. After the war, Butlin returned to England, with just £5 in his pocket. Investing £4 to hire a stall travelling with his uncle's fair, Butlin discovered that giving his customers a better chance to win brought more custom in, and he quickly became successful. Soon one stall became several, including prominent locations such as Olympia in London, and Butlin soon was able to purchase other fairground equipment, and started his own travelling fair. He proved successful in this endeavour as well, and by 1927 he opened a static fairground in Skegness. Over the next ten years, Butlin expanded his empire, all the time harbouring an idea to increase the number of patrons in his Skegness site by providing accommodation. Two years later he bought forty acres of land at Ingoldmells near Skegness for £3000, built his first camp and advertised it at £500 for a half-page in the *Daily Express*. Within a few days, he had received over 10,000 enquiries. It was opened on 11 April 1936 - Easter Saturday - by Amy Johnson, the first woman to fly solo from

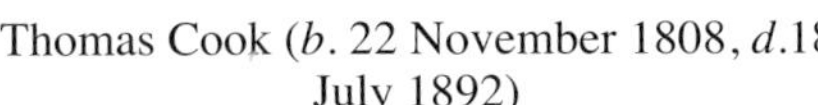

Thomas Cook (*b.* 22 November 1808, *d.*18 July 1892)

England to Australia.

An all-inclusive holiday at the camp cost between 35 shillings and £3 a week, depending on the season. Sports personalities coached campers at tennis, snooker and other games, while entertainers performed on the stage. Another of his slogans was 'A weeks holiday for a week's pay' - a clear indication as to where Butlins were targeting their market.

However, behind its jolly *Hi-de-Hi!* image, the Butlins empire flourished on a mixture of sex and violence. Little did the chalet guests know that Butlin was forced to carry a weapon to defend himself because he'd made so many enemies on his way to the top! It seems that Billy Butlin was a man who associated with many violent people in his early days, and was afraid of retribution, so behind the crisply starched handkerchief, he carried a cut-throat razor in his top pocket all the time!

Billy Butlin was also among the first to realise, that even in the 1930s, sex sells - so single people were targeted as prime customers - for the entrepreneur knew a reputation for bed-hopping among the chalets would pull in the punters.

Butlins' holiday camps provided apparently innocent fun in postwar Britain and built a reputation for wholesome family entertainment, but both the campers and their Redcoat entertainers enjoyed the seamy side of life, too. Britain was a staid society, but Billy knew many people wanted no-strings sex. Despite - or maybe because of - the camps' seedy side, Billy Butlin hit on a money-spinning formula - it was shades of Club 18-30 in the years to come! Indeed, he put in place some of the cornerstones of the embryonic package tour industry. Indeed, Butlins Ltd owned and operated several aircraft, and also ran at least one airfield at Ingoldmells for pleasure flying.

The Second World War may have brought foreign holidays to a standstill, but tour operators of the 1930s including Thomas Cook, ski holiday company Inghams and Travel Club of Upminster found there was latent demand – which would be boosted by ex-servicemen wanting to revisit places in which they had fought. Travel Club resumed holidays to Europe in 1947, and its

Above: Sir William Heygate Edmund Colborne 'Billy' Butlin MBE (*b.* 29 September 1899 *d.* 12 June 1980) seen at one of his holiday camps.

Left: Pictures like this subtly hinted at some of the pleasures that could be available if you took a Butlin's holiday.

Left: Horizon Holidays came into being on 12 October 1949 and initiated the package holiday industry. Its first home was to be on the first floor of 146 Fleet Street, above the Olde Snuffe Shoppe, patronised many years before by the 18th-century English writer and lexicographer Dr Samuel Johnson. The entrance was via Wine Office Court.

Below: Vladimir Gavrilovich Raitz (*b.* Moscow, 23 May 1922 *d.* 31 August 2010)

founder, Harry Chandler, recalled: 'I painted a glowing picture of what Switzerland was like – plenty of food, shops full of goods, virtually pre-war conditions and a complete contrast to England at that time with its shortages, electricity cuts and hard times'.

Travelling by rail or road across war-torn Europe was not easy, and when a Russian émigré named Vladimir Raitz set up Horizon Holidays in 1950, he decided that his customers would fly from London to Corsica rather than undergo the forty-eight-hour journey by rail and sea that he had made the previous year. By chartering a series of weekly flights to a beachfront campsite, he is generally considered to be the inventor of the package holiday.

He was later to recall that first holiday: '1949 - It was my first holiday after the war. I chose Calvi on Corsica because a friend of mine, a fellow Russian colleague at Reuters, not only knew Calvi well but had taken part in 1938 in organizing a holiday camp at Calvi run by an émigré Russian water polo club called 'Les Ourses Blancs' - the White Bears. Now, after the war and the occupation, this idea had been revived. One of the original White Bears, 'Poff' - Dimitri Filipoff - had formed the Club Olympique, a tented village on the beach at Calvi. A friend of mine from Reuters, Baron Nicholas Steinheil, was staying there and had invited me for a fortnight's holiday'.

By all accounts, the installations and living conditions were primitive, to put it mildly. The tents were 'furnished' with camp beds: two, three or four to each tent, standing directly on the sand. You were expected to keep your clothes in your suitcase throughout the stay.

Ablutions and other essential human functions were performed in a 'Bloc Sanitaire' consisting of washing and showering cubicles, and toilets. There was no main drainage. If the toilets were all occupied, one went out into the sweet-smelling Corsican shrubbery to relieve oneself.

The bar functioned beautifully. Drinks coupons were purchased by the booklet from Mario, the head barman. Prices were extremely low, and after half a dozen pastis and a few cognacs after dinner, who cared about the sanitation? The wine was included in the overall price and flowed freely.

In addition to the tents, sanitary block, bar, and 'restaurant' there was a small but perpetually crowded dance floor where the band that had greeted the new arrivals was performing after dinner to an appreciative audience. In 1949 tangos, paso dobles and slow waltzes were much in demand, so it was not surprising that romance flourished. It was a world away from, tired, dreary grey post-war Britain.

Towards the end of his stay at the Club in 1949, Vladimir Raitz was having a drink with Baron Nicholas Steinheil in the bar who told him that his father and another White Bears member, Tao Khan, had excellent connections with the Calvi Mayor and the Municipal Council, and could get a concession on a large piece of land right on the beach between the Club and the town. 'We'll get some tents and equipment, and you can get us some British clients to supplement the French. We'll advertise in the Metro stations in Paris, and it's up to you how you get your clientele. If you want, we'll even call it the Club Franco-Britannique. You can do the work in your spare time, and we'll pay you a commission on each client.'

The suggestion interested Raitz, but he was concerned about the travelling time: he knew it would be at least 48 hours in each direction. He asked if there was an airport nearby.

'Not precisely an airport, but there's a runway built by the American Seabees during the war. Mind you, there are no airport buildings - not even a shack. I'm sure the Municipality could provide something, though. Why don't you charter some planes when you get back to London? We'll be opening the Club in May next year, and you can have sole rights for the UK.'

Raitz was to hit problems with governmental approval for what he was proposing, but this was eventually overcome. In early March 1950, a phone call came from the civil servant at the Ministry of Civil Aviation: 'Come round as soon as possible, we have a decision for you'.

Raitz grabbed a taxi to Ariel House.' 'I'm not sure whether you'll like the decision, or even if you'll be able to proceed at all. But you can operate your flights if you carry students and teachers only.'

It seems that a way forward had been found to allow Horizon to fly, by the expedient of using the 1945 Labour Election manifesto which was to encourage 'adult education' and for '...people to enjoy their leisure to the full, to have opportunities for healthy recreation' .

The implications behind the decision eventually proved to be monumental. Thomas Cook started it all by taking groups of like-minded people on journeys. Here now was a civil service department acting on government instructions, dictating to a tour operator what 'profession' and 'interests' their clients could be and have, a concept that eventually became known as 'Affinity Group Charters'

The journey time by Douglas DC-3 aircraft, at a top speed of 170 mph, was a mere six hours, including a refuelling stop in Lyon. Horizon soon faced competition, but not from Thomas Cook, who preferred to operate cultural and adventure tours while acting as an agent for rail, sea, coach

Left: Air Contractors used Dakotas and Miles Aerovans, as shown here with G-AISI.

Below: Lancashire Aircraft Corporation's Halifax G-AKEC.
(both author's collection)

Railway Air Services Dakota G-AGZB coming in to land. This, and a number of other airlines would soon disappear, merged into British European Airways. *(author's collection)*

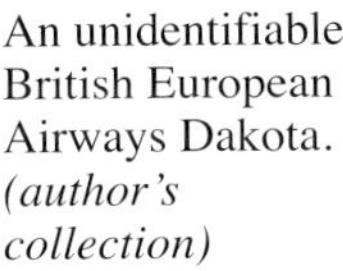

An unidentifiable British European Airways Dakota. *(author's collection)*

and air companies. The pre-war companies, including Sir Henry Lunn Travel and the Polytechnic Touring Association, which later merged to form Lunn Poly, also expanded into air travel.

Most pre-war British airlines had earned their living flying scheduled services: and for the post-war airlines, this remained their chief ambition. However, by prohibiting private airlines from operating these services, the Government hoped that it would stifle the infant industry, leaving the Corporations with a clear field. But in this, it failed.

There was a brief opportunity for so-called 'charter' airlines to exploit the enormous demand for travel as soon as the war ended.

Air charter was and is defined as the business of renting an entire aircraft as opposed to purchasing a ticket for an individual aircraft seat through a traditional airline. While the airlines specialised in selling transportation by the seat, air charter companies focused on individual aircraft and itineraries and any other form of ad hoc air transportation.

The Labour Government of 1945 under Clement Attlee proved one of the most radical British governments of the 20th century, enacting draconian economic policies, presiding over a system of nationalising major industries and utilities including the Bank of England, coal mining, the steel industry, electricity, gas, and inland transport (including railways, road haulage and canals). It developed and implemented the 'cradle to grave' welfare state conceived by the economist William Beveridge.

On 12 October 1945, Air Commodore William Wedgwood Benn, 1st Viscount Stansgate PC, DSO, DFC the Minister of Civil Aviation in Clement Attlee's Labour Government placed a secret memorandum - C.P.(45)222 - before Cabinet detailing the Civil Aviation Policy, arguing for full nationalisation, with no participation by private interests in international services. In this document, under the paragraph describing the creation of the European Corporation that would eventually be British European Airways, there is one sentence that said much: 'I do not propose to find a place for the independent pre-war operators as I do not consider that they have a useful contribution to make'.

Not only is the arrogance of the man breathtaking, but it also shows the inherent Marxist mentality of the Labour Party where the State had to control all, and there was no place for the entrepreneurial spirit as demonstrated by those airlines who did so much to develop civil air transport during the 1930s.

These recommendations were embodied in the Civil Aviation Act of 1946, so there was a brief period when an operator could carry passengers with few restrictions apart from those imposed by a war-time bureaucracy, such as those covering the export of currency and the need for visas.

The act led to the merger of two divisions of the British Overseas Airways Corporation (BOAC) to form three separate corporations: BOAC for Commonwealth, Far East and the North Atlantic routes; British European Airways Corporation (BEA) for domestic and European routes and British South American Airways Corporation (BSAA) for South Atlantic routes. The corporations were to be subsidised for the first ten years, after which they were expected to be self-financing.

On 1 August 1946, the Civil Aviation Act 1946 was given Royal Assent and passed into law. It established BEA as a crown corporation in its own right and transferred primary responsibility for scheduled air services from the UK to Europe (including the British Isles) to BEA. To fulfil its role as the new short- and medium-haul British flag carrier, BEA was organised into two divisions based at Northolt and Liverpool Speke respectively, with the former responsible for all scheduled services to the Continent and the latter for all scheduled services within the British Isles. The Civil Aviation Act 1946 furthermore provided for nationalisation of private, independent British scheduled airlines and gave BEA a legal monopoly as the sole short-haul scheduled British airline. Due to BEA's inability to take over the UK domestic flights of independent scheduled operators such as Railway Air Services, Allied Airways (Gandar Dower) and British Channel Islands Airways on 1 August, these independents continued to ply their scheduled routes under contract to BEA until they were absorbed into the corporation in 1947.

The first flight operated by the newly constituted BEA departed Northolt for Marseille, Rome and Athens on the day of its formation at 8:40 am. It was followed by further route launches to Amsterdam, Brussels and Lisbon. Initially, BEA supplemented its ex-RAF Transport Command Dakotas with Dragon Rapides and Avro Nineteens.

With literally hundreds of war-surplus aircraft becoming available, at knock-down prices, many former RAF aircrew were intent on starting up their own charter airlines; so by the end of 1946, there were over eighty such businesses engaged in air charter work. These were the days of the flying buccaneers - often equipped with just one or two converted wartime aircraft. If you went to an airline looking for someone to fly your or your goods and the first 'airline' you went to did not want the business, you just went next door! Referred to as 'The Independents' by some, the charter industry had more than its fair share of characters. It was not long before the charter airlines formed their own lobbying organisation and support group, the British Air Charter Association (BACA), which first met on 28 August 1946 at the premises of the Royal Aeronautical Society at 4 Hamilton Place, London. The main problem they all faced - apart from Governmental and Civil Service obstructionism - was a shortage of fuel and a shortage of aircraft.

The demand for overseas travel could not be met by scheduled services alone; there was only very restricted availability of seats on passenger flights which were, in any case, erratic. The situation regarding surface shipping was no better. Most shipping was required to carry returning

Lancashire Aircraft Corporation not only flew freight, they were amongst the many independents that made use of the uniquitous Dakota. *(author's collection)*

Air Kruise used Bristol Wayfairers for short-distance passenger services across the channel. *(author's collection)*

forces' personnel from the various war zones. Vessels were in a very run-down condition, and passenger vessels would need extensive refitting before they could be returned to regular service. British companies with overseas interests required to send staff out to resume contacts that had been either ruptured or curtailed during the war. As a result, there were many select charter flights out to China, the Far East, the Middle East and Africa, some involving epic journeys in quite a small aircraft. There was a more straightforward demand for people to emigrate from war-torn Britain, especially to South Africa; a number of the air taxi operators took advantage of the lack of shipping space to fly small parties and families on the one-way journey south. Some pre-war business opportunities were quickly resumed, with charter companies again able to fly press photographers and newsreel cameramen at short notice; and newspapers returned as a staple on special early morning charter flights.

A proliferation of companies

Charter firms were not confined to the London area and centres of populations: a number developed specialised businesses around Britain's shores, exploiting seasonal holiday links - usually over water - helping export goods and products and bringing tourists in. Offshore islands were quick to benefit from the resumption of charter activities; doubtless, there was a measure of island pride in seeing a locally named airline established at the nearby airport. The Isle of Man boasted two charter airlines at Ronaldsway, Manx Air Charters and Manning Airways, both flying de Havilland Rapides, thus evoking memories of the pre-war Isle of Man Air Services. The Channel Islands, which had been especially hostile to the

nationalisation of what they saw as 'their' airline, ascertained that the Ministry in London had no powers to regulate inter-island services, so soon created Island Air Charters, operating Rapides between Jersey, Guernsey and Alderney; it was linked to another charter airline, Air Transport (Charter) (Channel Islands). In 1949 Welshman Maldwyn Thomas started air charter operations out of Jersey, also using Rapides. Discovering that he could not register the name Jersey Airlines as it was too similar to the late Jersey Airways, he called his airline Airlines (Jersey) and painted the titles 'Jersey Airlines' on the aircraft anyway.

Rival airports on the Isle of Wight had Bees Flight, flying Miles Geminis, operated out of Sandown (Lea) when it reopened in 1948. Renamed Isle of Wight Airport, Sandown became the primary commercial airport on the island. Ryde, the essential destination for Portsmouth, Southsea and Island of Wight Aviation (PS&IOWA) ferry services from Portsmouth before the war, had been closed but Somerton (Cowes) had remained open and was used by Somerton Airways until both closed down in 1952.

In Northern Ireland, Lord Londonderry founded Londonderry Air Charter, in December 1946. Based at Newtownards, where Miles Aircraft built the Messenger club aircraft, the airline relied on Miles for much of its work, carrying aircraft assemblies and spares between Newtownards and Miles' other base at Woodley, near Reading. Aircraft used included a fleet of Miles Aerovans and Messengers. By late 1947 production of Messengers had ceased and the airline had to look elsewhere for business. Two Rapides were acquired for passenger work, mainly weekend charter flights to the Isle of Man, and the

Right: Dr Graham Humby, Managing Director London Aero and Motor Services Ltd, and brother-in-law of the famous orchestral conductor Sir Thomas Beecham.

Below: One of a number of Handley Page Halifax bombers converted for use by LAMS. *(both authors collection)*

name was changed to Ulster Aviation. Further change came about in 1949 when Ulster Aviation and Mannin joined forces to form North-West Airlines, based at Ronaldsway, which took over the assets of the two airlines. It was short-lived, and North-West was to be bought out by Lancashire Aircraft Corporation.

Wales had Cambrian, its own flourishing airline, but in Scotland, the pioneering spirit so brightly lit by Captain Ted Fresson had been extinguished. BEA flew the internal services, but the inter-island network in Orkney was not resumed; Scottish Aviation Ltd, owner, developer and operator of Prestwick Airport during the war, was a respected charter airline, flying all over the world and specialising in contract services and had ambitious plans for developing a network of services post-war which were cut short by the Government's plans for nationalisation. Scottish Aviation lost out on both fronts, as the airport was taken over by the Ministry of Civil Aviation, and the formation of BEA precluded any scheduled service development, and its domestic services had been taken over. Nevertheless, under its energetic founder Wing Commander McIntyre an airline division was started, Scottish Airlines, which obtained Dakotas and Liberators for charter work. It operated contract services for BEA out of

Glasgow's two airports, Renfrew and Prestwick, and also flew extensively for European airlines, including Iceland Airways, KLM, Luxembourg and Hellenic Airways, besides developing its own holiday charter services to the Isle of Man. Its parent, Scottish Aviation, built up a formidable business maintaining and refurbishing former military transports.

In England, Air Charter was formed in 1947 at Croydon and operated Rapides and Geminis until 1950, when charter services were suspended. Operations resumed in 1951 when entrepreneur Freddie Laker, previously an Air Transport Auxiliary flight engineer, took over the airline, together with Surrey Flying Services and Fairflight which all eventually operated under the name of Air Charter.

Without a doubt, Freddie Laker was one of the industry's leading 'characters'. Laker, originally from Canterbury, Kent and an old boy of the Simon Langton Grammar School for Boys - albeit an expelled one - started working in aviation with Short Brothers in Rochester.

After the war, he worked for a brief period for British European Airways and London Aero Motor Services (LAMS). Having borrowed £38,000 from Bobby Sanderson, a wealthy friend to top up his own savings of £4,500, he went into business as a war-surplus aircraft dealer. The Soviet blockade of West Berlin in 1948-49, during which all available aircraft were needed to fly essential supplies into West Berlin, allowed his business to flourish as this provided more than a year's work for his aircraft and employees almost immediately. This period often saw Laker flying the aircraft himself.

Freddie Laker had founded Aviation Traders in October 1947. It was based at Southend Airport, Essex, and specialised in converting numerous war-surplus aircraft into freighters. This included the conversion of Handley Page Halifax bombers into freighters, six of which were sold to Bond Air Services, who based them at Wunstorf in West Germany to carry essential supplies into West Berlin during the Blockade of 1948-49. Bond Air Services furthermore contracted Aviation Traders to service these aircraft. In return, Aviation Traders received half of Bond Air Services' freight charges.

Following the end of the Airlift in 1949, Laker had most of the Halifaxes he had supplied to various independent airlines during the Airlift scrapped at its Southend facilities. He also made use of these facilities for the subsequent conversion of several DC-4/C-54 Skymaster airframes into Carvairs for various operators around the world.

In addition, Aviation Traders re-engined Argonauts, BOAC's Canadian-built Douglas DC-4s, with unused Rolls-Royce Merlin engines, which the company sourced from the eighty-eight spare engines Freddie Laker had acquired earlier along with BOAC's entire fleet of Haltons - former RAF Halifax bombers that had been converted to carry passengers and cargo - and several Avro Tudors purchased from the Government.

Wing Commander Hugh Charles Kennard DFC formed Air Kruise (Kent) at Lympne in Kent and was the first operator of the Miles Messenger, to which was soon added a Percival Q6 and a Proctor. The airline developed a network of cross-channel charter services. In 1950 Air Kruise opened a three times daily service from Lympne to Le Touquet, using Rapides, and Kennard quickly spotted the potential for offering a cheaper service between London and Paris. By catching a train at either end and using the Rapide connection across the Channel, the journey was an hour quicker than the standard rail-ferry-rail service and was marginally cheaper. Holidaymakers for Le Touquet also used the service, as did day-trippers.

Air Transport (Charter) (Channel Islands), was a small airline with a big name, merits attention

Right: 'Freddie' later Sir Frederick Alfred Laker (*b.* 6 August 1922 *d.*9 February 2006)

Below: One of Air Charter's Avro Tudors, sucessfully converted into a 'Super Trader' by Freddie Laker. *(both author's collection)*

East Anglian Flying Services operated a number of Miles Aervans during the early days, G-AJKM is seen here. *(author's collection)*

As with many other airlines, East Anglian Flying Services made good use of the classic DH.89 Rapide eight-seat mini-airliner. *(authors ollection)*

because its business activities and its subsequent fate serve as a template for the evolution of post-war charter operations. It started with Rapides and 32-seat Dakotas, carrying holidaymakers from the United Kingdom to the Channel Islands during the summer months; and at other times making long overseas trips, mainly to Africa, with freight, livestock and passengers.

Derby Aviation was formed as Air Schools in 1938, a reserve flying school established at Burnaston, near Derby, which was subsequently joined by a second flying school at Wolverhampton. Some 14,000 pilots and navigators were trained during the war, and afterwards flying training continued; and as so often happened, the light aircraft used by the school and the Derby Aero Club was made available for charter work. The first such commercial flight was made on 21 August 1947, when a Miles Messenger was chartered to take three passengers to the TT Races on the Isle of Man. The name Derby Aviation was registered in 1949 and operations continued with a Rapide and an Aerovan. Like many other small charter operators, the airline flew summer charter services to Jersey.

East Anglian Flying Services, started by Squadron Leader Reginald 'Jack' Jones, was registered as a company in August 1946 and was the first operator to be based at Southend's new municipal airport, taking up residence on 5 January 1947 with an Airspeed Courier, an Auster and a Puss Moth. At first, the company relied on pleasure flying, but Jack Jones soon began to look for charter work and bought a Miles Aerovan, once even sending it down to Cyprus. The expansion started with the arrival of Rapides and a regular series of charter flights across the Channel to Ostend. The business evolved into Channel Airways.

Don Everall (Aviation) came from a small operation started by a Midlands haulage contractor who bought an Auster for his own use, then began to undertake pleasure flying out of Wolverhampton. Following the acquisition of a Birmingham based operator, and some larger DH Rapides, Don Everall developed a mix of charter flying, joyriding and holiday services to the Channel Islands and the Isle of Man.

Eagle Aviation operated its first flight on 9 May 1948, carrying a load of cherries out of Verona in a Halifax. Started by Harold Bamberg, another young entrepreneur and pilot who went on to dominate the industry in the 1960s, the airline took over the Bovingdon based freight airline Air Freight, and continued to operate fruit flights; it

Derby Aviation went through a number of evolutions - Derby Airways, British Midland *et al*. This picture, from the days of their first DH.89 Rapide, when everyone had to turn their hands to anything, shows Frank Marshall, second from the left, who became their Engineering Director. *(author's collection)*

was well placed to serve in the 1948 Berlin Airlift. Bamberg's other company was Air Liaison, an airline passenger and freight agency which also acted as general travel agents.

Hunting Air Travel was formed in December 1945. Its directors, members of the Hunting family, also sat on the board of Percival Aircraft and based a fleet of three Proctors at Luton. Hunting Air Travel was in the air on 1 January 1946 as the ban on private flying was lifted, flying a charter for the *Daily Mail*. Several new Vikings and Doves were ordered to supplement the fleet, which grew to include Rapides and Ansons, and the company switched its base to Gatwick, then Croydon, before settling on Bovingdon. The mix of business was typical: fruit flights, occasional long haul charters and regular flights to holiday destinations.

Island Air Services started flying in June 1946 and was an early charter operator to and from the Scillies, carrying flowers to the mainland during the season. But by the end of 1948 its focus changed, when, under its redoubtable Chairman and Chief Pilot, Monique Marie 'Aggie' Agazarian, it gained the joy riding concession in London, first from Northolt, then at Heathrow, flying Rapides on pleasure flights from the public enclosure there, although the airline was based at Croydon. A woman in a mans world, Aggie was another of the industry's characters.

As a child Monique had ambitions of becoming a film star and was studying at the Royal Academy of Dramatic Art (RADA) in 1939 when she became a VAD nurse on the outbreak of war. Three of her brothers joined the RAF and her brother, Pilot Officer Noel Agazarian, told her about girls training as ferry pilots. Monique applied immediately, but it was not until 1943 that she was accepted for training. She passed her medical examination only by learning in advance from an RAF doctor that a minimum height of five foot five inches was required. She was not quite

Brooklands Aviation was one of a number of companies that survived the war and post-war interference by Government. Here their red and black Rapide G-AJHO loads more passengers on the south coast. *(authors collection)*

five foot four inches but knew as a nurse that it was possible to gain an inch for a few seconds by lying flat on her back until immediately before her height was measured. The examining doctor came into the room to find her lying on the floor.

'Would you mind taking my height straight away?' she asked, then jumped to her feet and stood against the wall. 'Not quite five foot five inches' said the doctor. Monique went to get back on the floor. '...just a minute, I can do better than that.' The doctor believed her - she passed the rest of the medical without effort.

Monique did her training and soloed in a Miles Magister. She shrieked with delight all through her first flight she told me years later: 'I suppose I always really wanted to do fly. After seeing Peter Pan as a little girl, I kept trying to fly by jumping off the bed, although I must admit I was never keen enough to try it out of the window.' Her flght training began in the autumn. She enjoyed the sports car temperament of the fighters and was disappointed that the end of the war brought only a return to RADA.

Monique gained her commercial flying licence and began to look for a job as a pilot. She wrote the same letter to every air charter company she found in a classified directory, recieving only five replies and no offers. An optimistic visit to Elstree Aerodrome in North London did lead to Monique becoming the London manager - at £5 a week - of a company called Island Air Services.

IAS had two Proctors - one operated a service between the Scilly Isles and Lands End piloted personally by the owner, Daughtey Hills-Grove-Hills. The other Proctor was leased to another charter firm, based at Elstree. By early 1947 Island Air Services had moved into Croydon Airport and

Monique was flying the second Proctor herself. Hills-Grove-Hills, a wealthy young man who had learned to fly since the war, was persuaded to let Monique develop the Croydon end of the business while he concentrated on the Scilly Isles.

Croydon was busier than at any time in its history. The big corporations, particularly BEA and Air France, were slow in establishing their passenger routes after the War; Island Air Service was typical of the way the small airlines rushed in to fulfil the need. In a single day, Monique flew a businessman to Southampton, a football manager and two directors to Leeds, a party of holidaymakers to Cowes then brought a group of people back to Fairoaks and returned to Croydon in time to squeeze in two pleasure flights for members of the public visiting the airport.

Monique was now managing director and chief pilot of her own charter company, Island Air Services (London) Ltd as Hills-Grove-Hills agreed to her taking over the London operations which she had built up, and his original company continued to work from the Scilly Isles. She set up in business with two pilot friends, Ray Rendall and John Phelps. They raised £5,000 as capital, and she borrowed a further £1,500 from the bank. A second Rapide was bought from BEA, and a third was available from a friend whenever he was not using it.

The company's first two summers were most successful, especially holiday flights to Jersey. But by early 1950 Monique had to admit that she had started her business in time to meet the biggest slump that the small charter operators were ever to know. 'The usual seasonal decline in work was particularly severe that winter. Even worse, BEA and Air France were beginning to win back

Hunting-Clan was an evolution of Hunting Air Travel. Seen here is one of their Dakotas on approach to Manchester airport. *(author's collection)*

passengers from us by offering increases and improvements in their scheduled services. We had just one charter all winter'.

In March 1950, Monique persuaded her partners that the company should spend their remaining cash buying her some new clothes and send her to France. The costumes were to boost her morale; the trip to France was to talk the casino owner at Deauville into the idea of establishing a regular air service for British gamblers wanting to play at his tables. The casino owner was impressed by her forecasts of the traffic, the seasonal peaks for passengers, and the costs of operating such a service. Monique proposed he should pay full charter rate for a daily service by Rapide between Shoreham, in Sussex, and Deauville, and look after all publicity in France. Island Air Services would pay him seventy-five per cent of all ticket revenue and publicise the service in England. If the service regularly flew with a full load of passengers the seventy-five per cent of ticket sales would more than cover the casino's cost of chartering the plane, leaving a twenty-five per cent profit for the operators. They were the kind of odds which appealed to the casino proprietor. Having personally been on the receiving end of Aggie's 'persuasiveness' many times, I can fully understand how the casino owner stood no chance in resisting her!

Island Air Services duly moved into the league of international scheduled services, operating an associate agreement with BEA and charging fares laid down by IATA. The Mayors of Brighton and Hove travelled on the inaugural flight. The Mayor

of Deauville, French aviation officials, and the casino executives were assembled to meet them. Monique flew as a passenger and led the way out of the aircraft in her capacity as managing director of the company establishing a link between the two countries. The dignity of the occasion was shattered when two of the French ground staff, waiting in oil-stained overalls to re-fuel the Rapide, recognised her from working flights into the airport. They ran forward to embrace her with cries of 'Madame Monique, tres bonne de te revoir! (Madame Monique, how lovely to see you again). The reception committee politely ignored the oil smudge on the tip of her nose when it was their turn to greet the airline's managing director.

She established the Deauville service as a complete success, achieving one hundred per cent regularity and carrying many stage and TV personalities on its flights to and from the gambling tables.

A different kind of passenger was being provided by another operation being developed by Monique at the same time. First at Croydon and also at Northolt, she found an eager demand for

Right: Monique 'Aggie' Agazarian (*b* 17 April 1920, *d* 7 March 1993).

Below: The silver, white and royal blue Rapide G-AFFB, one of a number of Rapides operated by Island Air Services. *(both author's collection)*

pleasure flights from members of the public visiting the airport to watch aeroplanes come and go. The opportunity to go up in one of those aeroplanes gave most airport spectators an active interest in aviation for the first time.

The big chance came when IAS won the concession for pleasure flights from London Heathrow. Her base was a caravan near a public enclosure which was little more than an open space, and pleasure flying was restricted to Sundays. Soon she had four Rapides making 100 flights a day for six months of the year.

It is for this reason that Island Air Services deserve a place in the history of the holiday airlines - IAS played a crucial part in the first-ever 1000 movements a day at London Airport. IAS opened up flying for pleasure to the mass market.

White-uniformed marshals formed the ever-present queue into groups of nine ready to board each Rapide. Nine, because Monique had approved a special modification for short-range pleasuere flying where the rear bench seat was fitted out for three passengers instead of two! Turnround averaged thirty seconds, and at peak periods the four Rapides would be landing, loading and taking off side by side. Whenever possible, Monique tried to time her aircraft's movements for them to pass in front of oncoming traffic and so miss the turbulence. 'If I were taking a pilot's shift, I would lead the other three Rapides along special taxiing routes to whatever runway control specified. We all had duplicated radio equipment in the aircraft covering all frequencies in use to ensure constant contact with the control staff'.

On reaching the edge of the specified runway, the four Rapides would take up a loose box formation. The formal message to control was: 'Ready immediate take-off.' Over the years, this became 'The Shower's ready to go.' Then the four machines would take off across the runway in the same loose formation, climb to 1,000 feet, make a five-minute circuit of the airport, request permission to land, touch down one behind the other, and turn off the runway at four different intersections, almost while their tails were still in the air. As a variation there was a more extended flight, costing 22 shillings a head instead of 11shillings, which offered a conducted tour of London at 1,500 feet. Pilots averaged six airport circuits an hour or three of the tours.

Even after paying £3,000 in advance to the airport authorities for each season's flying concession and being charged landing fees and parking fees, the company could make twenty per cent profit on the operation. The airport flights were also an effective advertisement for holiday charters to Jersey. Monique recorded a clear profit of £10,000 during six months of 1955, plus the prestige of chartering two fifty-seater Elizabethan airliners from BEA to cope with a sudden surge of business.

Then, in 1956, pleasure flying at London Airport was brought to an end. Monique carried her protests to the House of Commons and was assured the decision was taken on operational grounds. She was told of fears of an increased accident risk with airport traffic reaching new peaks and the prospect of the big jets to come. Monique preferred to believe that her little fleet was made a scapegoat for local residents' complaints about noise. A routine protest, made soon after her concession was withdrawn, brought a Parliamentary assurance that movements in and out of the airport had been reduced by 100 flights a day. The banning of the small Rapides presumably lessened the noise made by four-engined transatlantic airliners.

In other areas of the country, Lancashire Aircraft Corporation, owned by Eric Rylands, an important figure in the post-war airline industry, quickly established itself in 1946 at Squire's Gate, the new airport for Blackpool, flying DH Rapides. Bearing the red Lancastrian rose, the fleet

Another Dakota operator in the early 1950s was Morton Air Services. *(authors collection)*

expanded rapidly so that by mid-1947 there were over twenty aircraft: Rapides, Consuls, Proctors, Austers and the first of many Halifaxes. The airline's sister maintenance organisation converted the latter, and as there was insufficient work for them in the north of England, they were based at Bovingdon, mainly flying fruit from the continent together with the occasional ship's charter and other long haul freight flying.

Morton Air Services was the first charter airline to introduce the Airspeed Consul into service, but also made extensive use of the Rapide. Based at Croydon, and founded by Olley's former Chief Pilot, Morton's first flights early in 1946 included two return flights to Rome, a 17-day tour of Europe arranged for two British and two United States businessmen engaged in reviewing prospective markets, and a 5,735 mile flight from Bombay to London for an Indian Maharajah. In September one of his Airspeed Consuls flew four passengers down to South Africa, taking six days to cover the 7,000 miles. The Rapides were well adapted to air ambulance work, with a large door that allowed easy stretcher access, and Morton's operated many air ambulance flights from the continent, including skiing accident casualties from Switzerland during the winter season. In 1948 Morton's, together with Air Enterprises, was contracted by the United Nations Truce Commission in Palestine to provide seven Consuls for courier and patrol services, with an engineering base at Beirut. This contract lasted until 23 April 1949.

When Transair became the specialist newspaper carrier it bought a fleet of converted Ansons. The first newspaper services were to Paris, starting in October 1948, and were followed by further contracts to Brussels, Dublin and the Channel Islands. No doubt impressed by the efficiency and regularity of Transair's services, the Royal Mail also decided to start using the airline, awarding it mail contracts from 1950 to France, Belgium and the Channel Islands.

Skyways set out to challenge the Corporations and develop as significant a presence in the charter sphere with some big ideas and an impressive board including General Critchley, formerly Director-General of BOAC, and Sir Alan Cobham.

Skyways immediately obtained valuable contracts with the Anglo-Iranian Oil Company to fly personnel, stores and equipment out to Basra in the Persian Gulf on a twice-weekly basis. Anglo-Iranian, the fore-runner of BP, had over 5,000 expatriate staff together with their families based at its Abadan oil refinery in Iran; regular services were needed to take staff out there on appointment, on leave and for business travel. Skyways also launched so-called 'aerial

Right: An early Skyways flyer, announcing the commencement of their Coach Air Services. At the time the compnay had offices at 7 Berkley Street London W1.

Below: The pale blue, white and silver Dakota of Skyways.
(*both author's collection*)

cruises' on behalf of Sir Henry Lunn, precursors of the package tour. Travellers were flown out to Zurich in Switzerland, transferred to a hotel for a two-week stay and then flown back to England, all for an inclusive price of £75.

At the time of Skyways' first flight to Basra in May 1946, the Government had still not enacted the new civil aviation legislation and was nervous about the possible threat to the state airlines.

Another charter airline which was launched almost fully-fledged was Airwork; the company had spent the war training pilots and working on military maintenance contracts, overhauling aircraft at its engineering base at Gatwick, but soon included civil contracts also, converting military Dakotas to civil standards for BOAC and the Dutch airline, KLM. Under its managing director, Myles Wyatt, and its commercial director, Sir Archibald Hope, the company aggressively sought out new business ventures. With its extensive world-wide contacts, the company was asked to help develop a sales organisation overseas for British transport aircraft like the Bristol Freighter and the Vickers Viking; it sold six Vikings to its protégé, Indian National Airways. It was but a short step to acquiring some of those aircraft and operating them in its own right, flying out of Blackbushe. They were used by the Polytechnic Touring Association (PTA) for what were called tourist flights to the Continent, starting during the summer of 1947. These were among the first inclusive tours, and over 2,000 passengers were carried to Switzerland during that summer. The PTA was no stranger to promoting tourist flights abroad; as early as 1932-33 it had chartered a Handley Page HP42 from Imperial Airways for all-inclusive holidays to Switzerland, By the end of 1947 Airwork was also involved in the Hadj, the pilgrimage to Mecca, flying over 100

pilgrims between Mombasa and Jeddah. There was a Viking based in Kuwait to operate on behalf of the Kuwait Oil Company, and another Viking in Karachi to fly for the newly formed Pakistan Government. Elsewhere in the Middle East, Airwork continued its association with the major oil companies, forged before and during the war; maintaining and operating five Rapides and two Doves for Anglo-Iranian Oil at Abadan, and three Rapides and two Doves for Iraq Petroleum. The company also obtained a valuable three-year contract in South America, operating two Bristol Freighters and various smaller aircraft on behalf of Shell in Ecuador, flying heavy equipment as well as cement and food supplies into remote drilling strips.

Silver City Airways launched its services in December 1946, joining the growing number of long-haul charter operators, and flying Lancastrians and Dakotas on behalf of its parent company to South Africa, Burma and Australia. It is perhaps ironic that this well-respected airline found its real purpose operating some of the shortest of all routes, ferrying cars and their passengers across the English Channel. The airline was closely associated with British Aviation Services (BAS) which was backed by the constituent companies of the British Aviation Insurance Company which performed appraisals, accident surveys, aircraft ferrying and the like. Through BAS, Silver City acquired its managing director, Air Commodore Powell, formerly of RAF Ferry Command, the organisation which had ferried aircraft from the US and Canada during the war. Ferrying aircraft must have been in his blood because at first a large part of BAS's activities consisted of ferrying war surplus aircraft back to Canada and elsewhere. BAS managed the new airline for its original owners, the Zinc

Silver City Airways Lancastrian G-AHBV was used for long-haul charters. *(author's collection)*

Corporation of Broken Hill, New South Wales and the Imperial Smelting Corporation in Australia, which also had mining interests in Burma and South Africa, and needed to transport staff and freight between its various locations. Problems arose after the independence of India in 1947 when the Indian authorities began to make difficulties for South African engineers on their way to Burma, causing long delays and somewhat negating the whole point of these private flights. Later it became possible to route South Africans west-about to Australia on commercial airline services, obviating the need to transit India, at which time the Zinc Corporation no longer had a demand for such specialised charter services and the airline sold its Lancastrians. The Zinc Corporation, later to become Rio Tinto-Zinc, continued to use Silver City's aircraft both in the United Kingdom and Australia for a while, but early in 1950 decided to sell the airline to British Aviation Services.

The 'sky tramps' push ahead
The rapid development of charter flying worried the government. Its objective had been to guarantee State-controlled airlines a monopoly of all scheduled services, but in the hectic post-war rush it suspected that many passengers were being diverted across to charter airlines, seen by officialdom as 'sky tramps'.

'Mushroom development of charter services to cash in on the overflow from the airlines and the lack of shipping space is giving aviation a bad name' was the candid comment from Aeronautics, which complained about the 'couldn't care less' attitude of many pilots, who did not seem to rate passenger comfort and convenience very highly. 'The survival of the fittest operates in air transport quite as effectively as the jungle, and it is unlikely that many of these casual concerns will still be going in a year's time. Meanwhile, they are queering the pitch of the old-established charter companies who know the business from A to Z and give their clients service'.

A two-tier system had developed, riding on the back of the good old British class system. BOAC and BEA, being scheduled service operators established and ran by the government were utterly untainted of course; charter airlines such as Airwork, Silver City and Skyways were 'acceptable' - whereas many of the others were barely capable of sitting at the same table.

'Oh, so you're in the racket' remarked one politician to a Skyways employee, causing the latter to conclude in an article in Flight that this comment was borne '...of an inverted form of snobbery and ...a complacent smugness which rejoices in its own security, while condemning the foolishness of those unwary enough to seek their fortunes outside the realms of Government control'

Weekend services to the Channel Islands, in particular, were suspect; there seemed to be just too many 'charter services' and inevitably, not all of them could be legitimate. Having framed the 1946 Act under the Penal Code, the Labour Government could only test the Act in the Courts, so the Ministry started examining charter flights with a view to early prosecution. A questionnaire sent out to some charter airlines in 1948 asked numerous questions: 'How did the passengers know that seats were available? Was the first approach made by the passengers to your company, or by your company to the passengers? How was that approach made? Whom did the passengers pay for their seats?'

Editorial from the 'Commentator' in *The Aeroplane* on 31 December 1948 dismissed the questionnaire as '...a typical product of a Civil Servant who has nothing to do and all day to do it in.' Other questions included: 'whether the flights were systematic, that is, performed regularly;

Transair's high maintenance standards ensured that their fleet, such as Dakota G-AMRA seen here, had an annual usage of over over two thousand hours per aircraft. *(author's collection)*

whether spare seats could be sold off to fill up an otherwise properly chartered flight; and just what were 'members of the public'?

The Ministry was able to supervise the activities of charter airlines through its control of many of the airports that the airlines had to use.

The Corporations were not above making mischief either. '...I regarded this as a case rather of pique on the part of BEA who were annoyed at their prices being undercut in respect of flower trade', wrote a Treasury Solicitor concerning a complaint about some flights made by British Air Transport from the Channel Islands.

Following the first prosecution in May 1948, involving Ciro's Aviation, the magistrate had some sarcastic comments to make about the Air Minister as he fined the airline a nominal £10. 'These are terrific powers given to a Minister. No private individual shall compete with a nationalized undertaking. If they do so, they shall be required to give full particulars of the offence. They shall convict themselves at the arbitrary order of the Minister who can fix his own time for the information to be supplied.'

The Ministry then prosecuted Hunting Air Travel for regularly flying passengers to Jersey during the summer of 1948, but must have been disappointed when the Court stated that the airline had '...rendered yeoman service to the public in general', and fined them only one pound on each of the two summonses, rather than up to £5,000 that the law allowed.

The singular lack of success in the Courts was embarrassing, and the Ministry became reluctant to prosecute. In desperation the Treasury Solicitor suggested that Section 23 of the Act should be redrafted in the form of an absolute prohibition, subject to exemptions, but this proposal was turned down by the Ministry, which was unable, or reluctant, to determine exactly what activities the charter companies should - or should not - be allowed to undertake.

A different world...
Back in the early 1950s, only two million Britons travelled abroad on holiday, by train, car and scheduled airline services. By the new millennium that figure was closer to thirty million - which included a vast number who took package holidays by charter aircraft.

For those familiar with today's Mediterranean resorts, the world that Vladimir Raitz and Horizon Holidays were starting to reveal is hard to imagine.

Spain may have been in the firm grip of General Francisco Franco's dictatorship, but proved a most fertile ground for the fledgling package holiday revolution.

The country was barely fifteen years out of a vicious and barbaric civil war during which Benito Mussolini's Italian troops, sent to aid Franco's Nationalist cause, had marched into Alicante. which had divided families and friends and channelled all the polemic of twentieth-century politics - fascism, republicanism, communism, anarchy - into a bloody conflict which has been estimated to have cost over 400,000 lives.

There were hardly any hotels. Fishermen went after shoals in boats painted with an eye on the prow, to ward off evil spirits. The sea lapped on empty beaches, unviolated by the serried ranks of roasting sunbathers and noisy jet skiers.

In small, dark bars, behind beaded curtains which prevented flies from buzzing through open doors, Andalusian guitarists played traditional tunes with incredible dexterity, having no inkling even of the looming avalanche of rock and roll, let alone the pulsing strobe lights and mechanical beats of later generations.

Instead of pounding disco rhythms the evenings of the 1950s saw on dusky promenades, on which the daily paseo remained a bashful rite of courtship, boys following breathless girls until their passions were silently declared.

If only they knew what the future held - sunburnt, skimpily dressed British, Dutch or German alternatives, caution loosened by cheap alcohol and the heady escape from dreary jobs, to divert their intentions and provide release from stifled sexual desires.

Indeed, foreign women daring to venture out in revealing clothes would have found their holidays quickly 'cancelled', for to dress indiscreetly away from the beach risked arrest by the Guardia Civil, who always patrolled in pairs. It was little more than a decade since in Barcelona the Catalan language and the stately dance known as the Sardana, which visitors may now see performed in quiet squares, was banned. The pornography currently in plain view on the Ramblas in the centre of Barcelona would have been unthinkable, and the handbag snatchers who spoil tourists' innocent pleasure did not exist then.

Chapter 2

Form your own airline...

One tour operator who was worried about the quality of flying he could obtain for his clients was Captain T E D Langton, who ran one of the early inclusive-tour operations, Universal Sky Tours. Towards the end of the fifties, he had become so anxious about the effect this could have on the tour business that he commissioned a study to discover whether it would be possible to form a reputable airline, in association with his tour operation, to ensure he had the quality he needed to attract more customers.

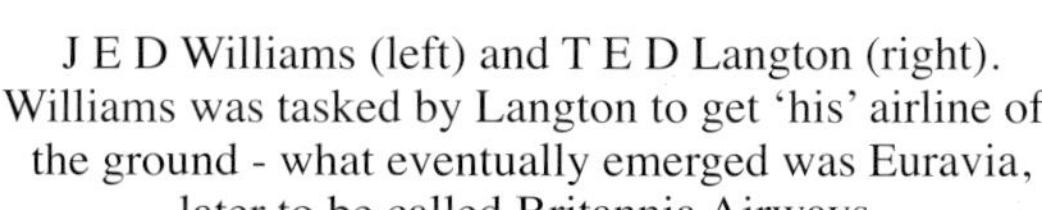
J E D Williams (left) and T E D Langton (right). Williams was tasked by Langton to get 'his' airline off the ground - what eventually emerged was Euravia, later to be called Britannia Airways.

Langton - who never received the recognition he deserved - was the archetypal swashbuckler-cum-businessman travel trade innovator and perhaps the most inventive and resourceful of all the early mass - market operators. He was something of a mercurial character who showed great personal creativity and imagination - not least being his adoption of the rank of 'Captain' - and he led something of a Jekyll and Hyde existence in both his business and private life.

His story started before the beginning of the 20th century, in the seaside village of Southport between Liverpool and Preston. Thomas Edwin David' Ted' Langton was born to a father employed by the Vesteys, a wealthy family who owned a large chain of butchers shops and he wanted his son to follow in his footsteps. His son, however, had other ideas altogether; he made his way to Liverpool Docks, where he found a job with a shipping company transporting Irish migrants to the USA.

Each morning, he would board the first train from Southport, to reach the office of the Galleon Shipping Line by 6.30 a.m. Here he would meet Irish passengers arriving from Dublin and Belfast and issue them with onward tickets to the USA.

Before long the Great War intervened, and Langton was sent off to serve in the Merchant Navy. It was not until 1926 that he decided to go into the travel business himself, opening up a firm which he hoped would provide competition for George Lunn and Polytechnic Travel, two firms located close to the Cadbury factory, at Bourneville, whose workforce generated a large slice of their custom.

Initially, Langton's operations were small scale; he set up a programme of rail and coach holidays to Ostend, Paris and Lucerne, and although this was not exactly a roaring success, he somehow secured an invitation from King Alfonso XIII of Spain to open a Spanish Tourist office at 87 Regent Street, in London.

It was 1927, and King Alfonso was one of the earliest and most enthusiastic promoters of his country as a visitor destination. He had discovered, when trying to accommodate guests for his wedding, how short Spain was of good hotels and he also threw his weight behind the creation of a network of Paradores, hotels located within historic and atmospheric old buildings.

It was always Langton's claim that his attachment to Spain stemmed from the time when he was a young boy, and a Spanish ship ran aground close to where he lived, its crew then choosing to stay on as an expatriate colony. This led to Langton's lifetime fascination with everything Spanish and him spending time learning the language and picking up something of the culture.

Langton's London office provided a convenient information portal for the fledgling tourist trade. For the next four years, then, Langton ran this little bit of Spain in London, during which time he was a frequent visitor to Barcelona and Seville, and became involved in many ventures aimed at stimulating relations between Spain and Britain.

At other times, when he was in England, he was tasked with visiting travel agents up and down the country, particularly those affiliated to Thomas Cook, the firm which provided sixty per cent of his trade.

Unfortunately with the collapse of the Spanish monarchy in 1931, all of this came to an end, and Langton, now married with a child, returned to Southport to live with an aunt. Within a week of his arrival, though, he had noticed that the town lacked a travel agency, so he decided to open one of his own. Key to getting that kind of business off the ground was securing a contract with one of the handful of major tour operators. An approach to George Lunn paved the way for Langton to become a Thomas Cook agent, but his big breakthrough came in a Liverpool pub.

T E D Langton had just turned thirty when he entered the travel business between the wars, setting up a firm called Happiways in his home town of Southport with a capital outlay of £500. It was the result of a conversation in a Liverpool pub, in which coach operator William Webster was complaining that business was painfully slow. Webster operated James Smith & Co (Wigan) Limited, but by 1935, the company was marketed as 'Webster's Tours', run by James Smith & Co. Langton asked Webster how much he would charge for providing a coach for the whole summer.

Sensing an opportunity, Langton offered to hire two coaches, and so was born his coach-tour programme: one-week holidays to Torquay, Bournemouth and Ilfracombe for four pounds nineteen shillings and sixpence and nine days to Newquay in Cornwall for six pounds nineteen shillings and sixpence.

Langton then scoured the West Country for hotels and guest houses similarly in need of business. Thus was born a concept adopted by the package tour business - with coaches taking customers from the north to Devon and Cornwall and bringing home those who had completed their holidays. A one week break - Happiways offered packages to Scotland, too - started at just under £5 a week.

He was quick to capitalise on his success. In his second year of operation, he set up a network of sales agents, offering them five per cent commission on every ticket they sold, promptly following this up with a programme of tours all over the Continent. All this was done with a minimum of overheads. All he did was rent a tiny kiosk in the Bedford Hotel, in London, and place a single-column classified advertisement in the Daily Express, calling himself Anglo-Continental Motorways. The response was overwhelming, and soon the kiosk was bursting with application-filled mailbags. Langton promptly sold Happiways to Roberts of Rochdale and used the £5,000 to fund a new operation. In 2019, Happiways is still around having passed through numerous evolvements and owners and is now known as Shearings.

The business expanded healthily, and in 1933 Langton decided to begin operating tours to Ostend and Paris. He formed a coach company in Belgium called Les Cars Bleus, to carry customers on the Continent. It was known in Britain as Blue Cars. Again, his travel offers caught the public imagination. In his very first year of providing Rhineland tours, he carried 3,000 paying passengers to Koblenz, taking them first by train to the coast, and then by bus from Belgium onwards. So lucrative did the venture prove, that he was able to afford offices in up-market Shaftesbury Avenue, just off Piccadilly Circus.

Next, he bought a Belgian coach company, thereby establishing a base in Ostend, followed by three custom-built Cruiser coaches, three more Leylands and six Morris Commercials. The increased volume of sales required extra representation overseas, so he either set up new companies, or bought existing ones in Milan and Paris, and moved into a New York office which his company shared with Frames Tours.

Next, he took to the skies. In 1936 he chartered four Rapide aircraft to fly from Lympne Airport in Kent to Le Touquet, in Northern France, where he

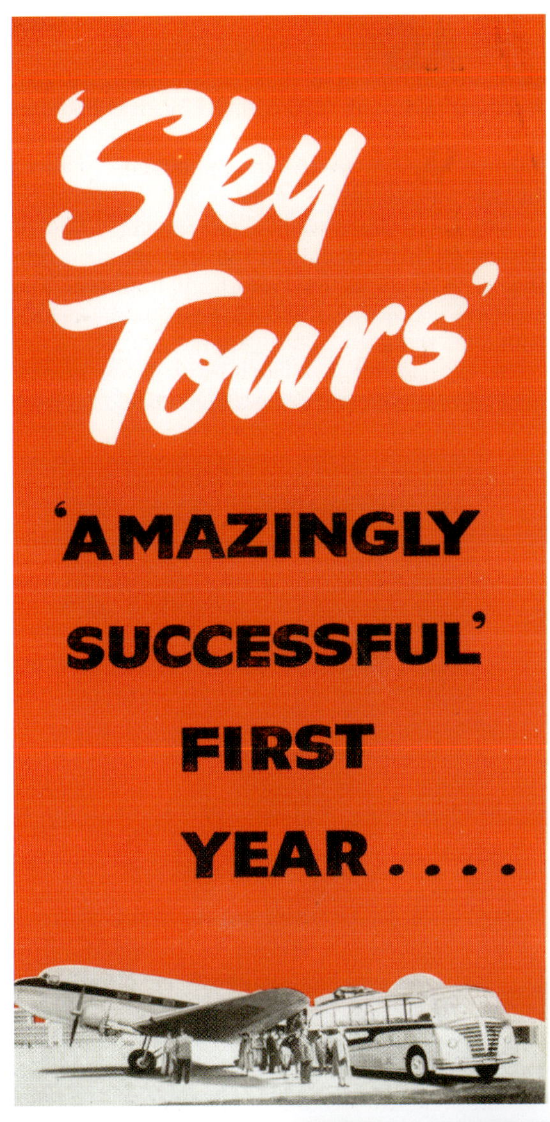

had stationed several coaches to carry passengers to Brittany, the South of France and on to Spain. Again, though, the outbreak of a world war got in Langton's way, for with Hitler's tanks rampaging across Europe, the demand for European jaunts came to a sudden halt.

Once the war was over Langton went looking for the remnants of his business. The good news was that his coaches in France were still mostly intact. The bad news was that their counterparts in Belgium and Italy had been destroyed. Instead of lamenting his misfortune, though, Langton sold the Blue Cars operation to British Electric Traction, in 1951, for almost a quarter of a million pounds. This then left him free to concentrate on his other operations, of which there were many.

No sooner had Langton sold off Blue Cars, than he started up Universal Skytours, a company specialising in air holidays to Europe. Even though he had signed a contract with British Electric Traction that prohibited him from forming a tour company for the next two years, Langton decided to ignore such a petty sanction. At which point British Electric claimed he had used the Blue Cars mailing list to kick-start his new operation and he was forced to return £100,000 of the sale price. With typical bravado, though, Langton referred to this sum as a 'fleabite'.

It was T E D Langton who had the airless, windowless office at 84 Piccadilly - now, in 2019 a Starbucks Coffee House - where he would spend around nine hours a day, six days a week, keeping his fingers on all items connected with Universal Sky Tours. He was everything from stamp licker to price fixer. But around 8 p.m each day he would

Above: T E D Langton's 1956 booking form, announcing just how good his 1955 year was!

Right: Universal Sky Tours called 'home' a various small locations in London's Piccadilly area, including this one, photographed later under totally different ownership.

Legend has it that J E D Williams office was behind the half-moon windows on the first floor, with T E D Langdon's office in the corridor outside!

leave for another of his business interests, the Blue Angel night club in Soho, where Danny La Rue occasionally appeared as a drag artist. Langton even bought an ocean-going yacht which he kept in the Mediterranean and on which he hardly ever sailed - but which is probably where his title of 'Captain' came from!

Six months after the sale of Blue Cars, and having recognised that air charter was the way forward, he formed his new company: Sky Tours.

It was clear that being in charge of a company involved in international aviation was going to be a lot more complicated than running coach tours. Anything to do with flights, including charter flights, was under tight government control, whether in the interests of safety or, has sometimes seemed to be the case, of commercial protectionism.

Sky Tours started with a mixed programme of stay-put holidays mainly in Majorca and the Costa Brava, as well as few air-coach holidays. The emphasis was on travel at the lowest possible prices, within the framework of the regulations.

The holidays that Sky Tours offered were seen as rather downmarket affairs and could be traced back

'Captain' T E D Langdon owned the tour company Universal Sky Tours, and in 1958 used BBC TV personality Jeanne Heal to promote his brochure, called the 'Programme of Air Holidays Abroad. Heal had begun her radio and TV career on women's war work and later in 'Forecast For Fashion' and often in her programmes, generally aimed at women and including 'Meet Jeanne Heal'. That year Langton was using Eagle Airways and BEA - the brochure was full of highly colourised artwork and some black and white pictures.

Holiday brochures can be used to trace a lot of what was going on behind the scenes, and so it is with the Sky Tours ones. Here it is possible to see the evolvement from just a tour company to that of eventual airline operator.

PASSENGER EMBARKATION

LUXURIOUS INTERIOR

GRACEFUL " ELIZABETHAN "

Langton applied the same technique overseas, knowing it was more critical for hoteliers than airline operators to ensure they had guaranteed pre-bookings. It was on this vulnerability that Langton played his ace card. He would go round the world looking at hotels, with the ability quickly to sniff out those having problems. The technique was to say he would take all the hotelier's beds for the season, and then screw, screw and screw again so that he could get an acceptable price. If the man could not be screwed, he would abandon the hotel and find another whose owner could be.

It was a technique that worked well with hotel owners and coach operators, but not with the airlines because, for by adopting the same procedure with them, he inevitably became mixed up with the 'cowboys'.

Something was wrong with his technique; he saw airline companies fail with painful regularity, their passengers ending up stranded at a resort. On the other hand, he did not want to pay the seat prices demanded by state airlines.

As a brand, Sky Tours appears to have started trading in 1953, and it was not long before what was offered to the public via the travel agents was seen as something of a success, as the following description of a 'junket' for the travel trade appeared in one of the trade magazines.

'When a new tours company sells ninety-seven per cent of its available seats during its first season, travel agents are always keen to know more, which is exactly why the directors of Sky Tours Services Ltd of London, took twenty-eight agents to Croydon Airport for the day.

'They were able to show them some of the reasons why, with ninety-three successful air-coach tours to nine major European centres during one short season, they had carried within three per cent of the total capacity'.

'One reason, of course, is the cost. Sky Tours, while lacking nothing in passenger comfort, service and personal attention, still cost an average of thirty per cent less than regular trips'.

'During their tour, however, agents saw numerous other reasons for Sky Tours' amazing success'.

'Plan for the day was to take the agents through the same routine as a Sky Tourist from the time of boarding the coach at Waterloo Air Terminal to the time he is winging his way south to Europe'.

'A London fog, however, blanketed the airfield and prevented a planned 20-minute local flight, during which cocktails and refreshments were to have been served just as on a normal Sky Tours flight.

'Everything else went according to schedule. The

to when Langton had initially been refined his concept in a land-based, UK setting. The idea for his system-designed holidays began in a Liverpool pub when a coach operator was bemoaning lack of business, and Langton asked him how much he would charge to put a coach continuously on the road throughout the summer. Armed with the low quotation he received, Langton toured Devon and Cornwall looking for hotel and boarding-house keepers who had difficulty filling their rooms. Selecting the most desperate, he offered a deal to give them continuous occupancy throughout the season. Thus was born the concept of 'hot bedding' whereby on what tour operators call 'back-to-back' packages, coaches from the north ferried holidaymakers to the south-west to fill the beds sometimes left only minutes before by departing customers whom they then coached back home.

35-minute trip from London to Croydon was made in a comfortable coach which I was told is the type used by Sky Tours both in this country and on the continent'.

'At Croydon, we were met by officials of Transair Ltd., the airline operating company in whose 32-seater twin-engined DC-3 aircraft Sky Tours passengers travel'.

'Later inspection showed why these aircraft were chosen; for the operating company has paid meticulous attention to every detail of a passenger's comfort. Galley and toilet are neat and spotless and, to ensure that passengers are warm in cold weather, hot air is pumped into the cabin for an hour before take-off.

'Every gleaming square inch of wings and fuselage has a weekly polish and paintwork is like new. Interior furnishing of these aircraft is of a high standard with carpets and seat upholstery of a warm red. By clever repositioning of bulkheads, the company has also managed to give more leg-room than I have ever before seen in this type of aircraft'.

'Such things count a great deal, and I firmly believe they go a long way towards comforting the mind of the first-time air passenger'.

'To prove that this was not all top show, however, Transair's chief inspector, Bill Richardson, took the party into maintenance hangars and workshops where every nut and bolt of every aircraft is put through stringent tests with unfailing regularity'

'An unusual situation this, for most travel agents, to see the back-room mechanics of the airline business and to watch bulky 1,200 horsepower Twin Wasp engines being stripped down in the engine shop during their regular overhaul after 900 hours; to see, too (a mental note for reassuring nervous clients), the automatic foam fire extinguisher system which is built-in as part of the engine itself'.

'Stacked neatly at the other side of the hangar they also saw a set of new armchair seats upholstered in red fabric by Transair's own upholstery section'

The legendary skytramp Captain Marian Kozubski.
(author's collection)

'Back in the terminal building agents were shown the reception lounges and even the customs hall before being driven to the adjacent Aerodrome Hotel for lunch, where they were welcomed by Mr S.Anderson, sales executive of Sky Tours. Plans for 1956, he said, included twice as many tours as during 1955, and full information of these as well as attractive window displays would soon be in the hands of all agents'.

'It was an agent who summed up admirably, in a short but sincere vote of thanks, when he said: 'The clients we booked on 'Sky Tours' in 1955 returned to us with glowing accounts of the wonderful holiday they had. They were full of praise for the way in which all the arrangements had been carried out- the comfort of the aircraft seating - the services of the hostess and the courier - the high standard of hotels used on the tours - the cuisine offered at these hotels - and also the excellent coaches used on the continent which from all accounts were all that could be desired. I have no hesitation in recommending 'SkyTours' and wish them every success in 1956.'

It seems that the more I dug, the more I discovered

Left to right: T E D Langton, Richard DeJudicibus and Leo Roupioz, founders of Unitours. *(author's collection)*

about T E D Langton. In 1957 he financed Richard DeJudicibus, formerly of American Express Travel of New York and Leo Roupioz of Paris with the sum of $10,000 each and instructions to open an office in Paris and New York and follow his lead in offering group travel experiences. Each of the companies was called 'Universal Travel' – but the name was taken in the US; thus, the name 'Unitours' was born.

The organisation became an international Catholic pilgrimage tour operator that has been in continuous operation and under the same management since 1957, with offices and partners are spread out throughout the world from headquarters in Port Chester, New York to Tel Aviv, Italy and Athens and is still trading in 2020.

Some abortive airline attempts?
It was this which convinced T E D Langton that the only answer was to start his own airline. For many years historians have always stated that the genesis of Britannia Airways came about with the creation of its predecessor Euravia which occurred on 1 December 1961 with a meeting of Langton, Captain J C Harrington and J E D Williams but events happened two years or so earlier that cast doubt on the accuracy of this. It was, in fact, the date that the new concern was registered with Companies House.

Entrepreneurs love to keep things close to their chests, and T E D Langton was no exception. It has proved impossible to locate any primary source documentation as to his plans and intentions. However, a close study of Universal Sky Tours' 1959 brochure drawn up in the latter half of 1958 and the aircraft registration documents in the files of the British Civil Aircraft Register, held by the Civil Aviation Authority reveals that Langton had been working towards this idea for at least the last two years. Sifting through this material reveals a mixture of holiday brochure hype, employment of a 'media celebrity' and cold bureaucratic recording of details - and several apparent mysteries.

The saga goes something like this. Anyone wanting to start operating air flights was required to jump through a number of bureaucratic hoops. Firstly, a licence was needed. Applications had to be submitted months before the annual hearings of the Air Transport Licensing Board, whose main objective appeared to be to safeguard the routes operated by BEA and BOAC. As an added complication, the organisations which had to apply for the licence, were not the operators, but the airlines, who, in order to avoid the all-but-inevitable refusal, expressed a preference for routes to apparently minor destinations that were unwanted by the major airlines - Perpignan for Barcelona, Alicante for Valencia, Rimini (a military airport) for the Adriatic. Plus an assortment of small airports in Italy, Yugoslavia and Austria, as well as in Belgium and France. Similarly, applicants had to avoid the significant British air hubs, with the result that smaller airports such as Croydon, Blackbush, Luton, Gatwick, Southend and Manston became essential to the success of any application.

In 1953 Langton set up an extensive programme for Skytours' debut season, and it required all his ingenuity to get around the various obstacles in his way. He had acquired a licence to operate out of Blackbushe airport, in Berkshire, but this required a lengthy coach journey out of London. At the same time, he had failed, despite repeated attempts, to obtain a licence to fly to Palma, in Majorca. Refusing to abandon the idea, though, he came up with the idea of flying from Manston, in Kent, to Maastricht in Holland, from where he could touch down and then take off again to Palma.

The way he then set about securing more licences was to team up with Marian Kozubski, an ex-Polish-army pilot, and create a firm called Independent Air Transport, flying a Dakota first out of Croydon airport, and later from Blackbush. However, Kozubski's methods and operations were questionable, and before long, the licensing board took away the company's licence.

Undeterred, Kozubski simply painted the aircraft in a different livery the next day, proceeding to pull the same trick over the following years, with   a

Douglas C-54A Skymaster G-APCW of Independant Air Transport. *(authors collection)*

variety of other surrogates. It was a ruse which kept his aircraft in the air, of that there is no doubt. At the same time, though, the stunt eventually wore thin in the eyes even of Langton, who realised that his continuing association with Kozubski would mean only perpetual conflict with the authorities.

But to the mysteries: the first is a simple one - that of the address used. Indeed, Universal Sky Tours material show that Langton was using 84 Piccadilly from at least 1959. However, other sources indicate that Langton was housed in 93 Piccadilly. It had not proved possible to discover when the company moved - if indeed they did!

Next, let us look at the aircraft. According to the UK Civil Aircraft Register, Langton's first attempt occurred when Douglas C-54A 'Skymaster' airliner G-APCW had its registration transferred on 11 September 1959 from Independent Air Travel Ltd to a new concern named Blue Air Ltd of 84 Piccadilly, which was Universal Sky Tours address in London. The registered owner changed again on 19 February 1960, when it was transferred to Universal Sky Tours - of the same address - remaining with them until the end of the year.

Independent Air Travel came into being in 1954 when a group of airline pilots purchased the London-based travel agents, Independent Air Travel. Operations were, in the main, from Blackbushe, with Hurn as a maintenance base.

The end of the 1958 inclusive tour season was marred by the crash of one of Independent's Vikings in Southall in Middlesex. The Viking (G-AIJE) had taken off from Heathrow Airport early in the morning of 2 September, bound for Tel Aviv with two Proteus turboprop engines aboard for the Israeli airline, El Al. The aircraft had been in flight for some time when an engine failed, the pilot electing to return to Blackbushe for repairs. However, although a slow descent was maintained the aircraft wandered north of its right track. The Viking crashed into a house in Kelvin Gardens, Southall, killing the aircraft's crew. At the Court of Inquiry the Solicitor-General, Sir Harry Hylton-Foster, submitted that the aircraft was above its permitted all-up weight on take-off at Heathrow; that there was a possibility that the aircrew's flight-time limitations had been exceeded; and that the two people who had worked on the aircraft's engines before the flight were licensed engineers. It led to Independent Air Transport becoming major headline news in the national press in March 1959, and the airline then underwent some drastic reorganisation. The company's Chairman and Managing Director, Captain Marian Kozubski, sold his majority shareholding in Independent and left the company to form another airline called Falcon Airways.

As a result of the departure of Captain Kozubski, a reorganisation of the board of directors took place,

The relevant entry for G-APCW within the Civil Aviation Authority files, showing the 'change of ownership' from Independent Air Transport to Blue Air to Universal Sky Tours.

CA 113

DESCRIPTION OF AIRCRAFT ...... *Skymaster C54A D.C.*

CONSTRUCTOR'S No. *10299*

NATIONALITY AND REGISTRATION MARKS

G-APCW

FILE No. *59.AD.6069/2*

FILE No.

SHEET 1

Certificate of Registration No.	Full Name and Address of Owner	Nationality of Owner	Date of Registration	From the Date Shown, Registration Lapsed on Account of:-		
				Change of Ownership	Destruction or Permanent Withdrawal from Use	Cancellation by the Minister of Transport and Civil Aviation
R.6069/1	*Independent Air Travel Limited* *Hurn Airport* *Hampshire* *Regd. Address: Waterloo Chambers, Fir Vale Road, Bournemouth*	*British*	*5-7-57*	*11-9-59*		
R.6069/2	*Blue Air Limited* *84 Piccadilly* *London. W.1* *Registered address: 23, Harcourt House, Cavendish Square, London. W.1.*	*British*	*20-10-59*	*9-11-59*		
R.6069/3	*Universal Sky Tours Limited* *84 Piccadilly* *London. W.1.*	*British*	*19-2-60*	*15.12.60*		

The next year, 1959. Langton used TV personality Hughie Green to promote his flying programme. The cover of the tour company brochure shows two views of Blue Air's C-54 Skymaster G-APCW, but it may be that the aircraft just wore the Blue Air titles for the photo-shoot. *(author's collection)*

with Conservative politician Albert Edward Cooper (b. 23 September 1910, d.12 May 1986), becoming the Chairman of Independent Air Transport.

The airline continued operations with the summer's inclusive tour charter programme in place. Independent still had a large number of inclusive tour charter contracts, including one with Universal Sky Tours. As a result of the adverse publicity attracted by Independent during the Southall accident inquiry, many of the aircraft acquired 'Blue-Air' titles overnight, while others flew without any titling whatsoever.

As with many of the charter airlines, come the end of the summer flying season and the general downturn in holiday traffic, Blue Air found itself in financial difficulties. Within days, Blue-Air's operations had all come to an end, with two Vikings returning to Bournemouth on 16 October 1959. G-AMNR arrived from Blackbushe at 11.55 and forty minutes later G-AJCE also landed at Hurn after completing its last positioning flight from Blackbushe in the colours of Blue-Air.

It is here that something of a mystery surfaces. Of the Blue Air fleet, the three DC-4s - G-APCW, G-APID and G-APNH - underwent a change of ownership to Universal Sky Tours. Intriguingly, I can locate no evidence that Universal Sky Tours gained an Air Operators Certificate, a document essential to allow the legal operation of an 'airline' even one with just one aircraft, despite the events occurring precisely at the time when legislation was brought in that forced the gaining of such a certificate!

In 1960 Aviation legislation had been transformed. To carry paying passengers one required an Air Operators Certificate from the newly created Director of Aviation Safety - a man who had enormous personal powers, including the right to withdraw a certificate in the middle of the night without warning - and a licence for the particular service from a new Air Transport Licensing Board (ATLB). They issued permits having regard to the public need, the diversion of traffic from existing licence holders and fitness of the operator (except in matters of safety), particularly in the issues of financial fitness.

Langton saw this legislation simply as a bag of tricks designed to entrench British European Airways and put people like himself out of business.

Today, an air operator's certificate (AOC) is the approval granted by a Civil Aviation Authority (CAA) to an aircraft operator to allow it to use aircraft for commercial purposes. This requires the operator to have personnel, assets and systems in place to ensure the safety of its employees and the general public. The certificate will list the aircraft types and registrations to be used, for what purpose and in what area-specific airports or geographic region.

The requirements for obtaining an AOC vary from country to country, but are usually defined as:

- Sufficient personnel with the required experience for the type of operations requested.
- Airworthy aircraft, suitable for the kind of activities requested.
- Acceptable systems for the training of crew and the operation of the aircraft (Operations Manual).
- A quality system to ensure that all applicable regulations are followed.
- The appointment of critical accountable staff, who are responsible for specific safety-critical functions such as training, maintenance and operations.
- Carriers Liability Insurance - Operators are to have sufficient insurance to cover the injury or death of any passenger carried.
- Proof that the operator has adequate finances to fund the operation.
- The operator has sufficient ground infrastructure, or arrangements for the supply of proper infrastructure, to support its services into the ports requested.
- The certificate is held by a legal person who resides in the country or region of application.

An AOC is a precious asset to have, but in itself, not having one would not be a problem many 'start-up airlines' make use of another's AOC until they are in a position to gain their own.

The public face of T E D Langton's Universal Sky Tours travel operation was its brochures, and the 1959 edition was to heavily feature TV personality and former Hollywood teenage star Hughie Green.

Hugh Hughes Green (b. 2 February 1920, d. 3 May 1997) was born in Marylebone, London and after his fathers business went bankrupt, his father encouraged his stage-obsessed son into performance, and by the age of fourteen, Hughie Green had his own BBC radio show and created and toured with his own all-children cast concert party called *'Hughie Green and his Gang'*. After an extensive tour of Canada, in 1935 Green appeared in his first film, *Midshipman Easy,* then went to Hollywood where he appeared in the film *Tom Brown's School Days* and at the Coconut Grove nightclub in Santa Cruz, California with his cabaret act.

Having been caught in North America on the declaration of war, during the Second World War Green served as a pilot in the Royal Canadian Air Force, ferrying aircraft across the Atlantic with RAF

Sunday best, bare shoulders and neat hand luggage just off the aircraft - the Sky Tours Air Holidays Abroad brochure for 1961. *(authors collection)*

Ferry Command. In 1942, he married Montreal socialite Claire Wilson and went on to work in the aircraft industry as both a ferry transport pilot and stunt pilot. From 1947, when he returned to London, he was involved in several business activities that included selling aircraft.

In 1949 Green devised a talent show called *'Opportunity Knocks'*, which was commissioned by BBC Radio. The show lasted for only one series, and Green was told it was 'too American' for the British audience. After the show was cancelled, Green sued the BBC, Carroll Levis, and six friends and family of Levis, alleging a conspiracy to keep his Opportunity Knocks show off the air to preserve Levis's rival show, Discoveries. The case came to trial at the High Court in May 1955, with Green represented by Viscount Hailsham. The trial lasted for twenty days, but on 27 May, after the retirement of only twenty minutes, the jury returned a verdict for the defendants. As a result of the costs in the case, Green's creditors filed a petition for his bankruptcy, and a receiving order was made on 8 May 1956. Green went back to work ferrying aircraft and working in the aviation industry. He was not discharged from bankruptcy until 18 June 1958. He was later to re-appear on British television with the record-breaking ITV quiz-show

CA 113					From the Date Shown, Registration Lapsed on Account of:—		
DESCRIPTION OF AIRCRAFT Skymaster C54B - DC		SHEET 1	NATIONALITY AND REGISTRATION MARKS **G-APNH**			FILE No. SG. AD. 6391/2	
CONSTRUCTOR'S No. 18.333					FILE No.		
Certificate of Registration No.	Full Name and Address of Owner	Nationality of Owner	Date of Registration	Change of Ownership	Destruction or Permanent Withdrawal from Use	Cancellation by the Minister of Transport and Civil Aviation	
R.6391/1	Independent Air Travel Limited, Bournemouth (Hurn) Airport, Christchurch, Hants. Regd. address: Waterloo Chambers, Fiwale Road, Bournemouth.	British	17-6-58	11-9-59			
R.6391/2	Blue Air Limited, 84, Piccadilly, London, W.1. Reg'd Address: 23, Harcourt House, Cavendish Square, London W.1.	British	15-10-59	9-11-59			
R.6391/3	Astraeus Limited, 167 Victoria Street, London, SW1. Registered address: 122 High Street, Hounslow. Middlesex	British	8-3-60	23-3-60			
R.6391/4	Air Charter Limited, 31, Wigmore Street, London, W.1. Portland House, Stag Place, London, S.W.1. Registered address:- 35, Piccadilly, London, W.1.	British	25-3-60	24-8-64			

The entry for G-APNH within the Civil Aviation Authority files, showing the 'changes of ownership' from Independent Air Transport via Blue Air right through to Air Charter Ltd - no Euravia Air Transport listed!

Double Your Money.

In what was obviously a ghost-written letter in the brochure Green expounded on the benefits of taking a Sky Tours holiday:

'Dear Langton,

'It was nice of you to let me have a preview of your Sky Tours programme for 1959, and I can only say it lives up to the reputation you have built up during the last four years. When I read through the many tempting holiday bargains you offer, I'm really jealous that I can't take all of them. You do spoil one for choice'.

'The value is amazing, and it is still a complete mystery to me how you can do it for the money. From experience I know that compatible with price, everything is of the best. As a flying man, I was particularly impressed with the standard of aircraft, the ace crew and not forgetting the charming hostesses. When you tell me that you have personally chosen and vetted the hotels, I'm not surprised that the quality is high - anyway you as a practical hotelier should know what is needed. Overall, the organisation is certainly something to marvel at'.

'Not unlike anyone else I want the sun and if I can have this together with blue skies, sparkling blue seas and soft golden sands - I'm nearly satisfied, although I shall miss those towering mountain peaks and placid lakes of Switzerland and Austria unless I'm lucky enough to have the time to enjoy both sorts of holiday'.

'In Spain, I know the sun will be with me every day, whether I choose the Costa Brava or the Balearic Islands, maybe I might go further afield to the Costa Blanca, even to the far south to the 'Coast of the Sun', with a peep at Tangier. On the other hand, so many of my friends recommend Italy, to the Riviera of Flowers - Alassio or San Remo - others tell me I'm missing something if I don't try one of the Adriatic Rivieras of Italy. I repeat I'm spoilt for choice. You yourself, tell me to try the other side of the Adriatic, at that I might take you up, which is it to be just Opatija Patijaor shall I combine Opatija with Lake Bled. I still hate to think of missing out Switzerland and Austria'.

'What about these new two-centre holidays - you seem to have struck a winner there, the combinations seem wonderful - Innsbruck and Opatija on the Adriatic, Palma and Barcelona, Palma and the Costa Brava, Rome and Capri, Madrid and Tangier. These certainly conjure up exotic dreams, and what bargain prices!'

'Seems I could go on forever - I'm getting more and more envious of your Sky Tours clients, they're certainly in for some good times'.

'I could do with quite a few copies of the programme when ready, everyone I know seems to want to book a Sky Tour for 1959'.

'In the rush, don't forget to save places for me!'

This is where another facet of the mystery surfaces - that of the dates. As already stated, the 1959 brochure must have been prepared in the autumn of 1958, ready for release to the public during the winter of 1958/9. Clearly, the aircraft is marked 'Blue Air' - and this is before the days of imaging software, and yet according to other known information, Independent Air Transport did not become Blue Air until April 1959, which creates something of a puzzle. What is known is that all three C-54s passed through ownership of a Blue Air company with the address of 84 Piccadilly in October/November 1959. G-APCW in particular then went to Universal Sky Tours ownership in 1960 using the same address.

This was not the only occasion or airline company Captain Langton appears to have become involved with around this time. A few years earlier, on 25 March 1957, France, West Germany, Italy, the Netherlands, Belgium, and Luxembourg signed a treaty in Rome establishing what was termed the European Economic Community (EEC), also known colloquially as the Common Market. The EEC, which came into operation on January 1958, was a significant step in Europe's movement toward economic and political union. Langton saw the potential of opening up the travel market. Indeed, the records are pretty murky and very fragmented - which is not surprising given Langton penchant for keeping things close to his chest, but it seems that Langdon, in partnership with Dutch businessman A J D Steenstra Toussaint, tried to get an Anglo-Dutch airline off the ground. It was called 'Euravia Air Transport' although some sources say 'Euravia (Holland) Ltd'. Legend has it that one DC-4, G-APNH, was contracted to the new concern, but it seems that the venture soon failed, apparently due to lack of financing. Clearly, though, the European-sounding name 'Euravia' stuck in Langdon's memory, and was to be used again on another

concern as we shall see.

A few years later Steenstra Toussaint tried again, this time with businessman George Richardson, a former shareholder of Belgian International Air Services. Together they set up 'Transavia Limburg'; a local company based in Maastricht, initially using a single Douglas DC-3. Again there were financial difficulties as Toussaint and Richardson failed to arrange proper financing, so Florida-based Boreas Corporation, a trader in second-hand aircraft, bought a controlling interest in shares. The owner of Boreas, the famous test pilot Chalmers' Slick' Goodlin, wanted to profit from the fast-expanding and lucrative European charter market. He had a more thorough approach; the DC-3 was cancelled, and three former TSA Transair Sweden DC-6s were flown to Amsterdam Schiphol Airport. The company name was changed to 'Transavia Holland' and plans were drawn to create the first Dutch air charter company.

A meeting of minds

It was two years later that John Ernest Derek 'Jed' Williams B.Sc, FIN, AFRAeS, then a London aviation consultant, evolved the concept of a vertically integrated system design of travel to create a holiday package. As far as is known, he wrote the first article to be published advocating the policy - one that was later so sucessfully exploited by Tom Gullick and Clarksons Holidays.

'I was full of my ideas, but I did not know that Langton, of whom I had never heard, had been working along these lines for some years in the charabanc business,' Williams admitted.

From 1952 until 1958, Williams had been Manager of Planning and Development for El Al, the Isreali airline, and later as technical advisor for the chairman and managing director. He had previously worked with Swissair and Aerolineas Argentinas and with Air Service Training at Hamble. Equally unknown to Langton, J E D Williams had been introduced to aircraft dealer Leonard Orman by Itzhak Shander who later became president of El Al. Within two months of that meeting, Orman came to J E D Williams' office asking him for help selling three surplus to requirement El Al Lockheed Constellations - the reward would certainly be worth the effort - half the commission El Al were to pay Orman would go to Williams if successful. It was only then that J E D Williams learned the name of the potential purchaser: Captain T E D Langton. Though the name meant nothing to Williams, he was soon to meet the full blast of the colourful personality behind it. He could not have had a more challenging or taciturn first customer.

Having negotiated a passageway between Universal Sky Tours' Piccadilly shop and the administrative office above it, Len Orman and J E D Williams found Langton's office which itself formed part of the passage.

The two sat there uncomfortably as office workers passed to and fro and T E D Langton read his mail. There was complete disinterest both in the visitors and their mission. Orman eventually grudgingly got the admission from Langton that he could be in the market for aeroplanes for a new Spanish airline he was starting with Spanish associates, being called Hispair.

As a result of that spark of interest, however, T E D Langton and J E D Williams flew to Tel Aviv and met Williams' old boss, General Ben Arzi, in his office as chairman of the board of El Al. Not unexpectedly, Langton showed no interest in buying the General's Constellations, and it became apparent to Williams that no deal was to be struck. However, surprising events were afoot: 'I went on my own to Israel Aircraft Industries, IAI, who had maintained the three Constellations for El Al, that was also government-owned, and suggested that they sell the aircraft to Langton, fully overhauled and converted to his high-density seating, in a package which would include ongoing engine and component overhaul business for them. Following a day of discussions and, we can be sure, some tough-talking behind the scenes between IAI and El Al, Langton and I met the managing director of IAI the next evening in the bar of the Dan Hotel. As usual, Langton said nothing.

'We got down to £90,000 for three Constellations, fully overhauled in 82 seater configuration, plus a consignment of spare engines and parts which would remain the property of IAI. The overhauls alone were worth more than £60,000.

'I stared helplessly at Langton. He had to say something. I was finished. Langton fished a scrap of paper out of his pocket and wrote some numbers on it. He stared at them for a couple of minutes and then read them aloud slowly. They were the dates at which he would make progress payments. He had bought them!

'On the flight back to London, Langton talked to me at length for the first time. Aviation legislation had been transformed in 1960. To carry paying passengers one required an Air Operator's Certificate from the newly created Director of Aviation Safety - a man who had enormous personal powers including the right to withdraw a certificate in the middle of the night without warning - and a

licence for the particular service from a new Air Transport Licensing Board. They issued licences having regard to the public need, the diversion of traffic from existing licence holders and fitness of the operator (except in matters of safety), mainly financial fitness.

'Langton saw this legislation simply as a bag of tricks designed to entrench British European Airways - the forerunner of British Airways - and put people like himself out of business. I disagreed. We argued.

'He saw Spain as the big growth area, and he would by-pass the whole system with his own Spanish airline to which it would be politically impossible for the British to refuse traffic rights.'

Now Williams realised what was in Langton's mind - the vertical integration of the components of the package holiday system.

'You will have to go to Madrid to see about getting these aircraft accepted. I accepted, as a consultant, and pointed out that my meter was now ticking to his account. He grunted acquiescence'.

Things changed a couple of weeks later: 'After boarding a Madrid flight at Heathrow, I was astonished to see John Bruno, Langton's right-hand man, sitting breathlessly beside me. 'Just made it,' he said, 'Captain Langton sent me to tell you that he wants your mission to fail. He doesn't want a Spanish airline now.' 'Doesn't he realise that he has bought the aircraft and cannot now back out?' 'That's not it,' replied Bruno. 'Now he wants a British airline, and he wants you to be the Managing Director'.

The only clue located as to the date of the fateful meeting between Langton and Williams appears in a set of Britannia's official documentation titled 'Britannia Airways Fact Sheet,' it was in December 1961 that T E D Langton contacted J E D Williams about the formation of an airline to be named Euravia.

The aircraft the fledgling Euravia obtained from El Al had somewhat chequered histories, and are worth looking at in some detail. The three former El Al machines comprised a single L.149 and two L.049s. They were placed on the UK Civil Register as G-ARVP (formerly 4X-AKB), G-ARXE (4X-AKA) and G-AHEN (4X-AKD).

4X-AKA was built as a standard C-69 in 1944 as the sixth production aircraft in the earliest Constellations built. Its construction number 1967 signifies this because the first production C-69 bore c/n 1962. The aircraft was delivered to the USAAF late in 1944, bearing the military serial 43-10315. The aircraft remained on air force strength until 1947 when, having been declared surplus by the US Government, was acquired by a Mr A. Schwimmer. After being returned to Lockheed for civil conversion, the airliner became N90827 on the American Register for International Airways Inc. The aircraft was then placed in storage until early in 1951 when El Al's management decided to replace their DC-4 fleet with L.049s.

4X-AKA was converted from 049 to 149 standards by Lockheed in 1953. Fuel tankage went up from 4,773 gallons to 5,770 gallons, and AUW increased to 100,000 pounds.

When Britannia 313s replaced Constellations on the company's North Atlantic route in 1958, the L.049s continued to be used on the European network and also provided extra capacity during the peak season between Israel and the USA on an ad hoc basis, as well as operating between Israel and South Africa. Finally, in the autumn of 1961, 4X-AKB was put into storage. Total airframe hours to October 1961 exceeded 34,000 with an approximate mileage of 10,500,000.

4X-AKB with c/n 1965 was the fourth C-69 built in 1944. Although destined for the USAAF and allocated the military serial 43-10313, at the time the aeroplane came off the production line, it was painted in Transcontinental & Western Air colours, with serial number 10313 on its tail.

Despite its colourful airline livery, this early Constellation never carried a single fare-paying passenger back in 1944/45: wartime regulations within the USA prohibited such experience to all but a select group of Government-sponsored civilians in contrast to many thousands in the Armed Forces! Sometime after VE Day, the airliner was repainted in USAAF wartime livery, making several hundred Atlantic and Pacific crossings, repatriating American military personnel.

In 1947 the machine was declared surplus, put into storage, and early in 1948 Mr. Schwimmer acquired the airliner. Like 4X-AKA she was painted in the colours of International Airways Inc., becoming N90828 on the Civil Register.

Undoubtedly the third Constellation G-AHEN had the most colourful history of the ex-Israeli trio. Having c/n 1980, it was initially built as the 19th C-69 early in 1945. Although never put into service with the USAAF, it was allocated the military serial 42-94559, The aircraft was then sold to BOAC and was delivered to the Corporation's Montreal Engineering Base on 31 May 1946, becoming G-AHEN, being christened "RMA Baltimore" by Lord Knollys, The last-named event, appropriately enough, took place at Baltimore's own Municipal Airport to where the aircraft was specially flown for the occasion.

In company with other aircraft in the original BOAC 049 Constellation fleet, G-AHEN logged 11,350 hours on North Atlantic schedules until 8 January 1951 when, having completed a crew-training flight at Filton, the aeroplane overshot the runway, hitting a fuel storage building before finally stopping. Amazingly, there was no fire in this accident, but G-AHEN suffered severe damage to the front portion of the airframe, including the undercarriage and the main spar. By agreement between BOAC and the insurance underwriters, G-AHEN was declared a 'write-off'', the badly damaged aircraft becoming the property of the British Aviation Insurance Co. Ltd., who paid the (then) record sum of $244,000 for the remains.

The badly damaged airliner was dismantled at Filton and taken by road transport to Avonmouth Docks, shipped to New York aboard a freighter, having been purchased from the insurance company by Mel Adams & Associates Inc., of New York (Aircraft Brokers). The task of completely rebuilding this 049 was carried out by Lockheed Aircraft Service International at their Idlewild Base. Twenty-nine weeks after the salvaged 049 had been unloaded at the New York Docks, a 'new' Constellation was delivered to California-Hawaii Airways Inc., bearing the registration N74192. Into the rebuilding went salvaged parts from two other machines; found in a US Air Force Hangar at Toulouse, France were the fuselage and other components belonging to a C-69, serial 43-10314, that was shipped back to the USA by Lockheed's, together with parts from salvaged Air France 749 F-BAZQ.

From April 1952 to October 1953, N74192 logged about 1,153 hours, mainly on charter flights between the Pacific Coast and Hawaii. The aircraft was then purchased by El Al and, after being overhauled in New York,

Adolph William 'Al' Schwimmer (b. 10 June 1917, d. 10 June 2011) was integral to Euravia obtaining their first aircraft.

G-AHEN of BOAC perched in a very undignified position at Filton following it's landing accident. *(Simon Peters Collection)*.

was ferried to Israel, becoming 4X-AKD. At Lod Airport's Maintenance and Engineering Workshops, the aeroplane was stripped down (including a 1,200 hours check) by El Al's team. The work done included the re-arrangement of all cockpit instruments to conform with the airline's other 049s; the rebuilding of the entire passenger cabin eliminating the two-class arrangement, creating a single all-Tourist cabin and seating configuration, new cargo holds, new toilets plus a whole series of lesser maintenance jobs. All this was completed in a record time of six weeks, after which the aeroplane was immediately put into service between Israel and New York, joining the airline's (then) three other 049s on these North Atlantic schedules.

Incidentally, there is a very great deal of doubt regarding the two Constellations registered to International Airways Inc. It seems that the Israeli Mission which bought these two aircraft negotiated the transaction through a company, which traded as Intercontinental Airways Inc., of Burbank, California. The head of the company was recorded as "Mr A Schwimmer".

Al Schwimmer was another of the legendary 'characters' who surfaced after the war. He was an American and later Israeli engineer and businessman. In 1939, Schwimmer began his aerospace career at Lockheed Corporation as an engineer and also received his civilian pilot license. In World War Two, he worked for TWA and with the Air Transport Command as a flight engineer.

During Israel's War of Independence, he used his war experience and his contacts to smuggle aircraft to Israel as that fledgeling state battled against the invading armies of its neighbours. Using circuitous routes, he also recruited the pilots and crews to fly the aircraft to Israel, many becoming the nucleus of the Israeli Air Force.

In 1949, Schwimmer returned to the United States

and, in 1950, was convicted of violating the US Neutrality Acts for smuggling the aircraft and aircraft parts into Israel. Schwimmer was stripped of his voting rights and veteran benefits and fined $10,000 but did not receive a prison sentence. Schwimmer refused to ask for a pardon, believing that smuggling weapons to help create a Jewish State was the right moral decision to make and that breaking the law was a proper form of principled civil disobedience.

In the early 1950s, Schwimmer, who was running an aircraft maintenance company in Burbank, California, was approached by David Ben-Gurion, Israel's then Prime Minister, who asked Schwimmer to return to Israel and establish an aircraft company for commercial and military purposes. Schwimmer acceded to Ben-Gurion's request and founded Israel Aerospace Industries, of which he became the first CEO.

'A birth is announced...'
1 December 1961 saw the formal establishment of Euravia (London) Limited with J E D Williams and Captain John Charles 'Jackie' Harrington OBE, FRGS, MInstT, AFRAeS as co-directors. Harrington had been involved in aviation since pre-war Imperial Airways days and was also a director of J E D Williams & Co (Aviation Consultants) Ltd. The company secretary was recorded as P C Ward, and Sales Manager A W F Selby-Lowndes.

J E D Williams became the Managing Director and share capital of £25,000 was announced with Williams putting up £5,000.

The main tasks which had to be accomplished speedily if operations were to commence on April 1962, were the building of a management team; the finding of an operations base; the procurement of licences and obtaining an AOC. The Chief Engineer's role was filled by M Sydney 'Sid'

Finnigan, who was hired from Pan American and formerly of El Al and as such became the first employee of the company. The post of Chief Pilot was given to 39-year-old Captain Derek H Davison, who had worked as a Training Captain with El Al. Operations superintendent was Mr W. M. Strangeways, who was responsible for crew rostering, traffic and ground services. Mike Strangeways was previously with Silver City, Britavia, Aquila and helicopter services and had considerable experience of high-intensity short-haul operations.

Captain Derek Harold Davison (*b*. 6 July 1923, *d*. 22 December 2007) seen posing for a photograph in the Captain's seat of a Britannia 737. *(Britannia Airways)*

Derek H Davison - who was later to become Managing Director and Chairman of Britannia Airways later recalled the formation in Issue 12 of *'Britannia News':* 'I wasn't present at conception - which is a pity as it must have been quite interesting, conceptions usually are - but that was the joint privilege of Captain T E D Langton of Universal Skytours and Jed Williams of the consulting company.

The period of gestation was reasonably short, and I came in towards the latter end of February 1962. The birth took place in May 1962 if one understands by 'birth' - and we certainly did at the time - the obtaining of the Air Operators Certificate and our first flight.

Captain Edwards (later a Captain with QANTAS) was in command for a week's tour of the Holy Land. A fitting destination we thought.

I was with El Al out in Israel at the time when I accepted the position of Chief Pilot to commence 1 April 1962. El Al agreed to my release and well before 1 April, and I became involved with the preparation of Constellation emergency duties at the request of Roy McDougall, who had been appointed Deputy Chief Pilot. He was back in the London office, setting out an Operations Manual. Mike Forster had

been appointed Chief Flight Engineer, and while we both were sure we had met before on the Comet I fleet of BOAC, neither of us could recollect the circumstances. As soon as we saw each other at Lod Airport - Mike having arrived to collect one of the three ex-El Al Constellations which had been acquired from Bedec, the Israeli Maintenance and Overhaul organisation - we were immediately able to recollect the circumstances under which we had met - in Rome some eight years earlier, but that is another story'.

'After some very high cylinder head temperatures during full power Segment II climbs with cowl and oil cooler gills set to achieve the required performance, we accepted the first and subsequent two aircraft; and they were placed on the British Aircraft Register'.

Sid Finnegan was appointed Chief Engineer and Mary-Ann Allen Chief Stewardess, which completed the new executive team. I emphasise executive team because it was really one team with everyone in the airline contributing their utmost to get 'this thing' off the ground.

Derek Harold Davison was born in Kirkby-in-Ashfield, in Nottinghamshire, on 26 July 1923 and

Chief Engineer Mike Forster, who was instrumental in obtaining Euravia's AOC. *(Britannia Airways)*

educated at Queen Elizabeth Grammar School, Mansfield, where he was the shot and discus champion. He joined the RAF on leaving school and trained as a pilot in South Africa.

He joined 614 Squadron flying B-24 Liberator heavy bombers from airfields in southern Italy. Many years later his wife, an art historian, was horrified to learn that the purpose of his first visit to Venice had been to sow mines in the lagoon.

After leaving the RAF in 1947, Davison flew converted bombers on long-range transport routes before joining, in August 1948,

British South American Airways (BSAA), an airline established by the former Pathfinder leader Don Bennett.

Davison soon found himself involved in the Berlin Airlift, flying Avro Tudors from RAF Wunstorf, in Germany, with supplies for the beleaguered city.

When BSAA was taken over by BOAC in 1949 Davison became a First Officer flying the early post-war airliners before transferring to the Comet 1 fleet. With the chances of command remote, however, Davison joined Pakistan International Airlines as a captain, and four years later, became a training captain with the Israeli airline, El Al, flying its newly-acquired Bristol Britannias.

In the last few days of 1961, the company submitted their first group of applications to the ATLB - then under the chairmanship of Professor Daniel Jack - for 'B' licenses for the summer of 1962. A 'B' licence is held in conjunction with the tour organiser for a regular series of flights - such as every Tuesday afternoon to Mahon - for the exclusive carriage of passengers for the tour organiser on a specified holiday, usually with provisions as to the cost of the holiday. The ATLB was, in turn, required to satisfy itself as to the suitability of the applicant, concerning financial resources, the insurance arrangements and condition of service of employees.

The records at the Kingsway, London, HQ of the Civil Aviation Authority, successor to the ATLB, show that Euravia (London) Ltd, were applying for a licence in conjunction with Seamarks Bros Ltd (Airtours) of Luton'...for the carriage of inclusive tour passengers between Luton and Palma, the licence to be in effect from 26 May to 29 September 1962. The service would be operated at a frequency of one flight weekly in each direction on Fridays or Sundays with Constellation aircraft. The tariff to be from £53.11s.0d. to £72.19s.6d.'

Deputy Chief Pilot Captain Roy McDougall. *(Britannia Airways)*

Captain Jim Watret *(Britannia Airways)*

Submissions were initially made in a private hearing and by correspondence. Then it was time for a public hearing - opened on 20 February 1962 - to consider the need for the proposed services and the effect this would have on other airlines.

The Board decided that a day would be set aside for the first hearing, the morning to be devoted to a public airing of Euravia's case on the need for their services and the objections to them, and the afternoon to be a private session on the airline's fitness to undertake the flights.

The list of the objectors reads like a directory of British airlines. One objection was that the proposed charters would divert traffic from the proposed scheduled service for which no license had been issued and for which no evidence had been heard by the Board. The records show that one Board member accused sky Tours as the tour organiser of asking for licenses for which it didn't have passengers, or trying to get passengers for flights for which it didn't have licenses! Both requests appeared to be heinous crimes.

J E D Williams recalled the hearing: 'The whole thing was silly and the debate on a low intellectual level. It was stupid for three reasons. Firstly, we would not divert traffic from scheduled services, we would stimulate it, but the government and the Board would not entirely accept this argument for another three years or so. Secondly, the question of diversion of traffic from one charter airline to another was an issue between tour organisers, not the airlines they happened to have contracted that year. Thirdly, everybody present knew that if Langton wanted to fly to Spain, nobody in Britain could, and nobody in Spain would, stop him from chartering a Spanish airline. One objector said he would not mind because the British public did not like flying by Spanish charter airlines. I wondered whose side he was on'.

' The afternoon session was very different. I had, of course, given the Board, in advance, documentation with lots of appendices which purported to show that our operation would be viable, our cash adequate, our fleet ideal for our purpose, and that we in Euravia were splendid chaps at running airlines especially with the vast resources of Universal Sky Tours behind us. This time Jackie Harrington, the company secretary and I occupied the centre of the front row in the enormous empty hall. The Board outnumbered us more than two to one'.

' The questioning started, courteous and deadly efficient. Almost immediately the accountant rushed to the loo and did not return, a consequence apparently of the deplorable pub lunch we had shared. Jackie sat relaxed, casual, strong and silent, looking just the chap to start an airline on £25,000. The trouble, of course, was the complete absence of any hard facts about those vast resources of Universal Sky Tours. The man they wanted before them, would always want and never get, was of course Langton'.

'The claim that our fleet was ideal for our purpose was not entirely risible. At £30,000 per aircraft, we could afford to keep our aeroplanes on the ground much of the time if necessary. It was a telling point at a singular moment in aviation history.'

As the hearings dragged on, Euravia had the distinction of being refused - on the grounds of traffic demand - more licences than any other two airlines put together. However, they were also granted more than any other airline except British United. That year the new airline paid over two thousand pounds in licence application fees.

The rights to international scheduled air services were agreed between the governments concerned, and their nominated flag carriers had to offer identical fare structures. Since the airlines could not compete with each other on price, they were all obliged to buy jets as quickly as they appeared. Most of the world's pre-Boeing 707 fleets came on the market within three years. Charter airlines sprang up everywhere and disappeared as quickly. Established charter airlines were in trouble because they had paid too much for equipment suddenly obsolete.

J E D Williams again: 'We got about eighty per cent of the licences we sought. In my opinion, against the background of those times, the Board would have been entirely justified in rejecting us entirely. That they did not is a tribute to the courage and insight of the members of the Board, distinguished old gentlemen without any knowledge of aviation between them.'

There were more applications the following month, but now existing operators were beginning to take note of this unknown airline called Euravia. When it applied for a route from Gatwick to Palma and Barcelona, there were objections from British European Airways, British United Airways, Cunard Eagle, and even East Anglian Flying Services of Southend. Nevertheless, the request was granted subject to the flights leaving from Luton rather than Gatwick.

Along with this were also early signs of Euravia's forward ambitions. In the next month or two, they had already submitted 34 applications for summer routes the following year. The broadening of UK departure points was shown by requests to fly from Glasgow, Belfast, Luton, Liverpool, Manchester and Cardiff to destinations including Palma, Valencia, Tarragona, Ibiza, Perpignan, Nice, Genoa, Alicante, Malaga, Tangier, Gerona, Barcelona and Tenerife.

There was also a need to make sure that all the aircrew were licenced for the type they were flying. Several of the flight crew who were being taken on did not have Constellation experience, and it seems that the El Al book on the aircraft was not acceptable with the ARB examiners. It was not the appropriate background in the eyes of the British authorities who informed Euravia that they based their examinations on the 049 model Constellation input used by Gatwick-based Trans-European Aviation who were operating this sub-type.

Euravia's Deputy Chief pilot Roy McDougall's visit to Trans-European drew a complete blank; they saw Euravia as a competitive threat and firmly declined any assistance. Fortunately, one of Trans-European's flight engineers, Andy McGill, was known within the Euravia camp. Like many flight crew in those days, his wife augmented his airline salary with a business of her own. In this case, it was a hairdressing salon in Richmond, Surrey. Roy McDougall went to see McGill, and he agreed to supply books and run classes for Euravia crew in the evening after the salon closed. It was possibly the strangest of aviation classrooms ever - men sitting on swivel-chairs under inactive hairdryers with notebooks perched on empty sinks until 10.30 pm on dark winter evenings learning the subtler points of how to fly Constellations.

Though Euravia still needed an Air Operator's Certificate, at least they could now offer routes to potential tour operator clients. But the biggest disappointment came from the chief shareholder. The level of bookings from T E D Langton's Universal Sky Tours indicated an ominous excess of supply over demand both in the licences awarded by the ATLB and in the number of aircraft they were about to accept. There was not enough business even for two of the three Constellations.

With the climate of opinion surrounding charter operators at that time, it is not surprising that the rumour mill - which always operated at the speed of light - had already encompassed Euravia. Tour operators were ready to bet the airline would not get off the ground - and they were not willing to risk their clients being stranded on a windswept Bedfordshire plateau rather than enjoying themselves on a Mediterranean beach.

After grudgingly admitting at the last minute that he only needed two aircraft, Langton came up with what proved to be a telling lead, telling Williams he knew of a tour company that had not yet chartered its summer programme, Williams immediately rushed to the Midlands to see the prospect. As a result, Williams came back armed with a whole summer programme to fill one of the Constellations. Not only that, the rate he negotiated was ten per cent higher than Langton was paying for his charters.

Then there was the matter of finding a base. At first, the fledgeling airline considered Gatwick Airport, to the south of London. Gatwick was then, as it is now the home to a number of the charter airlines. A visit to the airport commandant revealed that although the flying would not create any problem, there was a distinct lack of facilities and that maintenance and handling would have to be contracted out to established operators there. These problems led to a visit to Luton Airport, perched on a plateau above the town and close to the then newly opened M1 motorway, where the local authority had provided a good runway and hangar facilities to attract business.

So the advertising campaign for Campari aperitif by Bliss Films Advertising Agency under creative input from Vernon Howe placed 'Luton Airport' well in the public's mind for a generation as a 'bucket and spade' holiday airport. It was followed up, and the image was reinforced by 'Cats UK' a British four-piece all-girl band who had a hit on UEA Records in October 1979 with the single 'Luton Airport', written by Paul Curtis and John Worsley.

The airport itself had it's origins back in the mid-1930s when, with the aid of a government loan, Luton Corporation bought the 329.5-acre site for £100 per acre, and the aerodrome was under way. Even in these early days, Luton was thinking big.

'Aviation fever' took hold and, in February 1936, the Corporation created a twelve-member Airport Committee. It would not be long before they would see the fruits of their labours. Edgar Percival's Percival Aircraft Ltd, then based at Gravesend's London - East airport, enquired about the possibility of establishing an aircraft factory on the town's new airport. This was an early realisation of Luton's dream - not only an aerodrome but a site of aircraft production! A ten acre site was made available at advantageous all-inclusive rates with an option to purchase the site after ten years when a negotiable set of landing fees would come into force.

The aerodrome was officially opened on 16 July 1938 by the Right Honourable Sir Kingsley Wood, Secretary of State for Air. The Air Minister was greeted by airport committee chairman Alderman Oscar Hart, who later presented him with a golden key to commemorate the occasion. The VIP party who arrived with Sir Kingsley from Hendon included Transport Minister and Luton MP Leslie Burgin and Lieut-Col Sir Francis Shelmerdine, Director-General of Civil Aviation.

With the outbreak of the war, the progress of civil aviation from Luton was slow. Research and development of military aircraft were in abundance with Percival taking the lead. After the

Setting up at Luton Airport

'Were you truly wafted here from Paradise?' asked Jeremy Clyde, who was playing the suave, upper-crust young man as a glamorous young couple paused for refreshment on the terrace of an exotic villa drinking Campari... 'Nah... Lut'n Airport' replied cockney-girl actress and model Lorraine Chase.

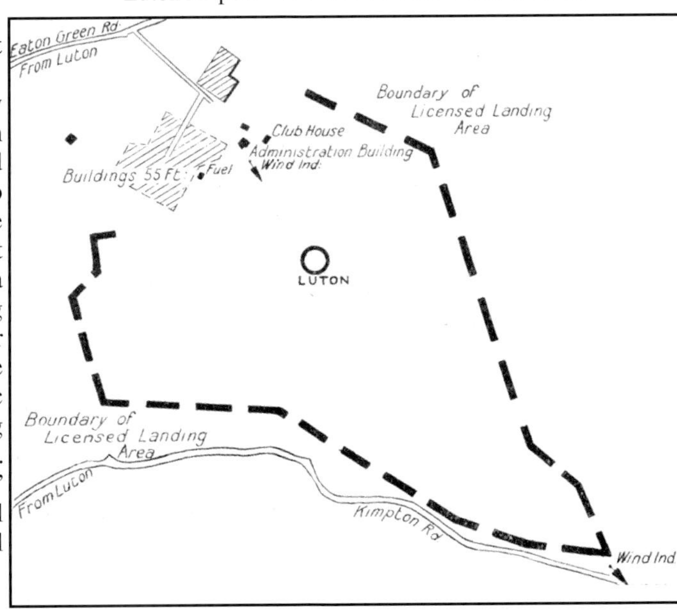

Luton Airport - as seen in the *Air Pilot* of 1937.

Right: The original Passenger Terminal at Luton Airport around 1951 showing the airside entrance for arriving passengers.

Below: The inside did look slightly better, as this shot of the HM Customs Hall' shows.
[both Simon Peters Collection.]

first flight of the Percival Proctor, it came to play a vital role in the war effort, providing both the RAF and the Fleet Air Arm with much needed wireless trainers. But after 122 Proctors had been built at Luton, the Ministry of Aircraft Production (MAP) concluded that the Percival plant was better suited to the manufacture of larger aircraft and the Proctor was moved out to F. Hills & Sons of Manchester.

In March of 1940 D. Napier & Sons - the engine manufacturers - established its Flight Testing Department at Luton, an annexe to their successful engine manufacturing plant at Acton in West London.

The appearance of post-war Luton looked very good, for it seemed to be a very successful commercial concern with two well established manufacturers, an extended aerodrome and four additional hangars. The Corporation accepted the Government's new proposal to purchase additional land and buildings. There was one major problem for the airport though - the continued lack of Customs facilities of any kind at Luton.

It was in September 1950 that the Airport Committee decided to build its new control tower on the north side of the aerodrome and, the following year, the aerodrome was granted a one-year trial of customs facilities. At last, Luton had an Airport. The new control tower was opened in September 1952 by Alan T. Lennox-Boyd, Minister of Transport and Civil Aviation, who promised that the airport would receive as much Ministry help as

possible for forward development.

The new five floors high tower replaced the old wooden structure. The ground floor housed a reception and the airport enquiries office, and the first floor was reserved as a future office, the second was to be home to the meteorological room and records and, on the top two floors, were generating equipment and the actual control room. By now there were three grass runways in use -1,800,1,650 and 1,550 yards.

In May 1959 Mayor Alderman Mrs F. M. Brash blew a whistle and sounded a klaxon which started construction of Luton's new concrete runway. The Lady Mayor was Chairman of the Airport Committee in 1947. She said that Luton should '...seize the opportunity to advance towards an airport worthy of such original vision, commensurate with the industrial importance of the Borough'.

The new runway designated 08/26, was to be 5,432 feet long, 150 feet wide, took seven months to build and required 80,000 tons of concrete to make the ten-inch thick pavement. The east-west siting would allow for ninety-five per cent operational use in cross-winds of up to fifteen miles per hour. It was planned that the runway would later be extended to 8,000 feet to handle larger aircraft and that this would require the acquisition of further land. The runway would have a fifty feet wide taxiway linking the runway with the enlarged parking apron. It would be operational by 21 December 1959. Work was undertaken to install new runway lights, full visual glide path indicators, displaced threshold, high- and low-intensity approach lights, taxiway centreline, holding bay and apron floodlighting, illuminated windsock and identity beacon. The lighting was supplied from GEC, and the revised expenditure was around £35,000. In all, the new lighting took eight months to complete.

White, high-intensity approach lights stretched 1,400 feet into the approach from the threshold, together with a further 1,000 feet of red, low-intensity approach lights. At intervals of 200 feet, were white bi-directional runway lights with green threshold lights. At each end of the runway, visual glide path indicators were installed. Later, these were to be renamed 'VASIS' or Visual Approach Slope Indicating System. Each unit contained red and white lights which appeared to be pink when the approach was made on the correct slope. It was the first full VASIS system to be installed at any UK airport, although it had undergone trials at Southend as a prototype.

The airport also installed a new Decca radar system which gave a clear radar approach for one aircraft at a time coming into the main runway. This 'Talk-Down' radar was operated by the controller to position the aircraft on the extended centreline of the runway while the gave verbal height information direct to the pilot until he could actually see the runway and visually land at Luton.

Luton had laid plans for the erection of a giant hangar at the airport. At this time, there were plenty of available sites, and Luton based operators could more or less choose their hangarage positions quite freely. But the Corporation's Hangar 61, was approved and building work was commenced on a 200 feet clear span structure. There were also plans for a new terminal building which would house airline offices, freight sheds and the customs office. Initially, the terminal was to be rather basic in design but would allow conversion to alternative usage when the proper terminal was completed.

Although Luton's customs facility had been earlier withdrawn, it was re-instated on an initial trial basis. The Ministry agreed to sanction permanent customs for Luton this time, provided sufficient business could be demonstrated. It was a blessing to international travellers inbound to Luton as, previously, there had been a forty-minute stopover at Southampton to clear passengers through customs. A customs shed was erected adjacent to the terminal building, next to the control tower, and cost £2,000. With the advice of HM Customs & Excise, the Airport Committee established a duty-free bonded store.

A conference was staged at Napier's which took as its theme the subject of 'Air Charter Passenger and Freight Traffic'. It was recognised that the airport's catchment area had a 30-mile radius plus the south Midlands - more if the newly-opened M1 motorway was a success - and embraced a population of some four million people. It was stressed that Luton should be developed by the independent airlines for charter, inclusive tours,

Luton Airport in 1960. Even with the new runway, the site managed to retain something of an aerodrome look, despite the industrial development around. *(Bill Armstrong Collection)*

vehicle ferrying and private executive travel. Many of the local businesses, represented by the Luton. Dunstable and District Chamber of Commerce, had still to realise the potential of having an airport on their doorstep.

At this conference, the airport disclosed its five-year plan, including a 5,000 feet north-south runway, a permanent terminal building with shops, bank and public enclosure, further hangars and additional apronage.

J E D Williams and Captain Harrington made at least two visits to the airport to inspect the facilities and talk things over with Peter Rushton, the Airport Commandant who appeared to be welcoming. The arrival of Euravia's first Constellation shattered the rural peace of the nearby village of Caddington, a little under three miles west of the runway, but the sound of Euravia's aircraft was to become a very familiar one as the airline made Luton its main departure point, operations centre and maintenance base.

The new runway was undoubtedly suitable for operations, but the existing passenger facilities were hopelessly inadequate. Three days after Christmas 1961 JED Williams and Jackie Harrington met with Luton's Mayor, the Town Clerk and a group of other councillors and officials. It did not take long a proposal to be made for a new, but temporary passenger terminal that could handle 250 passengers at a time and be ready within four months.

The extension to the passenger terminal was undertaken between January and April 1962 and Euravia started the move into its hangarage in February, allowing the airline the much needed workshop space, stores and offices. The relocation was completed in March.

On completion of the terminal building, Euravia was feeding through almost 250 passengers each morning and evening. The terminal was bulging with even more passengers during the high season as Derby Airways and Autair routed their own traffic through.

Immediately, the airport put forward plans for a

Left: JED Williams is seem on the left with Luton Airport Commandant Peter Rushton, who was an early enthusiastic supporter of Euravia.

With the increase in passenger numbers passenger accomodation was created at the base of the Control Tower. The remodelled terminal building consisted of two prefabricated wooden buildings. It doubled the space available and lent the much needed extra capacity in the departure lounge. There was a buffet and bank and a number of other new facilities for passengers to enjoy.
(Simon Peters/Bill Armstrong Collection)

more permanent terminal building. It was scheduled to open in 1964 - but did not come into use until 1966. Because of the increase in air traffic, Luton started to monitor aircraft departure and arrival noise levels. The village of Caddington, three miles to the west was suffering most so, from September 1963, departing traffic made a twenty degree left turn after take-off to avoid the village.

The airport formulated a five-year plan which included improved access, the first phase of the new terminal building, twenty-nine stands for aircraft up to Comet size and a heliport.

As J E D Williams was later to recall: 'We took to the Luton people, and they took to us. They had a nice long runway and a lovely big empty hangar — and enthusiasm. I knew I could sell Luton to T E D Langton because of that new M1 Motorway, which made it nearer to London than Gatwick. That was critical because, in those days, charter travel began, for most people, in Central London. Euravia had established a town terminal in an old Avon tyre works near Euston station from where passengers were bussed to the airport. That was particularly convenient for holidaymakers travelling on the overnight trains from Scotland and the north'.

If the financial deal with Don Harvey, the Town Clerk of Luton, and his airport committee was an ace for Euravia, the trump card deftly played by JED Williams was an astute arrangement that the airport would not have a duty free shop. That perk - and it was a big one - to was be Euravia's, and they exploited it to the full.

It was time to concentrate the corporate mind on securing the Air Operator's Certificate without which Euravia could not start their aircraft flying or cash flowing. It had to be won from the Directorate of Aviation Safety by satisfying the officials on its operational performance and facilities - and that it has the resources, equipment, skills and standards to carry passengers safely. It included the preparation of comprehensive manuals covering airline operation.

To help achieve this within the timescale, stewardesses were press-ganged into duplicating and collating the necessary manuals, but it was deputy chief pilot Roy McDougall who, at the outset, accepted the bulk of the task. As a line captain, he had no experience of paperwork or administration generally. The first need was for an operations manual.

Mike Forster, the chief flight engineer, was given the task of pushing the manual along to secure the necessary Air Operator's Certificate. He still had his home in Bournemouth and, as a former BOAC Constellation flight engineer, he retained his manuals in the attic of the house there. He rushed down to the South Coast, brought the volumes back to Luton, and by the simple method of deleting 'BOAC' and substituting the word 'Euravia', handed the sheets out for typing.

Within the wooden shack which became Euravia's first Luton Airport base, there was one office for Williams, one for Harrington, and the rest shared a room - and one secretary. She could not possibly cope with all the input needed for that manual, so McDougall's wife, who was working

Lockheed Constellation G-AHEN...

...along with company sister aircraft G-AHEL

A pair of Euravia Constellations are made ready at Luton for another trip. *(Bill Armstrong Collection)*

elsewhere, typed much of it helped by the other girls in her office who earned a few pounds by typing the sheets after hours.

Euravia had to satisfy an enormous group of people - the Air Transport Licensing Board, the officials who issued the Air Operator's Certificate, the Air Registration Board, and an almost endless list of other civil servants who had to be satisfied with every full stop and comma, and also that every dotted line had to contain a signature.

Captain Davison was later to recall the delivery flights of the airliners for Euravia: 'El Al agreed to my release, and my first task was to carry out some test flights on the Constellations in Israel before accepting delivery. To meet the required two-engine-out climb performance, the aircraft required a delicate handling balance of bank angle to relieve the rudder, with the cowl gills and oil cooler flaps closed to reduce drag to the point where both engines were on their temperature limits.'

The delivery flight of the first aircraft, Victor Papa, took 10¼ hours and it was necessary to change the crystals in the radio set because of the then shortage of frequencies as they passed through the Cyprus control area to Athens, to Italy and so to Heathrow. The flight engineer on that delivery was Mike Forster.

The last of those Constellation test flights in Israel was the day before departure for Heathrow where formal clearance into the UK was to be given. Because the aircraft left Lod Airport, Tel Aviv, at 1.30 a.m. on 11 April, it was a very tired Captain Davison who arrived back in England. Even then there was a mix-up over clearance, so Davison decided to call it a day rather than fly on to Luton as had initially been planned. They overnighted at Heathrow.

'I remember feeling how green the countryside was after Israel - and also how difficult it was back then to spot the runway.' By the time he brought the remaining two aircraft in, Echo November twelve days later, and X-ray Echo on 12 May he was beginning to feel at home.

According to the *Britannia Airways Fact Sheet*, there was a welcoming ceremony for the new airline at the airport on 17 April.

Two weeks after delivery of the first aircraft, Captain Davison had a meeting with the Directorate of Aviation Safety to provide them with the information they needed for the issuance of the all-important Air Operator's Certificate.

'We had not done enough, and we did not satisfy them. But before they said 'no', I jumped up and said: 'You want to see more of what we have done and be told less of what we are going to do.' The reply was that that was precisely right. I asked for another meeting in a week's time, and we then got the certificate. If I had not done that, we might not have got the certificate at all.'

But getting that certificate was just one milestone reached on a long journey of activity still required to achieve first commercial flight. Another was training the crews and converting many of them to a new type of aircraft as well as carrying out various checks. There were two aspects to checking the pilots. One was the standard line flying - route familiarity, heights, navigational elements and the whole scenario surrounding whether a pilot can fly safely. The other was the ability to deal with an emergency - be it engine failure, a three-engine landing, an engine fire, or, if necessary, evacuating the aircraft of its passengers. There was also parallel work to be done in engineering terms.

Derek Davison was working until the small hours of the morning, then facing an hour's drive home and snatching a few hours' sleep ready to be back in his Luton office by early the next day - the pace was punishing, but it needed to be done. The reward was the   sight of the first commerical first flight taking off - albiet a positioning service to Manchester.

With all licences, Certificates of Airworthiness and Air Operators Certificate in place Euravia began its summer-season series on schedule on 5 May 1962, with a Birmingham-based Midland Air Tours holiday flight from Manchester to Perpignan and Palma under the command of Captain Peter Edwards. Chief Stewardess Marianne Allen remembered that the aircraft took off without oxygen masks on board. She asked the handling agent for some when they arrived at Manchester. He could produce only one - but fortunately, the rest of the first flight went smoothly.

By all accounts that first flight was completed incident-free, but the second one - on the same day - was certainly not without drama. It took off in the early evening from Luton for Barcelona and Palma with seventy-seven passengers under the command of Captain Don Tanton, who was recruited to Euravia from Skyways on 1 April. After half an hour's flying in the rain, the windscreen-wipers stopped owing to a jammed motor. It was just the beginning, for at Barcelona the wheel brakes failed. It proved impossible to take the Palma passengers to their destination, so G-AHEN limped back empty to

A line-up of Euravia Constellations at Luton, seen from under the tail of another. *(Kaz Ale Collection)*

Lockheed Constellation G-AHEN in flight *(author's collection)*

Luton two days later.

It was not long before the name Euravia in blue and black lettering on a white fuselage - presented in what today would be regarded as an inelegant typeface, could be seen on the fuselages of Constellations G-ARVP, G-AHEN and G-ARXE at a growing number of European airports.

It did not mean that the company was starting to take-off in a corporate sense. A capital of £25,000 offered precious little liquidity or manoeuvrability with staff, fuel costs, landing fees, and passenger, hangar, engineering and other facilities needing to be paid.

The economic reality was that they were achieving around 1,200 hours a year of flying out of each of the Constellations. It was mainly within a six-month operational window because the holiday market being, of necessity, concentrated on the summer months. A few weeks' flying to South America or the Middle East was about all that was available outside that, but for the rest of the winter, the aircraft was in hibernation. Things were so tight that it was rumoured that when it was necessary to obtain another engine for a Constellation, the money was not there, so J E D Williams had to come to the rescue with a personal guarantee of £5,000.

One period when there was undoubtedly no flying was Christmas Day - and then the terminal building was turned to festivities with a staff party with refreshments provided by the airline's catering department.

During the formative period whilst crew training was carried out, and the company's Air Operator's Certificate was obtained, Euravia set up a flight operations department and associated administrative organisation, moved into a new terminal building at Luton, took over a new £200,000 hangar, and set up its own catering, traffic and engineering divisions. Within a few months, there was created the complete nucleus of a self-contained international airline - a unique achievement in itself, as Euravia was the only British independent formed at the time to establish itself to full airline scale as a self-contained entity. The developmental problems and difficulties were soon overcome, and the three Constellations operated a very satisfactory first summer season. Following an appraisal of that season's operations, it soon became apparent that

One of the company Constellations parked at a remote area of Heathrow, with the BEA building just visible in the background. *(author's collection)*

Not the best of images, but pictures of the interiors of Euravia/Skyways aircraft are very hard to find, likewise any photographs of the hostesses. Here Stewardess Lanteala is seen in her uniform with passengers on a Luton - Malta service.

The picture shows that the 749 Constellations were configured with five-abreast seating, and had no overhead racks.
(author's collection)

additional capacity was required, so the problem of further or new equipment was studied.

Another incident that involved Captain Tanton was in Valencia when he could not start the number four engine. It was found that the flywheel would not engage with the crankshaft. Tanton remembered that when he was flying DC-3s, the meshing could be achieved by pulling a chain underneath the engine. He suggested to his flight engineer David Brown, who was later to run the airline's training school, that, perhaps, there was a similar chain on the Constellation's engines. After taking all the cowlings off the engine, a lever was found on the back of the flywheel. The only way the engine could be started, however, was for Tanton to energise the starter from the cockpit while Brown actually stayed up in the engine and manually engaged the starter motor when it had reached the correct speed.

'Passengers slipped on hydraulic fluid as they ran to board their aircraft - there was no seat allocation in those days. Hordes of airmen rushed out with drip trays and placed them in position around the aircraft whenever we visited RAF Lyneham to protect their beautiful new white concrete!'

Nevertheless, only three months after their first flight, Euravia found itself in active discussion to take over Skyways, another UK airline, and were talking to Martins Bank, which had a debenture for more than the company's assets could realise.

In the autumn of 1962, the well known and old-established independent Skyways suddenly found itself with relatively modern Constellation 749s for their services. As the sole UK operators of Constellations, both Euravia and Skyways were simultaneously faced with equipment problems. Euravia, with only three aircraft, and limited

Euravia Constellation G-AMUP is photographed at Manchester. This aircraft remained in service with the airline until it was permanently withdrawn from use in January 1966.

W M 'Mike' Strangeways, Operations superintendent, confers on an operational problem with Captain J C Harrington, deputy Managing Director.

capacity. Skyways with three Constellations and four Yorks and a general all-year-round business had just lost, quite suddenly, a valuable BOAC contract to operate scheduled freight services between London and Singapore. Apart from the passenger services between London, Tunis and Malta, and general charter work, Skyways' fleet was now dramatically under-employed.

Universal Sky Tours' chairman was Air Commodore Sidney Smith, who was hired by T E D Langton. Smith was the public persona of the company; any irate customers or inquisitive journalists were directed his way, as Langton hated the public relations aspect of the business.

Sidney Smith had previously worked for Skyways, and it was through that connection that an approach was made to Euravia. In addition to the charter airline, there was Skyways Engineering at Stansted Airport, which had diminished from whole aircraft overhaul to less ambitious component overhaul, and Skyways Coach Air, which ran a ferry service across the English Channel. Despite the obvious decline, the company was still being run with style and corporate grandeur.

The initial groundwork may have been through Sidney Smith, but the creator of the deal which took the ailing company into Euravia was Victor Doel, Skyways' finance director. Firstly, Skyways Engineering was hived off for the benefit of Martins Bank. Though the coach-air operation did not have much future, Skyways owned the airfield they used at Lympne in Kent, and that had real estate value.

Skyways owned traffic rights to Malta, though these were later sold to British European Airways.

A spectacular night-time shot of one of Euravia's Constellations about to depart Luton. *(Simon Peters Collection)*

Constellation G-ALAK, formerly of Skyways. The aircraft went to Ace Freighters.

G-ALAL, another former Skyways machine.
(*both Britannia Airways Collection*)

Even the Yorks brought contracts with them, including emergency service for Pan American to get spare engines to unserviceable aircraft stranded anywhere between Iceland and Iran.

The core company, complete with a £250,000 overdraft, was sold to Euravia for just £1. The deal was that Euravia employed the assets after deducting their costs and make a contribution to overheads. The rest of the revenue went to reducing the overdraft.

Doel's deal turned out to be a good one for virtually all the parties concerned. As J E D Williams was to comment later: 'About thirty British airlines had gone bankrupt since the war, and this was the only deal I am aware of where a civilised arrangement was made resulting in everyone being better off.

The shareholders and the unsecured creditors all received something out of it, and Martins Bank - later taken over by Barclays - got most of their money back. We had a lot of static from the Air Transport Licensing Board because of our lack of capital against our ambitious plans, having doubled the size of the fleet in the first four months. Any change in the share capital would, of course, have diluted my twenty per cent holding in Euravia.

So the aircraft which initially belonged to Universal Sky Tours had their titles transferred to the airline during the first year, and Euravia paid the £90,000 by an instrument of subordinated debt that kept the ATLB happy because now £115,000 was shareholders funds instead of £25,000.'

It was apparent to Euravia that, as the Skyways 749s had freight doors, these aircraft offered non-seasonal regular trade with the added advantage of aircraft capacity so urgently required to meet the 1963 summer season commitments. The eventual solution was for Euravia to take over Skyways and the share capital was acquired in early October 1962. Both companies remained legally as separate entities but were fully integrated and respective aircraft operated from a shared pool. Without a doubt, there were problems with assimilating Skyways' staff into their new parentage. Though

Engineers work on one of Euravia's Constellations in preparation for service. (*Simon Peters Collection*)

A delightful snapshot of G-ARVP outside the hangar at Luton. (*Kaz Ale Collection*)

there was, for instance, no equivalent opening for either the Skyways' operations director or its chief pilot, so both readily accepted positions as line captains. Not only that, they gave strong support to their new superiors.

There was a good tailpiece for J E D Williams himself. He bought the business of Skyways Engineering from Martins Bank, with money the bank loaned him, turned it into the Canford group of companies, and sold it to advantage to Rio Tinto Zinc in 1983.

The winter of 1962-63 found the now established organisation concerned with problems of rationalisation and organisation. The fleet now consisted of six Constellations and four Yorks, all of which were integrated at Luton, the Skyways aircraft moving over from bases at London Heathrow and Stansted, although a small Skyways operating base was maintained at Heathrow. Major annual checks were carried out by Euravia, Marshalls of Cambridge, and Israel Aircraft Industries at Lod.

The management of the company, although closely associated with the Sky Tours organisation, was entirely independent; indeed, traffic generated by Universal Sky Tours accounted for less than half of Euravia's revenue. Undoubtedly the application of Euravia' energies to the rapidly developing specialist inclusive-tour holiday traffic, supported by scheduled passenger services (as exemplified by the Malta service) and by the general world-wide charter work, consolidated the companies position and provided a firm base for further expansion.

Most importantly, these events created new dimensions for Euravia. Derek Davison: 'Skyways was a real turning point in the company's history. It more than doubled the size of the airline in one sweep, and it told the public that this small company was here to stay. I think it was very much a stepping-stone to the next stage.'

The acquisition of Skyways
The organisation was considerably reinforced by the acquisition of Skyways, which brought into the organisation, in addition to three mixed passenger/cargo Constellations, along with trained Constellation crews, considerable maintenance capacity, IATA membership and the benefit of the already licensed scheduled London - Tunis -Malta service. Assimilation of the organisations took place over the winter so that a settled entity emerged that was well equipped to operate the 1963 season.

Skyways had been around since 1929, but it did not emerge as a proper airline entity until 1946, and its previous history before the acquisition by Euravia was typical of the independent airlines of the time. Three aviation pioneers were responsible for Skyways' resurrection, Brigadier-General A C Critchley, Sir Alan Cobham and Captain R J Ashley. formerly Chief Pilot of Aer Lingus and also a senior test pilot for Lockheed, became Skyways' Chief Pilot, and Lieutenant Commander Leslie Castlemaine was appointed the Commercial Manager. The airline's first contract was with the Anglo-Iranian Oil Company and involved the carriage of all Anglo-Iranian personnel and freight between the United Kingdom and the Persian Gulf. From London, the Yorks plied twice weekly to Basra via Malta and Cairo. The first flight under this contract (and also Skyways' first commercial flight) left London on 14 May 1946. The airline's first York, G-AHFI, being christened as 'Skyway' the previous day by Lady Heath-Eves, the wife of the Anglo-Iranian Oil Company's Deputy Chairman. This ceremony took place at Langley Aerodrome, and it was intended that the aircraft would then use Northolt as its London base for its operations to Basra. However, the Ministry of Civil Aviation would not allow a private company to use either Northolt or Hurn for its services, and as a result, Skyways was forced to load the passengers onto the aircraft at Langley. As there were no customs facilities at Langley, the York then had to fly to Manston to clear customs, and later on to its first stop at Malta. By the end of the first day, the York had reached Cairo, and during the second day, the York reached Basra, loaded aboard its new passengers and then flew back to Cairo. The third day saw the York returning to England, and after the first few flights, Skyways was allowed to operate these services from

Skyways' Constellation G-ANUR, formerly of BOAC. Skyways was later bought by Euravia.

Heathrow and Northolt.

Skyways' first two Avro Yorks were each fitted with thirty red leather armchair type seats, and apart from the services to Basra, these aircraft were also contracted for a series of aerial cruises to Switzerland. Organised by Sir Henry Lunn Ltd., the first of these cruises began on 31 May and subsequently, two journeys were flown each week by a Skyways York. Each passenger paid a fare of twenty-five pounds, and from London, they were flown to Zurich on Fridays and Saturdays until the end of August.

In November 1946 Skyways. had bought Dunsfold airfield from the government, and here it established its main base.

Throughout the summer of 1947, Skyways continued to undertake tourist flights to Switzerland on behalf of Sir Henry Lunn Ltd. With the steady increase in the amount of work undertaken by Skyways, the company acquired a fleet of four Douglas Skymasters from the Dutch airline, KLM.

At the end of 1947 the Drayton Group of companies purchased a substantial holding in the company, and Brigadier S K Thorburn, of the Drayton Group, became Skyways' Deputy Chairman. During 1948, Skyways acquired a financial interest in the Croydon-based Morton Air Services, and this interest was retained until 1950.

Civil participation in the Berlin Airlift began fully on 4 August 1948, but the first Skyways aircraft did not take part until 16 November 1948. On this date, three York freighters (G-AHFI, G-AHLV and G-ALBX) all started flying sorties into Berlin from Wunsdorf Aerodrome. The Berlin Airlift was a memorable operation for Skyways, and while the Yorks and Lancastrians had been plying their way along the corridors into Berlin, the other members of the fleet had also been particularly active. Early in December 1948, the size of the airline's Dakota fleet increased when the Dakotas flown by Air Contractors were taken over by Skyways. Skyways now held several contracts necessitating the use of Dakota aircraft, with one of these aircraft opening a new service on 14 May 1949 under charter to East African Airways.

That same day Skyways celebrated its third birthday having completed more than seven and a quarter million revenue miles. For the year ended 14 May 1948, Skyways carried 9,662 passengers and a total of 651,840 lb of cargo. For a similar period ending 14 May 1949, the airline carried 13,786 passengers and 1,184,960 lb of cargo.

In March 1950, with little work available for its long-range aircraft, Skyways was placed into voluntary liquidation by its owners. This sad event was followed on 31 March by the registration of a

Skyways' York G-AMGK at Stansted. *(author's collection)*

Another view of Skyways' Constellation G-ANUR, possibly at a snowy Luton. *(authors collection)*

new company named Skyways with a share capital of £157,000. The new Skyways acquired the business activities of the old company. Operations restarted in April with six Dakotas based at Dunsfold, and the board of directors remained, for the most part, unchanged, consisting of Brigadier-General A C Critchley, Brigadier S K Thorburn, Captain R J Ashley, Group Captain C A B Wilcock and Major General Sir Drummond Inglis.

However, in January 1952 Skyways sold its last two Dakotas and all charter operations were suspended, although the company itself continued in existence. For the first three months of the year, Skyways remained dormant as an airline company, but in March it was bought out by Eric Rylands and David Brown of the Lancashire Aircraft Corporation. The price paid for Skyways and all its assets was approximately £157,000, and changes started to take place almost immediately. The Lancashire Aircraft Corporation decided to transfer the responsibility for the operation of its fleet of four-engined long-range transport aircraft to Skyways. As a result, Lancashire's large fleet of Avro Yorks was painted in full Skyways colours, and Skyways moved its operating base to Bovingdon. From here, Skyways continued to undertake the War Office trooping contracts previously flown by Lancashire, and in June Skyways was awarded a further trooping contract that required the carriage of four thousand troops, their families and various civilians between the United Kingdom and the Caribbean.

Another major operation by Skyways during 1952 was the transport of competitors from England to Helsinki to take part in the 1952 Olympic Games.

The major event of October, however, was the move of Skyways from Bovingdon to a new base at Stansted Airport. Previously, the customs facilities at Stansted had been withdrawn, but with the arrival of Skyways, these facilities were re-introduced. One of the company's first ad-hoc charters from its new base was a flight to Colombo on 28 October with forty-four passengers on board.

On 25 November Skyways bought out Eagle Aviation's fleet of five Avro Yorks for a price of about £160,000. Included in the sale was an Air Ministry contract to fly Air Force cadets from the UK to Rhodesia. Although this contract had been running for ten months, it still had a further fourteen months to.run. Skyways was now, by a wide margin, the world's largest commercial operator of York aircraft, and at the end of the year, it was announced that Skyways had carried forty thousand troops on its aircraft during 1952. The Yorks covered a total of 2,960,000 revenue miles during the year.

For the year ending 30 September 1953, Skyways returned an impressive set of figures for its British based operations. A total of 71,736 passengers had been carried, and the company's Yorks had flown some 139,382,700 passenger-miles. These figures do not include the considerable amount of flying then undertaken from the company's bases in Cyprus and Malta. These bases had been set up in support of the flights to the Middle East, and a large number of civilian charter flights were also made from these important island bases.

At the end of 1952, Skyways had applied to the ATAC for several long-range scheduled services. The first application was for a colonial coach-service between London and Salisbury, Southern Rhodesia. The route requested included traffic stops at Malta, Nicosia, Wadi Halfa, Khartoum, Nairobi and Mombasa. Skyways also applied for similar routes to Accra (Ghana), Kingston, Jamaica, and Nicosia, Cyprus. The first approval was received in 1953 for the route linking Stansted with Nicosia, and Skyways named this service the 'Crusader' service.

Skyways announced a variety of ambitious plans for future services by the company. The airline proposed to open high frequency scheduled services from Lympne to Beauvais and Ghent using Dakotas. Skyways planned to operate several services daily in each direction, and these were to be flown in conjunction with British, French and Belgian coach operators.

Skyways' Hamburg based York continued to fly many European flights from its German base throughout 1954, and regular services were flown to Berlin carrying both passengers and cargo. The airline planned further German operations in the spring of l954 when it announced the formation of a new German airline, Deutsche Lufttransport Gesellschaft (DLG). Although the majority of the finance for this company came from local German interests, Skyways held a minority shareholding and proposed to transfer three Dakotas, and their crews, to this new airline. Another ambitious plan put forward at this time was for the formation of a Middle Eastern based airline to be known as

Kuwait Independent Airline. The purpose of this airline was to take over the interests of Gulf Aviation and to open scheduled services between the Persian Gulf and Cyprus to connect with Skyways "Crusader' service from Cyprus to Malta and Stansted. However, neither the German nor the Kuwait company ever got off the ground, and Skyways continued operations normally.

Early in March 1955, the Bibby Line bought a financial stake in Skyways resulting in the increase of the company's capital from £157,500 to £315,000. Two directors of the shipping line, Derek Bibby and Leslie Harding, joined the board of Skyways, but no other changes took place as a result of the injection of the extra capital by the Bibby Line. In July 1955, Skyways was awarded an Air Ministry contract for the carriage of twelve thousand troops annually between the United Kingdom and Cyprus. The introduction of the Hermes fleet also led to Skyways undertaking several inclusive tour charter contracts including a Stansted to Treviso service flown on behalf of Travel Planning.

During December l956, the Lancashire Aircraft

Constellations at rest! A pair of Euravia machines, with G-AHEL, a former Trans-European Airways machine closest to the camera. *(Simon Peters Collection)*

What appears to be a bright, if cold day on the apron at Luton, with three Euravia Lockheed Constellations parked up. Closest to the camera is G-AHEN, the other two thought to be G-ARVP and G-ARXE indicating that these were the three initial aircraft obtained from Isreal. *(Simon Peters Collection)*

Corporation was bought out by British Aviation Services, but Skyways was not included in the deal, and the company's operations now continued apart from those of the Lancashire Aircraft Corporation.

By 1957, Skyways was operating a regular freight service using Yorks from London to Singapore under contract to BOAC. In addition, a scheduled livestock service was now flown from Blackbushe and Stansted to Beauvais using Yorks, and this service mainly carried horses.

In June 1959, Skyways agreed to lease-purchase four Lockheed Constellations from BOAC with these aircraft, the airline operated the former's all freight scheduled services from Heathrow to Hong Kong, Singapore and Sydney.

The airline's operational fleet for 1960 consisted only of five Yorks and four Constellations. The Yorks were often chartered by BOAC and Pan American to fly aircraft engines and spare parts to stranded aircraft abroad, while the Constellations operated all of Skyways' passenger schedules and the BOAC scheduled freight services to the Far East. During the 1960 summer season, the Constellation fleet also undertook the operation of a regular inclusive tour charter flight from Gatwick Airport.

With the rundown in the airline's operations, changes took place within the airline in September 1961. Eric Rylands purchased the Bibby Line holding in Skyways, and although this purchase had been agreed late in 1960, it was not announced until September 1961. Eric Rylands Ltd., became the holding company for three subsidiaries, namely Skyways, Skyways Coach-Air and Skyways Engineering. All the aircraft were now owned either by Skyways or Skyways Coach-Air (with the exception of one Constellation), while Skyways Engineering was only engaged in aircraft overhaul and maintenance.

By the end of 1961, Skyways' operations had been considerably run down, with the four Constellations flying most of the airline's services. One of these was returned to BOAC, but the other three were now owned by Skyways. However, overnight Skyways had lost almost three quarters of its revenue with the loss of this important contract. Subsequently, the 1962 season was spent operating ad-hoc charters with the Yorks, and the scheduled services to Cyprus, Malta and Tunis with the Constellations.

By August 1962, an agreement had been reached with Euravia, and Skyways was taken over on 1 September. The Yorks continued to fly in Skyways colours and ended their days flying cargo charters for Pan American and BOAC.

At the time of Skyways' take-over by Euravia, the board of directors consisted of the following personalities. Sir Wavell Wakefield was Chairman of the airline, and the other members were J Eric Rylands (Managing Director), Charles F Dickson and David Gaunt. The senior executives of

A typical Sky Tours newspaper advert from 1964. the price of '28 Gns' is equal to £29.40.

Skyways were D J Davies (Secretary), Donald MacQueen (Commercial Manager), R Birkett (General Manager of the Coach-Air division), Victor Doel (Financial Controller), Mrs E Whittaker (Public Relations Officer and personal assistant to the Managing Director), Captain J Michie (Operations Manager) and H R O Stephens (Traffic Manager).

After the take over of Skyways by Euravia, just one further aircraft appeared in Skyways colours. This was Constellation G-ARXE, which was painted up in full Skyways livery in October 1962 to operate the services from Heathrow to Cyprus, Malta and Tunis. On October 21, this aircraft was chartered by Cunard-Eagle for a flight from Heathrow, and for the remainder of 1962, and all of 1963, this aircraft continued to operate the schedules to the Mediterranean. However, in April 1964 these schedules were finally closed down, and the Constellation returned to Luton to undertake inclusive tour charter work for Euravia.

The 1963 summer season saw Euravia operating a combined fleet of eight 82-seat Constellations on scheduled inclusive-tour services to twelve regular holiday destinations: Tenerife, Valencia, Ibiza, Palma, Barcelona, Perpignan, Genoa, Venice, Rimini, Klagenfurt, Dubrovnik and Maastricht. These flights originated not only at Luton but on a similar scheduled basis from Manchester, Glasgow, Liverpool, Newcastle and Birmingham. In addition, a twice-weekly return Luton - Malta - Luton service was flown in association with BEA. This particular service, operated as a night tourist service on Monday and Wednesday nights, and were flown with very high loads in the peak season.

In addition to the scheduled holiday flights carried out from early May until late October, principally on behalf of Universal Sky Tours, Ellis Air Tours, Universal Coach Tours and SPES Travel, a large number of passenger charter flights was made to destinations all over Europe and the Near East. Also, Skyways Yorks and Constellations carried out freight charters outside Europe, including to South America, Africa and the Far East.

The Constellation crew complement comprised Captain, First Officer, Flight Engineer and two stewardesses. On all flights, meals, refreshments and bar service was supplied to full airline standards. Holiday flights such as to Palma, Barcelona and Venice, averaged four hours - during this time passengers, many of whom were making their first flight, received a full meal, along with hot coffee or tea, full bar service and drink and cigarette sales. Special attention was given to every passenger comfort.

Many regarded them as lovely aircraft - certainly very good to look at, but they caused plenty of problems for the baggage handlers wherever Euravia flew. The hydraulic fluid was

Trans-European Airways initiated charter flying from Gatwick in 1961, although the airline had been formed in 1959. It flew a pair of L-049E Constellations, G-AHEL seen here. In the summer of 1962 it flew charter flights from West Berlin, but due to financial problems the carrier went into receivership that July and operations ceased in August. *(Simon Peters Collection)*

Above: Two of Euravia's Lockheed Constellations in the hangar undergoing undercarriage retraction checks - the floor bears plenty of evidence of the airliners propensity to leak fluids! *(author's collection)*

This was especially noticable as Euravia's first hangar was shared with Vauxhall Motors and often car components were stored under the wings, resulting in the metal receiving an unexpected rustproofing! Here Barry Crossland and Brian 'Queenie' Price undertake a Check III on a Wright Cyclone.
(Karoly Ale collection)

everywhere, and as the aircraft sloped from forward to aft when it was on the ground, the fluid ran along the whole of the underneath of the fuselage. On the Constellation the hold entrance was underneath the aircraft, which meant that the baggage handlers who were loading and unloading the baggage were constantly covered in hydraulic fluid as they climbed in and out of the hatch.

Although expected to be commonplace today, Euravia saw each passenger as representing valuable repeat business, and considerable emphasis was placed on punctuality. All flight schedules were carefully integrated with coach arrival and departures at the respective airports as outbound aircraft invariably return with homecoming holiday parties. It soon became the company's experience that more late aircraft departures from Luton were due to the late arrival of coaches, as a result of traffic-jammed roads than to any other cause.

Although satisfying in terms of guaranteed and known load factors, inclusive-tour flying even back then had many peculiar problems. A distinctive feature of Euravia's operations was that the peak flying days of each week were Saturday and Sunday for six months of the year. The weekend peak built up from around eight flights on Friday to fourteen on Saturday, twelve on Sunday, six on Monday, and never more than four per day for the week. There was a simple explanation - at this time employment regulations and practices meant that people could only take their holidays from the end of the working week - a Friday, to the start of the next - a Monday.

During the 1964 season, an average of forty-five return flights per week were scheduled with a total of eight aircraft, often depleted by virtue of the fact that one of the 749s is away on a long-haul charter. This weekend peak caused problems of crew rostering, maintenance and aircraft positioning, complicated by the flights terminating at provincial airports such as Manchester, Glasgow or Newcastle, with resultant positioning of crews. Throughout the 1963 average of thirty-five services a week was operated, and the eight Constellations flew approximately three hundred hours per month. The company's crew establishment consisted of nineteen captains, eighteen first officers, three radio officers - for the York fleet - fifteen flight engineers, two navigating officers and twenty-eight stewardesses.

This meant that considerable ingenuity had to be applied to the flight schedules, which were tailored to cut out night-stops as far as possible. Also, BEA domestic flights were used for positioning crews to provincial airports. The Constellations were popular with both crews and passengers alike. Operated at a normal height of between 13,000 and 20,000 feet according to ATC requirements, the aircraft was fully equipped for pilot navigation and rarely carried a dedicated navigator or radio officer except when engaged on extended over-water charters. All the fleet had been extensively refitted and equipped with up-to-date communications equipment and were usually on airways when flying in Europe. The three 749s had larger flight decks than the earlier models and in addition to the pilots' and engineers' positions, had provision for a navigator officer and were fitted with bunks.

The peak weekend demand of Euravia's services, operated to planned schedules although they were charter flights, called for considerable planning of aircraft and availability, yet at the same time aircraft availability had to be adaptable to last-minute changes. The fact that the peak regularly occured each Saturday precluded scheduled maintenance that day, yet the intensity of flying called for the utmost speed in-between-flight servicing, ground handling and turn-round. In practice, schedules are arranged so that a reserve aircraft was always available within one hour.

The number of employees grew from two in January 1962 to two hundred and twenty-four at the height of the 1963 summer season. It was the policy of the company to keep skilled tradespeople and flying crews engaged permanently although some small number of aircrew, particularly stewardesses, were employed on a seasonal basis.

The airline found itself doing a number of 'out

Another view of the apron at Luton - two of Euravia's Lockheed Constellations undergo turn-around checks. From the 'ground equipment' it was the usual alterations as usual during business hours! *(author's collection)*

of season' charter flights - one example being a convoluted two aircraft flight around Europe during November and December 1962 for the famous American ballet impresaro Martha Graham, along with the Martha Graham Dance Company who were touring Europe with the ballet Clytemnestra, based on the ancient Greek legend.

The US State Department-sponsored tour was part of an international cultural exchange programme of the United States during the Cold War. This liaison of politics and dance created an unusual situation, in which political forces were at work in the introduction of a new dance style of the modern dance genre to Eastern Europe. The media gave the visit considerable publicity, and this analysis of the reception of the Graham Company shows how critics, influenced by a climate of receptivity to Western cultural ideas and a domestic critique of free dance as undeveloped - as well as by Graham's carefully planned publicity and promotional materials - responded to Graham as a legend of dance. They particularly valued the technical and expressive advances she brought to the genre of modern dance. It was not surprising that Euravia carried the entire ensemble to Athens, Belgrade, Zagreb, Warsaw, Munich, Cologne, Stockholm, Oslo, Helsinki, Amsterdam and Massatricht.

As was typical for the time, the flight crews carried a large amount of hard currency - predominently US dollars - to pay for everything as they went, including the fuel, for in many of the counties visited, the fuel carnet was not accepted. From a charterers point of view, the trip went smoothly, from the airline's viewpoint there were problems. In Cologne, during a two-day stop one Constellation experienced an engine problem; Jamie Alderman decided to fly the aircraft back to Luton on three engines for a change of unit, returning the next day to pick up the next leg.

Euravia needed to gain more utilisation out of its fleet. With the gradually lengthening duration and greater liberalisation of timing, for workers taking holidays in Britain, In those days, aircraft costings were based on the principle of DOC (Direct Operational Costs), which only took into consideration weekend flying, from Friday midday to Sunday night, i.e. the times that the vast majority of package tour passengers could manage. This, of course, rendered the planes redundant during the rest of the week, and Langton's next priority was to find a way of making use of them.

It was a man called Peter Sinclair, owner of a small company called Flightways, who had first recognised the advantage of midweek flying; low aircraft costs, and no deposits or contract penalties. He set up a ten- and eleven-day holiday operation, flying into Madrid, and then taking passengers onwards by coach to Malaga or Tangier.

Back then, though, both were still obscure destinations, and the programme had failed miserably. Langton, however, saw that the basic idea was sound, and had been let down by the combination of remote destinations, high ticket prices and the gruellingly long coach journey. He spent the next few months tinkering with the component parts, and, the very next year launched his own 11- and 12-twelve day programme to the Costa Brava.

This proved to be tremendously popular and was soon oversubscribed. encouraging him to

Lockheed Constellation G-ANUR is seen at Luton, in what appears to be one of a number of different Skyways of London colours. In fact the blue-grey cheat line appears to have faded in the sunlight. Operated by Euravia from 1964 to 1966, it has previously flown with QANTAS as VH-EAB *Lawrence Hargrave* and BOAC as *Basildon*. (Simon Peters Collection)

A snapshot of a Euravia Constellation with a pilot and cabin crew including Stewardess Gill Kirk. Headscarfs, forholding a hat on the head was de rigueur for any girl on an airfield! *(author's collection)*

expand the principle to Majorca and other resorts. Thereby making maximum use of his aircraft, and allowing him both to reduce his weekend prices and at the same time increase profits. Other operators soon flocked to follow his example, and in next to no time, midweek travel became an established business practice. But it was not before there was another battle with bureaucracy.

This was theoretically superb for both travel company and airline but, in practice, it came up against the intractable 'Sir Humphrey Appleby' mindset of British Government bureaucrats. Firstly, there was what was termed Provision 1. This proclaimed that no packaged holiday could be offered at a lower price than the normal economy scheduled return air fare to that particular destination's airport. Secondly, the Air Transport Licensing Board had traditionally supported the scheduled carriers' view that charter traffic diverted passengers from their services. J E D Williams strongly believed that this stance was untenable.

'The point I kept making was that our product was not like a scheduled airline ticket. Our product was sea, sun, sand and secondary sexual stimulation. And that was a completely different product from anything the State airlines had ever dreamt of offering. We were not in the same line of business and, therefore, not competing.'

There was a plethora of protests led vigorously by Henry Marking, the chief executive, on behalf of British European Airways.

Williams was assisted in the battle by Donald McQueen, an ex-Royal Navy commander, who had been sales manager for the original Skyways company and retained the same role for Britannia gaining many ad hoc charters. When the Air Transport Licensing Board finally conceded the merits of the airline's case in 1965, BEA appealed not just against Britannia's licences but against those granted to all the independents.

Williams decided that now was the time to assume leadership of the independents in their battle, and so he employed professional advocacy in Geoffrey Rippon, QC, who had been a Minister of Aviation in the Conservative Government.

'Rippon was a delight to work with...' wrote Williams. 'Having disposed of both of the State corporation's case and its counsel, he demanded costs on the High Court scale against the corporation for wasting everyone's time. That was turned down, but the central argument for restricting 'B' licences, otherwise than under Provision 1, was abandoned forever. The practical significance was that we had the security of tenure and security of the right to grow.

So incensed was J E D Williams about the need for this kind of application that he once wrote in Flight magazine: 'The first delusion is that aviation is in some special way connected with national prestige and the national interest.

The second delusion is that air transport is a delicate plant which needs careful regulation and control if it is to grow up sturdily. Nothing could be further from the truth. In the first place it is big business; the world's airlines turn over thousands of millions annually. In the second place the regulatory bodies do not nurture it; they throttle it. No case can be made that control is in the interest of the nation, the travelling public, or the industry. The world is full of sane businessmen anxious and willing to provide the risk capital to operate public services, given the freedom to do so.

Whether in Skyways or Euravia's colours, G-ANUR was an oft-photographed airliner, seen about to depart from London Heathrow! *(author's collection)*

It is strange that people who are not doctrinaire socialists of the old school and whose general philosophy and political orientation is towards a limited laissez-faire in a capitalist society believe that British civil aviation, for some reason, needs to be strangled by red tape in a manner unparalleled in any other industry of modern Western culture. Aviation is no different from any other industry of comparable magnitude and importance. It follows the common economic rules and reacts in the same way to commercial stimuli and government control.'

1965, thanks to the lifting of those restrictions through the Air Transport Licensing Board victory, was another turning point for Britannia Airways and was also crucially significant for the airline in a more direct corporate context.

Hardly was the ink dry on the Skyways coup than another operator of a couple of Constellations, Trans-European Aviation, also became financially embattled, and that well-known City of London corporate 'doctor', Sir Kenneth Cork, was appointed receiver. The arrangement that Williams came to with him was to lease Trans-European's two Constellations, G-AMUP and G-AHEL, for £20 an hour, with a guaranteed minimum of 600 hours' flying a year.

So it was therefore that Euravia rapidly grew from a three-Constellation operation to a company with eight Constellations and two Yorks. Though J E D Williams was not happy with the fleet: 'The Constellations had high direct operating costs, poor mechanical reliability, and were slower than the Douglas DC6s and DC7s of the competition. They were not attractive to charterers which was the reason we acquired them on such advantageous terms. The Yorks would already have been scrap were it not for that valuable Pan Am contract'.

'There was no possibility of making much profit, but without any investment, we were developing a viable business, not dependent on Universal Sky Tours, in preparation for the next stage which would be profitable.'

By 1964 the engineering organisation, were operating from a new £200,000 hangar capable of housing three aircraft and employed over one hundred people, allowing Euravia to perform all Check Ones and Check Twos at Luton. The company had also been approved by the Airworthiness Registration Board to do major checks, performed during the winter months. As Euravia engineering did not have the capacity to do two or three major checks concurrently, this was contracted to outside organisations, Air France, Marshalls of Cambridge and Israel Aircraft Industries, were engaged for this work.

At Luton, all ground handling, traffic handling, aircraft cleaning and cabin servicing were carried out by the company's own staff. Passenger Reception, ticketing and baggage handling was similarly handled by the company's own traffic staff. No traffic, ground or engineering staff are employed at outstations or terminal points abroad; all handling was on the company's behalf.

The summer 1964 season saw Euravia flights operating to the following destinations from a number of UK airports:

Tenerife:	Luton
Malaga:	Manchester
Palma:	Luton, Liverpool, Manchester, Cardiff, Newcastle.
Valencia:	Luton, Manchester, Liverpool, Newcastle.
Barcelona:	Luton, Manchester, Newcastle, Glasgow.
Ibiza:	Luton.
Perpignan:	Luton, Manchester, Glasgow, Cardiff, Liverpool.
Malta:	Luton.
Genoa:	Luton, Manchester.
Rimini:	Luton, Manchester, Newcastle, Glasgow.
Venice:	Luton, Manchester.
Ljubljana:	Luton.
Dubrovnik:	Luton.

The next stage of the airline's development would need money - and that, Williams discovered, presented a problem. At the launch of Euravia, Universal Sky Tours' bank had required that the airline use only them as bankers. Initially, that did not seem unreasonable, but a limit had been placed on the overdraft facilities for the group. With T E D Langton acquisitive to buy his own hotels, as well as the needs of organic growth, Universal Sky Tours grabbed every penny of overdraft for itself.

J E D Williams: 'The problem was how to build up an airline without using money, and at the same time provide Sky Tours with low-priced transport of acceptable standard to enable Langton to realise his plans. Those plans were, of course, important to us, too, but also they were the only reason he formed the airline in the first place - and the source of the only interest he ever showed in it'.

'Naturally, I consulted him about every major step, but all he ever said was, at worst, 'I hope you know what you are doing,' or, at best, 'You seem to know what you are doing.' T E D Langton was precisely the patron the airline needed in those days. He starved us of cash and was our most demanding customer. Within the restraint of these excellent disciplines, I could develop the airline as I pleased so long as nothing went seriously wrong'.

By the summer of 1965 Euravia was carrying 185,000 passengers, Of course, the sudden increase in visitors from Britain and elsewhere put considerable pressure on European hotels, particularly in Spain and the Balearics, so in response to this, Langton built a new hotel in Majorca, the Arenal Park, and invested heavily in the 900-bed Taurus Park Hotel, on the Costa Brava. And because the Taurus Park was in an isolated location, he took the bold step of including nightly entertainment in the price. He also decided to employ his own, on-site management team, on the grounds that it distinguished Skytours from its competitors.

And it didn't stop there. T E D Langton was the

Future echoes! The six BOAC Bristol Britannias in open storage at Marshalls of Cambridge. They would later create a name change and appear in new colours. *(author's collection)*

first operator to move into Benidorm, using the Avenida Palace, the Bristol and the Alameda, all of which remained popular, despite the new hotels being built on the neighbouring beaches. Wherever possible, too, he obtained exclusive use of hotels, which meant he could price his holidays without fear of being undercut by other operators. At the same time, he developed a reputation for reliability, and fulfilling his contracts year after year; as a result, hoteliers were happy to stay with him, even if he did have a tendency to chisel away at the prices, once the business started to flow.

Elsewhere, he gained an early foothold in Cala Millor and Cala Bona, in Majorca, and he was the first to fly into Tenerife, Klagenfurt (Austria) and Ljubljana (Yugoslavia).

A Change Of Type, Change of Name.
In the couple of years since the launch of Euravia, the business had been increasing. In 1962, Euravia carried less than 20,000 passengers, but in 1963 this had grown to more than 50,000 when new routes were pioneered including one of the then most popular of destinations, Ibiza.

With this broadened base, the Constellations were becoming less attractive. It just so happened that the British Overseas Airways Corporation had several early-model Bristol Britannia series 102 airliners mothballed in storage.

J E D Williams opened negotiations to obtain some of those idle aircraft, and the resulting deal meant that, for less than the cost of a new Britannia 310, he bought six of the earlier models together with engine spares on a 'buy now, pay later' scheme. Another two followed later.

When Williams told T E D Langton that the contract was signed, the dour head of Universal Sky Tours had only had one question: was the seating plan, unlike the Constellations, the same for all six Britannias?

On being told it was, he made a conscious demand which foreshadowed later thinking in aircraft passenger flow: 'Right, I'll need a copy of the seating plan to put on the booking form so that my clients can apply for their seats when they book their holidays. You'll have to print the same plan on the back of the tickets so they can see what seats they have got. You can use it as a kind of boarding card if you like'.

But before they were printed, another issue had been exercising J E D Williams' mind. He had always regarded Euravia a terrible name for an airline, mainly as the UK was still many years off

Left: the original Articles of Association for Britannia Airways.

Below: Britannia G-ANBF at a wintry Luton one day in January 1968. The aircraft wears the ititial BY colour scheme with red fuselage lettering.

An early Britannia Ticket, Baggage Check and Seating Plan/Allocation. This one, according to the Passenger Coupon counterfoil was issued on 23 April 1967, for Flight BY3605 on 11 May from Luton to Nicosia in Cyprus. It also answers another mystery: Britannia's Series 102s were fitted out to carry 117 passengers!
(author's collection)

membership of the European Common Market and there were divisions in the country over the whole advisability of joining. So, perhaps, a pan-European sounding name was also not a promising marketing title. What better to mark the new Britannia aircraft era than to adopt the name Britannia? So, on 16 August 1964, Euravia (London) Ltd became Britannia Airways, and the airline gained the famous BY flight code prefix.

'It was the most extraordinary thing that the name was available. Everyone wanted to have a name that did not sound like any other in the industry and suggested a responsible airline. We found that the name Britannia was lying there to be picked up. It was clear that British passengers liked the idea of flying a British airline.'

The Britannias were pulled out of mothballs, serviced, and crew training began. Flight crew technical training was undertaken for Britannia by BOAC in their Cranebank school at Heathrow Airport. The first candidates for flying training on Type 102 were Captain Davison and Captain Tanton who were instructed by Bristol Aeroplane's test pilot Willie Williamson. The two captains undertook the airline's inaugural Britannia flight from Luton on 6 December 1964, carrying pre-Christmas holiday-makers seeking Tenerife's winter sun. But, returning the next day, they had to redirect to Heathrow owing to strong crosswinds at their Luton base.

Wearing a simple blue and white colour scheme, with red titles, the aircraft carried the emblem of 'Britannia', a concept that dates back to the Roman

Above: Hangar 89 at Luton takes shape for Britannia Airways, seen here through the undercarriage legs of a company Britannia one misty morning. Taxiing in front of the new structure on its way to the runway is a BKS Air Transport Britannia.

Right: Christmas time at Luton. *(both author's collection)*

times, but in this case, the emblem related back to the time of Queen Victoria. Still depicted as a young woman with brown or golden hair, she kept her Corinthian helmet and her white robes, but now she held Poseidon's three-pronged trident and often sat or stood before the ocean and tall-masted ships representing British naval power. She also usually held or stood beside a Greek hoplite shield, which sported the British Union Flag: also at her feet was often the British Lion, an animal found on the arms of England, Scotland and the Prince of Wales.

It was not long before the staff disparagingly knew this proud emblem from the days of everything British as 'the old lady in a wheel-chair'!

The Bristol Britannia gave the airline another opportunity for a 'first'. They became the first charter company to provide hot in-flight meals. The staple diet in those days was cottage pie - sometimes referred to by some passengers as 'Shepherds Pie' - and its aroma often greeted passengers as they entered the cabin. 'I can smell the pie' became a regular remark of boarding passengers. Perhaps intending to take the cuisine up-market, the caterers decided to change the dish's name to 'Italian Cottage Pie' which much annoyed the passengers

who wrote to the press indignantly asking why Italian food was being served, the ethnic description was quickly dropped!

Things moved swiftly in the airline right from its inception. Williams had seen the inevitability of finally going jet, but both the Constellations and Britannias had the advantage of being the cheapest investment possible while giving the required capacity. Williams had dabbled - as any ambitious non-scheduled operator did at the time - with the idea of freighting and scheduled services. But as he said at the time, he was 'far too busy managing an explosive expansion into the relative void of IT work' to progress the schemes very far.

By now the 'vertical integration' concept, pioneered by T E D Langton and developed by J E D Williams was starting to show dividends. In his 1968 Brancker Memorial Lecture given to the Institute of Transport in London, Willams expounded on the theory - and its results. When this system was well organised he said, the savings on costs were spectacular. Williams illustrated that during the winter 1966/67 season, Sky Tours offered a seven day holiday in Palma the cost of which to the company was less than half that of a BEA/Iberia return fare.

By August 1965 the last Constellation was withdrawn from service, and the summer fleet consisted of five ex-BOAC Britannia I02s: G-ANBO, G-ANBE, G-ANBA, G-ANBL and G-ANBB.

Disposal of the earlier aircraft provided some exciting moments for Bob Muckleston, who had joined the airline from English Electric: 'We managed to sell some of the Connies, but no one wanted the Yorks, so they went to the breakers. As the aircraft were mainly alloy framework and had

plenty of useful equipment and other materials, there were scrap merchants who were interested in doing the job. Unfortunately, they were not very savoury people, as I found out to my cost. Some of the most notorious criminals in London were involved in the scrap business. The firm we finally chose to scrap the Yorks seemed to be respectable and started on the job well and disposed of the aircraft. They had paid some of the money upfront, and I waited for them to pay the balance. The money did not come. I then contacted a debt collector who went to see them. He could not find anyone there. Shortly after, I had a visit from the police, who asked me who had removed the aircraft.

They turned out to be one of the most vicious of the London gangs, and the police advised me to stay well away from them. I wrote off the debt!'

Not all the Constellations were sold off. Some were towed out to the edge of Luton Airport for the attention of the scrappies. *(Kaz Ale collection)*

Above and below: G-AMUP meets its fate during the summer of 1965 - not only did the aircraft received the attentions of the scappies, but also the local vandals. *(Kaz Ale collection)*

Above: I have never been able to work out the identity of this particular Constellation, but clearly from the wreckage surrounding it, the aircraft was not the first to be scrapped at Luton. *(Kaz Ale collection)*

Another picture that time has not been kind to, but an interesting one nevertheless! The date is almost certainly 1967 and this grubby postcard shows the passenger terminal at Luton, with an Autair Ambassador parked on its stand and in the foreground an early scheme Britannia Britannia, surrounded by the usual airline ephemera of the day - ground start cart, passenger steps mounted on a Commer pick-up truck and three engineers working on one of the prop-hubs from a gantry. *(author's collection)*

Flying 'the Whispering Giant'

At the time of the Britannia, Elizabeth Harrison was the Chief Stewardess. The qualifications for being a Britannia Air Hostess included weight proportional to a height; Candidates should not be any shorter than five feet four inches and had to be neat in appearance. They also had to be able to swim. A first aid qualification or the ability to speak a second language was an additional bonus. Many have reported that the Chief Stewardess was exceptionally well-spoken, and the bigger the plum in your mouth, the more chance you had of getting into the airline.

The holiday period within the UK was very seasonal, and despite a growing demand for 'winter sun' and skiing holidays, there was still a need for aircraft and crews to be utilised during the winter months.

The peak season for flying in those days ran from April to October. Typically all training, both safety and cabin service, took between seven and ten days, in advance of that, with one day dedicated to safety and emergency training. Trainees had to learn and understand all about the emergency equipment and drills, and how to get passengers out of an aircraft in a hurry. They all undertook a written examination to check that they all met both the company and the Civil Aviation Authority's standard requirements. If they did, they were ready to start in-flight training.

The Britannia had a flight deck crew of three, and four Cabin Crew, ranked one, two, three and four. The new Stewardesses usually flew as a number four stewardess and sometimes as a number three. The

Britannia Britannia G-ANBO at rest. *(author's collection)*

first duties as a number four stewardess consisted of packing the duty free goods into metal bar boxes, then collecting the passengers from the terminal and leading them out to the aircraft. They also had to lead them to the terminal when the aircraft landed.

Once in-flight, their primary duties were to help serve the food - usually a cold meal on the way out and a cottage pie on the way back. The passengers used to love it; the smell of the cottage pies heating in the ovens was always a source of pleasure to them. The Britannia had two galleys, one at the front and one midway to the rear.

Details of the ubiquitous cottage pie were provided by Britannia Catering Manager, David Douglas, who found himself heavily quoted as he explained the reasons behind the dish in the *Reading Evening Post* of September 1967. The airline prepared 347,520 meals during the year, of which 176,500 were full meals. During the peak times, Britannia used 12,000 bread rolls a week; around 1800 pints of milk a month; and 200,000 sachets of salt and pepper. Outward bound menus were always chicken dishes while return flights were 'typical English dishes' of beef, cottage pie or steak and kidney pie.

We often get the comment, 'We have had a wonderful holiday and what we need to finish it off beautifully is a typical English meal.' So we give it to them'.

Some of the most vivid memories of the airline's flight crews flying Britannias were of the charter work they carried out for Iran Air, taking Moslems to Mecca for the annual pilgrimage of the Hadj.

The Hadj is the largest annual gathering of Muslim people in the world. It is one of the five pillars of Islam, and a religious duty which must be carried out by every able-bodied Muslim who can afford to do so at least once in their lifetime. The state of being physically and financially capable of performing the Hadj is called istita'ah, and a Muslim who fulfils this condition is called a mustati. The Hadj is a demonstration of the solidarity of the Muslim people, and their submission to God (Allah). The word Hadj means 'to intend a journey' which connotes both the outward act of a journey and the inward act of intentions.

Pilgrims generally travel to Hadj in groups, as an expression of unity. Various institutions and government programs, such as the Hadj subsidy offered in India or the Tabung Haji based in Malaysia assist pilgrims in covering the costs of the journey. For many airlines, including Britannia, 'working the Hadj' was an excellent way to bring in extra money and increase aircraft utilisation; these were mainly return trips home for the pilgrims to various destinations in Iran such as Tehran, Shiraz and Abadan.

Janice Fitzjohn, neé Munt remembers flying for Britannia on the Hadj. 'We bunny-hopped around the Middle East on both Hadj flights and doing work for the holiday clubs. When carrying Arabs on the hadj, we had to be constantly aware of two things prayer-mats in the isle and galleys and Arabs brewing up mint tea on little spirit burners on the cabin floor!'

Janice also remembers one trooping flight back from Germany when Britannia brought a whole aircraft full of Parachute Regiment personnel - the famous Red Berets. 'They were directly off manoeuvres, still in all their combat gear and stank the aircraft out! Despite this, they were all perfectly behaved and wonderfully well-mannered'!

Everyone acknowledged that T E D Langton was a brilliant thinker about travel, and knew the business inside out, but they also knew that he had no management skills whatsoever and no understanding of the need for those skills. J E D Williams, '...things had reached a stage where the existing structure had to come to an end. Life with T E D Langton could be more than slightly hairy!

As an example, the man who kept the general ledger was not a qualified accountant, and there was no one managing the group cash flow. Universal Sky Tours would suddenly stop paying its bills because Langton had impulsively gone out and bought another hotel! Ted was a one-man mafia operating

G-ANBA taxies out for another flight. *(author's collection)*

The interior of a Britannia looking aft, showing the mid-section galley on the right *(author's collection)*

from a completely separate building, and there was no real control. From my point of view, this was terribly worrying and very frightening'.

To make matters worse, Langton was into his sixties and had already had heart trouble. If he died, Britannia Airways and Universal Sky Tours could well have been put into the hands of a receiver in a matter of weeks. Langton also owned racehorses, nightclubs, restaurants, coaches, and hotels, yet he cut an unremarkable figure, the ash from his cigarette forever poised and ready, like some crooked grey finger, to tumble messily down the front of his jacket.

In April 1965 he sold Skytours and Britannia Airways lock, stock and barrel to the Thomson Organisation, which was looking to invest in a business unrelated to newspapers. However, it was not a smooth transaction, by any means; the Thomson hierarchy, for whom Langton had nothing but contempt, found him unhelpful and uncooperative. Indeed, the sale went ahead even though the auditors maintained that profitability was minimal, and management almost non-existent, with virtually every decision, no matter how small, being made by Langton.

For his part, T E D Langton's only regret was to have sold Skytours too cheaply. The deal was based on a lump sum in advance and the rest, limited to £700,000, to be related to performance under the stewardship of Thomson's, who, in their first year of operation, made a profit of over £1 million. Predictably, perhaps, the relationship ended sourly, with Langton returning one day to find the new owners had changed the locks on his office. However, Langton was from an era where dirty washing was never aired in public. As always Langton was a man of few words, but he told *The Travel Trade Gazette:* 'All I can say is that I have not fallen out with Thomson and they have not fallen out with me!'

His last solo venture was to resuscitate a cruise programme which had been sidelined at the time of the sale to Thomson; this involved hiring the *Queen Frederica* from the Chandris line and setting up a schedule of Sovereign back-to-back fly-cruises. It failed – he was just too early.

Upon which, he retired to Majorca, where, unable to resist the temptation, he bought the small Hotel Morocco in Palma Nova, where, in his latter days, he could be found drinking steadily at the bar, accompanied by his dog Zeke. There, he died suddenly, but peacefully.

Chapter 3

Under New Ownership

Even with a fleet 'upgrade' to turboprops, J E D Williams was looking for a more stable platform - a sale of Universal Sky Tours and Britannia Airways into an appropriate corporate setting which could encompass its managerial and growth needs. It just so happened that there was another out there who was able to make it happen, and furthermore was in the market looking for just such a project.

Roy Herbert Thomson, 1st Baron Thomson of Fleet, GBE (*b*. 5 June 1894, *d*. 4 August 1976) was a Canadian newspaper proprietor and media entrepreneur.

During the Great War Roy Thomson attended a business college and owing to poor eyesight the army rejected him. He went to Manitoba after the war to become a farmer but was unsuccessful. Thomson travelled to Toronto again, where he held several jobs at different times; one of which was selling radios. However, he found selling radios difficult because the only district left for him to work in was Northern Ontario. To give his potential customers something to listen to, he undertook to establish a radio station. By quite a stroke of luck, he was able to procure a radio frequency and transmitter for $201. CFCH officially went on air in North Bay, Ontario on 3 March 1931. He sold radios for quite some time after that, but his focus gradually shifted to his radio station, rather than the actual radios.

In 1934, Thomson acquired his first newspaper. With a down payment of $200, he purchased the Timmins Daily Press, in Timmins, Ontario. He began an expansion of both radio stations and newspapers in various Ontario locations in partnership with fellow Canadian, Jack Kent Cooke. In addition to his media acquisitions, by 1949 Thomson was the owner of a diverse group of companies, including several ladies' hairstyling businesses, a fitted kitchen manufacturer, and an ice-cream cone manufacturing operation. By the early 1950s, he owned nineteen newspapers and was president of the Canadian Daily Newspaper Publishers Association, and then began his first foray into the British newspaper business by starting up the *Canadian Weekly Review* to cater to expatriate Canadians living in Britain.

In 1952, Thomson moved to Edinburgh and purchased *The Scotsman* newspaper. In 1957, Thomson launched a successful bid for the commercial television franchise for Central Scotland, named Scottish Television, which he was to describe as a 'permit to print money' (often misquoted as a 'licence to print money'). In 1959, Thomson purchased the Kemsley group of newspapers, the largest in Britain, which included *The Sunday Times*. Over the years, Thomson expanded his media empire to include more than 200 publications in Canada, the United States, and the United Kingdom. His

Britannia G-ANBO about to depart from Manchester for another flight to the sun! *(author's collection)*

Thomson Organization became a multinational corporation, with interests in publishing, printing, television, and travel.

By many standards, the group's financial resources were limited, so the search was for a business with short and long-term objectives: to create quickly a significant new profit centre at relatively low cost, and to lay the foundations for a big profit earner of the future where the development costs would not be high.

So Gordon Brunton, the Group Development Director of the International Thomson Organisation was tasked by Roy Thomson to find a business that required relatively low initial investment; in an area not needing too much technical know-how that had substantial growth potential and was in an area where Thomson's skills, particularly in marketing, could contribute. It had to be an operation with a different cash-flow from that of newspapers, which was poor early in the year and at its best at the end of the year; and a business which could use the organisation's newspapers and magazines to deliver messages to consumers at a low cost. Whatever he found had to have the right 'synergy'.

By research and analysis, Gordon Brunton eventually courted the package holiday business. He decided it was a reasonable prospect on several grounds. A few had seen the opportunities in packaged holidays but had only just tested the water, because they did not have the financial resources to dive in more deeply. Workers in Britain were going to have longer and more frequent holidays, aided by higher discretionary income for leisure spending. Jet aircraft were the pathfinders for cheaper, faster and more efficient leisure air transport. It was apparent to a man steeped in publishing that the increasing attention to travel abroad, both through the printed word and television – especially if the charges were low enough.

Sir Gordon Charles Brunton (*b*. 27 December 1921, *d*. 30 May 2017) was born in London and was educated briefly at Cranleigh School, Surrey and then at the London School of Economics, where he studied under Harold Laski, John Maynard Keynes, RH Tawney, Joan Robinson and Eileen Power. It was Laski's arguments, and ideas which had a particular influence on Gordon Brunton's thinking.

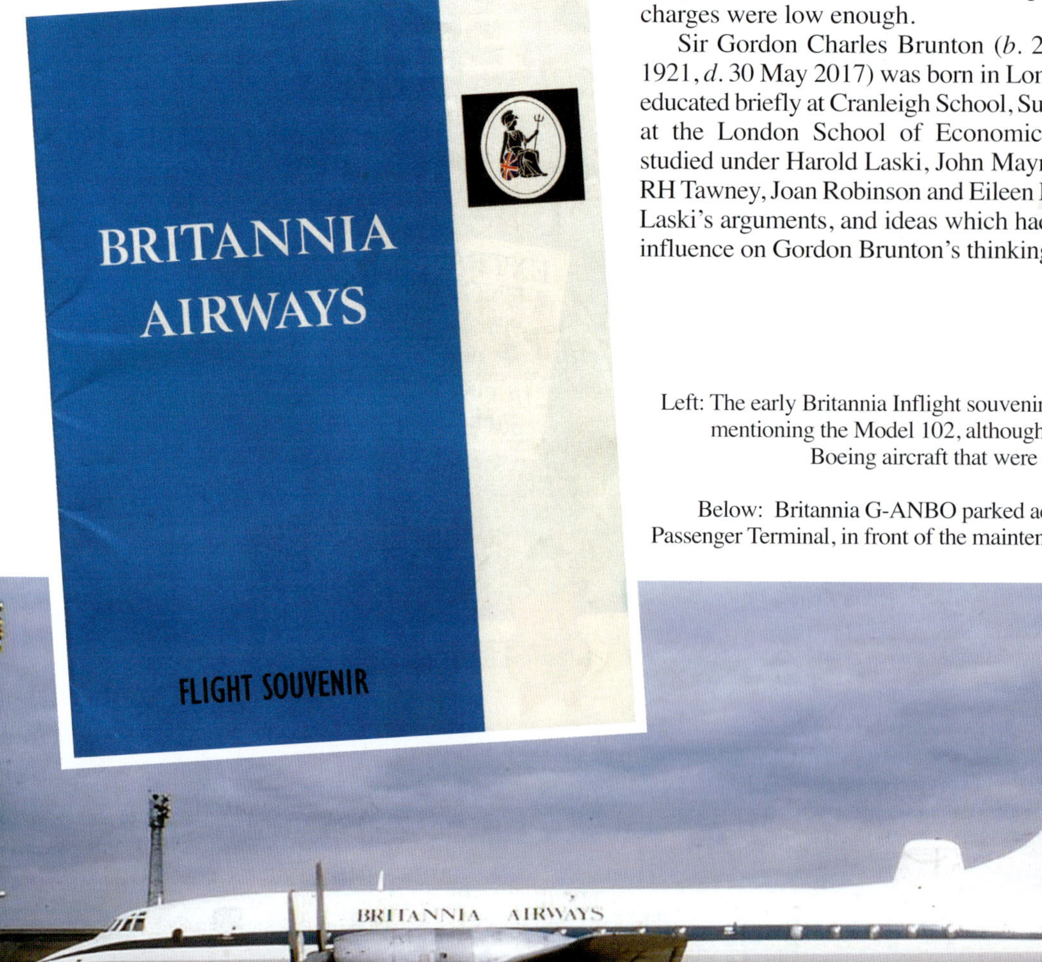

Left: The early Britannia Inflight souvenir booklet, only mentioning the Model 102, although hinting at the Boeing aircraft that were soon to come.

Below: Britannia G-ANBO parked across from the Passenger Terminal, in front of the maintenance hangars.

Above: Lord Thomson about to take his first Britannia flight, meeting Chief Ground Strewardess Lavinia Welicombe.

Below: Britannia 'on the Hadj'.

During the onset of World War Two, Brunton left university prematurely, was commissioned into the Royal Artillery in 1940 and went onto serve as a Captain in the Indian Army and Royal Artillery. For much of the war, he fought in the Burma campaign before joining the British Military Government in Düsseldorf and Hamburg, working on the reconstruction of local infrastructure.

After the war, Brunton worked as a door to door salesman selling classified advertising space to small businesses outside London.

In 1961 Gordon Brunton had been working at Odhams when he was hired as Managing Director of Thomson Publications by Roy Thomson, 1st Baron Thomson of Fleet founder of the Thomson Newspapers and the International Thomson Organisation Ltd (ITOL) Thomson Corporation.

Brunton served as Chief Executive of ITOL from 1966 to 1984 during the Thomson period of global expansion and diversification into travel, oil, print, book, magazine, newspaper, trade and technical press and local directory publishing and was set to become one of the largest and most influential companies in the world.

Of particular note was during the late 1960s, with Gordon Brunton leading the diversification into the package tour business for Thomson. Brunton believed Thomson had certain advantages in entering the travel market, at a time when tastes were changing for British holidaymakers with shifting aspirations for overseas holidays.

Gordon Brunton, later to become Sir Gordon, at the top of the stairs, along with Roy Thomson, deplane from Britannia G-ANBO.
(author's collection)

The significant expenses for travel companies were the print brochures and the PR and advertising space needed to promote package holidays. Brunton argued that Thomson held an advantage over their competitors with their printing presses, free access to their media empire with advertising and editorial capacity in their national and regional newspaper network. It put Thomson ahead of other package tour operators. This gamble, despite considerable opposition within Thomson management, proved highly successful.

Brunton realised that the package tour business would fit perfectly with Thomson's other interests. Holidays were paid in advance at a time of the year when newspaper revenues tended to be low - and conversely, the holiday bills paid by the holiday companies had to be paid when newspaper revenues were high.

So it was then that the Thomson board accepted the Brunton recommendation; now the need was for quick action to find the right vehicle or vehicles to enter that fledgeling inclusive tour business.

Vladimir Raitz had been at the London School of Economics with Gordon Brunton, but on being approached, Raitz expressed no interest in selling; instead, he suggested T E D Langton. Langton was happy to be wooed. Like all astute businessman, his philosophy was that everything had a price.

Thomsons sent investigators to Luton who were given a profit projection for the airline of £180,000 for 1965. But despite this, all sorts of objections were raised by members at the board meeting to discuss the potential purchase.

At the time there were two companies up for consideration; Universal Sky Tours and Riviera Holidays. Accountants Price Waterhouse were asked to investigate the books of both companies. The reports could scarcely have been worse, as Gordon Brunton later recalled: 'I shall never forget that meeting on the top floor of Elm House in Gray's Inn Road, London. I remember giving my views on why I thought there was an excellent opportunity for the future. Price Waterhouse responded with a formidable report analysing the companies' appalling performance, their unconventional, unstructured management style, their total lack of a track record, our complete inexperience of that business, and they put forward an unanswerable case. The marketing director jumped in, had his two-penn'orth, rejecting the whole crazy idea.

It was then up to Roy Thomson to take the decision. He listened carefully and had, up to that point, not opened his mouth. He said very quietly and very simply, and I'll never forget those words: 'I think Gordon may be right. We shall go.' We did.'

So the two businesses were bought, Universal Sky Tours costing, in total, £900,000 The signatures of agreement had to be applied rapidly because the Wilson Government had announced the introduction of capital gains tax, and a deadline had to be met to avoid the sellers having to yield a hefty portion of their cash rewards to the Exchequer.

In May 1965 Thomson Industrial Holdings Ltd - itself a subsidiary of the UK Thomson Organisation - acquired both Universal Sky Tours and Britannia Airways, and Thomson Holidays was then formed to incorporate Sky Tours. Thomson Holidays and Britannia Airways later both became subsidiaries of Thomson Travel Ltd, which in turn was just one company in the Thomson Organisation plc.

Besides acquiring Skytours (and Britannia Airways) from Captain Langton, the Thomson Group also purchased Riviera Holidays from Aubrey Morris, a former taxi driver, along with two other companies, Luxitours and Gay Tours, from Norman Corkhill. The result was what can only be called a gallimaufry of travel companies, each located in a different part of the country and each specialising in various spheres of activity.

The significance of the Thomson-Langton deal as far as the future of Britannia Airways was concerned cannot be understated, and is summed up by Derek Davison, who was to become its chairman and chief executive.

'The advent of Thomson was a change in the fortunes of the company in a very positive way. There was a limitation at that time to the potential growth of the company because airlines were moving into an era requiring significant capital. To be able to expand was going to be extremely difficult in the company as it stood on its own. Against that, I suppose there was the loss of freedom which had come about with the setting up of a really, really independent airline. We were now part of a massive conglomerate organisation.'

Langton walked away, believing that the Thomson Group did not know what they were doing, and he was probably right - at least at the start. At first, these separate companies were allowed to develop as they had under their original ownership, but it wasn't long before some parts of this disjointed empire began to falter, not helped by Thomson using managers with no experience of the travel trade.

Soon, other companies were romping away, leaving the Thomson group of companies to flounder in their wake, both in terms of product spread and overall passenger numbers. It became clear that instead of four companies separately marketing what was ultimately the same product, there should be just one. So which of the four companies was to be the flagship? In the end, an ingenious solution was found by Thomson's David Walker: the different companies' brochures would be published with titles featuring the Thomson name – Thomson Skytours, Thomson Riviera and so on – but with the word 'Thomson' at first being displayed in a very small print font, and then, over time, becoming steadily more substantial and more extensive, to the point that only 'Thomson Holidays' would remain.

When the Thomson group took over, it was clear that the strategy of the airline had to change. It had to be part of the Thomson Organisation, which meant that many more resources were involved. The objectives had to change; Thomson was not interested in running a small group. Everything they did had to be significant. There was a feeling in the early days from some in the airline that they did not want too much involvement with Thomson; they wanted the money, but not necessarily the relationship. That went on for quite a few months before it gradually began to change and they realised the sense of involvement with Thomson. This type of behaviour and thought process was typical of most acquisitions; nobody wants a new master. Once everyone got over that hurdle, matters started to develop very rapidly.

Working the Synergy...
The buzz-word 'synergy', so beloved by marketing men and business consultants alike could be defined thus: synergy: noun: synergy; plural noun: synergies; synergism; plural noun: synergisms. The interaction or cooperation of two or more organizations, substances, or other agents to produce a combined effect more significant than the sum of their separate effects.

It was this concept that was sought by Gordon Brunton to find a perfect match between the

'Come fly with me, let's fly, let's fly away...' By the mid-1960s brochure covers had changed and were starting to relect the 'swinging sixties'.

publishing and printing businesses of the Thomson Organisation and the travel trade aspects of Universal Sky Tours and Britannia Airways. It all came together in that most transient of items - the holiday brochure - and Thomson Travel and Britannia Airways were one of the leaders in the genre.

The symbiotic relationship between tour company and airline was one that had an impact in both directions; each fed from and off the other, both in terms of business and publicity. It was especially true when looking at the closely linked inclusive tour companies and their associated airlines. A holiday, although a product, is not something - like a can of baked beans - that the public can be made aware of with a single, simple advertisement. One company may offer a range of fifty or so destinations with a whole range of different accommodations available within each. Thus the concept of the holiday brochure was born. For Thomson Travel - and therefore Britannia Airways - the brochure was one of the cornerstones for business and as such deserves looking at in some detail.

In the days before websites and online bookings took off, in the mid-1990s the travel industry was churning out an estimated 120 million brochures for the UK alone - a report by the environmental group Green Flag in 1993 showed that more than fifty million brochures were thrown away each year, many unopened. The mass of marketing material which had been selling package tours since their explosion in

Two views of Benidorm, about fifty years apart. Before the 1960s, Benidorm was a small village. Today it stands out for its hotel industry, beaches and skyscrapers, built as a result of its tourist-oriented economy. The town had a long history of fishing which created the myth that before tourism Benidorm was a charming fishing village when in fact it never was. Today Benidorm has three major beaches: Playa de Levante, Playa de Poniente and Playa de Mal Pas; all of them have a blue flag since 1987. Britannia Airways and Thomson Travel played a huge part in its development.

the mid-fifties had primarily disappeared into skips - a sorry loss. Racial attitudes, sexual mores, class structures, social and economic patterns, environmental changes, as well as the varying literary skills of the brochure writers, all call out from the glossy pages that have survived.

Battle of the Brochures and 'Brochureland'.
Development of travel brochures soon evolved into something of an 'arms race' that created thirty years of intense rivalry, skullduggery and being 'economical with the truth'. Britannia may have been the first to integrate brochure production for travel tours that incorporated its own airline all under the same corporate structure, but it was Thomas Cook who sowed the seeds of the modern brochure, beginning with his Excursion Advertiser, a small black and white pamphlet, which promoted trips to the Great Exhibition in 1851. The Holidays With Pay Act in 1938 may have provided the impetus for serious holiday business, but it was not until the nineteen fifties, with the war well out of the way, and jet travel beginning to get going, that the company transferred its advertising to a coloured magazine format. Holidaymaking first appeared in 1953. 'Holiday Recipe Ingredients,' offered one issue 'One blue lake, assorted mountains, snow dressing for tops of mountains, green valleys, flowers (all colours), one good hotel. To make: bake in the sunshine and add... yourself.'

The term 'brochure' was not yet in common use but travel company' books', as they were usually called, were already putting on weight. Cook's Wintersports programme for 1953-4, for example, ran to 120 pages and Sir Henry Lunn's covered over 100 resorts in 72 pages.

Below: Britannia G-ANBL is 'turned around' at Manchester, with a number of BOAC ground vehicles in the foreground.

Left: a early, and decidedly formal Britannia Airways 'Flight Souvenir' from around 1967
(both authors collection)

The visual style of the time was railway timetable meets dress pattern. Holidaymakers featured mainly as line drawings, young, fully dressed and elegantly affluent, ladies in dirndls and pearls, languid young men with cravats and cigarettes in holders, unencumbered by families. The copy was hyperbolic: full of wonder and the joy of discovery, unfettered by the spectre of the customer complaints department. 'You really ought to see Rhineland'; 'Lucerne - Gay Swiss Resort'; 'All that the Spanish do is done with elegance'.

Favourite adjectives were always 'gay' - as in the original sense of the word - for the resort, and, somewhat strangely to today's eyes, 'limpid' for the water. The emphasis is on tradition, glamour, the Alpine resorts, the Rivieras - 'Doesn't the hotel look sumptuous?'

Sumptuous, well yes, old certainly. But there was never a modern building in sight, nor a picture of a holidaymaker interacting with a local. Company hand-holding was prominently on offer, helped by primly dressed 'hostesses'. 'John involuntarily handled Cook's ticket case in his pocket...' begins a photo story describing how Cook's made life safe and secure for John and Mary on holiday.

The lure of sun, water and price over scenery and refinement was rapid. 'New hotels spring up overnight, and they have no reputation to guard,' Cook's brochure warned in 1957. 'What will everyone seek this year? Just one thing - a generous sun.'

Sex, in the shape of bikini-clad cover girls, had not been used as a marketing magnet; then the first cover girl in a swimsuit appeared, and the first picture of a swimming pool. By 1961 new white

Spain as a holiday destination soon became about tower-block hotels that were barely finished before the tourists moved in and more coach trips than you could shake a stick at - mock bullfights, wine-tastings and general sightseeing.
(both author)

Above: A Britannia Britannia in flight.

Right: 'Summer breeze, makes me feel fine. Blowing through the jasmine of my mind...' By 1966 gone were dresses and hand-luggage, in were bikinis, beachballs and 'Sun and Fun Holidays'!

hotels are emerging and in 1963 the brochure euphemistically explains: 'Sometime ago it was Majorca that was 'away from it all'. It is so gorgeous that everyone went there and it became tremendously gay.'

Prices become larger, photographs bluer, models closer to nakedness in an ever-deepening shade of orange. Flying was regarded as 'exotic', and the brochures pushed that aspect. Everyone got dressed in their Sunday best to travel - it was an exceptional, unique experience, but not often in the way they were expecting, as Rose Robinson recalled: 'My first ever flight was the promise by my Grandad that we would go on a jet to the Isle of Man. Bad weather changed all that, and instead of a jet from Leeds Bradford (Yeadon as it was then), we went by Dakota from Blackpool! I remember my Dad being so cross as he'd paid for a taxi for us from Ilkley to Yeadon and an hour or so later we were on a bus travelling back through Ilkley to Blackpool. We did come back on a jet, and I have to say. Poor Grandad, he'd told us so much about their holiday, that's why we'd booked! I can remember it was like climbing a mountain to get to our seats, and I was poorly (only nine-ish at the time) how times have changed in a lot of respects. I love flying, providing I'm next to the window, especially on a clear day!'

January was always traditionally been the time of the travel industry's annual assault. Thousands of glossy brochures were launched at the public on the not unreasonable assumption that our resistance to images of sunny foreign places is at its lowest in the cold winter months.

By 1974, the first cracks had started to appear that the brochures were finally starting to go too far. On page 60 of Clarksons' brochure was the assertion that Benidorm was '...a charming little fishing village'. This was a literary way of describing what the photographs quite clearly showed looked like a Sheffield housing estate.

So how did the significant change come about? It cannot merely have been that Britain was fed up with the grief of war and the rationing which lingered on after it. Also, there must have been more to it than the fact that Britons had travelled abroad to fight, and were anxious to visit in peacetime. There is some truth in both theories, but, more likely, there was a

Curfew time at Luton - Britannias rest overnight between holiday flights. *(authors collection)*

cocktail of reasons. The Education Act of 1944 raised the school leaving age to 15 in 1947 and resulted in an explosion of grammar schools, which raised the aspirations of a whole new stratum of society. Demand for labour created higher bargaining power for workers, pushing up their wages sharply. Between 1955 and 1960, average weekly earnings rose by thirty-four per cent, while retail prices increased by only fifteen per cent. Television - mainly commercial channels which encouraged the 'live now pay later' society - fanned the flames of longing for destinations more exotic than the British seaside. And into this general atmosphere of opportunity, the feeling that anything was possible for anyone, from any background, gave berth to 'youth culture' and the sexual revolution of the 1960s. By 1959 a survey was noting that teenagers spent an average of 4s 6d a week on holidays - or seven per cent of their total annual expenditure. That compared with 6s 10d a week on cigarettes, 4s 3d on going to the cinema and 3s 10d on alcohol.

The 1960s were a period when the travel industry and its clients almost came to blows when the industry seemed to exist in the period of the American wild west, teetering between lawlessness and the arrival of the US Marshall. Brunton and the Thomson Group were up against a serious 'image problem' that reflected down on to Britannia Airways.

The difference was that all along the Spanish Costas, the cowboys were more real than mythological. These were years of such explosive growth in package holiday sales that consumers inevitably fell victim to over-optimism and risky enterprises and, just as inevitably, as consumers began to fight back, the holiday industry was forced to start putting its house in order.

There was a sense that mass travel had reached awkward adolescence, that it was on the cusp between childhood and maturity which manifested itself in other ways, too. The reins of regulation on airlines were loosened but never removed. The rule

that package holidays should not be sold for less than the standard return airfare was abused and eroded, but not completely abolished.

These were heady, exciting days, with the youth culture in full bloom and the prospect of unlimited horizons and vast riches for the holiday industry. England's World Cup triumph at Wembley in the summer of 1966 had put a new spring in the nation's step which not even the economic woes that beset Harold Wilson's Labour Government could dampen.

One significant problem came from Britannia's and the Thomson Travel Group's great rivals Clarkson Holidays and Court Line.

The rise of Clarksons had been meteoric. From 1965 through to 1973 the firm expanded from a small operation carrying 4000 customers a year into a giant providing package tours for 1.1 million holidaymakers. That expansion took place mainly in Spain, where the Franco government was subsidizing the growth of its tourism industry through a system of credits to hotel developers to enable them to build the accommodation needed to cope with the ever-increasing demand.

The man driving it all was Tom Gullick. He was born at Westgate-on-Sea in Kent in 1931, was evacuated to North Wales during the war, entered the Royal Naval College at Dartmouth as a 13-year-old cadet, and in 1948, aged 17, joined the Navy. After 14 years in the service, he left, using his naval contacts to get a job running a small travel agency called H. Clarkson (Air and Shipping Service), owned by the prosperous London City company Shipping and Industrial Holdings (SIH).

Through Gullick, Clarkson's decided to expand into longer holidays, despite Gullick's doubts that many people would go for anything but the shortest of these tours, and that most would be previous short break customers. Nevertheless, the programme was a sell-out.

The first brochure offered packages of eight, eleven, twelve or fifteen days - with prices from 26 guineas: 'We realized we could do it more cheaply than anyone already in the market. I think one reason for our success was that we had established great contacts with the Women's Institutes and that they included the next generation of young holidaymakers. At that time, we made very few sales through travel agents - virtually all holidays were sold directly to the customer following word of mouth recommendations.

More than any other, the firm was responsible for the creation of Benidorm, which became Spain's most popular resort. Clarksons' customers took up some six thousand of the total of ten thousand or so beds there in the late 1960s. It singled out hoteliers who had shown excellent management skills and lent them money over five years to build new properties to its own specifications. But even this system proved inadequate to keep up with its mushroom growth, so Clarksons formed its own development company in Spain and built eight large hotels, each with 600-800 beds, in significant resorts.

The constant ferment of new ideas intoxicated those who worked for Clarksons. Gullick used Clarksons to pioneer a new business concept into the travel trade: 'vertical integration'. Hence Clarksons involvement in Barbecues, Hotels, Coaches, Excursions, Land Development, Travel Agencies and English-style Pubs and a whole range of other things.

A vivid example of this was the Clarksons chicken farm. At that time British holidaymakers were still not entirely happy with Spanish cooking, so Clarksons felt it necessary to provide them with a blander alternative, such as an omelette, on standard hotel dinner menus. It was not long before Gullick began to suspect that somebody was profiteering at his expense, for the egg dishes began to cost more than he knew they should. So a friend of his offered to set up a farm near Benidorm so that several

The views in the travel brochures could be very different in reality. The views all the brochures shown of the Greek island of Corfu always included the classic shot of Pontikonisi - Mouse Island - and the Vlacheraina monastery seen from the hilltops of Kanoni. What they failed to show was the view from the other direction - final approach into Ioannis Kapodistrias Airport!
(both author)

In the 1960s many holiday snapshots were printed on textured paper that has something od a orange-peel effect that are notoriously difficult to reproduce in a book. One such example of this is this shopt of Britannia G-ANBE about to board another load of passengers at Luton. *(Kaz Ale Collection)*

thousand eggs a day could be supplied at a controlled price. 'We knew that we could always pull down the farm and sell the land at a profit later.'

Poor standards provided by some hoteliers, coupled with having holiday clients arriving at unfinished hotels was a public relations disaster, as was the practice of 'switching'. If a particular 'package' in a brochure failed to attract an acceptable load-factor, it was likely to be 'switched' to other resorts, sometimes at the very last minute - some clients placidly accepted a change of holiday destination, others didn't and complained - long and loud - to the Press. Also, recurrent reports of unfinished hotels heavily tarnished the reputation of package tour operators in the late 1960s and early 1970s. The use of 'artists' impressions' became commonplace in brochures.

Other problems that faced passengers were air traffic control delays, sometimes brought on by sheer demand, but usually by strikes, often involving the French. Passengers could be stranded either at their departure airport, or overseas, which resulted in yards of lurid newspaper headlines, and long delays in overcrowded airports, often in terminals with limited seating and no air conditioning!

At Thomson Travel there were still problems with their management team. Gordon Brunton worked on the assumption that a manager was a manager was a manager, and after a lot of searching for a Managing Director for Thomson Travel, he brought in Bryan Llewellyn, who was Marketing Director of Thomson Regional Newspapers, and a great deal of the success of the Thomson Travel operation could be ascribed to him. He knew nothing about the travel business but was an extremely able marketing man. He took over the whole thing and transformed it, and he brought in a significant number of bright young men who were able to help with the success.

Things became quite cut-throat behind the scenes - espionage between major tour firms was rampant. For example, a 'mole' in the printers used by Thomson's had managed to smuggle out a proof copy of the brochure. Clarkson's combed the pages to see if they could push the prices of some packages through the psychological £100 barrier. They searched the price panels to discover that their rivals had done just that. In a world where price comparisons were so sensitive that they could mean life and death to a tour operator, it appeared that Clarkson was safe to follow suit. The rivalry became intense.

Clarksons' Tom Gullick had decided to make some dramatic cuts in their rates, which were causing severe damage to Thomson's market share. Hambros Bank effectively owned Clarkson's and Gordon Brunton went and saw them to discuss the matter. He told them that in his view, the cut-throat operation was quite stupid and that no one would make any progress if it continued. Hambros told Brunton that their view was, and the advice they had been given was, that Thomson would not be able to stand the heat of the kitchen and they would be able to see any battle out.

Brunton is supposed to have retorted that Thomson was undoubtedly not without resources and it would certainly not happen that way. Usually, everybody put their holiday prices out at about the same time, but on this occasion, Thomson Travel waited until Clarksons had produced their brochures - and then undercut them by ten per cent.

Throughout the 1960s and into the early 1970s it became traditional for the airline to be featured on the front of the brochure to give glamour to the forthcoming journey, and then again in the rear - this time in the small print that provided information as to airports and flight times. It had the effect of indelibly linking the airline the travelling public used to the name of the tour company and by default the experiences they had. So it was with Britannia Airways and Sky Tours, although slowly the brochure identity evolved into just 'Thomsons'.

Although this is getting slightly ahead of the story, to complete this explanation, brochure layout - and even online websites - has remained remarkably unchanged since then, certainly in the mass market. The white or yellow background is still there, the unfeasibly blue and white photos, of pool, sea and apartment, the friendly local or donkey, the people who will be your new friends on the lovely holiday. Clients became much more aware of their rights, and the law protected them to a much greater extent. It forced the removal of the more shall we say 'decorative' descriptions from brochure-speak.

Attempts to sell the Greek islands to an already sophisticated market in the 1980s began to show companies that lowering expectations could make life easier. Charles Vyse and Vic Fatah created SunMed, who were the pioneers of a new, brutally frank style. At startup, SunMed carried 360 passengers in the first year but soon rose to one of the most recognisable tour operating brands taking 250,000 clients per year. Recalled Fatah: 'I've been in the aviation and travel industry all my life, right from going to 'help out' at my Dad's travel agency at the age of three. I started as a travel counter clerk, where I learnt the fundamentals that underly the industry, but primarily I discovered what the customers wanted.

I then became a 'bucket shop' co-owner and sold charter tickets across the Atlantic and to the Far East for a while until I recognised the market was so price competitive we needed a unique product. For me, this was package holidays to the Greek Islands, considered exotic at the time. It was the birth of Sunmed Holidays and was my baby for the next decade.'

'We told it like was, if something was rubbish we said so,' says Charles Vyse, One particular instance of this was the tale of a decrepit Greek hotel with an owner clearly suffering from dementia, which SunMed promptly marketed as the Hotel Fawlty, much to the disgust of the Greek National Tourism Organisation, who complained. There were rumours of diplomatic incidents and that SunMed might get thrown out of the country, but it had little effect on clients: 'It sold out. The more the guests complained about the facilities, the more demented the owner became. They called him 'Basil'. We had no end of letters from satisfied customers saying they couldn't believe the place was as bad as we'd portrayed it in the brochure.'

Brochures started to follow trends: tour operators discovered that women book most holidays. The result - the disappearance of the bronzed beauty on the cover, in favour of the happy family. Then came what was called 'fragmentation'. In 1994 Thomsons had more than fourteen different brochures ranging

'Beach baby, beach baby give me your hand...'... an almost deserted beach with a few palm beach unbrellas for shade - it had to be 1967!

In the summer of '69... The heady days of being spoilt in a SkyTours hotel - and this one even looks finished!

from 'Small and Friendly' to, well, big.

Tour Companies also become self-conscious about clichés. It was alleged that some companies developed software that asked the brochure writer 'Are you sure?' whenever they attempt to use the words colourful, bustling, golden, lapped, fascinating or majestic. There may well be a golden sand beach lapped by a shimmering blue sea next to a charming, colourful, bustling, market beneath majestic mountains, but it had reached the point where that could not be used because the business has already debased it.'

The result of the fragmentation and cliche-watching, though, was more desperate forays than ever into the realm of creative writing. The writers became tireless in their quest for new countryside adjectives: 'delightful countryside', 'enchanting countryside', 'exquisite countryside', 'breathtaking countryside', 'blissful countryside', 'strikingly beautiful countryside', 'beautiful rolling countryside', 'superb distinctive countryside', 'most glorious countryside', all appear within a few pages, before you even got to 'Tuscan countryside' and 'surrounding countryside'.

The Club 18-30 brochure went in a different direction and got itself far into an imaginary world of ravespeak: 'Take a little attitude, make a statement,' it exhorted. 'Life isn't a rehearsal - Hit the ground running!' It claimed that Tenerife was suddenly, somehow, 'breaking the barriers of light

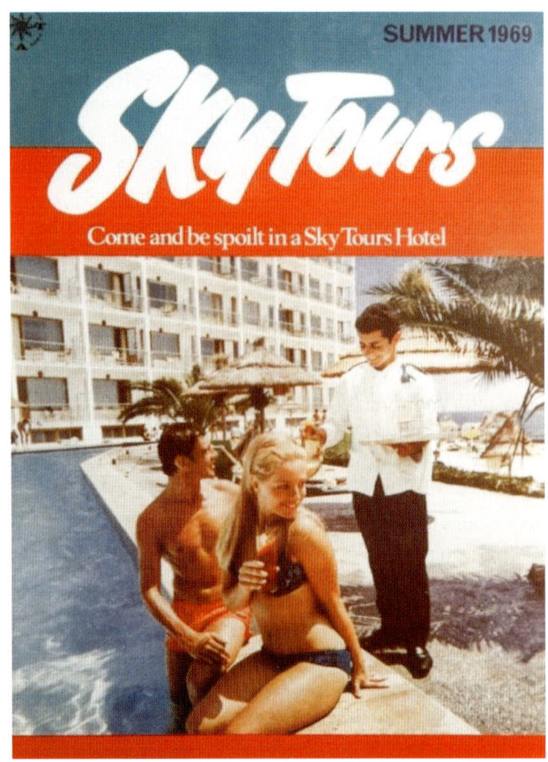

and sound', and a boat trip had become a 'journey into the Third dimension'.

Nevertheless, the copywriter euphemism concept stayed as healthy as ever: 'vibrant' was decoded as 'Ambient Sounds under your room all night'. 'Rapidly developing resort' meant staying in a building site; 'A good base for exploring further afield' - was the place is as dull as a brick; and of course, as ever 'Ideal for sun-worshippers', meant 'Absolutely nothing else to do'.

Nowadays everybody knows that 'lively' means a night club under your room, 'golden' depends on whether you are talking about a beach or showers, and 'fascinating' is shorthand for somewhere with either a nasty dictator or a particularly enthusiastic police force.

We all know that Brochureland doesn't exist, but that doesn't stop us from dreaming. While we've become immune to hanging around un-air-conditioned airports waiting for delayed flights, we still imagine the happy families who go on holiday in Brochureland, where the sky is the same unnatural shade of turquoise as the countless swimming pools, and where, for the winter months we imagine that is we would prefer to be. Without doubt, Brochureland is alive and kicking with the 'All-Inclusive prison-camps' - oh, I'm sorry, I mean Holiday Resorts!

That said, there could still be moments of genuine delight when reading the holiday brochure, something that sadly now does not happen with

internet booking sites. A few years ago prospective holidaymakers leafing through the summer brochure of one of the larger tour operators may have noticed what appeared to be a rogue photo caption. Among the several hundred other sensible ones, 'The pool at the Hotel Lloret', 'The swimming pool at the Lloret Hotel', 'Lloret Hotel Pool', was one which said: 'Two fat Germans on a slide.' 'It kind of slipped through the net...' explained one of the writers of the brochure. 'When you're captioning 500 virtually identical photos of pools you start to feel urges to break the monotony.'

But that is getting somewhat ahead of things, and away from the main thrust of the story. Britannia Airways was expanding, and the Thomson Travel organisation were using its marketing tools to their best advantage - then came tragedy.

A catalogue of errors...
Britannia G-ANBB was scheduled as Flight BY105 for a Universal Sky Tours charter flight to Ljubljana Jože Pučnik Airport - known then as Brnik Airport -

Yugoslavia. The aircraft departed Luton at 21:10 hours GMT on 31 August 1966, with a crew of seven and one hundred and ten passengers.

The en-route part of the flight was uneventful. After overflying Klagenfurt, the crew contacted Ljubljana Aerodrome Control. The controller supplied the crew with meteorological and other necessary landing information: 'Wind is calm, visibility 5 kilometres, shallow fog over the runway is forming now, clouds 2/8 strato-cumulus 1800 metres, QNH 1011, QFE 968 millibars. Temperature 10 and dew-point also 10 degrees. The runway will be 31. After Dolsko make left pattern holding, descend down to 4500 by QNH, report inbound.'

The crew acknowledged receipt of the information. When the pilot asked the controller if the Instrument Landing System (ILS) was operating, the controller answered that he had radar contact at a position twenty nautical miles south-east from the airport and advised the crew to make an approach to runway 31, and to report after descending to 4500 feet.

Left: When not engaged on holiday flights to the sun, Britannia Airways worked the Hadj. Here a group of Mecca pilgrims return back to Rabat in Morocco.

Below: G-ANBF outside the hangar at Luton awaits another load of passengers.
(both Kaz Ale Collection)

The crew acknowledged and reported they were at 4500 feet and would call over Dolsko inbound for the outer marker and asked again if the ILS was operating and if it was serviceable. The controller answered affirmatively, adding that the ILS was working normally.

He then gave the position as 'abeam Dol', and after the crew acknowledged that he asked if they had visual contact with the runway. The crew confirmed that they had contact. The crew then reported having passed Dolsko continuing and descending towards runway 31. The controller acknowledged this information and requested the crew to 'check final for runway 31', and gave the aircraft its position as seven nautical miles from touchdown on the centre line should be passing 3300 feet and repeated 'check final for runway 31'. The crew acknowledged this message and one and a half minutes later reported having passed the outer marker inbound. The controller issued clearance for landing and advised that he had set the approach and runway lights to maximum intensity. He then left the radar console and went to the light control console at the same time glancing towards the approach and the runway. He could not see the aircraft, but the approach and runway lights were clearly visible. At that moment, the crew requested radar assistance. The controller returned to the radar console and started to supply them with radar information. After giving the crew two aircraft positions of 3,5 and 2 nautical miles from touchdown, he observed that the aircraft signal was turning to the right and gave a correction of three degrees left. Noting that the aircraft did not make any correction, the controller informed the crew that its position was one and a half nautical miles from touchdown, and asked the pilot whether he was making a short right turn to the Menges radio beacon. The crew did not reply, and there was no further contact with them although the controller continued calling. Radar contact was lost at 00:47 hours local time on 1 September 1966 (23:47 hours GMT on 31 August 1966). Rescue services, reported that after fifteen minutes, they had found the crashed aircraft on fire, in a wood, nearly two miles south-east of the threshold of runway 31 and nearly half a mile north of the runway extended centreline.

Derek Davison and a team from Britannia flew to the crash site. The airline's Chairman, Gordon Brunton, together with his wife and family, were on their way home from a holiday on his boat off Majorca. When Brunton arrived at Palma Airport, he was greeted by Britannia staff with sad faces who gave him the news that an aircraft had crashed. Brunton immediately flew straight to Luton and then to Italy and collected a convoy of vehicles and people who could help, before driving to Ljubljana.

It was a tough and grim time. The burns unit at the local hospital was doing a magnificent job. They worked round the clock for two weeks treating the severely injured. They needed a variety of specialised equipment and drugs, and hospitals in London primarily provided it. Brunton arranged for special equipment to be flown out from the UK to help the doctors in their work. Everyone in Ljubljana was magnificent; kind and generous people. The women worked all night making Union Jacks to drape over the coffins, and a burial site was earmarked close by if it was needed.

The relatives wanted their loved ones sent back to the UK, and so it was arranged that the RAF would

With the increase in traffic, facilities at Luton expanded. *(author's collection)*

Above: The distinctly grubby-looking Britannia G-ANBB is moved from years of storage at Cambridge Airport to be prepared for service with Britannia Airways. 'NBB flew into Luton in November 1964, and made the first passenger flight for Britannia when it took holidaymakers to Tenerife. This was the same month the Constellations were withdrawn from use.

Below: The same aircraft after being repainted in Britannia's colours. Tragically this machine was to crash Ljubljana, Yugoslavia on 1 September 1966. *(both Author's Collection)*

provide aircraft to fly the bodies back to Britain.

Later, as thanks for the unstinting help of the people of Ljubljana, the Thomson Organisation presented scholarships for Yugoslav plastic surgery students to spend six months at a time in London hospitals to help further their training. The organisation also paid for the burns unit in the town to be re-equipped.

The subsequent investigation revealed that 'The probable cause of the accident was that the pilot-in-command did not set his altimeter to the QFE-968 Mb in accordance with the information passed by the controller. However, the whole approach to the airport was made as if the altimeter had been set to the QFE, and resulted in the path being about 1250ft lower than procedural safety altitudes, so that the aircraft's approach was too low, because although it was a moonlight night he could not distinguish any visual landmarks, which might have warned him of the low altitude, due to the nature of the trees covered terrain over which they were flying. As the altimeter error passed unnoticed by both pilots and because they were not carrying out cross-checks of the two altimeters in accordance with the relevant operations manual instruction attachment No. 15, the error was not corrected by climbing to a safe altitude.

This disregard of the procedure laid down in the checklists and operations manual for approach and landing was explained by the fact that the approach was carried out on a moonlight night in calm weather and with visibility of approximately ywelve nautical miles, which reduced the crew's concentration on precisely following the prescribed procedures and checks.

The visual effect of the runway slope made the situation worse, giving the pilots a wrong impression of the aircraft's approach angle. The co-pilot's altimeter was found set at 1005,5 Mb. The difference between the QNH and QFE passed to the aircraft was approximately equivalent to 1000ft. A figure which might have led to further confusion.

Aircraft maintenance accommodation was reaching full capacity during 1967, and while a new terminal at Luton eased passenger congestion, there was a need for extra hangar space. Britannia reached an agreement with Luton town council that the latter would construct to the airline's requirements, which would then be leased to Britannia Airways. The new hangar was opened in 1970.

With company titles painted out, Britannia G-ANBF meets its fate outside the hangar at Luton. *(author's collection)*

Between 1965 and 1970 the integration of Sky Tours and Thomson operations continued to grow and the main task was to relate aircraft availability with Thomson and the other tour operators requirements. Meanwhile, as the airline grew in importance, it became a larger contributor to the profits of The Thomson Organisation.

The airline continued to grow throughout 1968 with services to the holiday destinations of Europe and North Africa being operated on behalf of many tour operators, including such reputable names as Global, who had commenced flights from Bristol for the first time, Horizon, and Sky Tours. To meet the increasing demands, two Britannias were leased from Laker Airways and BKS Air Transport. The Britannia aircraft were now being flown in a 117 seat passenger configuration. By the end of 1968, the Britannias were carrying more passengers on Inclusive Tour holiday flights than their rivals, British Eagle.

The Britannias were given a new field of destinations when the airline obtained a 402 Foreign Air Carrier Permit for trans-Atlantic operations, by the United States Civil Aeronautics Board. This allowed Britannia Airways to enter the lucrative market of affinity group charters to Canada and the United States.

During the spring and summer of 1969 Britannia completed the final six months of a British United Airways contract with the Ministry of Defence (MoD), for the carriage of service personnel and their families to and from Royal Air Force bases in West Germany. BUA had been forced to drop these flights due to an increase in commitment to scheduled services and an MoD stipulation that aircraft be equipped with rearward facing seats. Britannia then successfully negotiated a new contract with the Ministry of Defence for these flights, and subsequently also for similar flights to Gibraltar, forcing the Ministry to reverse its stipulation on rearward facing seats.

Since these flights were operated midday and midweek and did not interfere with existing charter services, Britannia's aircraft utilisation rate immediately improved.

The remaining Britannias were also being kept busy during 1970 - what was to be their final summer of operations. As well as operating the Ministry of Defence flights, they continued to work ad-hoc passenger and freight flights to many destinations, including North America and the Far East, where affinity group charters continued to be the only mode of cheap transport to such faraway places. In addition to this, the Britannias were actively engaged in flying tourists to such events as the Munich Beer Festival and the Oberammergau Passion Play in West Germany, from British departure points.

The days of the Britannias were numbered, and on 29 December 1970 the last survivor of the Britannia fleet, G-ANBL, returned to Luton from Brussels for the last time. On the flight deck were Captain Adrian Coleman, First Officer Wilkinson and Flight Engineer Charles Tett, who was also retiring. 'It will be sad to see the old Brits finally fade away' he said. 'They have been good servants to many an airline. But times change. They just have not got the passenger appeal any more. Once people have flown in a Boeing, they don't want to know'.

Chapter 4

Going with Boeing

To the operational team at Britannia, it was clear that there was a new generation of aircraft coming. They were not yet proven, but there was a definite indication that competition was going to grow and that the old concepts of comfort and flying were going to disappear. The future was going to be all about productivity.

When they had been operating Constellations with eighty-two passengers on board, it took eight hours to fly to Palma and back. The move to Britannias saw 117 passengers take six hours for the same journey. It began to look possible to carry 117 in just four hours and gave the ability to achieve around 2,600 hours a year flying ultra-modern jets.

In those days, it was virtually unheard of for a charter operator to order brand new aircraft, let alone state-of-the-art aircraft which were not proven. The tradition among these companies was to buy second-hand aircraft from the leading scheduled airlines at a time when these were moving towards the obsolescent period of their operational life. They were not necessarily old in lifespan terms, but they were starting to be superceded so that that charter airlines could buy them at lower capital cost. By increasing the utilisation, they could gain a very competitive asset.

In the teeth of fierce resistance from the UK Government – who wanted the airline to order the British-built BAC 1-11, the Britannia team had set their heart on the Boeing 737-200, which was to become the workhorse of the UK package holiday business for many years to come.

The Britannia team had heard glowing reports about the Boeing 737 jet airliner and suggested that the Thomson Group should consider the possibility of buying them for Britannia. The team presented a good case, and it was also evident that something was needed to modernise the airline and help it provide the service that was required by the package tour holiday companies.

Britannia Projects Manager Peter Swift was tasked with looking into the possible introduction of the 737 into the airline. In November 1965 he presented a detailed report to the board, showing passenger miles increasing from 27 million in 1962 to 184 million in 1965 and a projected 258 million in 1966.

It was primarily associated with the growth of Universal Sky Tours in a joint operation, the success of which depended on offering the public a better buy in terms of price and quality of service.

There was no reason to believe that the future growth rate of Britannia Airways could not be forty per cent per annum - that is doubling every two years - provided the group continued to maintain two key features; the integration and coordination of planning with the associated tour organiser and very low-cost operation.

Studies demonstrated that a typical 737 schedule for the peak summer inclusive tour programme, showed that three return trips to a Mediterranean resort could be carried out per aircraft per day and still permit suitable times for passengers to arrive and depart, making use of public transport both to arrive at and depart from the London terminal.

Squadron Leader John Sauvage DSO. OBE (*b.* 9 Feb 1919, *d.* 2 April 2019) was appointed Managing Director of Britannia Airways in February 1967, and was later to become both Chairman and chief executive of the Thomson Travel Group. *(Britannia Airways)*

Enter the 'Baby Boeing'

Boeing had been studying short-haul jet aircraft designs and wanted to produce another aircraft to supplement the 727 on short and thin routes. Preliminary design work began on 11 May 1964, and Boeing's intense market research yielded plans for a fifty to sixty-passenger airliner for routes of fifty to one thousand miles long.

Although many airlines worldwide had historically expressed their faith in Boeing products, the company had been late coming into the short-haul twin jet scene. While both Douglas and BAC had been in the market with 'twins' for some time, Boeing had been scooping the pool with their three-engined 727 which, at one stage, became the world's top-selling aircraft.

The 737 design was presented in October 1964 at the Air Transport Association maintenance and engineering conference by chief project engineer Jack Steiner, where its elaborate high-lift devices raised concerns about maintenance costs and dispatch reliability. The launch decision for the $150 million

Two views of the fuselage of what was supposedly Britannia's first 737 at Boeing's Wichita plant. From here it would be sent by rail to their Seattle plant for final assembly. The minor mystery is the number '41' on the forward bulkhead - thought to be what is known as a 'line number', indicating the position of the aircraft in the production line sequence. However, if this is the case, the number for G-AVRL, their first aircraft, should be 38, suggesting that this was a publicity shot whereby the 'Britannia Airways' piece of card was quickly taped on the nearest available aircraft for ease and convenience! *(both Boeing via Britannia Airways)*

G-AVRL, Britannia's first 737, in the fitting out hangar at Boeing Plant 2, Boeing Field. *(Boeing)*

development was made by the Boeing board on 1 February 1965.

Never has an airliner had so many nick-names that thankfully the travelling public has never heard: 'Baby Boeing', Pocket Rocket', 'Fat Albert', 'Tin Mouse', 'Maggot', 'SLUF' (work that one out for yourself!), Light Twin, Fat Freddy, Thunder Guppy (series 1/200), Yuppy Guppy, Super Guppy (series 3/4/500), 'Pig', 'Bobby' (as in BOeing BaBY)... When Boeing decided to enter the two-engined market, their philosophy was to incorporate the same body cross-section as the Boeing 707 and 727, with six abreast seating. A controversial decision was to have the engines slung directly underneath the wing rather than the then more accepted practice, adopted by their Douglas and BAC rivals, at the rear of the fuselage. It caused a certain amount of comment because of the belief that engine ingestion from nosewheel debris could add expensive maintenance costs. Further developments, however, allowed the aircraft to operate even from unsealed runways.

Boeing decided to produce two versions of the 737, both powered by the Pratt & Whitney JT8-D, which itself became the world's most successful commercial jet engine at the time. The 100 series 737 got the production go-ahead on the strength of an order from Lufthansa, who became the launch customer on 19 February 1965 with a request for 21 aircraft with an increased capacity of 100 seats. The design was ideally suited with their intra-German network feeding into the Frankfurt international gateway airport. In parallel with this aircraft, Boeing was proposing a 200 series with a better range and even higher capacity. It attracted United Airlines who on 5 April 1965, announced that they had

ordered forty 737-200s. It was this version that appealed to Britannia.

The dilemma facing the Thomson hierarchy had several facets. The first was financial. At a time when the group's debt-equity ratio was one for one, they were being asked to commit multi-millions to heavy asset buying. Another disadvantage was that the group still had little knowledge of the airline business on which to form a sound judgment. And as though these were not enough greasy managerial poles, getting to grips was made more difficult by political intervention.

At the time the Luton men began to assess their jet options, to the south at the Weybridge, Surrey, headquarters of the then British Aircraft Corporation, managing director Sir George Edwards and his team confidently believed that they had the inclusive tour market virtually captured with the existing 200/300/400 versions of their BAC One-Eleven twin-jet. They had launched the aircraft on order from British United Airways and had since sold to Eagle Aviation and Court Line. They were flushed with success when news of the emergence of a 737 concept filtered through from the Boeing base at Seattle on the west coast of the United States.

Despite presentations from BAC, there was a growing synergy developing between Luton and Seattle. The Britannia exercise was an exciting challenge for the Boeing team because it was the first time they had worked to the concepts and needs of a one hundred per cent charter/inclusive tour airline.

Richard W. Taylor, then involved with the 737 programmes, and was later to become Boeing's vice president in charge of government technical liaison, recalled that what was needed to suit Britannia was

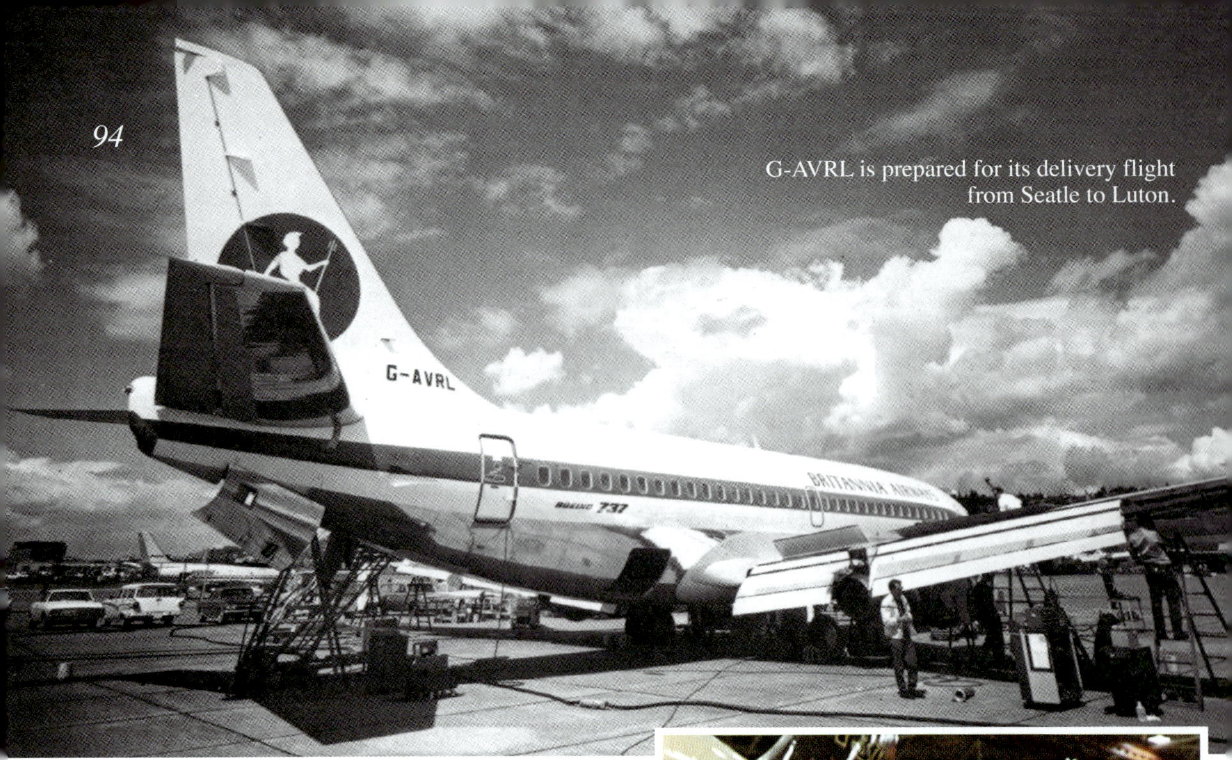

G-AVRL is prepared for its delivery flight from Seatle to Luton.

an extension of the fundamental design of the 737-200 airliner, particularly in the requirement for more extended range. From a performance aspect, the airflow was improved, but they also had to study the passenger cabin to achieve more seats, more closets, and room to store the then-unknown phenomenon in the United States - duty-free goods.

BAC still did not consider the cause lost. Sir George offered to stretch the One-Eleven, but then later he confided to Gordon Brunton that it could not be done. When Brunton told him, in that case, the Boeing would win, Sir George retorted: 'If you buy the Boeing, I'll fight you all the way on the political level.' Soon afterwards, Anthony' Tony' Crosland, (*b.* 29 August 1918, *d.*19 February 1977) who was a Labour Party politician and author and also President of the Board of Trade, was guest at a Thomson House lunch. Afterwards, Crosland asked to see Sir Gordon and Roy Thomson alone and told them what their patriotic duty was in the matter of buying their new aircraft.

Not only that, he affirmed that, even though BOAC had been allowed to buy American aircraft without penalty, Britannia would be charged fourteen per cent duty on every 737 they imported. The contention was that there was an equivalent British aircraft available, but Williams stoutly maintained that, on efficiency grounds, that was not the case.

Edwards and Crosland were not the only adversaries stacked up against Britannia in their planned purchase of 737s. Air Commodore Francis Rodwell 'Rod' Banks CB, OBE, Hon. CGIA., Hon. FRAeS, Hon. FAIAA., FlMechE., Flnst Pet., FRSA, CEng., MSAE, (*b.* 22 March 1898, *d.*12 May 1985). Banks, a British engineer who was involved in the development of the internal combustion engine. In the post-war years he held numerous posts, including as a director of the Bristol Aeroplane Company, and after the merging of Bristol Aero Engines with Armstrong Siddeley, their overall 'Director of Sales'

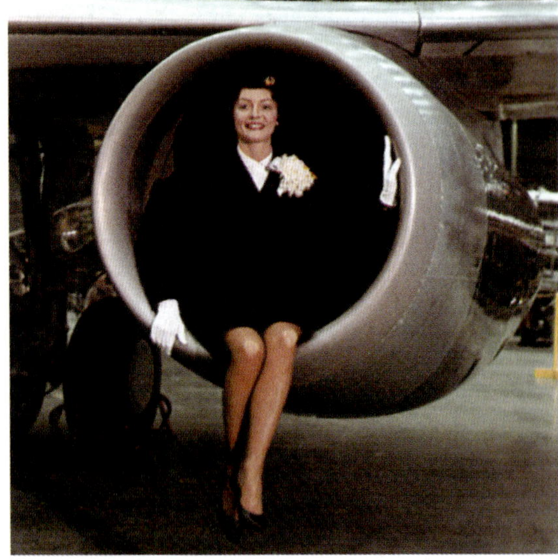

Chief Stewardess Liz Harrison in a classic pose for the early 737s - sitting in one of the intakes of the JT-8D jet engines - in the case, one fitted to the Boeing 737 demonstrator at Seattle.

in 1959. With the later mergers within the British aircraft industry, Banks became involved with the Hawker Siddeley company, in 1963, becoming Assistant Managing Director and Chief Executive (Civil Aircraft) at Hatfield, the former home of the de Havilland Company. He was to become something of an implacable foe for Britannia by championing the cause of the british aviation industry.

The first time anyone outside learned of the final choice was at another luncheon in Thomson House. The guest of honour was the then Minister of Aviation, Roy Jenkins. J E D Williams was asked to give his views on the industry, and, introducing him, Lord Thomson added a sentence of five significant words: 'We just bought the 737'. Britannia was contracted for three 737s with an option on a fourth.

When contacted by the press, Britannia claimed they had bent over backwards to buy British, but after the months of negotiation, the BAC One-Eleven remained economically unattractive when compared with the 737-200.

With 737s now ordered and Britannia now a vital cog in the Thomson Organisation, J E D Williams decided that the time had come to relinquish his role as Managing Director. A small and highly efficient management team, including Technical Director Jimmy Little, Financial Director Bob Muckleston and Derek Davison, who had become Operations Director as well as Chief Pilot, made sure that the airline and its eight Britannia aircraft continued along the right path, and the search started for a man to replace J E D Williams, who had decided to move from Managing Director to Chairman, and then, by June 1967 had taken full retirement. Sir Miles Thomas replaced him.

As J E D Williams told *Flight International* at the time: 'Lord Thomson and his colleagues have always treated me with the greatest consideration, never interfering with Britannia Airways, and when I wanted nearly $20 million to buy American jets they backed me unhesitatingly. It is just that, reaching last year the mid-point of a normal adult working life, I decided that this was not what I wanted for the second half. I have been working for months with my closest colleagues in Britannia and with the Thomson Organisation to get Britannia into the right posture and with the right industrial structure of Thomson

When Britannia Airways first announced their order for the 737, this image did the rounds of the media. It certainly shows a 73 interior, but there are aspects that just feel 'wrong'. The bulkhead does not appear correct, as does the location of that door behind the passengers. It is thought that it is the interior of the 737 mock-up in Seattle. *(Britannia Airways)*

Industrial Holdings to be able to realise the full potential of the airline. In my opinion, Britannia and its present team have a value second to no independent in Europe'.

William Miles Webster Thomas, Baron Thomas DFC (*b*. 2 March 1897, *d*. 8 February 1980), known as Sir Miles Thomas was a Welsh businessman. He was Managing Director of Morris Motors, from 1940 to1947, Chairman of the British Overseas Airways Corporation from 1949 to 1956, Chairman of the merger broker Chesham Amalgamations, and President and

Chairman of the National Savings Committee.

In 1956 he resigned after a row with Harold Watkinson, then Minister of Transport, and Thomas was elected as Chairman of the board of Monsanto Chemical Ltd. He later took other board appointments including Britannia Airways.

Introduction of the Boeing 737 was not without its problems. Rumours began to circulate that Boeing was having issues with their 737 programmes. These concerned both the structure and performance of the aircraft, demanding modifications to the wings. The need was to optimise lift and drag, even though the overall performance of the aircraft was exceeding the original expectation.

By 1970, Boeing had received only thirty-seven orders. Facing financial difficulties, Boeing considered closing the 737 production-line and selling the design to Japanese aviation companies. After the cancellation of the Boeing Supersonic Transport, and scaling back of 747 production, enough funds were freed up to continue the project.

The original engine nacelles incorporated thrust reversers taken from the 727 outboard nacelles. They proved to be relatively ineffective and tended to lift the aircraft up off the runway when deployed. In turn, it reduced the downforce on the main wheels, thereby reducing the effectiveness of the wheel brakes. In 1968, an improvement to the thrust reversal system was introduced; a 48-inch tailpipe extension was added, and new, target-style, thrust reversers were incorporated. The thrust reverser doors were set 35 degrees away from the vertical to allow the exhaust to be deflected inboard and over the wings and outboard and under the wings. The improvement became standard on all aircraft after March 1969, and a retrofit was provided for active aircraft. Boeing fixed the drag issue by introducing new longer nacelle/wing fairings and improved the airflow over the flaps and slats. The production line also introduced an improvement to the flap system, allowing increased use during take-off and landing. All these changes gave the aircraft a boost to payload and range and improved short-field performance. In May 1971, after aircraft #135, all improvements, including more powerful engines and higher fuel capacity, were incorporated into the 737-200, giving it a fifteen per cent increase in payload and range over the original -200s. It became known as the 737-200 Advanced, which became the production standard in June 1971.

In a bid to increase sales by offering a variety of options, Boeing offered a 737C (Convertible) model

Left: another poor quality, but historic image - Captain Davision, Peter Swift, 737 project manager ,and Captain Tanton with G-ARVL at Luton after their delivery flight from the USA.

Below: The old and the new! On the left is Britannia G-ANBA, while on the right is 737 G-AVRL, just having had its engine intake plugs removed in preparation for another service.
(both Kaz Ale collection)

in both -100 and -200 lengths. This model featured a 134-inch × 87-inch freight door just behind the cockpit, and a strengthened floor with rollers, which allowed for palletised cargo. The 737QC (Quick Conversion) version, with palletised seating - designed for quick conversion from passenger to general freight carrying allowed full advantage to be taken of the growth in the market. Amongst the varied cargoes carried, Britannia flew the celebrated racehorse Nijinsky - regarded by many experts to have been the greatest flat racehorse in Europe during the 20th century - to all his significant races except one. He won both the Derby and the 2000 Guineas after Britannia flights. However, the airline did not carry him to Paris for the Prix de l'Arc de Triumph, and unhappily he lost!

The short term result of all this was a delay in delivery of the first aircraft. For a scheduled operator, this news would have been unwelcome, but for a charter business which had pre-sold its summer flying programme for 1968, it could have been little short of disastrous. The answer was to lease aircraft to fill the gap. John Sauvage, who had become the Managing Director in 1967, turned to Freddie Laker, and the result was a deal for two of Laker Airways'

Left: a Britannia Airways inflight magazine from the early days of the 737, when they operated just eight of the type, alongside a number of Bristol Britannias.

Below: a 737 climbs away from the airstip at Boardman in Washington State. Here Britannia pilots learned the short-field technique required to safely operate the machine into and out of some of the more challenging European airports.
(both author's collection)

Bristol Britannia fleet. The blow was softened when Boeing agreed to pay for their short-term leasing.

John Sauvage was born in the Seychelles but left the warmth of the Indian Ocean in 1939 to face the chill of wartime Britain. His service with the famous Pathfinder Group of Bomber Command earned him the Distinguished Service Order, the Distinguished Flying Cross and bar. Like so many ex-RAF pilots after the war, he gravitated into commercial flying. Sauvage took part in the Berlin Airlift, and then became the chief pilot of Harold Bamberg's Eagle Aviation, rising up the Eagle management tree to become operations director, chief executive and managing director.

When Sauvage decided in 1966 to begin looking around to further his career, the spectacular crash of what became British Eagle, was still two years away. He had talked to J E D Williams and knew he wanted to ease out of Britannia and look to other challenges. Sir Miles Thomas was then on the Thomson board, and Sauvage had met him in the days when he was Chairman of the British Overseas Airways Corporation. He had two meetings with Thomas and Gordon Brunton. They agreed that Sauvage was the man to take Britannia forward.

Those old guard in Britannia kept track of J E D

As can be seen in these pages, Britannia's InFlight magazine evolved from something that was quite formal and staid, to more colourtful, stylish designs. *(all authors collection)*

Williams' activities outside the airline, but it still came as a shock when they heard that he had passed away on 30 Setpember 1992 in The Hague. He was survived by his wife Marianne.

Preparation to start work

The original 737 had been designed for route structures of relatively short stage lengths. A survey of the market-determined that most commercial customers interested in this airliner would be operating from field lengths of more than 5000 feet.

Continuing improvements to the 737 design resulted in the Advanced 737-200 - sometimes referred to as the -200ADV - which featured lower take-off and landing speeds, shorter stopping distances and, as an option, the more powerful Pratt & Whitney JT8D-17 engines with a thrust rating of 16,000 pounds. Automatic brakes became standard equipment and assured immediate braking on touch-down with a pre-selected rate of deceleration through the landing roll-out. The engine thrust reversers had been redesigned to improve their capability. Leading-edge high lift devices and trailing-edge wing flap improvements provided more significant lift and reduced approach speeds by four to eight knots compared with the original 737.

The improved performance made the airliner attractive to airlines which previously were unable to operate jet transport equipment because of limited runway lengths on their routes. Boeing 737-200ADVs began to be worked on unimproved

runways 5000 feet in length, and were certificated for operations on runways only 4000 feet long.

For an airline - including Britannia - making its first purchase of any Boeing airliner type, Boeing Commercial Airplane Company included in the Sales Contracts at no added cost a flight crew training programme. It consisted of ground school, cockpit procedure training, simulator training, transition flight training, and finally post-delivery route and line flying assistance and checks. The magnitude of the programme varied with the number of crews trained, but the course and the quality of training were standardised and resulted in fully qualified crew members.

Stewardess Sue Lloyd adds a touch of glamour to the inside of a 737-200 engine. *(Britannia Airways via authors collection)*.

The change from Bristol Britannia to Boeing 737! G-AVRL, seen here, brought a whole change of performance to the airline. This picture is thought to be an early image taken somewhere over the coast of Washington State - interestingly it shows an 'all blue' Britannia logo on the vertical fin. The photo was almost certainly taken in late June, early July 1968, just before delivery. *(author's collection)*

Boeing flight crew training for the 737 was based at Boeing Field International in Seattle, Washington. The Flight Crew Training Department, however, took advantage of the favourable weather, lower population density and excellent runways and airfield control facilities at Grant County Airport, Moses Lake, Washington, about twenty minutes by 737 from Seattle. There, a 13,000-foot runway - as well as tower personnel oriented to Boeing and airline flight training activities - made possible landings and take-offs at higher frequencies than would have been possible at any other base. The result was more training per flight hour.

In the case of the Advanced 737, the greater capability of the aeroplane had opened to jet operations fields with runways of 5000-foot length or less. Pilots making the transition directly from propeller-driven aircraft to jet-powered airliners, therefore, would be called upon to carry out line operations on runways a third as long as that stretching in front of them at Moses Lake. The need to give them the confidence to meet such an operational environment was viewed as necessary by those involved in instructing them at the Boeing Flight Training Center.

Many of the airports that Britannia intended to operate the 73 into and out of had runways between five and seven thousand feet in length - seemingly quite adequate for the new jet. It was complicated however by the poor condition of many of the runway surfaces - a number were quite bumpy - and often the airports only had a single, dual-direction runway that could impose quite a severe set of crosswind performance circumstances on operations.

Fortunately, Boeing already had a 'typical' field of such a length available on the sunny side of the Cascade Mountain range at Boardman, on land held under a long-term lease from the State of Oregon.

Boardman was used for US Navy flight training during World War II. It was about twenty minutes flying time from Seattle and about ten minutes from Moses Lake. The runway was hard-surfaced, 138 feet wide by 4200 feet long. There was no control tower or approach aids at the strip. Situated on a plateau above the Columbia River, it was surrounded by sagebrush and was far from any community that might object to the sound of jet airliner operations.

The runway at Boardman had Boeing-developed markings painted at each end. There was a broad white band on each edge 200 feet long, which began 500 feet from the threshold. It was the touch-down aim point. The narrow marking ended 500 feet further down the runway and indicated where touch-downs could be made with enough runway remaining for a safe stop.

Flight training consisted of a series of landings and take-offs such as those typically used in 737 pilot training. Fullstop landings, missed approaches, touch-and-go landings, approaches and landings with one engine throttled back, rejected take-offs from V_1 speed (the calculated 'go - no go' speed) and simulated engine failures at V_1 speed with continued take-off, were all accomplished. Each pilot made eight landings.

By the time the new 737 pilots got to the actual flight training, they had undergone ground school which included the material to prepare them for short-field training, and they had completed their simulator training. They were aware by now of the need for correct rotation technique where delayed or insufficient rotation could result in using too much runway. They knew that accurate and prompt response in case of engine failure at V1 meant adequate margins for stopping or continuing the take-off. They had been shown the importance of the correct approach path and approach speeds. They knew that too high an approach speed could waste available runway. Positive touch-downs and prompt use of brakes, spoilers, and reversers were pointed out to be essential.

They possessed the information, and they were about to get the experience!

Boeing 737 flight crew training always followed the same pattern. Each instructor pilot was assigned, two airline pilots. He began working with them in the simulator. Actual flight training sessions were each four hours long and were staggered so that each instructor pilot and his two pilots-in-training flew at different times of the day on subsequent days - morning, afternoon or night. Each flight session was preceded by an hour's pre-flight briefing and followed by an hour's post-flight discussion.

When short-field training was scheduled - always as part of a daylight session - the sequence began with a briefing that covered the material discussed earlier in ground school.

Regarding take-offs, Boeing instructors reviewed engine pressure ratio (EPR) settings, go/stop decision execution, refused take-off transition and implementation, and proper rotation which resulted in the earliest liftoff and best climb out. EPR settings are essential in short-field take-offs because settings even 0.10 low can result in 210 feet more runway

Left: Chairman of Britannia Airways during the early days was Sir Miles Thomas.

Below: Passengers board Romeo Mike for another service from Luton.

From Britannia Airways' early jet age comes this ticket and luggage label.

being required to reach V1 and less altitude gained in a given distance. If the go/stop decision is delayed even a second, more distance is needed to stop after an engine failure than would be necessary if the decision were made and executed promptly.

Boeing instructed the pilots to set proper EPR for take-off; execute go/stop decision promptly because mis-execution of 'stop' could result in overrun and mis-execution of 'go' could result in reduced clearance height; rotate on schedule; rotate at a proper rate and rotate to appropriate attitude.

In preparation for the short-field landings, the instructors emphasised to the Britannia pilots that the approach should be at the proper rate of descent and that the touchdown should be controlled, with the aircraft placed accurately on the runway and not allowed to float. They pointed out that while landing margins are large enough to allow for most additive errors, to ensure safe and comfortable operation, such errors should be minimised by proper aircraft operation and cockpit discipline.

Britannia had to accept a six-week slip in delivery, which meant that jet operations effectively missed the peak of the current season. The first delivery was a few days early, according to the revised contract.

So, instead of arriving in the spring as the herald of the seasonal inclusive tour programme, the first Boeing 737 - G-AVRL captained by Derek Davison - touched down at Luton from Seattle on 7 July right in the middle of summer schedules.

The flight from Seattle to Luton turned out to be a record-breaker. Boeing had designed the 737 to fly for 1,200 miles at a time. Captain Davison, along with Captain Donald Tanton and Peter Swift stayed in the air for 2,700 miles - 300 miles further than any 737 had previously flown. Boeing did not believe it was possible, but with careful flight planning and the installation of most internal fittings at Luton, it proved it could happen. The crew made just two stops out of an already scheduled three - the first at Montreal, the second at Goose Bay. Due to the following wind and light load, they managed to abandon the planned Reykjavik in Iceland stop and made the last leg a five-and-a-half-hour flight from Goose Bay to Luton.

As Derek Davison commented: 'The development of the operational capability of the 737, both in performance and range terms, enabled the aeroplane to meet logistically the increasing requirements Britannia had for flying further afield to more southerly latitudes and from airports further north. The elastic was being pulled at both ends.'

Boeing was the first to admit that this elasticity, allied to the performance of the 737 generally in the hands of Britannia, catapulted them into future orders for their airliner. Vice president Dick Taylor maintained that Britannia was a leader as far as the 737 was concerned.

'They were the first to get long hours out of the plane. We started to see the things we needed to improve the aircraft, and by incorporating them, we both produced a better plane and reduced maintenance. Also, we learned a lot from Britannia about improving despatch reliability of the aircraft - if they took 120 people out to the aeroplane, and it was not ready to go, because of their high utilisation they did not have another aircraft sitting around ready to call up.'

Peter Swift was Britannia's projects manager, for whom the delivery marked the culmination of three years' intensive effort to bring the jet operation plans to fruition. The contract had been signed in February 1966, seven months after the re-equipment programme was initiated.

Among the difficulties encountered along the way was the impact of the devaluation of sterling, resulting in a sixteen per cent increase in the price of the aircraft. The financing of the first four aircraft was tied up by Britannia at the end of 1967. The US Export-Import Bank was lending eighty per cent of the $15,535,000 price (about £6.5 million in 1968 terms). Britannia had to pay £150,500 import duty on each aircraft-a tax which, incidentally, was levied even on the cost of the delivery flight. The fifth aircraft was obtained on a long-term lease from Kleinwort-Benson, the London merchant bankers. The total cost of the fleet was estimated to be £8 million, including spares.

So impressed was Boeing with both performance and flight deck attitude of the Britannia team that, when there was a presidential commission in the United States into the advisability and safety of two-man cockpit manning, instead of the trio normal at the time for larger aircraft, they asked three European airlines to give testimony. They were British Airways and Lufthansa and Britannia.

The chairman of the commission was particularly taken with Derek Davison's candour on how they liked the airliner from piloting, training and safety aspects. 'I do not doubt that his testimony had a very great influence on the outcome of the commission's findings'.

It is worth noting that although the first five Britannia flight crews completed part of their conversion training, including all the ground-study syllabus, with Boeing in Seattle, they finished their flying training in the UK under four Boeing pilots on loan to the airline. The next six crews, needed when the second aircraft came into service, did their ground training at Luton under Seattle-trained instructors, and also did their flying training in Britain. Boeing had trained a nucleus of licensed engineers, and Britannia would do its own maintenance, with engine overhauls initially contracted out to SABENA.

Britannia pilots took very kindly to the 737. It was quite clear that the handling of the aircraft through all its routine and emergency procedures was comfortably within the capability of the two-pilot crew. This aspect had been convincingly demonstrated to the FAA by the manufacturers during about one hundred hours of flying on the highest-density routes that the USA could offer. Britannia expected to achieve an annual utilisation with the 737s of 2,500 hours. While Britannia had no plans for automatic landing at the time, the aircraft was equipped to be capable of coupled approaches to Category 2 and possibly lower minima.

Introduction to Service, and Training the crews.
Crew training on the new 737 took many forms - some which deserved reporting in the local papers. 'One hundred and twenty-two passengers and crew leapt from a blazing Boeing 737 airliner at Luton Airport yesterday. No one was hurt' screamed the headlines. The reality was that the aircraft was not on fire - and had not crashed. In fact, it was the evacuation of G-AVRL in the hangar at Luton. It took forty-six seconds for 122 people to unfasten their seatbelts, dive for the exits and warm their bottoms on the self-inflating escape chutes.

Some said that it was something of a record to empty an aircraft that quickly: the Ministry of Transport officials watching the exercise had allowed up to ninety seconds for the complete evacuation before they would grant the Boeing its UK certificate of airworthiness.

Ministry regulations insisted that 'passengers' who take part must be ordinary people with no previous experience of the event. This prevented airlines from using flight attendants,

Bryan Llewellyn, Managing Director of Thomson Travel Ltd and former Vice-President of the Travel Industry Marketing Group. *(Britannia Airways)*

Another a newspaper cutting, this time showing a group of Britannia Airways' flight attendants standing around the hangar at Luton in their stockinged feet before or just after the evacuation test of G-AVRL. *(Britannia Airways via author's collection).*

pilots and others who had done it all before. So it was that well over one hundred employees of nearby Vauxhall Motors, some who had never been in an aircraft before - found an unusual way of spending their lunch break!

There also had been concerns expressed in the area around Luton that the new 737s would do local night training flights from there, but Luton Corporation announced that these would not be allowed. Instead, Britannia Airways moved their training flights to Shannon in Ireland, in order to conform to their agreement with Luton Council. A Corporation spokesman told the press that '...people are more bothered about the noise from training flights than from regular operations because in training the aircraft take off, turn and then come into land again almost immediately whereas on regular flights they take off and are gone'.

The cost of modifying the 737 to obtain a British certificate of airworthiness was about £60,000 per aircraft. Britannia 737s were initially in a 117-seat all-tourist passenger configuration - particularly convenient since the Bristol Britannia fleet was also laid out for 117 passengers. Seat pitch on the 737 averaged thirty-two inches; however, it was planned that in 1969 to reduce that pitch to thirty-one inches to allow 134 passengers to be carried. The seats were manufactured by Flying Service Engineering and Equipment of Chesham, Bucks. A complete set was submitted to the Federal Aviation Administration in the USA, and both the seats and the Britannia seating layout received the FAA's approval. The most pressing reason for obtaining this was the airline's hopes of chartering its 737s in the American market during the winter - perhaps as many as three when

the full fleet was in service. Other British equipment included the galleys, from C. F. Taylor, Wokingham, Berks and galley equipment from Herman Smith, Dudley, Worcs. The galley facilities were concentrated in the forward compartment, and the toilet facilities aft, an arrangement suited to the high load factors encountered on inclusive-tour flights.

In line with a policy of fitting British equipment where practicable, the cockpit boasted twin Marconi ADF and a Cossor transponder. The fitting of British equipment did, in some cases involved the airline in additional costs, and the policy was limited by the fact that, while Boeing produced a standard aircraft at a highly competitive price, the cost of introducing non-standard items tended to be very high. One cockpit item which endeared itself to Britannia Airways pilots who flew those early 737s was the Sperry autopilot with control-wheel steering. This facility allowed the pilot to make adjustments in pitch and roll by merely moving the control wheel. Instead of being bound to a preselected rate of turn, the selection of an appropriate angle of bank by use of the control wheel enabled any turn rate (within limits) to be obtained to fit the circumstances. The net result was the relief of pilot workload, particularly in flying air traffic control patterns. The stick loads encountered in adjusting the flight path were similar to those when flying the aircraft manually.

The actual inaugural flight of the Britannia 737 compared to the inaugural service is something that appears to be different and open to conjecture. According to company files, the maiden flight was a special 'jolly' for Lord Thomson of Fleet and a large group of specially invited VIPs to hear Lord Thomson address a dinner given by Yugoslav

G-AXNC departs the busy apron area at Luton, heading out 'up the hill' to the runway. *(authors collection)*

hoteliers and travel executives in Dubrovnik.

With Lord Thomson was his son, the Hon Kenneth Thomson who was with his wife and a large private party. Amongst the passengers was the Yugoslavian Ambassador, His Excellency Mr I Sarajic, the Mayor of Luton, Councillor Cyril Jephson and Mr Will Howle, MP for Luton. Also on the flight was Gordon Brunton, managing director of the Thomson organisation, Harry Henry, deputy managing director, Sir Miles Thomas, Hillary Scott, chairman and managing director of Sky Tours and John Sauvage, managing director of Britannia Airways.

Britannia helped Boeing in another way by demonstrating the 737 to other potential customers. At around this time, British military trooping contracts to Germany had begun. These proved to be a useful revenue earner with flights a week bringing soldiers and their families on leave. They also provided useful sectors for pilot training. Later, a contract was won for troop movements to Gibraltar.

Both the Far East charters which John Sauvage instigated, and the trooping contracts were part of his double aim of not having too high a reliance on Thomson Holidays' business and trying to secure as much work as possible in the commercially hollow winter months: 'I was trying to achieve a balance and not to have too many eggs in one basket',

Yet the basket in question, Thomson Holidays,

had been undergoing its own metamorphosis with a policy that was to hatch many more 'eggs' for Britannia Airways.

Despite this bold entry into battle, the new holiday empire was slow to exploit its advantages. By the end of the decade, its parts were locked in internecine rivalry and staff were depressed and demoralised. Because of bickering over charter seat rates, the heads of its tour operating companies were hardly speaking to executives at Britannia. This was because of divergent views on the prices charged for airline seats. The Thomson board viewpoint was that the travel business did not necessarily have to be the biggest to be the most profitable.

The man credited with turning it around was Bryan Llewellyn, educated at Charterhouse and Cambridge, who had taught at a school in Paris, worked for Fisons the fertiliser manufacturer, for BOAC as a counter clerk, and for a West End furniture business. After joining Thomson, he rose to become marketing director of the group's regional newspapers division. Appointed Thomson Holidays' managing director in 1979, he came to be regarded as one of the industry's brightest lights. Llewellyn realised, to quote his own words in 1971, that the firm needed 'to establish ourselves in the public's mind as a big, solid, stable operation capable of operating successful holiday programmes... .while at the same time creating credibility and trust.'

A line-up of Britannia 737s, with G-AVRM closest to the camera. *(author's collection)*

In the early days of the 737, Britannia had a pair of 737-200QCs - this one thought to be G-AXNA - the QC standing for 'Quick Change' which with the large freight doors and roller-floor system allowed for the carriage of oversized loads such as thoroughbred horses or palletised passenger seating which facilitated a rapid conversion between roles. It is seen here in Seattle, being prepared for its flight to a new home at Luton.
(Britannia Airways via authors collection).

Clarksons, as the dominant operator at that time, was masterminded by Tom Gullick, whose philosophy was to create more business by cutting frills and prices to the bone. When Llewellyn arrived on the scene, the 1970 Thomson summer brochure had been produced, so it gave him a breathing space to assess the market. By the spring of 1970 he was ready to go to Gordon Brunton and tell him, confidently, that the only way to go forward was to enter the price market, go for volume, and fight Clarksons head-on.

Llewellyn won his way, prices were chopped and the result was that he had the dubious honour of recording, in 1971, the biggest loss of any Thomson group company. But from then onwards, Thomson's share of the holiday market began to climb to such effect that, in 1975, Clarksons collapsed in the UK's then biggest ever travel bankruptcy.

So Thomson's quality image, which was to become all the more critical in the wake of the Clarksons debacle, was born. By the start of the 1970s, the firm was Britain's second-biggest tour operator but was considerably smaller than Clarksons. In 1971 it was licensed to carry 350,000 customers, while Clarksons carried 750,000. But Llewellyn was already laying foundations which would see Thomson secure and hold its position as the market leader, cutting out the duplication of brands and overseas resort reps and aiming specific brochures at particular segments of the market. As the industry grew and became more complex, the need, as he saw it, was to make decisions which would stand a five or ten-year test and 'to create the right product at the right price through thorough market research backed up by really punchy, hard-hitting promotion and top service standards'.

Thomson Travel produced more than half of the Thomson Organisation's profits. An element in this was the creation of the Thomson Holidays brand name, as the biggest in the business, instead of trading under several disparate entities such as T E D Langton's original Universal Sky Tours, which was re-branded by the simple expedient of changing 'Universal' to 'Thomson Sky Tours'. But another was undoubtedly the relationship between the holiday business and Britannia Airways.

'John Sauvage and I got on together immediately because we saw eye to eye, He needed aircraft utilisation and if we got the holiday prices right, we would generate the volume. After we removed all the individual holiday brands we then owned, we marketed everything as Thomson Holidays and planned the best aircraft utilisation for them. We were after brand loyalty, and the 737s became part of the total holiday experience with their hot meals, bar prices, and duty frees'.

'The holiday airline business, however, was a very different beast from the scheduled market. It existed on competitive charters drumming up business which, in some ways, was more difficult,

Right: Maybe not the best of pictures, but then it was taken at 3am en-route from Corfu to Luton without the benefit of flash! It shows that the early 73s did not have the 'wide body' interiors, but were fitted with coat racks instead of overhead bins!

Below: G-AXNC departs on another charter. The aircraft demonstates one flaw of the early 737s - a darkened area on the aircraft that came from the amount of 'soot' deposited on the rear fuselage from the use of thrust reversers fitted to the JT-8Ds.

but if you got it right it was much more profitable. The secret of getting it right was the extent to which you could increase utilisation of the aircraft by taking more work. Having done that you were then able to offer highly competitive rates which, in turn, meant that holidays could be planned at lower prices than ever before - which increased the utilisation.

'Of course, the per-seat rates were less than the yield on a scheduled route, but if you are pumping 3,500 hours or more a year into a jet it makes a great deal of economic sense - costs were less per hour, overheads were reduced, and the only values that did not mitigate were the direct overheads such as flying the aeroplane. The more flying you do, the more you pay for fuel, you use more engine hours, you pay for more catering, but the costs associated with the support of the airline are greatly amortised.

'So we were able to offer, from that high utilisation, good commercial rates for the tour operation allied to an excellent aircraft in the 737 with its speed, comfort, outstanding reliability, and good catering and other cabin facilities.'

The result was that from the first year in which the 737s were introduced, when the passengers carried was 463,000, the numbers nearly doubled the following year to 826,000. By 1971 they had passed the million mark at 1,266,000.

Bryan Llewellyn summed up how he saw the industry - and Britannia Airways - in an article he wrote for The Spectator in November 1974. 'A natural and entirely realistic conclusion to the opening chapter of a new industry still in its mid-teens. The future cannot be described as unclouded. But there are signs that some of the knots can begin to be untied, a determined attempt made to increase flexibility by using more technically advanced systems. An answer does not lie in greater government regulation through minimum pricing. Capacity control, perhaps, but it has been amply demonstrated that price control has precisely the opposite effect to that intended.

Next year will be one in which capacity has been sharply reduced following the Court Line collapse, assuming that it is not also an economic disaster for the UK with unemployment at the two million mark, then there is every reason to expect those tour operators will return to at least some semblance of profitability. They deserve it.

'Leaving on a jet-plane…'

Anne Dobbs remembers as a teenager flying out of Luton with Britannia Airways on a Thomson SkyTours holiday in September 1970 with her sister Jane. 'It certainly was a dress-up-special kind of adventure! Harold, my dad, decided we were going to have one last holiday as a family as both my sister and I were starting to have boyfriends; previously we had all been down to Cornwall, but he made up his mind we were going somewhere special. My mum Beryl got a pile of brochures from Frames, our local travel agent, and we all decided that it was going to be Spain.

It was not until I started reading through the brochure Mum had saved many years later that I realised just how much was included in the price, and how much was explained to the holidaymaker. 'Flight arrangements and Coach connections - the aircraft used by Sky Tours are all superb jet aircraft. Most passengers will travel on Britannia Airways Boeing 737. Everybody on a Britannia Airways flight has a reserved seat on both the outward and homeward journeys. Sky Tours flights by Britannia

Above: The SkyTours Summer 1970 from which Anne Dobbs parents booked their holiday.

Left; Sisters Anne (left) and Jane Dobbs (right) deplane from the rear door of 737 G-AXNB *City of Birmingham* at Gerona Airport, having had their pictures taken by the Tourist Police, a normal practice at the time by the Franco Government.

Below: the same aircraft awaits another flight at Luton.

Souvenirs of a holiday! Bag tag, boarding card and ticket counterfoil from BY145/146 and the relevant page from the brochure. *(via Anne Dobbs)*

Boeing 737 operate directly from Manchester, Liverpool, Newcastle and Glasgow. Other aircraft used from Manchester include BAC 1-11's and the Boeing 707 to Tenerife. For those who do not wish to travel directly to the airport, coach services are as follows: From Liverpool, Prescott, Warrington, Leeds, Bradford and Huddersfield to Manchester (Ringway) for which there is no charge, please indicate on the booking form. Seats must be reserved at time of booking.

From Manchester, Chorlton Street, Bus Station to Manchester (Ringway) 7/6d each way by standard schedule airport coach service. Seats are not reservable.

From Glasgow Scotia Air Terminal, Bothwell St. and Edinburgh Scottish Omnibus Ltd., Waverley Street to Glasgow (Abbotsinch) Airport for which there is no charge, please indicate on the booking form. Seats must be reserved at time of booking.

From Newcastle Sky Tours Town Terminal, Newmarket Street to Newcastle (Woolsington) Airport each way for which there is no charge, please indicate on the booking form. Seats must be reserved at time of booking.

Duty-Free Goods - If you are flying on Britannia Airways, you will be sent with your confirmation a special leaflet on duty-free goods (and prices) available on the Boeing 737. You can use this leaflet to order from Britannia Airways, vouchers with which to purchase duty-free goods on the aircraft both outward and homeward. These vouchers are in addition to your travel allowance of £50 and £15 in sterling notes. You may order as many vouchers as you wish and any remaining unspent will be redeemed by Britannia Airways on your arrival back in the United Kingdom. Also, the airline will accept on board, personal cheques to the value of £5. The duty-free shop, at Manchester (Ringway) Airport, will accept personal cheques up to £5 per person for payment of duty-free goods.

'Dad decided that we were going to drive down to Luton; he parked the car in the long-term car-park, and we all trooped into the terminal, cases piled on a luggage trolley'.

'It seems that everyone in the terminal was wearing their Sunday best - there were no booty shorts, flip-flops or shell-suits! A long line of check-in desks stretched down the whole length of the building; I remember Court Line, Monarch, British Midland and quite several Britannia desks, all with their names above each desk on illuminated perspex signs. All the passengers lined up in orderly queues, and it was not long before the girl behind the counter had weighed our cases, and the four of us were checked in. At that time, the Departure Lounge was behind the check-in area, and while mum and dad went to find the bar, my sister Jane and I looked around the small duty-free shop'.

'We must've been in there for around forty-five minutes; then time to board the flight. Everyone walked out to the aircraft - we boarded by the rear door and found our seats - mine was 11C, and unlike nowadays, we had to retain the boarding card as we had the same places on the way back!. The inside of the airliner was long and tube-like, with rows of seats stretching forward. There were no overhead lockers, and no-one had carry-on cases like today - just a few coats, hats, jackets and small bags placed in the racks above by passengers before they took their seats and strapped themselves in.

'Looking back on it all, the one thing I do remember was that everyone seemed to be in such a good mood - everybody on board seemed smiley and cheerful! I guess it was the holiday mood that it seemed the passengers were in and was picked up by the cabin crew. Although it was my first ever flight, it was certainly one that stuck in my mind and was very different from other scheduled service ones I've experienced!'

'Leaving Luton was done without any fuss within five minutes of when we were supposed to. Not long after take-off, the stewardesses came around with an evening meal, followed by drinks and finally the duty-free trolley for cigarettes, spirits and perfumes! The flight to Gerona was just under two hours, and by the time we had crossed the Pyrenees, it was dark outside. Just before landing one of the Stewardesses

Sleek styling, shoulder bags and white gloves - it is not hard to see why the public saw glamour in the Britannia Air hostesses.
(Britannia Airways via authors collection)

came on the PA and warned us that 'there will be increased noise from the engines just after we touch down - this is due to the use of the thrust reversers for braking, and is quite normal'.

'Gerona Airport was chaotic, there were about five flights on different nationalities arriving almost together that evening, and tour representatives were trying to gather together their chicks to get on board the right coaches'

'The journey back was very similar, everyone being met on board by the delicious smell of cottage pie drifting out from the galley!'

'Oh, one final thing: in digging through my late mum's documents to bring the memories back, I discovered the original paid invoice - the total cost for the four of us for a 15-day, full board trip? £172!'

During 1971 Britannia continued its expansion of local departure points. From 17 April East Midlands Airport near Derby - also known as Castle Donington - was added to the list, with flights to Ibiza and Palma being operated on behalf of Horizon Holidays. The configuration on the 737s was once again increased: this time to a maximum payload of one hundred and thirty passengers, offering a total of forty-eight extra seats in Britannia's fleet at no real additional cost.

The increase in the use of Britannia's fleet of

Above: the 1966-opened passenger Terminal at Luton. At the far end was a small Barclays Bank, The main check-in concourse served, from left to right ; Court Line, Britannia, Monarch and British Midland Airways.

Below: from the foreground: the car-parking, passenger drop-off areas and then the Terminal at Luton. Aircraft parking was in an arc on the apron. *[both Bill Armstrong]*

Britannia Airways' Fleet

For the last decade the world of aviation has been completely dominated by the famous Boeing Company of America.

Every few seconds of every day, somewhere in the world, a Boeing jetliner either takes off or lands, and aircraft from this company have flown more passenger miles than any other.

The most famous of these the Boeing 707 which completely changed the face of continental air travel has now been joined by the 727, 737 and in the last two years, the famous Jumbo jet the 747. For their particular operation, Britannia Airways chose the Boeing 737 which seats up to 130 people in comfort and is eminently suitable for shorter journeys of up to approximately $3\frac{1}{2}$ hours flying time. This fleet has now grown to a total of eight aircraft, and Britannia Airways was the first independent airline in Europe to introduce the 737 aircraft. This model has now become synonymous with comfort and speed coupled with reliability. When Britannia Airways made the decision to enter into the field of Trans-continental flying, it was to the same 'family of jets' that they looked for their larger aircraft and a giant Boeing 707 capable of carrying 189 passengers at ranges of up to 5,500 miles has been acquired this year. This aircraft will be used to fly Britannia passengers all over the world.

TECHNICAL NOTE

Boeing 707 320C jet

189 passengers are carried, plus a crew of 10 comprising Captain, First Officer, Flight Engineer, Flight Navigator and Six Stewardesses.

Engines   Four 18,000 lbs static thrust Pratt and Whitney JT3D-3B turbo fan engines

Length   145ft 6ins

Wing span   145ft 9ins

Maximum Take-off Weight   323,500 lbs

Maximum payload   96,000 lbs

Maximum Cruising speed   .84 mach or approx. 600 m.p.h.

Maximum Range   5,500 miles

Boeing 737 Six 737—204 Series

Two 737—204C Series (cargo convertible)

130 passengers are carried, plus a crew of six comprising Captain, First Officer and Four Stewardesses.

Engines   Two 14,500 lbs static thrust Pratt and Whitney JT8D-9 turbo fan engines.

Length   97ft

Wing span   93ft

Maximum Take-off Weight   110,000 lbs

Maximum payload   35,000 lbs

Maximum Cruising Speed   .82 mach or approx. 550 m.p.h.

Maximum range   1,800 miles

Britannia Airways Limited, Luton Airport, Bedfordshire. Telephone 0582-21461

Another view of the new Passenger Terminal at Luton, this time taken from airside, overlooking the short and long-term car parks. Luton Flying Club was on the extreme left of the picture. *(author's collection)*

Opposite page: from a 1970 inflight magazine comes this page detailing the fleet - and the unfulfilled Boeing 707 colour scheme.

aircraft continued during 1972. To meet this demand, a further Boeing 737 was obtained from United Airlines in the USA.

1972 marked yet another remarkable year not only in Britannia Airway's history but also that of British charter aviation. On 2 November, Britannia Airways became the first British charter airline to operate Inclusive Tour charter flights to the USSR. Flight BY663 landed at Moscow airport from Luton with its first load of Thomson Holiday clients to visit the Soviet Union; starting a trend which continued for many years.

1973 also saw the arrival of two more Boeing 737s, increasing the airline's fleet to eleven. Demand continued to grow, most notably from Gatwick, Birmingham and East Midlands. However, one departure point which was dropped was Blackpool, whose weekly flight to Palma ceased.

A change of colours
When the airline started as Euravia in 1962, those first Constellations were painted in black, blue and white using what, in those days, was considered to be an exquisite style. However, in the early 1970s, with the application of that scheme to the Boeing 737s - partly because of the aircraft shape, partly because of changing attitudes to design - the 'look' was thought to have become old fashioned. Indeed,

it did not suit the long Boeing 707s then joining the Britannia fleet. Elegance was abandoned for modernity, and a new red, white and blue livery with the complete logo of Britannia on the tail-plane was introduced. Within the airline, the Britannia symbol was known, affectionately, as 'the old lady in her wheelchair'. It was under her steadfast symbolism that, for more than a decade, millions of holidaymakers had journeyed happily to the sun.

In fact, the 'old lady in her wheelchair' is something of a pointer towards roughly dating any picture of the early Britannia 737s. The initial scheme shows a bare metal lower fuselage, white upper half with a mid-blue cheat line and monotone logo on the tail. Finally, the airline name was in black. It soon evolved into a slightly more colourful scheme with red aspects added to the union flag on the shield.

This scheme did not last for long - it was time to liven up the somewhat staid colours for something a bit more lively. Out went the almost 'classic' look, and in came a red, white and blue scheme that when it was first launched was very distinctive, and the upsweep of the red and blue cheat lines up the vertical fin really suited the series 200 737s which did not have the later fin-fillet fitted to later versions. Variations of the scheme soon became used in similar forms by other airlines.

Britannia News

Issue No.1
February 1974

Something new in the air

It's here! Britannia's gleaming new Boeing 737 has just been delivered — straight off the production line in Seattle.

The new 'wide bodied look' jet G-BAZG is the first of three new 737s to join Britannia's existing fleet of eleven Boeing 737s. The other two aircraft G-BAZH and G-BAZI will be delivered to Britannia in February and March this year.

G-BAZG was flown from America to Britain by Captains David Hopkins and Eric Turner. Also on board were First Officers Christopher Clark, Christopher Norman and Chief Navigator George Berrisford.

Apart from being one of the most comfortable and operationally flexible aircraft in the charter business the new 737s score full marks when it comes to quietness of operation.

Each of the three new aircraft is fitted with 'extra quiet' engines with noise levels certified to America's Federal Aviation Authority standards — the most stringent in the world. The new 737s will also have an increased range.

One of the aircraft's main features is its abundance of storage compartments — for all those personal carry-on items and souvenirs of the typical holidaymaker. These will give passengers increased leg room and comfort.

The new spacious interiors are designed to create the holiday atmosphere the moment passengers step aboard with the colour emphasis on varying shades of brown, yellow, orange and gold.

Interior picture of the new 737 inside

737s over the pond.

The 737 delivery flights from Seattle to Luton became almost commonplace - so much so, in fact, there was practically a standard procedure.

The flight crew reported to Boeing Field at 09.00 hours local time (17.00hrs GMT). Departure was scheduled for 19.00hrs. After completion of the formalities signing the new aircraft over to Britannia, the crew boarded the aircraft and were immediately aware that this was not to be an Atlantic crossing of normal consequence. Just a few passenger seats were on board, and neither bulkheads nor galleys were present as the economics and efficiency of Britannia's engineering facilities, dictated that these would be fitted at Luton. Final preparations for departure were made, but a last-minute technical problem gave a short delay. The 737 was basically a short-to-medium range airliner, and this meant that at least one refuelling stop would be required, and this was planned to be Goose Bay on the North East coast of Labrador. It was a distance of 2,424 miles or five hours forty-seven minutes flying time in still air conditions. The route would take the 737 across places with such evocative-sounding names as Medicine Hat, Swift Current and Sioux Lookout.

The aircraft was soon declared serviceable. Pre-startup checks confirmed a full fuel load of 16,040 kilogrammes or approximately 4,450 Imperial gallons and shortly after clearance to start both engines were winding up for the first time in the hands of a Britannia crew. Permission to taxi to Runway 31L was given, and the aircraft trundled away from the flight line down the bumpy taxiway to the holding point. EPR (engine pressure ratio) was set at 1.99 (thrust setting), and take-off speeds were calculated at V_1 - 123 knots - the rate at which take off maybe abandoned without exceeding the take-off distance available. V_R - 134 knots rotation speed, and V_2 141 knots, the speed at which take-off may be continued with one engine inoperative.

Throttles were advanced and with a take-off weight of only 43,700 kilogrammes - well below the maximum of 55,111 kilogrammes, the aircraft accelerated rapidly down the runway seemingly to positively leap into the air. Climbing out over Puget Sound the 737 was cleared initially to Flight Level 290 (29,000 feet) direct to Cranbrook and on crossing the Canadian FIR boundary, broke through the top of the cloud layer and was then cleared almost immediately on up to FL 370, the requested level, for the Trans-Canadian crossing.

Level at 37,000 feet the flight time was calculated, with forecasted winds taken into consideration, at five hours twenty minutes. True airspeed at this point was estimated at 411 knots, using the PDCS (Performance Data Computer System). The PDCS was a computerised data store and memory bank which permitted the crew to retrieve this information for efficient and economical flight management. The system was linked to the various cockpit instruments and would indicate optimum performance settings for given conditions; also providing such information as correct fuel quantity, temperature: airspeed, groundspeed. Headwind or tailwind component etc. was displayed on a small VDU screen.

Once established at cruising level, the crew were only required to report their time overhead the various beacons, unlike Europe where accurate ETAS for the next reporting point were needed.

Two hours after departure the last of the Rocky Mountains had been left behind, and the cloud below had cleared to reveal the wheatfields of Saskatchewan and later still the frozen lakes and forests of Manitoba and Quebec. At 01.00 hours GMT and the last of the remaining daylight rapidly faded behind.

The crew, continually monitoring the en-route weather, soon became aware of a steady headwind and their ETA for Goose Bay was extended. At the same time, the weather at Goose Bay itself and, as was often the case, the alternate Gander, was steadily deteriorating. At 03.30 hours with one and a half hours to go. HF (High Frequency) contact with Gander was established, and the latest weather situation monitored. Nearing Goose, power was reduced, and with a turbulent descent through the heavy overcast, the crew intercepted the ILS of Runway 09.

A quick refuel and it was time to depart. The flight time from Goose Bay was estimated at 5 hours 40 minutes, but the predicted winds indicated a strong tailwind, reducing the crossing time as well as giving a healthier fuel reserve. For the delivery flight, the 737 was not fitted with either INS (Inertial Navigator System) or Omega (this would later be installed at Luton). Because of this, the maximum permitted flight level for the majority of the Atlantic crossing would be restricted to FL270, below the MNPS (Minimum Navigation Performance Specification).

Due to the lack of radar coverage and conventional navigational aids such as VOR. DME. ADF etc. pinpoint navigational accuracy could not be guaranteed without such sophisticated equipment - or a traditional navigator! Remember, this was before the days of Global Positioning Systems (GPS) - so unequipped aircraft were kept at this lower level out of the way of the 'Big Boys' up above so as to allow for inevitable minor deviations.

Above: G-AXNC seen at London Gatwick, before the construction of the North Terminal. *(authors collection)*

Below: The same aircraft at Gatwick, but in the new colour scheme.

The route would take the 737 over the southern tip of Greenland to a point 63°N 30°W then south of Iceland and down into UK airspace over the Outer Hebrides. It was a route that gave good en route alternates in Iceland and Scotland in the event of a refuelling requirement.

At 06.00 hours, after just one hour on the ground, the crew were once again airborne and contacting Gander to establish crossing clearance. It would be 700 miles before the next landfall at Prins Christian Sund, Greenland. Flying towards the sun, daylight appeared as quickly as it had faded. Above appeared a telltale line of a cloud almost certainly signifying a jetstream and although it was several thousand feet higher, the 737 was soon benefiting from its effect.

With little or no traffic on the frequency at this point- the HF was tuned to BBC Radio 4, in time to catch the early morning news from London.

At 07.00 hours, the weather radar tuned to its mapping function began to paint a landfall some 120 miles away but with icebergs and ice flows also being reflected a clear outline was not discernible. Soon after, as if on cue the cloud cover below rolled away to reveal a superb view of the tip of Greenland, its inhospitable looking mountains covered in snow and the surrounding water barely visible between the pack ice.

Iceland was visible on the port side at 09.00 hours

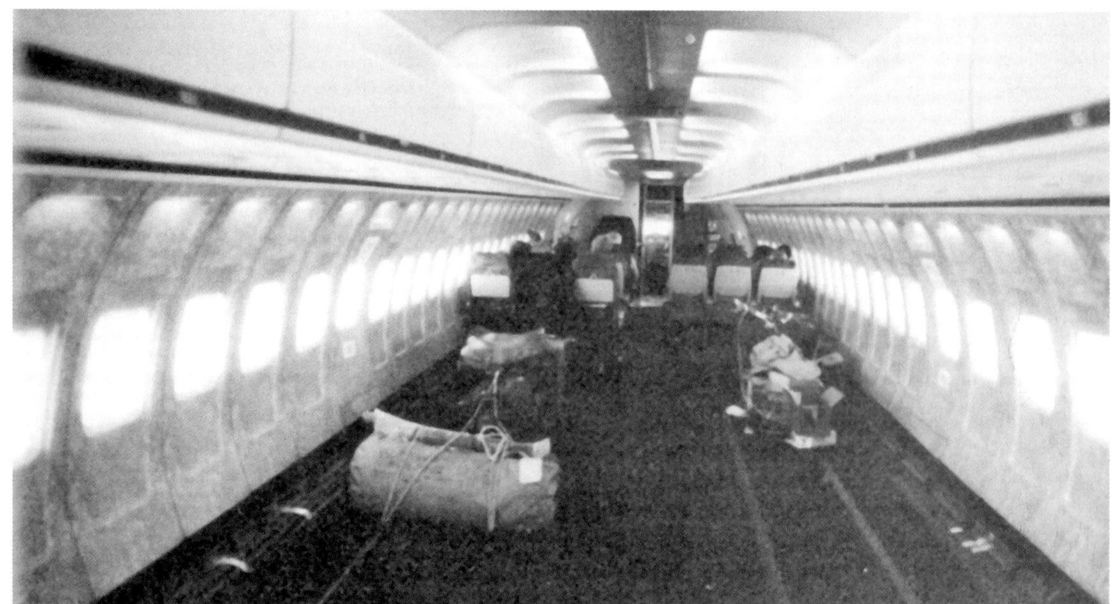

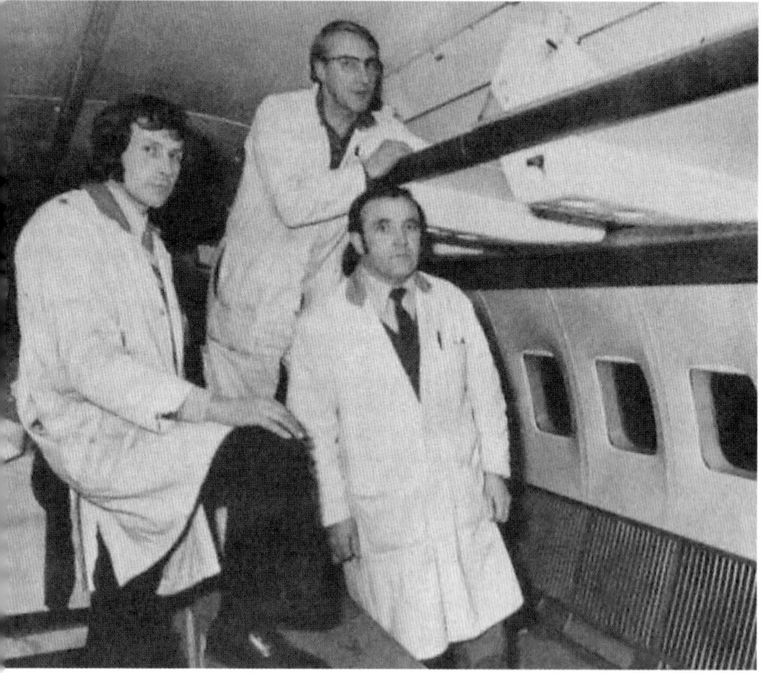

Above: the interior of a Britannia Airways 737 on its delivery flight from Seattle to Luton, with the barest of interiors fitted, the package closest to the camera is survival equipment 'in case of emergency'.

Left to right: Norman Lambert, Bill Bushell and David Roll, three Britannia engineers responsible for 'fitting out' the interiors of the new 737s on arrival, and also the installation of an £88,000 facelift to the existing fleet using British materials and the airline's own resources that saved the company thousands of pounds. Usually, such a renovation meant buying a modification kit from the aircraft manufacturers or returning the aircraft to the factory, which was considerably more expensive. New cabin sidewalls. carpeting and seating were fitted and twenty-eight overhead compartments introduced to provide valuable storage space for holidaymakers.
(both Britannia Airways)

and with a healthy fuel reserve, plus a tailwind of 79kts showing, the crew turned away and headed 'downhill' to home. Soon after they cleared the MNPS boundary and were cleared up to a more economical flight level of 370 (37,000ft), where they stayed for the remainder of the flight over the Scottish Isles and the length of Britain. The familiarity of a clear and concise 'English' speaking air traffic controller was in itself a great welcome home.

Runway 26 at Luton came in sight, followed by a smooth landing and the aircraft came to rest at its new found home, five hours twenty minutes after leaving Goose Bay. The total flight time from Seattle was eleven hours thirty minutes.

Following a certificate of airworthiness air test shortly after arrival, the aircraft remained in the hangar for ten days while it was fitted with seats, galleys, Omega and other items before operating its first revenue-earning flight.

The 707 and 'Affinity' or 'Bent Charters'

Those 1971 performance figures were aided by a short-lived, yet remarkable phenomenon for operators who could fly long-haul to and from the USA. For Britannia, it demanded the introduction of another Boeing type - the 707. The new market that was sweeping the travel trade industry was called Affinity Group Charters.

At this time, as a protection to the scheduled carrier, these were the only types of charters allowed into North America, and they involved all the passengers being members of a specific group for at least six months. These charters, if appropriately operated, were advantageous to the airline, as they guaranteed a full load of passengers on long-haul routes; something which could not, and indeed still cannot, be secured by either scheduled or charter airlines. However, back in 1969, according to the Britannia Airways Fact Sheet, the airline had been awarded a 402 Foreign Air Carrier Permit for Trans Atlantic charter operations by the American Civil Aeronautics Board.

The story of the development of this aspect of the travel trade in the late 1960s is interesting, if complicated, and deserves some explanation, The potential appeared so enormous to Britannia that they dived into the market and leased one Boeing 707 from World Airlines for $6 million, and then another from Executive Jet Aviation.

The ex-World aircraft, now registered G-AYSI, also registered two' firsts' when it arrived at Luton in February 1971. It was the first aircraft to enter Britannia's newly constructed hangar, and while there it was the first aircraft to receive the revised livery with a new red stripe to accompany the blue line along the fuselage, together with a modernised name and tail logo.

The inaugural flight of the 189 seater Boeing 707 in Britannia's colours was on 27 April 1971. Captain Roy McDougall took a party to Tenerife for the official opening of the Hotel Atlantic in Puerto de la Cruz. There Lord Thomson was able to tell his assembled guests that Britannia was by then the second biggest independent airline in Britain having a turnover, which would that year exceed £11.5 million. 'We are proud of the service we have built

Above: Boeing 707 G-AYSI outside the new Britannia hangar at Luton.

Right: Celebration time! The team on arrival of the first 707 - left to right: Jimmie Little, John Sauvage and Derek Davison, all representing Britannia, along with Brian Cook and Ed Daly of World Airways. Finally, on the right is Peter Swift of Britannia.

A favourite spot to take pictures was in the short term car-park at Luton, by the cafe. Here one of Britannia's 737s is seen just passing the fire station and trundling down the taxitrack to the parking area. *(author)*

up over the past decade and feel it compares very favourably with that of the State-owned scheduled-service operators.'

That trip gave Roy Thomson a liking for those resort hotels in the sun, for afterwards, he would occasionally travel incognito in the back of a Boeing 737, reading detective stories on his way to stay for a couple of days by himself in Tenerife, or sometimes in Majorca.

Although the 707s were obtained primarily for use on the now booming trans-Atlantic affinity charters from Luton, Manchester and Prestwick, it also opeated many Inclusive Tour flights from other provincial airports. Also, the new acquisition allowed Thomson Holidays to organise tours to the Far East and holidays in the Caribbean for the first time. This demand for capacity resulted in Britannia acquiring another 707 - G-AYEX - leased from Executive Jet Aviation which arrived on 1 October 1971.

The 707s were worked hard. The affinity group business was flourishing, and Britannia brought thousands of Americans to Europe. On one of John Sauvage's sales missions to the West Coast to drum up this business, Lord Thomson accompanied him to help sell the profitable charters.

Affinity Group Charters - quickly nicknamed by some as 'Bent' Charters - dated back to the days of the permission granted to Vladimir Raitz to fly his 'teachers and students' to Calvi, but were soon by no means restricted to just Europe. The concept was expanded in the 1960s into a rule crafted by IATA concerning the permissibility of chartering aircraft to operate flights across the North Atlantic for the sole purpose of carrying so-called 'affinity groups'. These could be at fares below IATA's officially agreed minimum fare for any given route by the organisation's member airlines through their wholly-owned, non-IATA subsidiaries came to the attention of a determined group of mainly non-IATA airlines, which sought to exploit these legal loopholes for themselves.

IATA - The International Air Transport Association - had been formed in April 1945 as the successor to the International Air Traffic Association, which was established in 1919 at The Hague, Netherlands. At its founding, IATA consisted of fifty-seven airlines from thirty-one countries. Much of IATA's early work was technical, and it provided input to the newly-created International Civil Aviation Organization (ICAO), which was reflected in the annexes of the Chicago Convention, the international treaty that governed the conduct of international air transport.

Civil aviation increased over the following decades and IATA's work duly expanded. It transformed its trade association activities to take account of the new dynamics in aviation, which was seeing increasing demand from the leisure sector.

The relevant rule stipulated in legalese that transatlantic charter flights were permissible provided that the only reason to transport a group of passengers who wanted to travel together on the same aircraft was those passengers' shared interest and that all of them were members of the same club. It was compared to the carriage of a group of 'unconnected' individuals on a specially chartered aircraft whose sole purpose of travelling together on that aircraft was to avail themselves of a cheap flight. That rule furthermore stipulated that anyone who wanted to purchase a ticket for an 'affinity group' charter flight needed to book at least three months in advance of

Right: The crew who operated the innaugural 707 flight: destination Tenerife. It was commanded by Captain Roy McDougal, second left.

Below: 707 G-AYSI ready for service. The location is thought to be Manchester. 'SI was the first aircraft to recieve the new livery with a red and white stripe together with a modernised name and tail logo.

Bottom, the 707 flight deck, showing the first officer and the flight engineer. *(All Britannia Airways)*

their intended date of travel and be a bona fide, paid-up member of an officially recognised organisation.

Although some of these 'affinity groups' were genuine, an overwhelming majority of these 'common interest associations' were fake. The sole purpose of their existence was to sign up as many members as were needed to profitably fill a contemporary long-haul jet airliner for a transatlantic charter flight by issuing each prospective passenger with a back-dated membership card of a non-existent organisation, sometimes on the day of departure itself. In some cases, this was openly done in the offices of 'specialist' travel agencies that had sprung up on both sides of the Atlantic to cash in on the new cheap flights' bonanza. These travel agents unscrupulously sold thousands of tickets to people falsely representing themselves to the aviation authorities in Britain, the US and Canada as members of an ever greater variety of imaginary affinity groups.

On 20 May 1963, the US Civil Aeronautics Board (CAB) granted Caledonian Airways a foreign air carrier permit for three years under Section 402 of the US Federal Aviation Act. It became effective on 17 June 1963 when it was signed by President John F. Kennedy, making Caledonian the first overseas charter carrier to obtain this permit. The so-called Caledonian Case established a precedent and constituted the legal basis for all airlines that had always wanted to operate charters to and from the US and Canada but had been unable to overcome the objections of the established airlines, such as Pan Am and BOAC, before the enactment of this law. Caledonian's US breakthrough led to it being granted Canadian affinity group charter permission as well.

The UK Air Transport Licensing Board (ATLB) licensed Caledonian to begin North Atlantic IT charters in September 1964.

Caledonian Airways had tapped into a demand for very low fares across the Atlantic, a concept that Harold Bamberg of Eagle Airways had first dreamed up in the nineteen-fifties. In making his case, he proposed tariffs to the West Indies and the Far East less than half the then-current tourist fares. Prophetically, Bamberg wrote: 'The airlines of the world have developed, and by now fully exploited, the market represented by the wealthy and the business traveller. It must find new markets among more modest travellers. The answer is to reduce the cost of air transport. ...if fares were reduced many more people would travel.'

IATA imposed further restrictions on airlines seeking to exploit this loophole by insisting that any agent booking these flights had their commission capped at five per cent, that the affinity group's membership could not exceed 20,000 and that those seeking to avail themselves of these offers must have been members for at least six months prior to the commencement of travel. These restrictions were designed to protect IATA members' transatlantic scheduled traffic by preventing non-members from undercutting them.

To comply with IATA's arbitrary transatlantic charter rules, independent charter operators insisted that anyone who wanted a cheap transatlantic charter flight needed to be a bona fide member of an affinity group, and that the prospective traveller required to be a member of such an organisation for a minimum period of six months. As a result, clubs and associations with names like Friends of Clan Albion, Anglo-Scottish-American Group, Anglo-American Families Association, Rose and Maple Amity Club, Paisley Buddies, British American Club, Canadian US Pacific Association etc. sprang up on both sides of the Atlantic.

As early as 1964 in the UK the Midlands Dahlia Society had been forced to cancel its planned excursion to the USA for a return fare of £66 because it had advertised in the personal columns of *The*

Two views of Britannia's leased 720 TF-VLC. Above it is shown parked up away from the terminal. In the background is the famous Vauxhall Motors vehicle parking area. Below: the airliner, leased from Eagle Air during 1979, is seen in a partial Air Malta scheme, with Britannia stickers. *(both author's collection)*

With everything 'down and out', Britannia Boeing 707 G-AYSI comes in to land. *(author's collection)*

Sunday Times for people to fill its empty seats. It received a reply from a Mr Hamilton asking for details and inquiring whether he could join at Manchester or would he first have to journey to London. It could scarcely have been more effectively worded to make clear that Mr Hamilton's sole reason for joining the Midlands Dahlia Society was to obtain cheap travel to the USA and that he was not yet a member, far less one of more than six months' standing. The dahlia growers accused Hamilton of being an agent provocateur from a rose-growing society - how else could BOAC have learned of the letter? The breach, however, of government regulations covering affinity travel, was in the Midland Dahlia Society's advertisement.

Another hint as to what was happening came in an article in the *London Financial Times* by its travel correspondent, Arthur Sandles: 'An American girl I know in London has a sick mother in the United States. She almost commutes between Heathrow and Kennedy Airports - and has yet to pay the full fare.

Membership of numerous aflinity groups gives her access to regular flights at rates upwards of £40. When one of her groups does not happen to have a suitable trip, she knows the ropes well enough to pick up a ticket on someone else's charter.'

The only way she could pick up a ticket from someone else's charter at short notice was by breaking the rules about membership duration. It was easy enough. Knowing the ropes meant knowing a 'charter consultant' like Aitex Travel, which was offering economy travel to Europe, North America, the Middle East, the Far East, Australia and Africa. Once in its Regent Street office, potential travellers were told they could buy return tickets to New York in about one month. '...Technically speaking you have to be a member of a club, but we can arrange that. We have several clubs and we can back-date your membership to six months. You do it our way, and everything will be all right.'

Strictly speaking, they were committing no offence, until the charter flight took off. The responsibility for policing charters rested on the shoulders of the airlines.

Watching to see whether they carried out their police work was the Department of Trade in the UK and the CAB in the States. The CAB was already extremely disillusioned about the whole business. By the beginning of 1970 its enforcement bureau chief, Richard O'Melia, had concluded that all but the closest affinity groups, like nudists or bishops, existed entirely for cheap travel and were being widely misused.

As soon as this scam had come to the relevant authorities' attention, they began policing the departure areas of the main departure and arrival airports on both sides of the Atlantic to catch bogus affinity group members and prevent them from boarding their flights. As a result of these actions, an increasing number of passengers hoping to board a cheap affinity group charter was denied boarding their aircraft. There were also reports about raids the authorities conducted on a particular airline/charterer only after having been tipped off by a jealous IATA member or by a fellow independent competitor. Also, the authorities fined the airlines operating these flights for each bogus passenger whose name happened to appear on the passenger list of an affinity group charter.

In the end, the authorities, as well as the industry, admitted that the absurd affinity group system worked to nobody's satisfaction. They also agreed that the real purpose of travel of an overwhelming majority of those who were travelling under the old affinity group rules was to avail themselves of a cheap flight. It was therefore decided to scrap the entire system and to replace it with a new system that recognised as well as legalised the growing demand for cheap transatlantic air travel at fares below the official IATA minimum fares.

The resulting compromise led to the framing of a set of new Advance Booking Charter (ABC) flight rules that did away with all of the onerous rules that had governed affinity group charters other than a four-week advance booking period, that was subsequently reduced to two weeks.

Above: With the blow-in doors in full use, this unidentifed 707 claws it's way into the sky on another long-hall trip from Luton.

Right: 1972 saw the 'Britannia Airways Flight Souvenir' InFlight magazine change in design and style to the 'Wanderer' which reflected the airlines more wider sphere of interest. *(both author's collection)*

For a while, Britannia Airways managed to avoid the worse of the negative publicity stirred up by the national flag carriers, but others were not so fortunate. Freddie Laker was becoming increasingly concerned. He called his lawyer and asked for his advice on how to protect Laker Airways against the illegal operations: he received a blunt, two words reply 'stop operating'.

So Freddie decided to clean up his business. He put his faith in his belief that the ordinary man or woman did not lie. He asked every passenger on his flights to put their hand on the Bible and swear they had been members of their affinity groups for a year. The rules required only six months, but Freddie decided to demand a year. They also had to swear they had not joined for purposes of travel. Freddie's lawyer had box-loads of affidavits in his office. No one flew on Laker Airways unless they signed these affidavits. Everybody happily perjured themselves. Lawyers, doctors, accountants, everyone signed the affidavits.

There was one story that did the rounds regarding one of Laker's US-based staff watched a group of priests lining up to check in for a flight to the UK. He went across to one of them and said, 'Father, do you know what you are going to have to do when you get to the check-in point?' 'Yes, I do...' replied the Priest. 'You are going to have to swear that you have been a member of this organisation for a year and not joined for travel.' 'Yes,' said the Priest, 'I know.' 'Father, don't you feel in danger of committing a mortal sin?'

It did not take Freddie long to realise that it was a waste of time. Crooked charter organisers in New York were selling tickets to any takers. In London the centre for illicit trade in charter tickets was the Earls Court Road and Haymarket. Noticeboards appeared covered with cards advertising cheap tickets. Most of the buyers were students with a youthful contempt for bureaucracy of any kind. They regarded affordable air travel as a right and breaking the regulations as about as dangerous an offence as smuggling a few cigarettes in from abroad.

At the end of August, the CAB and the Department of Trade began to crack down on the illicit charters. The CAB began demanding more details and imposing fines on airlines which were proved guilty of infringing the rules or even who failed to provide proof of their innocence.

Laker was raided once more by the Department, again due to a tip-off from the travel agent. This time a spot check of the one hundred and fifty-eight passengers on Laker's 707 revealed that forty-six of them were not bona fide members of the US Left Hand Club, which had chartered the flight through a

Britannia Boeing 707 G-AYSI at Luton not long after its arrival. The lighter 'oval' on the fuselage below and slightly aft of the flightdeck glazing is where World Airways - the aircraft's former operator - used to display its logo. *(author's collection)*

New York agent. The aircraft left with the remaining one hundred and twelve after a three-and-a-half-hour delay while the Department's inspectors interrogated the passengers.

The raid was filmed by Independent Television News, which had also been tipped off. As the bewildered passengers stood there, among them an old lady in tears, Laker was furious. He accused the Department of telling the television company of its plans and said that if it had not been responsible, it should have called off its investigation when it saw the TV cameras. The Department was equally perturbed at the presence of the TV cameras and realised that its officials, too, had been 'set up'.

Clearly the regulations needed reform and that everyone was entitled to cheap travel without having to belong to irrelevant affinity groups.

The previous November the delegates at a conference of the Association of British Travel Agents in Rotterdam were told that the rules governing cut-rate charter flights by affinity groups were 'the biggest can of worms on the travel scene'. BOAC had already put up proposals for an 'Earlybird' booking system, and it and British Caledonian were being granted exclusive charter rights to the Far East that took them clear of the need for affinity traffic.

Britannia's 707s were not, however, used just on these high-profit runs. Freight was a useful activity, two examples being a service between London Heathrow and Nairobi for Simbair, the cargo subsidiary of East African Airways, and the carrying

737 G-BABP banks away from the camera, revealing something that many did not realise - the 737 had no main undercarriage doors! *(author's collection)*

World wide in the 70's

A page from a company brochure, extolling the virtues of Boeing Products. *(Britannia Airways)*

The Britannia livery, illustrated here on the tail of the Boeing 707, is as familiar a sight at the company headquarters at Luton as it is at ten other departure points in the United Kingdom flying to destinations throughout the world.

In April 1972, Britannia Airways, Britain's second largest independent airline celebrated the 10th anniversary of its first flight. In just one decade, the company has made giant strides. It is a member company of the Thomson Organisation Limited.

For the 70's, Britannia has an all-jet Boeing fleet . . . nine Boeing 737's and two long-range Boeing 707's The entire fleet has been painted in a new livery– white with a distinctive blue and red line.
The 1,500 mile range and 550 mph of the Boeing 737 makes it ideal for flights to sunny Mediterranean resorts with tour operating companies such as Thomson Sky Tours, Horizon Midlands and Inghams, who use Britannia all year round.

The Boeing 707's, with a range of 5,500 miles, are capable of flying the Atlantic comfortably and have enabled Britannia to widen its commercial cargo and holiday flights to North America and the Caribbean. From May this year, Britannia Airways will fly 189 holidaymakers to Jamaica every fortnight on the first ever inclusive charter holiday to the West Indies.
Also new for 1972—the Boeing 707's will be used for charter flights for recognised clubs and associations from Los Angeles, San Francisco and Vancouver.

As well as the superbly comfortable, efficient fleet of Boeings, Britannia are looking closely at the development of wide-bodied aircraft such as the European Airbus and the Lockheed Tri-Star.
On the ground, too, Britannia has made important new changes to keep up with the 70's. There's the new, streamlined Britannia air terminal. It's conveniently placed in the centre of London so that holidaymakers can get out to Luton Airport quickly and easily.

At Luton, in the new million pound hangar, Britannia has some of the most modern facilities in the country where rigorous checking and servicing can be carried out quickly and efficiently. Britannia is the parent company to Luton Aircraft Engineers–and they have a skilled team of Boeing-trained engineers. Each Britannia jet is checked after every flight every twenty-four hours and after every 100 hours of flying time.
With such a fine fleet—and such careful attention to maintenance and passenger comfort, it is no wonder that Britannia Airways goes into its second decade with confidence and justifiable pride.

of racehorses from Britain to Japan.

It was beginning to become a concerning venture, but it was also a very lucrative market, and every one of the independents - including Britannia - felt that they should have a presence in it.

Although several of Britannia's pilots enjoyed their days with the 707, it turned out to be a short honeymoon. Political and competitive rumblings were beginning to be heard.

It was Captain Roy McDougall who was to claim the unchallenged longest 'day' worked by any Britannia pilot in a 707. When the height lock on one of the aircraft's autopilots would not work, the captain, Don Tanton, said he was not prepared to fly without it from Luton to Los Angeles. McDougall told the captain he would be his human autopilot.

He rushed home, changed into uniform, and reported for duty to a somewhat surprised captain. On the first leg to Los Angeles, they reached the Scottish border when a stewardess said to the flight deck that she thought a passenger was dying. It was decided to divert to Manchester and, with emergency steps and ambulance organised, they were on final approach to Ringway when a doctor on board diagnosed that the passenger had epilepsy and that he would be all right to continue. There was just time to do an overshoot of the runway.

Keflavik, in Iceland, was the first stop and, after refuelling, snow began falling. Halfway down the runway, Captain Tanton could not see, so he aborted take-off. It was realised that with lights on, the glare obliterated all visibility in the driving snow. The second try, without lights, was successful. Then after a five-hour wait on the ground in Los Angeles, the return leg was completed.

In all, Captain McDougall was out of bed for forty hours - but the assignment was perfectly legal. He was not a member of the operating crew; just a human autopilot.

Airlines, led in the UK by BOAC, did not like what they regarded as a back-door method of undercutting their scheduled services across the Atlantic. One primary victim of attempted lobbying was Sir Miles Thomas, Britannia Airways' Chairman.

Gordon Brunton described him as a marvellous Britannia Airways chairman who loved the job, and the staff loved him, but he soon he became embroiled in the political machinations. The pressure, however, was not confined to Thomas. It was equally applied to Bryan Llewelyn and John Sauvage, the official mouthpiece for the unease being the Civil Aviation Authority. As a result, weeks were being spent by Britannia directors in hearings, and it became evident that the wisest course was to abandon the affinity group charters.

A time of change

By March 1973 there were growing signs that Britannia Airways was shying away from wide-bodied airliners despite previously considered them. When Britannia ordered the 737-200 in mid-1965, the aircraft had a guaranteed range of about 950 nautical miles from Luton's 7,000-foot runway with 112 inclusive-tour passengers and full reserves. While this performance was marginal for Britannia's requirements, the airline was confident that the 737 would follow the example set by the 727 and exceed the minimum guaranteed performance, which

The 'other side' of G-AXNA with the forward cargo door open and a container about to be loaded via a scissor lift. *(authors collection)*

initially it did not. According to Capt Davison, Britannia's operations director, the airline felt its confidence in the manufacturer was justified, and the latest Advanced 737-200 could fly 1,400 nautical miles out of Luton with 130 passengers. Britannia took delivery of its second Advanced 737-200 in that month, and in addition to these two airliners, the airline operated seven basic 737-200s, two 737-200C/QCs with cargo doors and two 707-320Cs. The 14,500-pound thrust JT8D-9s powered all Britannia's 737s, so the increases in payload and range out of Luton were the direct result of a reduction in empty weight, better brakes and thrust reversers and aerodynamic improvements to the wing. Much of this was brought about by the use of kits of parts supplied by Boeing to improve field performance and reduce drag. The modifications included the replacement of the clam-shell thrust reversers with the later target-type units; a 45 inch rearward extension of the engine nacelle; small changes to the wing vortex-generators; and improvements to the sealing of the slats and flaps.

When these changes had been incorporated the aircraft could carry 117 passengers for 1,000 nautical miles from Luton. The latest Advanced 737-200 had automatic brakes and a new anti-skid system. A revised metering pin in the main landing gear shock strut allowed the aircraft to be placed more positively on the runway surface on landing with minimum passenger discomfort.

Britannia Airways was to take delivery of its eleventh 737-200 on 12 March 1973. The airline had been in discussion with Boeing regarding the possible purchase of three additional 737s for delivery later that same year or early in 1974. In the light of this new purchase, it would appear that the airline's selection of a wide-bodied aircraft had receded. Captain Derek Davison reported to the media that Britannia's decision on a wide-bodied aircraft had decreased. If a further 737 order was placed it would be for aircraft equipped with acoustic linings in the engine nacelles, similar to those supplied to Eastern Provincial Airways of Gander and would meet the noise requirements of FAR Part 36. The airline would consider retrospectively fitting hush-kits to all its aircraft if there were operating advantages attached to flying quiet aircraft. The airline was also evaluating the economics of the Advanced 727-200 in addition to those of the Airbus A300B, DC-10 and TriStar. Although the 727 would probably not bring a substantial reduction in seat-mile costs, it would provide a more versatile fleet while minimising initial costs and allowing more extended sectors to be flown from Gatwick, Glasgow and Manchester.

While the latest wide-bodied types brought distinct advantages in terms of seat-mile costs, it was clear that there were problems of providing standby capacity with only a small fleet. Sub-charter would be difficult even in winter, and Capt Davison pointed out that it could take up to four 737s to substitute for a TriStar or DC-10. He believed that the British Airways and All Nippon orders, together with the decision by Delta to drop its DC-10 options, were particularly significant for the TriStar. The long-range of the wide-bodied trijets was seen as an advantage for any potential Britannia wide-bodied operation.

Britannia had also noticed a distinct change in the pattern of inclusive-tour operations - passengers were now demanding holiday flights from their local

G-BAZG *Florence Nightingale* photographed at Luton. *(Richard Vandervord)*

Left: Duty-Free sales on board were a very lucrative aspect to business

Below Britannia Boeing 707 G-AYEX.

Bottom: The cover of *'Wanderer'*, Britannia's inflight magazine for 1973/4. *(all author's collection)*

airports and were increasingly reluctant to drive long distances to the operator's headquarters. Although Luton was well placed to serve a large catchment area and is close to the A1 and M1 trunk roads, Britannia planned more operations from Birmingham than Luton during the 1973-74 winter season. The airline would have liked to use Gatwick, but there was insufficient airport capacity. The flexibility of service and the need to organise groups of up to 400 passengers from dispersed airports would be essential considerations in any choice of a wide-bodied type. Although Britannia had leased both its 707-320Cs to British Caledonian, it was hopeful of returning to the long-haul business in the then not-too-distant future. It was also possible, given the right opportunity and the prospect of achieving a worthwhile return on investment, that the airline might be interested in a scheduled service.

Other problems were surfacing in 1973. New charter regulations governing the operation of trans-Atlantic charters came into force. It meant not only that the affinity group charters would come to an abrupt end, but also the airline would be required to set up offices in North America to continue any charter operations. Although the Boeing 707s had proven themselves to be very profitable, the capital

wanderer

'*Wanderer*' - which became the company in-flight magazine in the early 1970s was different in size - being smaller than usual, and in content - meaning that being thicker, the articles were more detailed.

By Edition Three, for 1974/5, it was well established. It was not only being used to promote the airline but also some of its more esoteric products available to the travelling public that included its own speciality rose 'Lady of the Sky', To quote a caption on page five on the edition: 'Ladies of the Sky - surrounded by a sea of roses in Gregory's specialist gardens near Nottingham. Maxine, one of Britannia's team of experienced stewardesses, begins her tour of the various stages in the development of Lady of the Sky'.

'Maxine' was, in fact, Sue Lloyd, as revealed in Britannia News, the staff magazine. Ms Lloyd became the 'face' of Britannia Airways for several years in the 1970s.

In issue 4 which featured TV holiday commentator Judith Chalmers, the editor could not resist a certain amount of back-slapping; 'You may not be aware of it, but you are flying with Britain's leading holiday airline, and that's no idle boast. Britannia Airways carried more holidaymakers last year and flew more passenger miles than any other holiday airline in the country - and this year it looks like being top of the league again.

But sheer size isn't everything - reliability, service and comfort are equally important, and Britannia scores here too'.

Britannia New

Girl in a million

Attractive Britannia stewardess, S Lloyd, has suddenly developed gre fingers. Six months ago she hadn't clue about planting roses but she do now.

Sue, who comes from Potters Ba Hertfordshire, will feature in a millio copies of Britannia's new in-flig magazine 'Wanderer' which comes o in the Spring.

Sue volunteered for the job of promoti Britannia's own rose 'Lady of the Sk which will be sold to holidaymake through coupons in the magazine.

During lengthy photographic sessions Gregory's — the rose growers in Staplefor Nottingham — she got to know a gre deal about the 'thorny' art of ro growing.

THE BRITANNIA LOG

...et Britannia's New 737s
...may not be aware of it but
...'re flying with Britain's
...ding holiday airline, and
...'s no idle boast. Britannia
...rways carried more,
...lidaymakers last year
...d flew more passenger
...les than any other holiday
...line in the country – and
...s year it looks like being
...p of the league again.

be article also mentioned the 'crisp cool navy uniforms' which
ad been recently introduced for female Cabin Crew.

hey were designed by one of the airline's Senior Training
tewardesses, Herdis King, and were based on the mix-and-match
oncept which gave the girls a wide choice of wardrobe.
erdis researched the uniform, gaining valuable experience from
e girls themselves. 'Simplicity' was the key to the design. It was
tally important because one must have a uniform which adapts to
l shapes and sizes and still looks smart'.

But sheer size isn't everything – reliability, service and comfort are equally important and Britannia scores here too. You're flying aboard one of the quietest, most reliable and most operationally flexible aircraft of its kind in the world – the Boeing 737. Britannia operates fourteen of these aircraft – three of them just having arrived from the Boeing Aircraft Company in Seattle. The chances are you could be flying in one right now!

And if you are you will be able to savour the comfort and luxury of the new 'wide bodied look' created by Boeing for the 737.

And as you jet away to some distant land, spare a thought for those on the ground who aren't getting away on holiday.

Britannia already operates one of the quietest fleets in the country and its new 737s will be quieter still.
In fact, the new 737s will serve more holiday destinations more quietly than any other aircraft.

New Look for Britannia Girls
Britannia's new Boeings aren't all that's new in the air. Those crisp cool navy uniforms the stewardesses are wearing were a recent introduction.

NEW LOOK FOR BRITANNIA GIR[LS]

HERE is the new stewardess uniform which will be worn by 300 Britannia Airways girls for the first time this month.

In French-navy cool...

...information from the stewardesses themselves.

The uniform consists of a French-navy tery... jacket...

...a red, scarf, a has red match on the...

Britannia's Fourteen Point Plan for a Quick Jetaway

In its efforts to make air travel as convenient as possible Britannia now operates from a record number of airports in Britain to holiday destinations abroad. Now holidaymakers can jet from any of the following airports: Bournemouth, Gatwick, Luton, Birmingham, East Midlands, Manchester, Blackpool, Liverpool, Tees-side, Newcastle, Glasgow, Exeter, Bristol and Cardiff.

Britannia keeps in touch with current trends and puts the passengers comfort first, this is vitally important in the airline business. We hope you agree.

Right: Luton Airport - and also Britannia got its biggest, and perhaps most unwelcome, promotion in the form of a Campari ad on TV. Here Lorraine Chase is treated to a VIP tour of the airport.

Below: The infamous Luton Airport passenger marquee that was a stop-gap for 1974.
[Court Line via Ed Posey]

Bottom: Thomson's brochure from the summer of 1974, showing some of the price deals.

outlay involved in setting up offices for such a limited trans-Atlantic service meant that they were no longer commercially viable.

As Sauvage had agreed wholeheartedly with the existing policy of not wishing to get into long-haul scheduled services, Consequently, the leases on the two Boeing 707s were cut short and the aircraft were disposed of in the Spring of 1973 to British Caledonian Airways.

There was little disappointment at Luton as a result of the move. As Derek Davison said just after the 707s were disposed of: 'We all felt some relief. It was partly because of the intense competition to all the gateway cities. Afterwards, it became clear how right that decision was when the charter business on the North Atlantic collapsed.

Even with the demise of Britannia's Affinity Charters, Luton Airport was still bursting at the seams: something had to be done and done quickly. Britannia News explained what was about to happen in its February 1974 edition.

'The end of this month should complete the first

stage in Luton Airport's massive expansion programme. Here is a summary of the total development:- Stage One is a temporary two-storey prefabricated building which will provide much needed extra accommodation for the holidaymakers - particularly during the peak Summer period. This stage cost £83,000 and will cover an area of 9,900 square feet'.

'Stage Two will be a two-storey building which will replace the temporary structure. It will provide extra accommodation for passengers and will include extensions to the departure lounge. This stage will cost £568,000 and will cover an area of 30,000 square feet'.

'Stage Three will be a single storey building including extensions to the arrival and departure halls and an airside holding area for passengers within the UK and to and from the Channel Islands and the Irish Republic'.

'This stage will cost £34,000 and will provide an area of 3,150 square feet. Both stages two and three should be completed by March 1975'

Britannia was now free to concentrate upon what it did best, providing a good standard of charter flights for the holiday traffic between the UK and the Mediterranean basin. There were some extension in the geographical area covered, of course, to include, for example, the Canaries, Madeira, Alpine and Scandinavian destinations, and some West African and Soviet cities; but Spain, the Adriatic and the Aegean remained central to Britannia's activities.

Davison's aims were now to secure more aircraft and improve profitability. But within a matter of months of the ending of activity to the west, shattering news came from the east. The Organisation of Petroleum Exporting Countries - OPEC - dominated by the Middle Eastern oil producers, had decided to raise their prices astronomically. In aircraft fuel terms it meant a trebling or quadrupling overnight of the fifteen pence a gallon Britannia was then paying for their supplies. Surcharges had immediately to be imposed on the tour operators - not the best of marketing incentives because the value of the pound had also dropped so that potential customers were already feeling the economic draught.

The OPEC-created oil crisis could not have happened at a worse time for Britannia, for it was just as they had started developing winter holiday programmes. It was the beginning of the second-holiday revolution whereby people who had bought a fortnight in summer were being enticed to take a short four or five-day break to places like Majorca, for around for less than £20, during the cold English winter. The idea was the brainchild of Bryan Llewelyn and, of course, was crucial in helping the

Although the airlines complained about the marquee, apart from being difficult to keep clean and tidy, it did serve its purpose, although not the ideal option. *[Court Line via Ed Posey]*

Above: the view out of the cabin window reflected the red, white and blue cheatline of the Britannia colours on the engine cowling of the port Pratt & Witney JT8-D as this 737 descends through the murk into Luton Airport. This view was a calming contrast to some of the wild times had by holidaymakers only a few hours earlier. *(both author)*

winter utilisation of Britannia's aircraft.

On the tour operating side in those days, even a one per cent increase in load factor boosted Thomson Holidays profits by a staggering amount. The news from OPEC ruined that ambition. The following season, the inclusive tour market collapsed by twenty per cent.

1974 was only weeks old when oil prices rose dramatically, which, along with many other economic problems, caused the cost of holidays to rocket overnight. In consequence, demand fell, and many major tour companies were faced with possible bankruptcy.

Meanwhile, however, the Britannia team had to come to grips with their own immediate over-capacity crisis caused by the holiday turndown.

Bryan Llewelyn told John Sauvage that he would have to dispose of some of his aircraft capacity. The choice was either to lease 737s to other operators - in a not particularly favourable international climate - or aeroplanes would have to be sold. Sauvage managed to lease three of the aircraft to the Dutch airline Transavia, and another to Far East Air Transport of Taiwan, but a real breakthrough was created by the efforts of director Bob Muckleston and Derek Davison.

Conscious of the anxiety which the fuel crisis was causing throughout the Travel industry Managing Director, John Sauvage, explained the situation, and the airline's plans in *'Britannia News'*: 'In December and since then, our fuel supplies have

Above: G-AXNB low down and fast at the Royal Air Forces Association Air Display at North Weald, just outside London on 29 May 1972. In the 1970s it was not unusual for airliners to appear on the Air Show circuit. *(Richard Vandervord)*

been controlled and allocated by the Department of Trade and Industry'.

'Concurrently, for commercial reasons we took a decision to lease an aircraft overseas and by early Spring may be leasing two units abroad for the remainder of the year; thus it is unlikely that any more than twelve out of the fourteen aircraft will be operating in the UK this year. Against this background and the improving fuel situation, as well as the encouraging developments in the Middle East, it is likely that our aircraft will be operating without fuel restriction this year. What is more worrying is the continuing price increase of fuel and the effect that may have on our trade'.

'What is encouraging, however, is the fact that the 737 can more than hold its own on fuel economy with most commercial aircraft employed in the IT industry, but they can, of course, do much more besides in these difficult days. In any event, they continue to be much in demand overseas should the position in the UK become unduly tricky, which is far from being the case at the moment.'

Lease in - lease out!

Airlines lease aircraft from other airlines or leasing companies for two main reasons: to operate aircraft without the financial burden of buying them, and to provide a temporary increase in capacity. The industry has two main leasing types: wet-leasing, which is usually used for short-term leasing, and dry-leasing, which is more usual for longer-term leases. The industry also uses combinations of wet and dry. For example, when the aircraft is wet-leased to establish new services, then as the airline's flight or

Above: A classic air-to-air, this time of G-BGYL that appeared in many promotional items for Britannia.

cabin crews become trained, they can be switched to a dry lease.

A wet lease is a leasing arrangement whereby one airline - termed the lessor - provides an aircraft, complete crew, maintenance, and insurance (ACMI) to another airline or other type of business acting as a broker of air travel (the lessee), which pays by hours operated. The lessee provides fuel and covers airport fees, and any other duties, taxes, etc. The flight uses the flight number of the lessee. A wet lease generally lasts 1–24 months; a shorter duration would be considered an ad hoc charter. A wet lease is typically utilised during peak traffic seasons or annual heavy maintenance checks, or to initiate new routes. A wet-leased aircraft may be used to fly services into countries where the lessee is banned from operating.

They can also be considered a form of charter whereby the lessor provides minimum operating services, including ACMI, and the lessee provides the balance of services along with flight numbers. In all other forms of charter, the lessor provides the flight numbers. Variations of a wet lease include a codeshare arrangement and a block seat agreement.

A dry lease is a leasing arrangement whereby an aircraft financing entity (lessor), such as GECAS, AerCap, or Air Lease Corporation, provides an aircraft without crew, ground staff etc. Dry lease is typically used by leasing companies and banks, requiring the lessee to put the aircraft on its own air operator's certificate (AOC) and provide aircraft registration. A typical dry lease lasts upwards of two years and bears certain conditions concerning depreciation, maintenance, insurances, etc., also depending on the geographical location, political circumstances, etc.

A dry-lease arrangement can also be made between a major airline and a regional airline, in which the major airline provides the aircraft and the regional operator provides flight crews, maintenance and other operational aspects of the aircraft, which then may be operated under the major airline's name or some similar name.

The Arab Republic of Yemen covers just 75,000 square miles and in 1973 had a population of less than seven million. But its geographical position is strategic within the Middle East - its waddied coastal strip fronts the south-east extremity of the Red Sea

Above: G-AVRN, '*Captain James Cook*' is seen at London Gatwick in full Britannia colours. *(Richard Vandervord)*

Left: Margaret Egleton (left) from Luton and Sue Lloyd from Potters Bar pose for a press photo showing off the then new cabin crew uniform.

Below: G-AXNA is seen just returned from lease to Transavia Holland, still wearing that carrier's basic livery with Britannia titles. *(author's collection)*

Above: Leased out! G-BAZG in Yemen Airways markings. *(author's collection)*.

Opposite page: From *Britannia News* comes the story of the Yemen leasing project.
(Britannia Airways via Kaz Ale Collection)

and its northern border nudges the desert heartland of Saudi Arabia. Its potential resources had yet to be developed appropriately, so the income of its inhabitants was among the lowest in the Middle East. For this reason, thousands of Yemenis in the seventies left for work elsewhere in the Arab world.

At the time, this traffic was one of the leading platforms for the growth of the country's airline, Yemen Airways, later known as Yemenia, who then wanted to enter the jet era instead of operating a piston-engined Douglas DC-6. This presented Britannia with the opportunity of leasing aircraft to the airline.

The first to depart UK shores, in December 1973, was Romeo Lima, the first of the Boeing 737 fleet delivered to Britannia.

In December of that year, Britannia Airways reached an agreement with Yemen Airways whereby a single Boeing 737 was wet-leased to the latter during the winter - that is they were supplied with the full crew complement and ground support.

G-AVRL left Luton for a three month period in the Middle East and was replaced by another aircraft in March. The agreement was soon increased to two jets from August 1974 and continued as such until May 1976 when Britannia withdrew from the contract. World Airways took over using a Boeing 727 until the Yemeni Boeing 737 (4W-ABZ) was delivered in December 1976 after Britannia had undertaken pre-delivery checks at Luton.

The financial return was good if Britannia could handle the environment and could get the right deal. There was an adverse reaction from the aircrew and maintenance side. The aircrew did not want to be posted to the middle of nowhere, and the maintenance team did not want to support an aircraft in what was something of a hostile environment. However, Britannia's financial

Leased in! In basic Britannia colours is TF-VLM. *(Richard Vandervord)*

Yemen contract clinched

Britannia's G-AVRL — suitably adorned in Yemen Airways livery decants passengers at Taiz airport in the Yemen.

Mike Kemp, Britannia's Sales Controller who has been at the head of the Company's negotiations in the Yemen, has just secured an option to renew a contract leasing one of its Boeing 737 aircraft to Yemen Airways. The contract was first signed in December last year.

This option is good news for Britannia which, in common with other airlines, has had to face over-capacity as a result of increased fuel costs and the general economic situation.

Mr. Kemp said, "the impact of the 737 on the Yemen services had been quite remarkable and its passenger appeal is being emphasized daily. We were told only the other day one hundred and ten passengers had collected in the airport at Sannaa only to find that they were a day early for our scheduled service. The normal D.C. 6 was brought onto the tarmac to operate the load but all the passengers decided that they would sleep overnight at the Terminal in order to fly on 'Al Jet' — the name they have given to our 737."

Britannia's 'man on the spot' — Station Officer Martin Sterling.

Sales Controller, Mike Kemp.

G-BJZW was one of Quebecair's -296s, and appeared in a six month lease-in and is seen here at London Gatwick in 1982. *(Richard Vandervord)*

situation would be grave if they could not find work for the two spare aircraft.

Britannia put together a spares pack and sent down two engineers together with some three crews. Initially, the teams were sent there for a month and then rotated, but the working environment was hard.

Britannia had already taken delivery of further three 737s, which had been ordered when the tourist market was much more buoyant. Suddenly the airline was faced with a problem of overcapacity and rising fuel costs. Fortunately, they were well placed on leasing several of their aircraft: the Yemeni contract having been extended to two aircraft; two aircraft were leased to Transavia Holland, and a further 737 went to Far East Air Transport of Taiwan as B-2605.

Britannia managed to survive but many of her competitors did not. These included Donaldson International Airlines and, most notably, Court Line Aviation, whose multi-coloured TriStars and BAC One-Elevens left thousands of holidaymakers stranded throughout Europe. It now left Britannia at the end of the year as Britain's number one holiday airline.

All in all 1974 was not going to be remembered as a good year for the travel trade in general or the airline in particular, primarily due to the dramatic increase in the price of fuel, which began in October 1973. John Sauvage, the airline's Managing Director, took rapid steps to protect the airline, as he explained to employees in the April 1974 edition of Britannia News: 'There are now definite signs that business is picking up well, both in the passenger and freight

G-AWSY seen 'somewhere in Greece' in a partial new scheme, with a bare metal lower fuselage. *(Richard Vandervord)*

Above: HP-895-CMP of COPA in the Luton hangar.

Right: Yankee Juliet was leased for a while to Midway Express, whose titles it wears.
(both Kaz Ale Collection)

Below: G-BJXI in non-standard colours *(Richard Vandervord)*

G-BNIA in a hybrid red, white and blue scheme that somehow suits the -200.

charter business and in holiday bookings. The latter development will now improve our load factors on IT flights to a respectable level and is most encouraging, but we have to bear in mind that this improvement has come too late to make it possible for us to restore our '74 holiday programme to its original size. This indeed is the experience of most big Tour Operators who have suffered in various degrees from the effects of a decline in the market of some thirty per cent. Our own experience and expectations are, of course, better than average, and we are confident that the aircraft capacity which is surplus to the requirements of our Tour Operators will now be fully utilised on activities which include a fairly extensive charter programme in the UK and contract flying for at least one, and offers for more aircraft based abroad. I said recently that we are fortunate in having the 737 and recent events have certainly proved that they are very much in demand.'

He was also asked about the ongoing fuel supply problems: 'Fuel supplies for aviation have eased and will shortly be unrestricted. Prices are, of course, another matter although they have now stabilised for the next three months - albeit at a high level. This will continue to be a major problem for us, like other industries, and that is why we are continuing with our fuel economy programme, which is now paying handsome dividends.'

When questioned about the possibility of redundancy John Sauvage explained: 'I particularly regret the fact that recent uncertainties and the decline in our holiday business have meant that we have had to turn away a number of personnel - including twenty-one pilots -- who in some cases joined us and in others were awaiting recruitment in the airline for training as part of the fleet expansion programme.

A pair of America West Airlines 737-200s undergo maintenance at Luton. *(Kaz Ale Collection)*

Personnel intake will, this year, be kept to a minimum to satisfy only present needs. In the case of surplus pilots, most of them have now been found jobs abroad through the efforts of our Deputy Chief Pilot Roy McDougall, and I sincerely believe that our thoughtful and considerate policy in respect of all staff will result in the minimum disturbance and hardship to individuals'.

1975 saw a far more cautious approach by tour operators to their holiday programmes. Lessons had been learned, unfortunately at the cost of several carriers. However, confidence was slowly being regained in the package deal holiday market as a result of legislation to ensure that the events following the Court Line crash could never be repeated. Passengers were now given a guarantee when booking, that all monies would be refunded in the event of the tour operator become insolvent.

By 1975 Britannia operated a total of fourteen Boeing 737s and carried two million passengers. Part of this was through the introduction of the 'Advanced' 737-200, which came with two distinct advantages. First was that the new aircraft, although appearing almost identical to others in the fleet had an additional 300-mile range - giving 1650 miles in total, when operating out of Luton. From a good neighbour point of view, its hush-kitted turbofan engines meant a significant reduction in noise, so allowing the aircraft to be used for night-movements out of Luton. Britannia planned on refitting the entire fleet with hush-kits at the cost of £80,000 per aircraft something that had been discussed back in 1973, a programme that would not be complete until 1979.

This expansion and survival from the 1974 travel trade problems once again worried the scheduled operators, particularly British Airways (BA), which had been formed by the merger of British European Airways and British Overseas Airways Corporation. Their executives were almost constantly complaining to the government on a variety of matters, including Britannias so-called 'Wanderer' flights which they claimed were a 'gross misuse of the Britannia licence', because they used vouchers as well as cash. The more likely reason was that the Wanderer packages were considerably cheaper to the same destination than BAs.

Early that year Britannia realised that it would be required to use the Boeing 737s then currently on lease to Transavia Holland and Far East Air Transport. Consequently, B-2605 returned to its old identity of G-AVRO, but Transavia still needed the aircraft they had on lease. As a result, the airline leased two Boeing 737s from United Airlines which in turn were leased to Transavia allowing Britannia's aircraft to be returned. Britannia Airways now operated a total of fourteen Boeing 737s for the

CS-TMA for Air Sul at Luton. *(Kaz Ale Collection)*

Over the years Britannia flew many flights in support of the Hadj, sometimes putting the aircraft in lessors colours, sometimes just operating as charters.
Above: 767 G-OBYV in the colours of Garuda Indonesian on a very wet Luton Apron, and below; the same aircraft gets a welcome at Jeddah. *(Kaz Ale Collection)*

summer season.

The airline's route network continued to cover most of the popular holiday destinations in the Mediterranean, Greece, the Alps, Canary Islands, North Africa and the Soviet Union.

Departure points in Britain were still primarily based in Birmingham, Bristol, Cardiff, East Midlands, Gatwick, Glasgow, Liverpool, Luton, Manchester, and Newcastle, while ad-hoc charters took place from as far afield as Aberdeen in the north to Exeter in the south.

The final part of the evolution of Britannia Airways into a significant force in the European non-scheduled arena took place in 1975, and the airline was to consolidate upon this newly acquired premier position. There are many reasons why this occurred: luck had on some occasions been on the airline's side, but most of all it had changed with the times by adopting modern jet airliners and tailoring capacity strictly to its requirements. The airline had survived both its withdrawal from the North American market and the economic instability which had caused the downfall of many of its competitors. Britannia Airways was now looking ahead and planning further consolidation and expansion with an eye towards the next decade and beyond.

Chapter 5

Recovery, New Colours and a New Type

In 1976 Captain Derek Davison was appointed Britannia Airways' new Managing Director when John Sauvage took over as head of Thomson Travel.

Davison quickly set about expanding the fleet to a projected figure of twenty-seven Boeing 737s by 1981. This decision was taken as a result of the upturn in the Inclusive Tour market which was highlighted in a survey carried out by the Civil Aviation Authority, that portrayed Britannia Airways as the most profitable UK holiday airline; earning pre-tax profits in 1976 of £4.8 million. The airline's market share of the holiday traffic stood at thirty per cent, and for the first time, the company flew contracts for Ellerman and OSL in addition to Thomsons, Horizon and the Ministry of Defence. An extension of the contract with Thomsons called for departures from Leeds/Bradford Airport for the first time and operations have continued ever since.

During the year the airline placed an order for a Boeing 737 simulator with CAE for delivery in 1977 costing £1 million, simulator time being available not only for Britannia Airways but also for other Boeing 737 operators.

Despite being Managing Director, Captain Davison still did a great deal of flying whenever he could, especially on trooping flights, as they were reasonably quick to do. He kept his uniform in his office, so that he could change before going out to the aircraft.

By now Britannia Airways operations stretched from the Canaries in the west to Rhodes in the east and also to Scandinavia and Moscow. The airline had a fleet of sixteen Boeing 737s of which seven were advanced models, and its market share had risen to thirty-two per cent. The longest route then flown was Glasgow - Tenerife, some 1850 nautical miles; the performance of the Pratt & Whitney JT8D-15 engines enabled the advanced 737s to fly 1000 nautical miles with a full load even from Leeds/Bradford's short 5400-foot runway.

The beginning of 1978 saw Britannia Airways again heading the UK airline profit league with aircraft utilisation standing at 9.6 hours per airframe per day, the ultimate being to obtain an annual aircraft utilisation of 4000 hours.

The summer operation called for departures from fourteen UK airports, and around sixty per cent of departures were for Thomson Holidays; twenty per cent for Horizon Midland and the

G-BADP in the early red, white and blue scheme, with the airline titling in black. *(Phil McCrackin Collection)*.

G-AZNZ *Henry Hudson* in the later scheme with red 'Britannia' titling and almost horizontal cheat lines.

balance being represented by the Ministry of Defence, ad-hoc charters, cargo flights and aircraft leasing. Luton departures accounted for thirty per cent of total traffic although traffic through provincial airports was increasing. The airline assessed Southend Airport for the viability of operating the 1100 nautical mile flight to Palma, however, this route was not flown until the 1982 summer season, when operations commenced on behalf of Thomson Holidays. A newspaper contract during the year, resulted in a journey from Manchester to Belfast which was customarily flown by a passenger aircraft.

In July the airline celebrated the tenth anniversary of the introduction to service of the Boeing 737 when the first aircraft G-AVBL flew to Ibiza from Luton with Captain Tanton in command. The summer season was fraught with delays due to a dispute by French air traffic controllers and this resulted in the hire of many varied aircraft to operate delayed flights.

The year closed with Britannia Airways carrying thirty-two per cent of the UK holiday traffic, with a fleet of eighteen aircraft and a staff of 1250.

1979 saw the airline operating scheduled services three times weekly between London (Gatwick) and Gibraltar on behalf of Gibair. However, between November 1982 and April 1983 British Airways flew this service in addition to their service between these points.

Britannia Airways continued to expand during the year, leasing one Boeing 720 from the Icelandic airline Eagle Air and two Boeing 737s, one from Transavia Holland and the other from Gulf Air, for the summer season. For the second year running this season was marred by multiple air traffic congestion, caused by several disputes involving European air traffic controllers. As a result of these disputes, Britannia was forced to hire aircraft for one-off flights to relieve the congestion, including a Martinair DC-10 and a Trans European Airways A300B Airbus, which were seen operating Glasgow-Palma flights on Britannia's behalf.

During the year the airline carried three million passengers for the first time and captured thirty-five per cent of the holiday traffic, an increase of three per cent over two years. The year closed with the ending of the Horizon Midlands contract which had occupied three aircraft full time and had been in existence since April 1971. Horizon decided to form its own carrier, Orion Airways, to commence operations in March 1980 with three 737s based at Birmingham, East Midlands and Manchester.

A new dimension in vertical integration began in 1980. It was not a new concept, having been around since the very early days of package tours. It involved a process whereby all the elements of a package holiday - tour operator, airline and hotel - were owned and operated by one organisation. Consequently, G-BOSL was delivered to the airline in April 1980, one of two 737s ordered by

OSL Holidays, a leading British tour operator, but which would be flown in Britannia Airways colours, being operated and maintained by the airline. Britannia Airways had flown routes for OSL since 1976, and a close relationship had been built up between the two companies. The OSL aircraft was to be integrated into the airline's fleet, but OSL would allocate the time contract work. Britannia Airways flew three new routes for OSL in 1980: from Glasgow, Newcastle and Manchester to Jersey. These routes were not gained without a fight from the scheduled carriers operating to Jersey, who lodged objections with the Civil Aviation Authority. The CAA ruled that the airline may operate this route from northern gateways but not from Luton or Gatwick as scheduled traffic from these points was adequate and the increase in summer passengers compensated the scheduled operators for the leaner winter months.

The previous year had seen the introduction of 'direct sell' holidays in the UK for the first time on a large scale. Tjaereborg, a Danish operator, had pioneered them, and the concept involved the clients dealing directly with the tour operator, thus cutting out the middle man, in this case, the travel agent. Britannia Airways had operated a few flights for Tjaereborg during 1979 but the bulk of

In almost twenty years of operating from Luton Airport our association has been close and friendly. We have watched the airport grow and helped in its expansion to one of the country's principal airports, familiar to millions of holiday makers. As Britain's largest holiday airline we congratulate Luton International Airport on its latest development. Together we shall continue to provide the . . . . .

first steps to a happy holiday!

Britannia Airways Luton Airport LU2 9ND Telephone (0582) 424155

their programme was contracted to Dan-Air Services. Realising the potential of direct sell operations a new British company, Portland Holidays was set up as a sister company to operate flights from London (Gatwick), Luton and Manchester to European destinations using Britannia Airways as its carrier. This operation continued, and the airline also flew for Tjaereborg from London (Gatwick), Luton and Manchester. Another major tour operator using this concept was Budget Holidays, who had contracted around ninety per cent of its total operations to Britannia.

Meanwhile - at the parents...

The Canadian company Thomson Newspapers Ltd., which was separate from International Thomson Organisation Ltd (ITOL), had long restricted itself to owning small Canadian and US newspapers with circulations below 20,000; the strategy was in keeping with Roy Thomson's drive to contain costs while nonetheless being assured of near-monopolies in local advertising. During the 1950s under Kenneth Thomson, the group published the most significant number of newspaper titles in Canada. In the following decade, a US acquisition programme was launched. By 1974 the group owned more than 100 newspapers.

In 1980 its profile was transformed through the acquisition of FP Publications and its chain of newspapers in most of the big cities of Canada, including Toronto's Globe and Mail, which Thomson attempted to turn into a national newspaper along UK lines.

By the 1980s Thomson Travel ranked as the largest inclusive tour operator based in the United Kingdom (about three times the size of its nearest rival), owned the country's biggest charter airline,

and was one of the largest travel retailers. Within a few years of entering the US market, it became one of the top three US tour operators, although by 1988 it had withdrawn entirely to concentrate on its activities based in the United Kingdom. This same year Thomson strengthened its UK leadership in tour operating, charter airlines, and travel retailing with the acquisition of the Horizon Travel Group, which had been one of its major competitors.

For ITOL, expansion continued throughout the 1980s in Britain and the United States alike. With the 1986 acquisition of South-Western, the largest American publisher of business textbooks for schools and colleges, ITOL became second overall in US college textbook publishing. The following year saw one of ITOL's most significant British purchases when it acquired Associated Book Publishers (ABP), a group including the legal publisher Sweet & Maxwell and the academic publisher Routledge, Chapman & Hall. Purchased for US$323 million, ABP represented a significant advance for ITOL in legal, scientific, technical, and scholarly publishing in the United Kingdom, North America, and Australia.

This trend toward 'high-profit publishing niches,' was orchestrated by Thomson's right-hand man, Gordon Brunton, and furthered by then-president Michael Brown; both were keenly aware that its oil holdings were rapidly becoming depleted. The 1986 fall in oil prices dragged the North American petroleum subsidiaries into overall losses, and both were sold off in 1987. In 1989 ITOL finalised its move away from oil and gas by selling its remaining British interests. Although the immediate cause was the major accident on the Piper Alpha oil rig in 1988, the longer-term rationale was that the company had

Advertising Britannia's 'Little Giant'. Part of a brochure that promoted the 737 to the travel trade.

Below: The short-field performance of the 737 was put to good use by Britannia on a number of the Aegean airfields before they were expanded. Here G-BTZF comes in to land at Lesvos in October 1984; at the time the runway was only 5000 feet long with difficult approaches.

Inset: The thrust reversers from the passengers point of view.*(both author)*

been less and less dependent on North Sea oil revenue, which had fallen both absolutely and as a proportion of ITOL's business since its peak in 1982. At that time it had provided about seventy-five per cent of ITOL's profits, but by 1985, when the Scapa field in which it had invested came onstream, this proportion had fallen to just over fifty per cent.

By leaving the petroleum industry altogether, ITOL was able to concentrate even more resources and attention on its core activities of publishing and information services. In 1988, for instance, subsidiary Thomson & Thomson launched a database containing over 300,000 trademarks and logos; Mitchell International developed further its involvement in the computerising of motor car building and repairs, and ITOL acquired 36 free newspapers in Britain. By the end of 1988, after 54 years of growth, Thomson Newspapers was publishing forty daily and twelve weekly publications in Canada, and 116 daily and 24 weekly newspapers in the USA, representing the most significant number of daily newspapers of any press publishing group in either country. The daily circulation exceeded three million.

In March 1989, to remain competitive in a dawning era of mega-mergers among media conglomerates, ITOL and Thomson Newspapers announced preparations to merge as The Thomson Corporation, a $4.7 billion entity which began operations a few months later. Thus empowered, the new company then bought the Lawyers Cooperative Publishing Company for $815 million, at the time the largest acquisition ever by a Thomson company. In 1990 Thomson Newspapers purchased five daily newspapers and several associated weekly publications in the United States, its largest-ever single purchase. Eight more Canadian local papers and the Financial Times of Canada were also bought. Thomson newspapers were now being published in thirty-two of the fifty US states and eight of the ten Canadian provinces.

..but back at the coal face

1980 saw many decisions made by the airline. The first was in January when a 'seats only' scheme was submitted to the CAA. It involved the sale of a percentage of seats on each flight direct to the public on a one way or return basis. This scheme would aid passengers travelling from the provincial airports which had no scheduled services to southern Europe and consequently passengers would not need to go via London. Also, this scheme would make the most economical use of aircraft capacity since Britannia reckoned that many flights had a few empty seats which could be filled with either businessmen or leisure travellers seeking independent holidays departing from one destination and returning through another. Derek Davison: 'A member of the House of Lords said earlier this year that not one airline in Europe was making a profit. If he had said mainland Europe, he might have had a point. The whole of our operation is profitable, and these profits have been growing consistently. We have the biggest fleet of Boeing 737-200s in Europe, and it is increasing continuously. We were the first European airline to opt for the Boeing 767, and we now have orders and options on five of these new wide-body airliners.'

In these buoyant terms, Britannia Airways' current situation and future prospects were highlighted in 1981 by Derek Davison. He pointed to the company's substantial share of the UK inclusive tour charter market as an indication of the success of its operations and forecast that it would be well placed to benefit further from the primary impetus behind the growth of air travel.

'In 1980 Britannia carried 3.6 million passengers mainly on package holidays, from 22 UK airports to some sixty-five-holiday destinations,' said Mr Davison. 'This represented a thirty seven per cent slice of the inclusive tour charter market compared with our thirty five per cent share in 1979. Where once leisure travel was a negligible part of civil aviation, today it dominates the air transport market. No less than seventy per cent of all European air travellers now fly for 'leisure' reasons, and I quite confidently predict that by 1990 that figure will have risen to ninety per cent.'

This huge increase in leisure travel by air - less than thirty years earlier it had accounted for only about ten per cent of total passenger traffic - was attributed by Davison to the industry's achievement in reducing the price of air travel by a very thorough employment of capital assets; 'In Britannia's case our Boeing 737 utilisation of 11hrs/day is the highest in the world.'

Notwithstanding the extensive flying programme and the high load factors the independent airlines in Europe, like Britannia, at that time only accounted for only fifty-two per cent of the total passenger-kilometres flown within Europe. Moreover, the development of leisure traffic at the forefront of the business interests of these independent carriers was being hampered by restrictions which the Britannia chief executive claimed were designed to protect government-owned airlines - the so-called 'national carriers' - from the competition. 'The leisure passenger is not paying a high fare - he has been 'deregulated' for the past twelve years. But the low fares for airline tourist travellers are part of the holiday packages, and the independent airlines are restricted in offering the increasingly sophisticated leisure travellers what they want - a

Left: Britannia Airways' 737-200 flight simulator was built by CAE Inc - formerly Canadian Aviation Electronics. The sim was installed at Luton in 1977 and was 'flown' on average 11,000 hours a year, not only by Britannia crews, but the flight sim was leased out to other airlines.

This included the Austrian holiday airline Lauda Air, established in April 1979 by former Formula One world motor racing champion Niki Lauda - as seen below - and started operations in 1985, initially operating as a charter and air taxi service. *(both Britannia Airways)*

seat and then the freedom to organise their holiday at the destination.'

Britannia was advocating a liberalised, flexible low fare structure in Europe that would allow the independent airlines to compete more strongly with the scheduled carriers in pursuit of the leisure sector business; and a plan to this effect was the basis of a UK Department of Trade recommendation being considered by the European Civil Aviation Conference.

The airline's proposals were incorporated in an August 1979 application to the CAA was that they were allowed to sell up to half the seats in their aircraft without linking them to a package arrangement. This would give passengers the ability to choose any length of holiday, to fly to one destination and return from another if they so wanted, and to avoid being tied to accommodation. As a means of ensuring the occupation of any seats not utilised by package tour operators this scheme, says the airline, would also help to maintain cheaper airfares. But sensing that the constraints were of a short term nature, Britannia was continually planning for expansion in the market. 'The growth in UK air traffic for leisure reasons is sure to continue and government bodies, airport authorities, anyone who has a say in civil aviation and the growth of leisure traffic, should now be seriously planning for a future when almost all air journeys are made for a leisure purpose', said Derek Davison.

In 1981 Britannia flew five more aircraft than in 1980. Three more Boeing 737s were acquired, bringing the fleet total to twenty-six, and a further two 737s were leased from Eagle Air and Transavia for the 1981 peak season. With three new 737s ordered from Boeing, Britannia's fleet totalled twenty-nine by the spring of 1982, and the airline was looking at its needs for 1983. To improve fuel economy and performance, Britannia fitted Lear Ziegler performance data computers to every 737 in its fleet, becoming the first airline to do so. It was planned that this equipment would produce fuel consumption savings of better than two per cent in 1981, this percentage reducing the fuel bill by approximately £1million.

In 1981 Britannia Airways passengers were flown over an average sector length of 1,050 nautical miles, a distance which extended by about forty per cent over the previous eight years and which encompassed nearby destinations in Europe as well as locations further afield, such as the eastern Mediterranean.

While for the majority of Britannia's passengers travelling with the airline meant sun, sea, sand and sangria, they never realised - or cared - that behind the scenes the airline was just one part of a huge multinational corporation that had many other diverse interests, often with no links with civil aviation or the travel trade. 1982 also saw changes to the Britannia board. Captain Dave Hopkins - who had joined the company in 1967 and later became a chief pilot - was made a Director in January, and Derek Davison was appointed Chairman and Chief Executive. With two 767s on order, three more in the pipeline and thirty-four 737s already on the books, he was ready for expansion when he ran into a little trouble with his masters at International Thomson.

By this time Gordon Brunton had left International Thomson. He had always been able to see the importance of Britannia and the support

Sometimes the strangest things are found in aircraft hangars! A story from *Britannia News*.

How's this for supre protection? These magnificent alsation visited Britannia's gi hangar recently at th invitation of Chief Engineer, Geoff Parkins.

He is secretary of the Dunstable branc of the British Alsatia Association which h 140 members. Geof assures us that these dogs are as docile an friendly as you'll fin and I wouldn't argue with him. Would yo

Even in the days before Photoshop, airline publicity departments made great use of artists impressions, often without declaring the fact. One potential example is this picture - which appeared in both company inflight magazines and corporate advertising material.

it gave to the tour operation, and he knew that by putting the two together, it was possible to achieve the right result and always made a profit. After his departure, there was a specific difficulty at International Thomson in understanding how Britannia could perform so well and there developed an argument that it must be at the expense of tour operating.

The questioning of motives came about due to a gradual change in Thomson Holidays over the years from having a real pride in the performance of its sister airline to that of envy in its profitability record, not helped by the introduction of a bonus scheme. Britannia's history reflected the airline charter markets while Thomson Holidays' performance reflected the more unpredictable and more difficult tour operating market. The evolving management at International Thomson had been persuaded that the difference between the two financial returns was substantially due to capital for aircraft acquisition being used by Britannia on behalf of tour operators competing with Thomson Holidays.

Captain Davison: 'There had been some indication of this at a previous meeting with International Thomson, and I got a very definite impression that while I was politely listened to, I was not believed.'

'After the meeting, I felt a new face was desirable, and I asked Dave Hopkins, who was then the Deputy MD, to prepare a presentation showing how each and every aircraft in the fleet was being used by Thomson Holidays; he produced a bar chart which showed that in summer every aircraft in the fleet except one at Glasgow had been used sometime by Thomson Holidays. It also showed that we could not accommodate the Thomson programme with fewer aircraft.'

'At the subsequent meeting with International Thomson, I asked Dave to present the chart. They looked at each other and made it quite clear that they had not previously understood the situation. Seemingly we had made some progress in changing already closed minds.'

'It all came to a head when I was summoned to International Thomson's London HQ at Stratford Place for a meeting with the new President of International Thomson and two of his colleagues.'

'I had been warned that it was a meeting to discuss a fleet reduction, so I took Peter Brown, Britannia's Financial Director, along with me. To my amazement, they wished to reduce the size of the 737 fleet by 17 aircraft. The meeting lasted two or three hours, and in the end, I was asked to agree on the sale of three old 737s.'

'Typical internal politics, I suppose, but it did leave me wondering about the future. However, we had won the battle if not the war and importantly, the top people at International Thomson realised how we were looking after shareholders' interests as well as providing good profits. Subsequently, more aircraft and hangar capacity were approved'.

Evolving the livery

By the nineteen-eighties, what had seemed ultra-modern ten years earlier was starting to look

We don't believe in making a big noise about ourselves.

Britannia is well aware of environmental problems and is doing its utmost to minimise the inconvenience caused by aircraft to communities in and around airports.
It already flies one of the quietest fleets in the country and its new breed of 737 aircraft are quieter and cleaner still. The Boeing 737 will serve more holiday airports more quietly than any other aircraft.

dated. Not only had red, white and blue motifs been adopted by many other airlines, but the combination had permeated into other forms of transport.

Britannia's red, white and blue scheme had been through several minor variations and modifications, but now there were those at the company's Luton headquarters who were beginning to wonder if it was time for a new, bolder look at the livery.

It coincided with the forthcoming arrival of the new wide-bodied Boeing 767s that turned abstract thought into the need for decisive action. When the existing livery was applied, in outline, to the wide-bodied shape of the 767, the effect was, to say the least aesthetically anaemic. Something had to be done.

Boeing had an in-house design team which had historically created striking liveries for airlines and was willing to undertake similar work for Britannia. However, there were two reasons why the Britannia livery challenge was not entrusted to the men in Seattle. The first was that, in the words of customer services director Bob Parker-Eaton, who was responsible for masterminding the design input, 'We felt the name Britannia had unique significance to the British - may be old fashioned and emotional in some ways, but standing for quality, determination and honesty. Also, to the longer-serving staff, the 'old lady' had a special symbolism. The task was far more than a simple design exercise - it was thought that only a British design team could adequately capture that unique meaning'.

The search lasted eighteen months, the task eventually falling to the London design house of Peter Eaton and Partners. The design brief of the winner had to encompass everything from a sick bag to the Britannia logo now embellished in eight-foot-high lettering on the company's hangar at Luton International Airport, and there could be little argument that it was still the livery of those aircraft that was the most crucial.

An essential ingredient in the production of a

successful design scheme was an ability to relate to Britannia's engineers to ensure that the final design was practical as well as decorative. The then technical director, Geoffrey Parkins, and his engineering team had crucial inputs to make for the aircraft design to succeed. Their involvement was essential. That experience and the personality of the two designers helped swing the day, and Peter Eaton and John Piper won the design contract.

It was no easy task, as Peter Eaton was to later diplomatically put it: 'Britannia had strong ideas of what it wanted, and many concepts were eliminated as being interesting, but just not appropriate.'

The 737s - especially the early variants - were always regarded as a dumpy aircraft - it was not nicknamed 'Fat Albert' - or even SLUFF - for nothing! The designers sought a design which would make it appear sleeker, at the same time suit the larger, longer 767. The obvious solution was an old graphic designer trick - stripes. Stripes have existed on aircraft ever since they had windows. Early designers felt that windows were ugly and slowed down the eye, so they sought to create the opposite effect. That is why they were called 'cheat lines'.

The designers had been working with Britannia's then colours of red, white and blue, without achieving a breakthrough. One day Peter Eaton commented how, paradoxically, Britannia's earlier livery of blue and white was now less dated in design terms than the present, newer, red, white and blue scheme.

It was Derek Davison who suggested something approaching what was eventually decided upon 'Why not drop the red? Blue and gold, with the white would look very elegant'. A graded striping of horizontal lines was developed, but somehow the design still looked cold and clinical. So Peter Eaton added back thin red lines between the blue and gold. The effect was magic.

Another minor mystery resolved! This newspaper cutting from the Post-Echo shows the rough time period when Britannia started naming their aircraft - and that the 'names' came straight from the top! *(Britannia Airways)*

MEET the Sir Barnes Wallis, Britannia Airways' latest addition to their fleet of Boeing 737s.

Ground receptionists Lorraine Wagstaff, right, and Karyn Smith, are pictured welcoming the new arrival which landed at Luton Airport yesterday from the Boeing factory at Seattle. Its arrival brings the number of Boeings owned by Britannia up to 20. Another five are on order this year.

The plane, which can carry 130 passengers, will be going into service on Saturday.

It is one of the first of Britannia's Boeings to be given a name, and the decision to call it after the famous aircraft designer was taken at boardroom level.

On Christmas Eve 1981, Peter Eaton and John Piper presented their final designs to the full Britannia board at Luton - and held their breath. After a long pause, Derek Davison looked up, smiling, and said: 'We gave you a tough task and a tough time, but you have cracked it. That's our new livery!'

From that start, the livery was translated to the aircraft interiors, airline vehicles, check-in desks, signs, stationery and the thousand and one other items bearing the Britannia name or logo.

Finally, the name was changed from Britannia Airways to simply Britannia.

The reaction of Dick Bernard, of Boeing's marketing team, was that the new livery had lifted the design level of airline corporate identity. 'Its individuality is so striking that it will be a hard act to follow'. That may well have been the case, but coincidentally - or not? - the scheme in a very similar form emerged as Boeings house colours!

Along with a new livery on the aircraft, the cabin and ground staff would receive new uniforms - a project that was four years in the making. It was revealed to the staff by Terri Eastaff, writing in *Offchocks,* the cabin staff newsletter. 'The hats would be made in Luton - the largest hat-producing region in Britain.

Ideal Clothiers made a suit and coat in pure wool. A company, Leslie Whitley, was called in as they specialised in blouse manufacture. Their representative agreed to design a material using red, white and blue in lightweight polyester with particular emphasis on washability. It was in the same style as initially decided, long- or short-sleeved with a two colour choice - blue and white on red, or blue and red on white. Apron, shoes - in navy calf leather with a small gold chain on the front - handbag, belt, cabin bags, brevet and gloves were all details. A new uniform for male Cabin Crew was also planned.

Planning for the 767

In the spring of 1979, it was clear that business trends and a five-year forward projection indicated that Britannia, of which Derek Davison was at that time managing director, would need to start to replace at least some of its fleet by 1984.

The Boeing 737 fleet was proving excellent value and eminently reliable, and although the company still had more of the aircraft on order, it would not be competitively sensible to go on buying the type forever. The 737 entered service in 1968 and, although its seat-mile cost economics were still excellent, these would now have to be

measured against not only the new, advanced members of the evolving Boeing family but the competitors from McDonnell Douglas and Airbus Industrie. Boeing, by that time, had announced their 737-300 series. Fuel prices had risen significantly in 1974, and again in 1978. Technology had advanced, particularly in engine design. A reduction in performance diluted advantages gained by stretching the fuselage to achieve extra seating capacity, and so the improved economics sought by Britannia was just not there.

A direct 737 replacement would have been desirable, but it was apparent there was nothing on the market. The exercise was not one involving a 737 replacement, but a displacement - was there an aircraft which could be introduced to displace the -200 on the airline's densest holiday routes?

Robert 'Bob' Ginns was the Project Manager for Britannia's Commercial Division and the overall co-ordinator for the then-new aircraft evaluation project. He recalls that the management team decided that they should be aiming for a fleet of five new aircraft. 'I joined the airline in May 1977. Much of the work I did was directly for Derek Davison - things such as annual management plans although I was working for the commercial director Brian Christian in the family tree. Within two weeks of joining, I was in Seattle, where the 16th 737-200 was about to be delivered. In 1980 we commenced studies for future aircraft types and concluded that there was no suitable direct replacement for the 737-200. Hence we looked at aircraft to displace the 737-200 on the densest routes. The competition was between the 757, 767-200 and A310.'

'These, the management team believed, should be introduced in a short time to spread the significant investment necessary in training, tools, and test equipment as well as all the fixed costs associated with a move into a new breed of aircraft.'

'We wanted to use the aircraft to the best benefit by high utilisation and to be able to introduce a reasonable number of them in a short time. Though we saw the aircraft as a displacement for 737s, and that we would wait for a genuine 737 replacement, in the meantime we would be introducing a highly commercial aeroplane. We would be replacing our assets, but we would be maintaining the asset value and the profitability of the airline with this displacement fleet'.

Most of Britannia's tour operator clients had been telling them that they felt the need was for a 130-seat aeroplane - a similar capacity to the 737 - but with up-to-date technology. Not surprisingly, they also made it abundantly clear they did not want to pay more for their charters.

Bob Ginns again: 'At that time Britannia, together with Thomson Holidays and Lunn Poly the travel agent, all reported to Thomson Travel. One of my recollections of that time was the speed with which Britannia obtained approvals from the Thomson Organisation for new 737-200 aircraft acquisitions. A simple submission with estimated revenue from assumed use was given in around two weeks'.

Britannia held the view that a configuration of up to 300 seats could be justified in the mid-eighties for the most popular routes. This view removed the hurdle associated with a larger aircraft. And so for the second time, Britannia was, as a charter airline, set to lead the way.

Underwriting this view was an analysis of the effect or their biggest client, Thomson Holidays. The sister company put together a draft programme which showed they could already utilise two of this size aircraft in their following year's programme. In turn, Britannia themselves

One of the very few representations of the 767 - albiet in model form - in the earlier Britannia Airways colour scheme, along with a 737 model for comparision.

calculated that, for the year ahead, two bigger aircraft could be displaced for four 737s, without adversely affecting the complex dovetailing of holiday programmes. That this was acceptable in 1980 encouraged them in their fleet projections for four years later.

So the requirement narrowed the prospects down to three from two companies. Boeing had announced their narrow-bodied twin-engined 757, primarily produced for Eastern Airlines and British Airways, and capable of carrying up to 189 passengers, and the 767 wide-bodied twin medium-range aircraft offering from 200 seats, with United Airlines as the lead customer. Across the Atlantic, a derivative of the A300 European Airbus - previously eliminated from Britannia's studies - was the 210 passenger A310, which had gained Lufthansa and Swissair as initial customers. Whichever company could land the Britannia' fish' then they could swell a not over-endowed order book by at least $100 million.

Britannia was seeking an aircraft which could climb out from Luton with a full payload and reach 41000 feet above Paris, enabling high cruising altitudes with maximum fuel economy and minimum air traffic control delay.

Following the first appraisal, four committees were established to evaluate economics and performance, customer services, engineering, and flight operations. Initially, there was precious little hands-on material available - all the types under consideration were still 'paper' aircraft. It was, therefore, essential to ensure a level playing field in the evaluation, as each of the airliners had different specifications.

The staff responsible for the economics and performance report studied the specifications, particularly the weight breakdown. Each competitive aircraft had different features to be taken into account - one would have a big door as standard, giving it the ability to carry engine modules, and another a pallet system in the cargo hold. So these peculiarities, together with significant differences in the cabins, meant that various options had to be put into the mix to come up with a telling evaluation. In this, Britannia did not merely accept the brochure specifications of the aircraft manufacturers. Bob Ginns and George Berrisford, who were Britannia's performance and navigation managers, visited both the airframe manufacturers at Seattle and Toulouse. They wanted to ensure they were inputting the correct weights and specifications into the evaluation.

Some detractors criticised the 767 for its 156- foot wingspan. They claimed it would create drag, and so affect performance. Conversely, the wing assisted airfield performance giving better lift, and also had air traffic control advantages. The flight paths down through France to the Spanish Mediterranean destinations can be heavily congested in summer. Flying at altitudes of between 31,000 and 35,000 feet is usual for the majority of aircraft types. However, the 767 wing provided the ability to climb to 43,000 feet, so air traffic controllers could grant clearance to a 767 at a UK-departure airport by obtaining a flight 'slot' at a higher level over France when lower levels over the Continent were saturated.

Another important consideration was what is known as 'block fuel and time' - the precise art of studying the fuel burn from engine start through taxiing, take-off, cruising, descent, approach and landing. There can be significant fuel cost differences for them in each flight segment. The most critical for Britannia was a 1,000-mile sector due to the distance to those southern Spain destinations.

Defending the A310, Airbus Industrie officials - who although they conceded that the 767 was more economical at longer ranges, suggested that there was a cross-over point against the A310 making it more fuel-efficient over shorter distances. Britannia thought it much lower than that claimed by Airbus and much lower than the critical 1,000 nautical mile flight sector. The 767 produced a better fuel-burn performance per seat than the A310 on the majority of Britannia routes.

The full payload range was another critical area to evaluate. Britannia's team considered not just the nominal performance indicated by the manuals, but also the guaranteed performance being put forward by Boeing and Airbus Industrie. The same assurances had to be forthcoming in such areas as altitude capability and noise levels.

In the context of economics, the ground rules which Britannia had gained from their 737 experience were applied to the bigger aircraft. Britannia inserted their own crew costs, handling charges, landing fees related to aircraft weight, and a host of other considerations, plus, of course, the price of the aircraft into the calculations. To compare like with like, they even paper-fitted each aircraft with the same engines.

Britannia customer services had two main concerns; in-cabin layout and function along with ground handling and turnrounds. In both the challenge was to achieve equal timing and efficiency with the 737 fleet, despite having an aircraft which would be half as big again and carry twice as many passengers.

To be economical in flying competitively-priced IT passengers, whichever airliner was chosen had to be configured in a high-density layout, a factor that did not add to the ability to give efficient cabin service.

The 757 was a single-aisle aircraft, so it was impossible to add an extra seat abreast. But with the 767 and the A310, having twin aisles, Britannia was keen to add an additional place to the rows, making eight-abreast in the 767, and nine in the A310.

Another advantage of the 767 cabin which Britannia liked, was that it had constant seat rows with its 'rectangular' fuselage rather than the more cigar-shaped A310 which necessitated a reduction in the number of seats to a row at the rear of the aircraft, smaller galleys and offered no flexibility for the location of the toilets.

The ability to increase the seats in two of the three choices, thus achieving improved seat-mile costs started to have a negative effect on the 757, which would have to remain at three seats either side of the central aisle. However, the 767 had the width to incorporate a seat configuration of two-four-two, and the slightly wider A310 could accommodate three - three - three.

It meant about thirty extra passengers could be flown in each type, though with an admittedly adverse trade-off of slightly narrower aisles. To compensate for this, the committee proposed an improvement in seat pitch allowing thirty-one inches instead of the thirty inches the airline specified in their 737s.

Detailed analysis of seat-mile costs based on these changes, compared with the 2.66p achievable over 1,000 nautical mile sectors by a new 737-200, showed 2.55p for the 767, and 2.57p for the 757 and A310, even allowing for a later revised layout proposed by Airbus Industrie.

Davison played skilfully on the rivalry of the two competing manufacturers and successfully negotiated a favourable deal for the purchase of two 767s on the understanding that three additional aircraft would follow them. He was invited to the United States to attend a Presidential task force set up to determine the safety of two-crew operation for the new, large wide-body aircraft. His experience made a significant impact on the committee, which concluded that two-crew operations could be conducted safely. All wide-body aircraft developed since have been two-crew operated.

Britannia initiated the second round of negotiations with Boeing. The airline had liaised closely with Braathens SAFE in Norway, who were also interested in the 767, over a standard specification for the aircraft. Davison asked Boeing for a second negotiation based on this standard specification and the double order. It resulted in several Boeing concessions to both companies, including participation in financing a simulator, which eliminated costs associated with the two pilot crew and the high-density configuration including additional seat-rails.

The final specification on which the contract was drawn up based on decisions on literally hundreds of permutations for items of equipment and other 'add-ons' for the 767-200.

Here is a good a place as any to explain the difference between owner and operator. Airlines and enthusiasts alike often say that an airline 'owned' this or that airliner. Indeed, it was something I used to do until corrected by Captain Mike Russell of Britannia. He once said to me, ' unless you actually saw the suitcases of money change hands, never say 'owned by'. In reality, from the 1980s onwards, many airlines did not own the airliners they flew but leased them from either a conglomerate of banks or specialist organisations. The only evidence of this was a small stainless steel plate fixed somewhere on the flight deck. An example is this plate that was once affixed to 767 G-BNCW. It shows that the aircraft was operated by Britannia Airways of Luton, but was owned by the International Lease Finance Corporation (known as ILFC) of Beverley Hills, California.

Bob Ginns: 'We had to justify every item - either it paid for itself or we did not buy it. In theory, we wanted to purchase the standard Boeing aeroplane - everything extra had to be justified by the bottom line. We certainly did not buy anything for purely cosmetic effects. That would have been the worst of all reasons.'

Eventually, the original order for two 767-200s was doubled, another ordered for 1988 delivery, and an option to be negotiated.

Models and detailed plans of the aircraft were studied to determine the best cabin layout and baggage handling arrangements to suit the specific needs of a high-density charter airline. Britannia had to consider the galleys, the galley equipment, the follow-on cabin service and every facet relating to where the passengers were seated.

An off-the-shelf galley equipment system called Atlas - developed in Europe and adopted by many scheduled airlines was made. Atlas followed a modular principle and was relatively cheap compared with tailor-made competitors. It was based on a series of slots which have the flexibility to take an oven, boxes, an aisle cart, or a combination of them. So successful was its adoption by Britannia and Braathens, that Boeing made provision to include the system in production-line 767s.

On all their aircraft so far, including the 737s, Britannia had served meals on hand-delivered individual trays. Now came the opportunity to move to carts, progressively parked down the aisles, from which cabin staff serve new-style meal boxes. The new design featured a letter-box type aperture in the front of those boxes so that, instead of having to take each tray off its a shelf to place the hot dish on it from the oven, the cabin staff now just fed the meal in from the front - a great time saver. So successful did the whole system become that the 737s were partially converted to cart service.

Time-saving on the 767 was going to be very important. It was calculated that for a full load of 273 passengers, an average flight allowed just ninety seconds to serve each passenger with a meal, drinks, duty frees, and attend to any other individual demand. This narrow time-window meant that everything had to be done to ease the flow of service down the two aisles. Here toilets were going to be a problem because people walking towards them or queuing around them formed human barriers to efficient service. The solution was to have the galleys at each end of the cabin, and the main toilets in the middle. The cabin crew were divided into two teams, each servicing up to the centre of the aircraft from the two extremes so avoiding the jams around the toilet area.

Those toilets, incidentally, caused curious problems of their own in the early days of the 767. The lavatories were vacuum-operated, their efficiency depending on a rapid swirl of water followed by a sudden whooshing noise as the clearing vacuum came into play. The waste then passed down underfloor pipes to holding tanks at the rear of the aircraft. In the early days, there were complaints of disturbing clinking noises heard down the rear cabin. The phenomenon baffled investigating engineers until cabin crew were caught throwing away ice cubes down the pan. It was these that caused the noise as they rattled their way to the back of the aircraft!

To achieve Britannia's required forty-five-minute turnround, this only left a twenty-five minutes cleaning and servicing slot because arriving and departing passengers accounted for the other twenty minutes when disembarking and embarking. The airline also had to take into account that it needed to put the maximum number of passengers into a sophisticated aeroplane using unsophisticated systems compared with those for scheduled service operators because they - Britannia - would be taking the aircraft into less advanced to parts of the world such as Banjul in West Africa.

A difficulty was created by what was possibly the only minus factor about the 767 - its fuselage

Opposite page: The 767 final assembly line at Payne Field, Everett, WA. Closest to the camera is the first 767 for Britannia. (*Britannia Airways*)

The first airline identification to appear on the assembly line is the fitment of the rudder, as shown here with this 767 to appear in the new colour scheme. *(Britannia Airways)*

shape compared to other wide-bodied aircraft. Its curvature meant that the lower deck was not big enough to take standard baggage containers side by side, so the company came up with a system that used the smaller LD2 and LD8 containers for the rear hold with a walkway alongside. It permitted both containerised and manual loading, and a large Boeing container for the front hold, which would hold both large items and any overflow from the rear. These containers, more correctly called unit load devices (ULDs) were and are a pallet or container used to load luggage, freight, and mail on wide-body aircraft and specific narrow-body aircraft. It allows a large quantity of cargo to be bundled into a single unit. Since this leads to fewer units to load, it saves ground crews time and effort and helps prevent delayed flights. Each ULD has its packing list (or manifest) so that its contents can be tracked.

Britannia was always on the lookout for ways to speed up overseas turnarounds; one such idea was the underfloor stowage of all the rubbish in the aircraft. The cabin crew dumped everything into a fireproof container which was emptied and replaced at the home airport. It also proved to be a good flight safety point because on a long flight it removed the need to have rubbish bags blocking the doors of the aircraft, which previously had been the only place cabin crew could put them. By putting rubbish

through the hatch in the floor, it meant they did not have to be offloaded abroad, and there was more space for the cabin crew operating in the aircraft.

While planning for the 767, the decision was taken by Britannia to maintain a two-person flight deck crew the same as with the 737s, even though Boeing had designed the flight deck for three crew operation. Bob Parker-Eaton, Customer Services Director: 'It always annoyed me over the years that some of the overhead lockers in aircraft were taken up with overnight bags and other items for the cabin crew when they should have been available for passengers. I managed to get Boeing to design a cupboard to fill the space left by the smaller flight deck, for cabin crew stowage. Over the years that became a standard Boeing option'.

The Boeing 767 was selected, and in March orders were placed for two aircraft to be delivered in 1984, plus options were taken out for a further one for 1985 and two for 1986 deliveries respectively.

Subsequently, the 1985 option was converted to a firm order for two aircraft. In June an order was placed for a further three Boeing 737s for delivery in 1982, . Coinciding with this last order the airline also specified the General Electric CF6-80A as its powerplant for the new Boeing 767s.

Britannia opted for a 265 passenger capacity in its 767s, and it was the first airline to select the high-

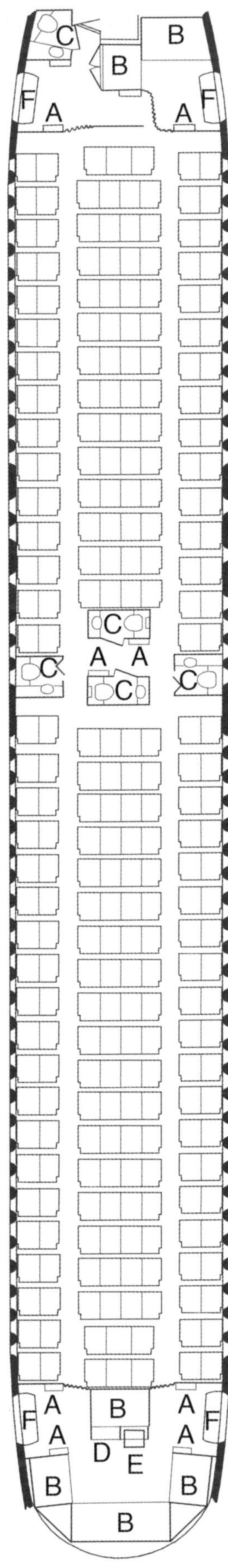

Left: The interior of a Britannia Airways 767.

A - Cabin crew station.
B - Galley unit.
C - Toilet unit with hand-wash basin.
D - Fold-down shelf in rear galley.
E - Waste chute into lower lobe.
F - Passenger door with escape slide in bustle.

Most of the seat-pitch in both cabins was set to thirty-one inches.

Each cabin had a video projector shing forward onto a screen for movies.

Below: a cross-section of the main cabin, showing the dimensions.

density version - the airliner was to have more doors, strengthened main deck floor, revised cabin layout. Eight abreast seating gave a 2+4+2 arrangement on the twin-aisle configuration, and the majority of the seats offered a thirty-one-inch pitch. The galleys were located at the front and rear of the accommodation - the main galley aft with all the toilets at the centre cabin except for one at the forward end. At maximum, the number of seats could have been increased to 290, but this would have involved the retention of only minimum galley facilities. Up on the flight deck, Britannia opted for a two pilot arrangement.

With the advent of the 2,600 nautical mile range Boeing 767, however, the average length of the airline's flights was set for a significant stretch. The new aircraft would be capable of reaching all Mediterranean and West African destinations non-stop from the UK, and of flying to points in East Africa with only one stop.

The customer complement of the 767 was planned to be just over double that of the 130 seat 737 so with the new aircraft representing, in effect, ten more 737s Britannia is projected its fleet size by 1986 at the equivalent of forty-two 737s, this implying the acquisition of three more of the smaller twinjets between 1983-1986. The first year of operations with the 767, 1984, was expected to see the aircraft rostered on the routes where the airline

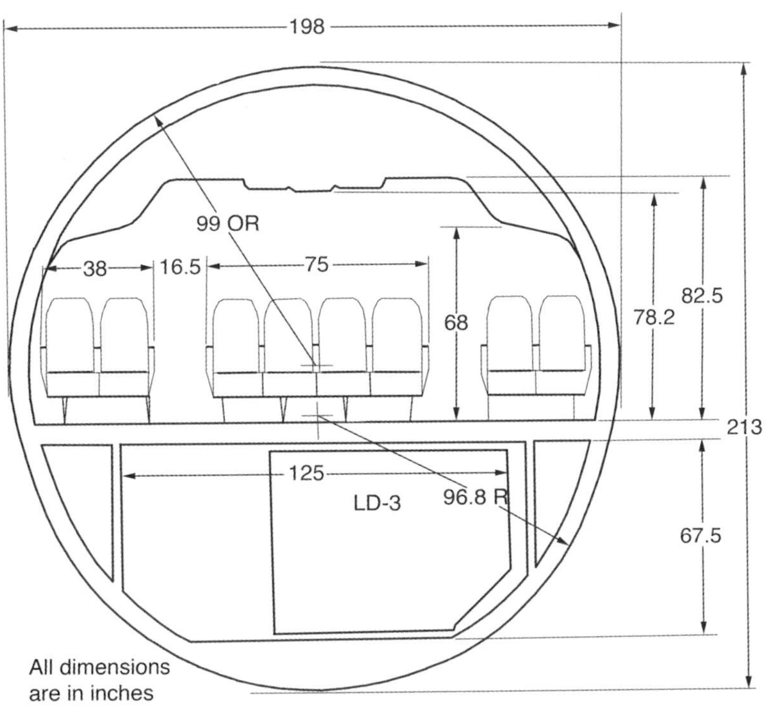

All dimensions are in inches

Right: The signing ceremony for the first 767. Left to right: Joe Sutter, Boeing executive Vice-President, Derek Davison, Boeings Lond-based chief Chris Longridge and Bob Brumage, Boeing Regional Director, Contract, Europe.

Below: One of the 767s is prepared for fitting out. *(both Britannia Airways)*

handlers and maintenance engineers, and the real size of the effort begins to emerge.

The 767 operating costs were meagre when compared to older generation aircraft. The 767 proved to be reliable and cost-effective, the GE engines of 48,000 pounds thrust enabled the aircraft to cruise at 540 mph at 43,000 feet with fuel consumption of 1,166 gallons per hour. With the arrival of the 767, Britannia moved forward considerably with passenger comfort and, despite the new aircraft's larger capacity, lost nothing in terms of ease of ground handling and speed turn round.

has more than five 737 flights per week, for example, to Tenerife, Malaga, Alicante, Palma, Corfu, Athens and other destinations from departure points such as Luton, Gatwick, Manchester, Glasgow and perhaps in 1985 - Birmingham.

Buying just one 767 left little change out of £30 million at 1984 rates, but that was only a part of the capital expenditure in which Britannia has been involved. Add on the costs of erecting and equipping a new hangar at Luton; of buying and installing as a joint venture with Europe's second 767 operator (Braathens SAFE of Norway) a Rediffusion simulator, also at Luton; of designing and introducing a new livery for the whole fleet which then had to be extended to a full corporate identity programme, and of training staff at all levels from the flight deck, through cabin attendants to ground

Britannia intended that 767 passengers would be kept happy with another advance through the introduction of unique in-flight entertainment. It was based on a multiplex system enabling all the commands for the entertainment programme to be sent down one channel.

Part of this included the introduction of an exciting innovation in the cabins, the use of PDADS (Passenger Digital Auto Display System), developed in the USA by the Colt company. PDADS offered the facility to display messages on small repeater screens, seven of which were fitted in the 767 cabins. They were used primarily to display aircraft ground speed and altitude throughout the flight, starting when the aircraft reached 50 mph. Time to go to destination, and local time at the destination, could also be displayed, and PDADS had the facility to store several messages, which could be scrolled or displayed statically in two rows of up to 20 characters each. Developed from systems used in business aircraft, PDADS was evaluated by Britannia in a Boeing 737 and proved so popular that a three-display system was fitted in all the airline's 737s.

Video screens in the 767 cabins were used to display a pre-flight emergency procedures briefing, an eleven-minute feature on 'Britannia's World' details of duty-free sales - which accounted for a substantial proportion of the airline's net profits - and short films featured comedian Tom O'Connor. There was also a 'Thinking of Your Next Holiday' clip - featuring Thomson Travel products of course - to be shown on inbound flights, and longer films could be displayed if flight times allowed.

Each passenger could receive six audio channels through the headsets provided - usually free of charge. On inbound flights, passengers were given a comprehensive review of the news they had missed at home during their fortnight's holiday. It was under an arrangement with Britain's Independent Television News, and the appearance of the news review was guaranteed to make passengers scramble for their headsets. These free headsets were provided another saving in cabin crew time by preventing the need to tour the cabin collecting a fee.

When the first of the 767s arrived at Luton on 8 February 1984, it was much more than being just the first new type added to Britannia's fleet for more than a dozen years: it was adding a new dimension to the whole of the airline's operation. Understandably, the popping of champagne corks came close to drowning out the fanfare sounded by trumpeters of the RAF Central Band as G-BKVZ nosed into the new £4 million hangar for the first

time. The building, formally opened on 1 March 1984 was named Parkins House, in memory of Britannia's former technical director, Geoffrey Parkins.

The 767 had flown non-stop from Seattle in 8 hours 42 minutes under the command of Capt Dave Hopkins, the company's flight operations director, accompanied by the chief 767 training Captain Eric Turner and the 767 fleet captain Nick Pennington.

Among the 43 passengers on board was Derek Davison, who had earlier accepted the keys of the 767 from Boeing chairman Thornton' T' Arnold Wilson in Seattle, and a group of Britannia staff who had completed Boeing's training courses. Britannia's chairman and chief executive explained some of the reasons that led to the selection of the 767, including 'the best fuel burn per seat of any available today' and the twin-aisle layout with toilets in the middle of the cabin and galleys at each end, helping to reduce conflict and congestion in the aisles. Moreover, the 767's performance and economics had actually improved since the order was placed; weight reduction, lower drag and better engine performance had combined to produce a five per cent improvement in overall economics, while clearance to go to higher operating weights would allow Britannia to fly full payloads over even higher ranges than the 3,000 nautical miles required initially - which was sufficient to enable the airline's longest route to Banjul, The Gambia, to be flown non-stop.

Compared with the 737, the 767 produced a

Below: The first two Boeing 767s are prepared for delivery at Boeing's Paine Field in Washington State. Right: The aircraft were fitted with Passenger Digital Audio Display Systems. *(both Britannia Airways)*

166

Former Conservative Secretary of State Sir Nicholas Ridley accompanied by Captain David Davison at the naming ceremony of Boeing 767 G-BKVZ *Sir Winston Churchill*. *(Britannia Airways)*

The naming ceremony for Boeing 767 G-BKPW christened *Earl Mountbatten of Burma* by Patricia Knatchbull, the 2nd Countess Moutbatten escorted by her sons Phillip and Timothy. To their left is Captain David Davison. *(Britannia Airways)*

twenty-seven per cent better figure for fuel burn per seat, based on a thirty-one-inch pitch seating arrangement. Capital investment per seat was calculated by Britannia to be some $130,000 for the smaller aeroplane and around $175,000 for the 767, and the direct comparative costs were put at 4.07 cents per seat-km for the 737, 4.09 cents for the 767. The economics of the big aeroplane were obvious, but in Davison's view, big was not necessarily beautiful; he stated that there was a too big airliner and a big enough one. The 767 was regarded as big enough for Britannia and could even appear to be too big in the eyes of tour operators, who had not previously had to think in terms of 273-passenger loads. There consequently was been something of a role reversal, with the airline leading the tour operator rather than merely responding to the latter's demands.

Britannia's second 767 first took to the skies in October 1983 and was used to obtain the British type certificate - costs associated with meeting British requirements totalled some $7 million. As the basic 767 had previously been certificated only for a maximum of 255 passengers, FAA approval also was needed to increase the maximum to 290, involving the use of two overwing emergency escape hatches over the wing each side, instead of only one each side. The second aircraft arrived at Luton later in February, and on 8 March was the subject of a naming ceremony by the 2nd Countess Mountbatten of Burma and her two youngest sons Phillip and Timothy,when it became *The Earl Mountbatten of Burma* after her father. The second 767 arrived in March 1984 and was named *Sir Winston Churchill*.

Revenue operations had already begun, however, with a flight from Luton to Monastir, Tunisia, on 18 February and the first operation from Manchester on

Boeing 767 G-BLKW is re-supplied and loaded with freight in the underfloor hold before another charter flight. (*Britannia Airways*)

25 February, to Faro.

While 767 flight crew training proceeded, just as much attention was given to the preparation of cabin personnel. Of more than eight hundred cabin crews employed by the company, only over two hundred were picked to operate on the 767, based on one month on the new type alternating with two months on the 737. Except for some ski flights, when short duration (such as 55 minutes to Munich) puts a heavy load on the stewardesses, the standard cabin staff totals seven on the 273-seat 767, compared with four on the 130-seat 737; nine were carried on the other flights.

A plethora of variants

With business increasing briskly, Britannia Airways leased a Boeing 737 from Transavia Holland for the summer season, this aircraft mainly appearing on

G-AVRN in the new colour scheme at the old Ellinikon Airport Athens, but with a 'raw nose' - for whatever reason the nose-cone has not been painted. (*Richard Vandervord*)

Left: two Flight Attendants in the new uniform (*Britannia Airways*)

schedules from Newcastle. Not all the expansion was in the air: the airline opened a new operations centre at its Luton headquarters during the year, again emphasizing the importance of Luton as one of the airports serving the London area.

During the 1981/82 season the airline carried four million passengers and ordered two more Boeing 737s for delivery in 1983. The fleet had now increased to 26 aircraft, and a further two were leased from Transavia Holland (PH-TVR), and Eagle Air of Iceland (TF-VLK).

In January 1982 a new contract was signed with Pilgrim Air. The agreement covered operations for three years and called for departures from Luton and London (Gatwick) to Bologna, Milan, Naples, Palermo, Pisa, Rimini, Rome, Turin and Venice. In addition, summer services were operated to Brindisi and Cagliari.

The following month saw the collapse of Laker Airways and consequently its two tour operators, Laker Air Travel and Arrowsmith, who operated from Gatwick and Manchester. Laker Airways also flew for many other tour operators including OSL and Ellerman; thus, many rival firms, including Thomson Holidays, increased their operations. The end result was that Britannia leased five aircraft for the summer season from Air Florida, Eagle Air, Transavia Holland, and two from Quebecair. The Air Florida and Transavia aircraft were generally based at Glasgow; the Eagle Air Boeing 737 at Gatwick; and the two from Quebecair at Manchester. With the sale of Arrowsmith to Greenall Whitley by the receivers of Laker Airways, Arrowsmith contracted with Britannia to fly its summer operations, the first flight taking place from Manchester on 12 March 1982.

Naming Names

By the early 1980s Britannia started naming their fleet of 737s after 'famous Britons', but was later to include those of other nationalities as well.

The names included Sir James Watt FRS FRSE, a Scottish inventor, mechanical engineer, and chemist; Sir Francis Drake, English sea captain, privateer, naval officer and explorer of the Elizabethan era; General James Wolfe, British Army officer known for his victory in 1759 over the French at the Battle of the Plains of Abraham in Quebec; Florence Nightingale OM, RRC, DStJ an English social reformer and statistician, and the founder of modern nursing: Sir Walter Raleigh, an English landed gentleman, writer, poet, soldier, politician, courtier, spy and explorer; Lieutenant-Colonel Sir Arthur Whitten Brown, KBE, navigator of the first successful non-stop transatlantic flight; Sir Barnes Wallis CBE FRS RDI FRAeS, an English scientist, engineer and inventor; Reginald Joseph Mitchell CBE, FRAeS, an English aeronautical engineer who worked for Supermarine Aviation, Jean Gardner Batten CBE OSC, a New Zealand aviatrix, John Eric Bartholomew, OBE is known by his stage name Eric Morecambe, an English comedian. The list went on and on. and was later to include the 757s and 767s after *Britannia Airwaves* ran a naming competition in 1998. (see fleet lists)

By the spring of 1982, Britannia's fleet of 737s had reached the impressive total of twenty-nine - in several sub-variants with different versions of the JT8D turbofan, different fuel capacities and different operating weights. With the collapse of Laker Airways, five more 737s were leased for the summer operations that year (two from Quebecair, two from Transavia and one from Eagle Air); this introduced still more variants so far as maintenance, flight deck and cabin arrangements were concerned, but the extra business that became available allowed the company to break the four-million barrier in passengers carried; statistics for 1979-1983 went like this:

	Rev pax/km	Passengers
1979	3,224,813	5,640,529
1980	3,478,492	6,353,030
1981	3,893,429	7,162,695
1982	4,084,410	7,215,814
1983	4,401,800	7,712,447

The Civil Aviation Authority approved Britannia's seat sale plan in April 1982 but ruled that only a maximum of fifteen per cent of the aircraft capacity - twenty seats - could be used for this purpose and that Gibraltar would be excluded from the operation along with all flights from Gatwick, Luton and Stansted airports. The airline felt that this was unfair to passengers residing in the south-east of England, but the CAA argued that the airline would distract passengers from other British scheduled airlines operating from Heathrow and Gatwick. Britannia produced details of its fares that represented dramatic savings over the scheduled airfares.

One aircraft, two colour schemes!

Cessna 421 Golden Eagle G-BRIT was used by the company to ferry crews and urgent spares around for a good number of years
(both Richard Vandervord)

Above: Sir Frank Whittle, inventor of the jet engine, with Britannia Managing Director Dave Hopkins (right) beside 767 G-BKLW.

Left: Jean Batten in the Captains seat of 737 G-BGYL which was named after her in March 1981. She is assisted here by First Officer Suzanne Eastbury
(both Britannia Airways)

Meanwhile, in July, the Boeing 767 demonstrator visited Luton during a sales tour of Europe and the Gulf States. In the same month, Mr Iain Sproat minister responsible for Civil Aviation opened a new £500,000 administration office block housing the Customer Services Department and Director's Suite for Britannia.

During October, after British Airways announced its latest route cuts, Britannia applied to the Civil Aviation Authority for leisure orientated scheduled licences from Glasgow, Manchester and Gatwick to Palma, Alicante and Faro; however, the application was subsequently withdrawn in early 1983. In the field of Customer Services, the airline produced a booklet designed for first-time fliers which stated that around seventy-five per cent of passengers on all UK airlines were travelling for leisure reasons. The booklet was primarily intended for travel agents and answered the typical questions put to them by first time

For instance;

Britannia	Scheduled Operator
Manchester-Palma £85	Gatwick-Palma £152
Manchester-Venice £77	Manchester -Venice £128
Glasgow-Lisbon £93	Gatwick-Lisbon £172

In May, Rediffusion Simulations Limited announced that a £4.5 million order had been placed with them for a Boeing 767 flight simulator for joint use by Britannia Airways and the Norwegian airline, Braathens. The simulator was installed and operational at Luton in 1984.

fliers. Mr Bob Hutchison, Customers Services Manager stated, 'It surprises many of us in the travel trade that as many as one in five of our customers are flying for the first time'. That was even though around twelve million Britons holidayed abroad annually.

Britannia's fleet of Boeing 737s reached a peak of thirty-one in the spring of 1983 with the delivery of its two newest aircraft, but the total reverted to twenty-nine in the autumn when two 737s that were owned by OSL but operated by Britannia in its own livery, were sold. Capacity was to be maintained and then increased, with the arrival early in 1984 of the first two Boeing 767s.

As would be expected, Britannia was closely identified with Thomson Holidays within the activities of the Thomson Travel Group, under the chairmanship of John Sauvage - who had preceded Derek Davison as Britannia's managing director. About fifty-three per cent of Britannia's flying in 1984 was for Thomson, this providing almost all of the latter's requirement; but Britannia also flew for many other tour operators, such as Ellermans, Arrowsmith, Budget and OSL. It also had contracts with the MoD for trooping flights to Gibraltar, an agreement with GB Airways to operate scheduled service between Gatwick and Gibraltar on the latter's behalf and a newly-won CAA licence to operate a scheduled service from Manchester to Palma. It had UK approval to sell up to fifteen per cent of capacity offered out of 'non-London' airports in the UK on a seat-only basis (not as part of a holiday package), but full use of this cannot be made until other governments gave similar approval.

Working the 'Troopers'

It was a surprise to many when they learned that Britannia also did MoD (Ministry of Defence) flights, flying military personnel to various airfields throughout Europe. The flights, which dated back to the very early days were known as troopers, flying mainly from Luton to destinations such as RAF Wildenrath (WID), Gatow (GWW), Gutersloh (GUT) and Gibraltar (GIB).

Many military personnel remember the 'Smith Air' desk at Luton where they would get checked in by a couple of squaddies in blazers and slacks as opposed to all the other offices where there were more attractive people, even if they were to go on a Britannia flight. The idea was that it wouldn't stand out as a target for the IRA, but there were so many lads with green hold-alls strewn about the place it was impossible to mistake it for anything other than what it was.

The flights were mostly short-haul except GIB, but all were very organised and disciplined, meaning the troops and their families knew precisely how to board and sit in their seats without any assistance from the crew. Indeed many cabin crews regarded it as a pleasure to watch. One anomaly on the troopers was that the aircraft had to have a specific set of inflight magazines specifically flagged 'Ministry of Defence flights only.'

Despite the discipline of the Services, not every floight was well-behaved. One passenger, who wishes to remain anonymous recalled one flight: The majority of the other passengers were undergraduates (UAS or UOTC), who had been drinking for most of the day in the air terminal bar because the aircraft had been delayed at Luton with technical problems. When we were eventually loaded, the movers could not reconcile the number of pax with the manifest. The movers called the roll with the inevitable result and were on the point of offloading us when the flight deck door opened and

Britannia flew so many 'troopers' that they had specific Inflight magazines for those services. (*Britannia Airways*)

they were informed that if the aircraft did not leave soon, the crew would be out of hours and would be staying overnight. Faced with the prospect of finding transit accommodation for a bunch of drunken officer cadets, the movers decided to close the door and let Luton sort out the problem!

Carrying Air Cadets was not an uncommon event, often to Cyprus or Gibraltar. Gavin Scott: 'Doing a GIB was a different kettle of fish, the roster would read LTN-GIB-???-LTN. Flying to GIB in the 1980s was not straight forward. Being classed as a military flight Britannia was not allowed to enter Spanish airspace due to the border being closed. We flew over part of France and Portugal to finally land in GIB, The scary part was not the landing, but looking out for stray cars as the main road crossed the runway, but the fighter aircraft already parked in the airfield. On our return we had to Tech stop for fuel somewhere in Portugal, I have no idea which airfield, but it was not the usual ones we were accustomed to, I am pretty sure it was a military airfield somewhere in the south of Portugal'.

The troopers continued for many years, but as the British bases in West Germany were downgraded in the Rhine area following German reunification, this work was passed along to other operators. That did not mean that all trooping flights ceased: Troops were flown out as part of the Falklands conflict and later Britannia took over trooping services around the time of the first Gulf War when the RAF were otherwise occupied. Legend has it that The 767 was met as it approached the Falklands by a RAF fighter escort. It seems that they had heard there were civilian aircraft coming with real air hostesses so were holding up cards with their names and phone numbers apparently!

With the withdrawal of British troops from Germany, a good number of bases and airfields closed, and with them the departure of the Britannia' troopers', usually flown in and out of RAF Gatow. The final weekly 737 rotation was operated by Captain John Crew, who had also flown some of the very early trooping flights back in 1969. During the turnaround, Captain Crew found time to accept a commemorative certificate from RAF Gatow Station Commander, Group Captain Feenan and Captain Culter of 62 Transport and Movement Squadron, Royal Logistics Corps. All returning passengers also received a similar certificate. The flights were replaced with discounted fares on scheduled British Airways flights out of Berlin until British Forces finally left.

The liberalisation of air traffic regulations within Europe, in which there were some encouraging signs of movement, were welcomed by Britannia. Less welcome was the forthcoming privatisation of British Airways unless some reins were placed on the latter's activities in the non-scheduled market. The fear is that British Airtours

Captain John Crew accepts a certificate marking the last trooping flight into and out of RAF Gatow.
(*Britannia Airways*)

Air Force escort! A 1435 Flight McDonnell Douglas Phantom FGR.2 escorts a Britannia 767 into the Falklands. The picture must have been taken before the end of July 1992 when the Phantoms were replaced with Tornado F3s.(*MoD*)

could undercut all the other carriers in bidding for Inclusive Tour business by using depreciated aircraft made available to it on favourable terms by parent British Airways.

As the holiday industry grew throughout the 1970s, the tour operators found that their clients were demanding more flights from airports more local to them. As a result, the number of UK airports from which Britannia operated grew, and as many as twenty-five departure points could be in use in the high season. During the summer of 1986, the airline flew from nineteen UK and Eire airports to seventy-six overseas destinations. As a primarily charter operator, Britannia sold seat capacity on its aircraft to tour operators who, in turn, sold these to the public, usually as part of a 'package' holiday. In addition to flights for its sister companies Thomson Holidays and Portland Holidays, Britannia also operated on behalf of many other well-known names including Global, Ellerman, Inghams, P&O Cruises, Swan Hellenic Cruises, Pilgrim Air and Tjaereborg. In all the airline flew clients from more than 100 tour operators and travel companies.

In 1985 Britannia began its first scheduled service with flights connecting Manchester and Palma. Three more services planned started in the Spring of 1986: Manchester - Tenerife, Manchester - Malaga and Gatwick - Tenerife. Services from both Manchester and Gatwick to Las Palmas were to be added later.

Scheduled services were easy to plan for due to their regularity; charter flights were less so. Forward planning for each summer season commenced in the previous June when the tour operators approached the airline with their flying requirements. In September a graph of the tour operators' requirements was plotted to show each aircraft's workload and the pattern of flights from each UK airport. Amendments were made to this graph as necessary, and when this had been finalised it was returned to the tour operators for their approval. Once this was obtained the slot times were submitted at the Airline and Airports Conference which takes place twice yearly in June and November. This conference enabled representatives from airlines and airports in all parts of the world to meet face to face and discuss or make adjustments to the slot times desired by each airline. When these were finalised, the airline can compile its draft for the following summer's operation.

Britannia did not allocate each individual flight number but instead issued each tour operator with a specific batch of numbers which the tour operator assigned to its flights. This information was then fed through the airline's computer and each aircraft is allocated its routes as dictated by operational and engineering requirements.

Mention has already been made of 'ad-hoc charters' that constituted a small but exciting part of the airline's business. Providing there was an aeroplane available, a Britannia Boeing could be chartered in a range of configurations; from 130 seats (in the case of the 737s) to 'executive' layouts or a mixture of passenger and cargo.

Catering for the flight could range from standard economy class meals to full cordon bleu menus with 'real' cutlery, glassware and crockery worthy of the First Class service of any

Boeing 767-304 parked outside the hangar at Luton. *(Britannia Airways)*

international airline. Customers for ad hoc charters have ranged from car manufacturers taking motor journalists to a launch of a new model to film companies taking crews and equipment to exotic and not-so-exotic locations in the world. One man chartered a 737 to take himself and some of his friends Halley's comet-watching!

Gavin Scott recalled one particular VIP charter: 'In late August 1982, my roster was suddenly changed to an early morning report at 0600 hours to crewing, where I discovered I was part of the crew doing LTN-ABZ-GVA (Luton - Aberdeen - Geneva). During the pre-flight briefing, we were informed that it was the Aberdeen Football Club going to Geneva, where we were going to lock up the aeroplane for two nights with the crew staying at The Noga Hilton Hotel, at that time their flag hotel.'

'Positioning empty to Aberdeen we were wondering what to expect, for the whole service was new to us all, free drinks, three course meal of smoked salmon, prawn cocktail, starter steak/fish main course, and some dessert, with a choice of tea or coffee, all to be served on most beautiful porcelain with stainless steel cutlery in approximately two hours.'

'The seating arrangement for VIP pax was, first six or seven rows Directors and guests, then seven to eight rows for manager, Alex Ferguson (now Sir Alex of Man. Utd fame) training staff, and players, the next two to three rows for supporters, and finally the press, being a European Game

there were quite a few of them. From meeting a few of them in the past, I knew they liked to participate in the art of libating! While we were planning the order of service it was decided to go with drinks, meals and duty-free. Being Scottish I knew what to expect - free booze to an aeroplane full of Scots, it didn't take much working out! I suggested a litre of vodka, a litre of Gin and a litre of Whisky for the press with ice and mixers, I can't remember if Chris Grace, our No.1 agreed or not, but I did it anyway. She left us alone to look after the real VIPs. Everything went as sweet as a nut, as they say. Inbound was precisely the same except when about ten minutes before the seat belt sign came on we were in the galley preparing for landing. It was not an everyday landing, for we had to separate 130 cups, saucers, plates and store them in separate air larders! While doing that, a journalist opened the curtain and said of all the flights he and his colleagues had been on, they had never been so well looked after and offered me a hand full of paper money - I had to explain to him that Britannia crew never accept gratuities of any description, so he returned to his seat shaking his head in bewilderment, Job satisfaction at the highest level (excuse the pun)'.

'Finally, two days in Geneva, what did we do? In the usual Britannia way, we visited a science museum, an art museum, the Toblerone factory, went to a ski slope, swam in Lake Geneva, and visited a cuckoo clock factory, by the time we found the Cartier shop it was closed'.

Chapter 6

Milestones and Going Long-Haul

The 1980s and 1990s were not only a time of expansion for the airline; it was also a time of reaching a myriad of milestones. According to published Press Releases, it was also a time when the airline was showered with awards. Some of these were marketing-driven, and of no great importance - others were authentic and something of which every employee could be proud.

An early 'milestone celebration' and a precursor of things to come occurred in 1978. It took the form if a small, four-page promotional leaflet that stated 'Britannia Airways celebrate the 10th Anniversary of the introduction of the Boeing 737 on their routes'. The booklet - which prominently featured G-AVRL - explained that '...in the ensuing ten years, we have increased our fleet to seventeen of these aircraft, and we have two more on order. In those ten years our 737s have amassed altogether some 360,000 flying hours covering over 160 million miles, have carried 15 million passengers and have consumed 250 million gallons of fuel. This year alone, we expect to fly 63,000 hours, carrying well over two million passengers'.

Coming of Age - and on to the Silver Anniversary
1983 saw Britannia celebrate its 21st Birthday with a cake, exhibition and a party.

Two years later there was another milestone. On Tuesday 26 November 1985 over seven hundred staff attended a special party and exhibition to mark the first million Boeing 737 flying hours - a feat achieved in just fifteen years at an average of nearly

Operating under the advertising slogan 'Pride in Service', in 1983 the airline celebrated 21 years of operation.
(Britannia Airways)

Banners in the hangar roof proclaim 'One Million Flying Hours', a sight that met the seven hundred partygoers who were addressed by Chairman Derek Davision standing on a somewhat rickety plastic chair! Apart from the party, there was also a exhibition of aircraft parts on display. *(all Britannia Airways)*.

667,000 hours a year!

Two years after that, on Thursday 30 April 1987, Britannia celebrated its 25th Anniversary with a party in Parkins House, otherwise known as the 767 hangar. Over nine hundred employees partied the night away below a colourful canopy of parachutes, with displays of photographs and momentoes chronicling the twenty-five-year history of the airline. Every member received a copy of the commissioned book *Flying to the Sun* by Geoffrey Cuthbert and an acrylic commemorative plaque. Before cutting a specially baked anniversary cake, Britannia's Chairman Derek Davidson said 'Our success over the last 25 years has been due to the way in which the whole Britannia team works together to achieve the objective of always being the best in the business. As it has been the recipe for success in the past, it will continue to be so in the future, and it goes a long way to guaranteeing that the next 25 years will be even more successful'.

Passengers on a Britannia 737 flying from Manchester to Palma also found themselves unexpectedly involved in the birthday events. The flight on 5 May duplicated the first-ever commercial flights by the airline between the same points on the same day in 1962. The flight received a champagne

Top: One hangar, one 767, one Chairman and 400 members of staff celebrate twenty-five years.

Above: Britannia Chairman Derek Davison 'cuts the cake' to mark the 25th SAnniversary celebrations.

Right: Geoffrey Cuthbert's company - commissioned book 'Flying to the Sun' and the acrylic plaque presented to each employee.

Above: Britannia Chairman Derek Davison and Gil Thompson, Chief Executive of Manchester Airport gives a champagne toast to Britannia's 25th Anniversary flight from Manchester to Palma on 5 May 1987. It was a quarter-century to the day that a Euravia Constellation operated their first commerical service.

Below: HRH Prince Charles is introduced to Britannia Cabin Staff by Head of Cabin Services, Margaret Johnson at Britannia's 25th Anniversary event for the airlines major customers at the Guards Polo Club, Windsor. *(both Britannia Airways)*

send off with passengers on the flight being offered a complimentary 'Bucks Fizz' to toast the airline. On arrival, passengers and crew received a special welcome from Palma airport officials.

Britannia also marked the 25th Anniversary for major customers by hosting a polo match at the Guards Polo Club, Windsor on 23 May. Heavy rain prevented play on the day - two teams were to compete for the Britannia Airways Trophy - but all enjoyed the lunch. His Royal Highness the Prince of Wales who was to have played in one of the polo teams attended the function after lunch and talked with guests.

Then we come to 1992. Britannia was voted Charter Airline of the year for the second year running by *Travel Trade Gazette*. Confirming the view that Britannia was 'Better By Far' than all the competitors, the award was just one of a whole host of awards received by Britannia that year...

In February leading international airline business publication, *'Air Transport World,'* presented Britannia with the Market Development award in its 19th Annual World Airline Awards held in Washington DC. The first time in the history of presenting the awards that a charter airline had ever won, Britannia was commended for providing outstanding 'value for money air travel 'and for its 'considerable record of aviation innovation', including its recent introduction of Royal Service.

Britannia was voted top charter carrier in the airline section of the *Daily Telegraph* Parent-Friendly Campaign. The campaign, established in May 1992, aimed to encourage businesses to improve the services and facilities they provide for parents and young children and involved a survey completed by more than 36,000 parents nationwide. And so it went on.

One milestone that certainly put Britannia in a new charter class with the passengers was the introduction of Inflight entertainment - or IFE as it's dubbed in the trade. Inflight movies had been around since the 1930s, when a projector would be set up in the aisle, and the sound blasted out from a single speaker, its volume cranked up to compete with the roar of the engines.

By the 1990s, movies became just one side of the elaborate IFE programming that the major airlines offered and something that was rapidly growing. On Britannia, passengers could choose between ten audio channels called Royal Service Radio, and at least four hours of continuous quality television termed Royal Service TV, as well as the latest feature films on long-haul routes. This line-up offeredBritannia passengers more choice and quality than on any other charter airline.

'Feel like a laugh?' asked the promotional material. 'Watch Jasper Carrott or Blackadder on television. Perhaps something more highbrow? Try some relaxing classical music by selecting 'The Great Composers' on channel 9. Need to amuse the kids? Choose the unique Jet Cadets cartoon programme. There is something for everyone'.

A pair of Britannia 737s, G-BADP closest to the camera, with G-AVRN behind. *(Kaz Ale Collection)*

But how is all this TV and music chosen, and by whom? The simple answer was that it was the passengers' choice. Britannia carried out continuous research to find out what customers want and kept abreast of the music charts and TV ratings to make the programming was contemporary as possible.

'The focus of our TV programming is on comedy,' explained Michael Earley, Britannia's product manager responsible for IFE. 'Detailed market research showed this to be a firm favourite with our passengers who, after all, are on holiday and in the mood to enjoy themselves'.

'Other popular strands include pop videos, cartoons, travel features and wildlife, though with the latter you have to tread carefully. Animals in the wild may look cute and cuddly, but they have a habit of killing and eating each other, which can be off-putting when you're tucking into lunch!'

'Every season I viewed anything up to a hundred hours of British TV programmes to select the very best line-upline-up,' said Michael Earley. Movies are selected on a route basis: on Florida flights with lots of children heading for Disneyland, the films screened will be quite different from the flight to, say, India, with its mostly adult audience.

Britannia offered a massive variety of radio shows stretching fifteen hours across the ten channels - more than any competing airline. These exclusive programmes are compiled for the airline by IFE specialists, Inflflight Productions, in London's West End.

The world of IFE has its very own 'Oscars', presented annually by the WAEA (World Airline Entertainment Association). More than ninety of the

Boeing 767s only just fitted in the hangar at Luton, as the clearance of the tail of G-BPFV shows. *(Kaz Ale Collection)*

Above: The Luton Airport apron, seen from overhead the runway with the two Britannia Hangars, the developed passenger terminal on the right, the Fire Station cenre left and, on the extreme right, 'The Spotters Caff', short term parking and Spectators car park.*(Kaz Ale Collection)*

Left: Skyscene inflight magazine from the Summer of 1993. The only sign it was from Britannia Airways was the tiny gold 'Royal' logo centred under ther 'Y' *(authors Collection)*

widebodies, and it seems that IT passengers particularly like big aeroplanes. But Britannia's 767s were the only charter widebodies which had their cabins designed to suit the particular task that IT airline cabin crew faced, and they even had video entertainment (a Boeing optional extra) wired-in at delivery. They also had seven flight information displays in the cabin, providing information on how fast, high, and how long to go, which made things easier for Capt Speaking and the cabin crew. Safety briefings were shown on video which reduced the chances of catcalls and bad behaviour towards cabin crew if there happened to be a group of 'yobbos' in holiday high spirits on board.

So what would we be watching as we jet into the 21st century from the viewpoint of 1992? The future of IFE looked very exciting, with 'interactive IFE' - Nintendo games, telephones connected by satellite to anywhere in the world, hotel and car reservations and shopping from inflight catalogues - already in development. There was even talk of an inflight casino for those who fancied a flutter!

By the time the 40th Anniversary rolled around, those within the company were starting to think that

world's top airlines compete for the honours, and Britannia claimed two golds, a silver and a bronze, as well as being nominated for Best Overall Inflight Entertainment. Just to be nominated rates the airline in the top five in the world; Britannia was the only charter airline to have won.

IFE had other advantages. Surveys of passenger reactions to the airline travel included in their holiday regularly gave Britannia highest marks among charter carriers and Britannia's 767s won highest marks of all when the questions become specific. The latter was easy to understand because Britannia was one of only three UK charter operators which flew

Long-haul IFE, 1990s style! Darkened cabins, drop-down screens and paper programmes.
(Britannia Airways)

forty years was a good long time to survive. Then, about six months before the event would have taken place, the attacks on the Twin Towers in the USA happened, and the world changed. As Kevin Hatton said in a letter to staff dated 3 May 2002: 'We had planned to mark the occasion in a number of ways. However, we are all too aware of the effect on the entire travel industry caused by the events of last September and that it is only sensible that we are prudent in our expenditure. That said, we have commissioned a book by Ian Ormes called 'A Chartered Success' which will be published in the summer and every member of staff will receive a complimentary copy. The book tells the story of the airline through the eyes of the staff who have made it and who have made it successful'.

The name was selected through a competition ran for Britannia staff. The eventual winning title from internal auditor Kevan Findlay was selected by the Communications Team and Managing Director Kevin Hatton from an entry field of over fifty.

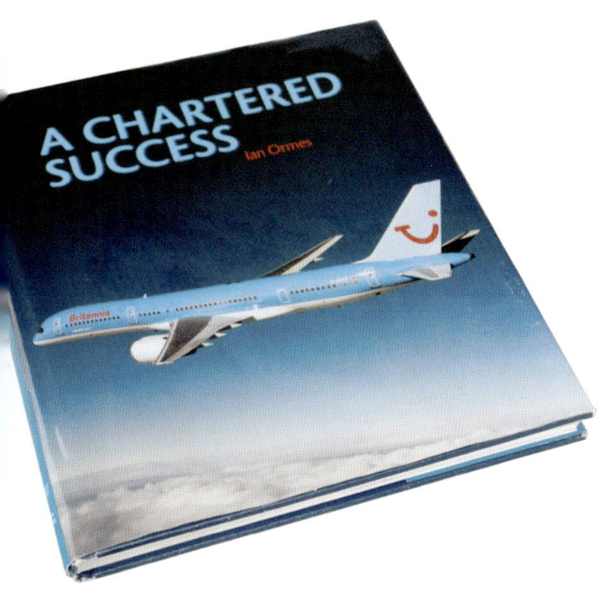

Roving further afield - and going 'Down Under'

As Captain David Hopkins pointed out in 1987. 'We are primarily wholesalers - even with the introduction of schedules, though that may mean things have to change.' Some 96 per cent of the airline's work was for operators in the inclusive tour (IT) holiday business, about two per cent was UK Ministry of Defence contract work, and two per cent is Britannia's then embryonic scheduled trade. Working in the IT business was altogether different from running a schedules-only airline. In IT charter operations the load factor risk was mainly with the tour operator, whether the tour operator ultimately retailed a holiday package or seat-only tickets. At that time about twenty per cent of seats purchased by UK tour operators were ultimately sold simply as cheap air travel, which means about two million seats a year. In many cases, the contract with the passenger included 'notional' accommodation to satisfy the rules in the relevant bilateral aviation agreement. This slowly changed.

In 1988 Britannia announced an increase in the 767 fleet, with the addition of three 767-200 EROPS aircraft. EROPS stood for Extended Range Operations, two for delivery that year and a third for delivery in 1989 bringing the fleet total up to eight. With a full load of 273 passengers and a still-air range of 4800 miles, the new type would be capable of operating non-stop flights to the USA, the Caribbean and much of Africa.

Although possibly not the true definition of 'long-haul', generally in Britannia terms it was going outside the confines of their European operation.

In November 1988, Britannia started flying ultra-long-haul - to Australia and New Zealand. It all came about when the new managing director, Dave Hopkins and commercial director Brian Christian came up with the idea of charter flights to Australia during the winter months. For years Britannia had been flying Muslim Pilgrims to Mecca for the annual Hadj from as far afield as Malaysia, which had provided it useful winter business but as the

Celebrations marking the tenth anniversary the flights to Australia were marked at both Gatwick and in Adelaide. *(both Britannia Airways)*.

pilgrimage dates slowly moved forward there was still a problem with winter aircraft utilisation. The two looked at the Australian possibility and pursued the idea of inclusive tour flights in association with the tour company TravelBag, This company had been formed in 1979 by Peter Wade, who opened the first store in Alton, Hampshire, specialising in tailor made holidays to Australia and New Zealand. Britannia also made use of another tour company called Austravel.

There was a reluctance in Thompson over the Australian flights because they felt that Britannia was very good at European operations but had little experience in long haul. However, the inital reluctance was overcome, and the service started to receive good reviews.

The long-haul charters to Australia and New Zealand could be something of an ordeal for passengers. The route was the UK - The Gulf for a tech stop, then on to Singapore. Here there was an option available for a two-day stop-over before continuing to either Perth, Adelaide, Melbourne, Sydney, Brisbane or Cairns. There was also the option to continue to Auckland in New Zealand.

Australia had a lot to offer both passengers known

BRITANNIA CELEBRATES 10 YEARS FLYING
DOWN UNDER

Britannia celebrated 10 years flying to Australia from Gatwick Airport for tour operator, Ausbound, on 1st November. Passengers on the first Perth/Adelaide flight of the winter season were treated to a bucks fizz reception and a slice of the 24 inch cake, made especially for the big occasion. The first charter airline to start flying down under with fortnightly flights from Luton to Perth and Cairns, Britannia now has three flights a week to Brisbane, Melbourne, Perth and Adelaide plus a weekly flight to Auckland.

Celebrating 10 years flying down under are (L to R): Dawn Mitchell, Britannia's Station Manager for Gatwick, Shell Jones, Britannia's Passenger Services Officer and Ausbound's Operations Manager, Jeremy Sweet.

With scenes like this it is not surprising that many deserted that cold and snow of the UK in winter for the warmth of destinations further afield. *(Kaz Ale Collection)*

in the business as VFRs (Visting Friends and Relatives), and the general tourist had been spotlighted recently, with Britannia attracting excellent media attention.

The breakthrough in such a dramatic reduction in fares was 'all thanks to the patience, determination and professional skills of Britannia Airways'. 'It was fine - more like a scheduled flight than a charter high praise indeed, but well-deserved'. 'I heard no one complaining of feeling cramped'. The food is equal to any scheduled flight and the starters much better'. So said the *Sunday Express*.

'Britannia Airways have managed to inject a high degree of comfort'... A big hand for Britannia's brand-new widebodied Boeing 767'. And on the subject of in-flight catering: scheduled airlines would have a job to compete', reported the *Evening Standard*.

'The plane was nearly full, but astonishingly, for an economy flight there was plenty of legroom'. *The Observer*.

'... Just as comfortable as an economy scheduled flight' *Today*.

' The first charter flight to Perth was opening up Australia for the package tourist'. *The Independent*.

On a technical note, May 1995 saw the announcement that the long-haul tech-stops to Australia would change from Sharjah to Abu Dhabi.

On a personal note, my in-laws Harold and Beryl Dobbs, were on one of the first of these flight to Cairns over Christmas 1988. They departed Luton for Abu Dhabi, then Singapore then Cairns. Not so comfortable compared with today but cheap! Two weeks including a hotel package cost £599. It was when you could not get a flight anywhere else in that direction for less than £1000!

But it was not all sitting back on their laurels and basking in the glory of long-haul. Britannia set up what was termed a 'Continuous Improvement Team', tasked with looking at ways of, as the name implied, finding methods making the product better. One of Britannia's largest continuous Improvement team studied and then presented the results of their project *Looking at Long Haul* to Roger Burnell and other senior managers.

The eighteen members who made up the cross-

Long Haul to Luton! A Britannia 767 returns back to base after another long-haul flight. *(Kaz Ale Collection)*

767-205 G-BNAX is seen at London Gatwick. *(Richard Vandervord)*

divisional Longhaul Project Team included representatives from Airport Services, Flight Crew, Engineering and Operations as well as service partners LSG Skychefs, Servisair and Alpha Catering.

The team, whose remit was to identify ways in which the airline's Longhaul On-Time performance could be bettered, studied all the tasks involved within a long-haul departure or turnround and identified over thirty areas where improvements could be made. Those involved in the project team included Iain Minns - Servisair; First Officer Chris Hope, Manchester; Captain Dave Calton, Manchester; No. One Cabin Crew Alison Green, Gatwick; Glyn Hale, Alpha Catering Manchester; No. One Cabin Crew Alison Salmon, Gatwick, Paul Reilly - Airport Services Manchester; Maggie Maslen, LSG Skychefs, No.Two Cabin Crew Tony Robertson Manchester; No. One Cabin Crew Karen Baker, Manchester; Greg Dawson - Ops Luton; Captain Dave Sweet, Manchester; Mick Naele - Engineering Gatwick; Chris Unwin - Airport Services, Steve Lowman and Mel Edwards - Continuous Improvement, John Knight - Engineering Manchester and Nigel Williams - Continuous Improvement.

In the summer of 1995 Britannia announced that the expected charter services to South Africa planned to start that winter had not materialised, as the charterer had decided not to proceed. However, it was expected that they would go-ahead for the winter 1996/97, which was indeed what happened.

The airline announced that it had been given the go-ahead to start charters to South Africa, with flights from London Gatwick to Cape Town and Johannesburg, with the expectation that they would be as popular as the Australian flights. It was in addition to flights to Dakar and Banjul in West Africa and Luxor and Mombasa in the east. The 1997/98 Winter season saw the South African charters continue with the necessasary liences granted by the South African authorities. Bluebird Holidays were the sole charterer using 767-200 aircraft out of London Gatwick via Mombassa.

Britannia had been operating for a number of years to the USA and the Caribbean with a significant destination being Orlando in Florida, home to more than a dozen theme parks. Chief among its claims to fame is Walt Disney World, comprising of parks like the Magic Kingdom and Epcot, as well as water parks. For many years the destination was Orlando International Airport (MCO) located six miles southeast of downtown Orlando. However, in 1997 the airline moved over to Orlando Sanford International Airport for two years, before returning to its previous destination. The airline was putting up to twenty flights a week into the area at peak season, from a number of European airports.

Florida was not the only transatlantic destination, the Caribbean, with Puerto Plata in Cuba, San Juan, St Lucia, Santo Domingo, Punta Cana, Antigua Jamaica and Barbados were all visited, as was Cancun in Mexico.

Chapter 7

Behind the Scenes

There were many departments in Britannia Airways that the public was not aware of - everything from aircraft cleaners to caterers, from ticket agents to accountants, from administrators to store-keepers. All had a vital part to play in the running of the airline.

That said, there were several departments whose day-to-day work could be considered as fascinating.

Britannia Ops...
In many ways, the heart of Britannia Airways - and indeed the holy of holies - was the Operations Room. 'Ops' of any airline has often been likened to the progress of the Battle of Britain on to blackboards at Fighter Command headquarters at Bentley Priory. So it was with Britannia. Any wartime RAF controller would experience a strong sense of déja vu were they able to penetrate Britannia's operations room just within the entrance to Luton Airport.

The battle, however, was not waged in shooting down the enemy but in shooting up the percentage of on-time departures. Surprisingly at first impression, all this was undertaken by writing on wall charts to update the latest movement of all the aircraft in the airline's fleet. It could have been thought that the only concession to progress was that the white chalk on blackboards for Spitfires and Hurricanes had given way to coloured felt pens on white melamine for Boeing airliners.

Each of the fleet had its own dedicated board so that, clustered in a semi-circular mural around the operations desk, were annotated movement charts for that day's flights, together with spares for aircraft of other airlines that might be chartered in to meet peak demands. Below these were the movement boards for the following day and, in the wings, like sentries waiting for the changing of the guard, were the skeletal schedules for succeeding days.

Initially, the operations room was a separate entity from crew planning which resulted in the controller shifting aircraft round and, in effect, claiming that if the crew could not be found to meet the change, then it was not his fault.

It was Roy McDougall, as operations director, who merged them into one department with 24 hours crewing. Many of the staff became dual qualified on both operations and crew rostering. Changes were no longer made to aircraft schedules unless crews could be found to operate them.

This system was introduced following a French air traffic controllers work-to-rule industrial action in 1978, which emphasised the weakness of not having a coordinated setup. Even then, the masterstroke of sending a Britannia executive to France to liaise with their air traffic control worked wonders for continued co-operation.

As duty staff climbed the dais to update movements of each aircraft, the obvious question was why all this was not computerised. The answer was simple. With a sweep of his eyes across the boards, the duty controller could immediately assess the state of the hundreds of sector flights that constituted a summer's day of operations. Substituting the embrace of the iris with a visual display unit would have entailed punching the keyboard many times to achieve the same breadth of knowledge.

The masterminding of all this activity came under under operations director Stu Grieve. His predecessor in the post, Dave Hopkins, regarded that 1978 French strike and its consequent delays as a watershed.

'Controlling and operating through that period accelerated a new look at the way operations were organised. It was a watershed: the day-to-day crewing on one side and the operation of the aeroplane on the other, and a supervisor effectively over the whole operation.'

The main change in those intervening years was the reliance placed on computers to store the total operational programme. Having a complete system also helped to avoid mistakes. Rosters for crews came out of networks, whereas before typists took two or three days to type them from original master rosters. And, invariably, mistakes were made.

Another computer-aid to efficiency and time-saving was that Britannia's operations supervisors

Right: Ops Manager Dave Cox, right with Ops Planning Offcer Dave Hills, left and Ops Supervisor Trevor Caveney. *(Britannia Airways via author's collection)*

The Britannia Airways Operations Building at Luton (*Britannia Airways*).

had direct input into UK air traffic control for aircraft flight 'slot' times. Previously they had to telephone the West Drayton centre, near Heathrow Airport, and ask for a slot. It could take up to an hour to obtain. Now the request is carried instantly over a computer network.

That is not to say that technology did not play its part. Captains were continually calling up the operations room with updates on their progress or to report snags with their equipment - those within a 200 miles radius used very high-frequency bands and those penetrating the more remote parts of Europe or beyond turned to single-sideband high-frequency radio. By the side of the controller was a computer terminal and should a captain, for instance, wish to divert to a non-scheduled airport for any reason, the availability of handling equipment and refuelling capability could be immediately keyed on to the screen. Behind the controller was a printer which punched out a variety of information including actual flight movement times for each aircraft.

The greatest asset a controller could possess, apart from calmness and judgment under stress, was the ability to act quickly to meet a crisis.

An excellent example of this 'thinking on your feet' was this extreme and unusual situation; an aircraft arrived in Tenerife just before midnight (all times in operations control are based on Greenwich Mean Time) with an unserviceable engine.

It was due to bring back a full load of passengers and take off in the early hours of the following day for Gatwick. If a replacement engine is needed, the passengers cannot be delayed awaiting the servicing of that aircraft as a new engine would have to be sent out in a freighter together with engineers to install it.

The duty controller would have to notify the engineering department of the problem, arrange to charter a freighter, secure a substitute aircraft to fly the stranded passengers home, and then, should the rest of the Britannia fleet be fully occupied, hope to secure the charter of an aircraft at short notice to carry out the succeeding day's programme of the out-of-action Boeing.

There is also the knock-on effect for the crew rostering department which has an office adjoining the operations room. At any one time, even without crises, they are scheduling crews for up to 1,400 different flights.

It was acknowledged by everyone within the company that the quality of their rostering affected morale to a higher degree than any other single discipline in the airline. A specific roster was completed at least four weeks ahead of the flight. This allowed crews to arrange their social and domestic life around it. Equally, judicious organising of staff would also have a significant effect on airline costs from the planning stage to the sort of hypothetical crisis typified by the Boeing in Tenerife.

The way they met the problems, from arranging crew hotel accommodation right down to transport to get them there can be financially critical.

Many said that if you wanted to test the pulse of the airline business, the best place to be was the Operations Room. One person who would undoubtedly agree was Britannia's Operations Manager Dave Cox.

For, over the years with the airline, Dave Cox has had his share of pulse counting - or heart fluttering ~ according to the state of play as he explained to *Britannia News* in early 1974.

'Twenty four hours a day, seven days a week, fifty-two weeks of the year the department maintained a constant watch, ever ready to switch an odd flight here or add a service there as the need arises.

It can be a demanding business since the best plans can be rendered useless by circumstances far beyond the control of Dave Cox or anyone else in the Operations Department - whether it be fog at Luton or a strike by air traffic controllers in Germany.

The aeroplane is a highly complicated piece of machinery. All of us who work in the industry have to be prepared to deal with trouble when it comes - and deal with it quickly.

To a certain extent, we can be prepared for it. We know, for example, that we're likely to get freezing fog sometime during the winter in England. The worst situations usually come with lousy weather problems, which can result in passengers having to hang around airport buildings for six, seven or eight hours at a time.

Things can get very congested and naturally there's a certain amount of grumbling from passengers. The most considerable difficulty was not being able to tell anyone anything.

A Thomson Passenger Ticket, Core Itinerary and pair of Flight Coupons from 1979.

PASSENGER TICKET
BAGGAGE CHECK & HOLIDAY ITINERARY

Thomson Holidays

Thomson Holidays — registered proprietor Thomson Travel Limited

SUBJECT TO IMPORTANT NOTICE AND CONDITIONS OF CONTRACT OVERLEAF

MR.M.SIMONS

WHITTLESEY TRAVEL
2A BROAD ST
WHITTLESEY
PETERBOROUGH

DATE OF ISSUE   30 JAN79
GREATER LONDON HSE, HAMPSTEAD
LONDON NW1 7SD. TEL: 01-387-93

PASSENGER NAME	HOLIDAY No.	BOOKING REFERENCE No.
MR.M.SIMONS	D1044	504486/342/4

AIRLINE	BAGGAGE ALLOWANCE
BRITANNIA AIRWAYS	20KGS (44LBS (None for infants)

OUTWARD JOURNEY

FLIGHT No.	DATE	TIME		LATEST CHECK IN DATE	TIME (LO
BY097A	01MAR79	07.55	*	01MAR79	06.5

HOTEL
SAHARA BEACH

ACCOMMODATION
SINGLE PB WC BL SV — ARRIVAL TIME AT RESORT (APPROX.) BEFORE LUNCH

BOARD ARRANGEMENTS
FULL BOARD — DEPARTURE TIME FROM RESORT (APP) AFTER BREAKFAST
WITH INSURANCE

RETURN JOURNEY

FLIGHT No.	DATE	TIME		U.K. ARRIVAL TIME (LOCAL
BY097B	29MAR79	11.45	*	29MAR79 14.5

* YOUR SEAT WILL BE ALLOCATED AT THE AIRPOR

FLIGHT COUPON No. 2
Any alteration invalidates this coupon

FLIGHT No. BY097B

DEP. DATE 29MAR79 (28)

FROM
MONASTIR

TO
LONDON (LUTON)

NAME
MR.M.SIMONS

BKG. REF.
504486/342/4

BAGGAGE		
CHECKED		UNCHECKED
PCS	KGS	KGS

M	F	C	I

FLIGHT COUPON No. 1
Any alteration invalidates this coupon

OUTWARD FLIGHT No. BY097A
RETURN FLIGHT No. BY097B

DEP. DATE 01MAR79 (28)

FROM
LONDON (LUTON)

TO
MONASTIR

NAME
MR.M.SIMONS

BKG. REF.
504486/342/4

BAGGAGE		
CHECKED		UNCHECKED
PCS	KGS	KGS

M	F	C	I

A typical week's operation for a Britannia Airways advanced Boeing 737

Flight Number	UK Airport	Departure time		Overseas Airport		UK Airport	Arrival time	Flight time
Monday								
BY741A	Manchester	0730	➤	Corfu		-	1100	3.30
BY741B	-	1310	-	Corfu	➤	Newcastle	1640	3.30
BY695A	Newcastle	1740	➤	Larnaca		-	0045	5.05
Tuesday								
	-	0145	-	Larnica	➤	Newcastle	0650	5.05
BY727A	Newcastle	1145	➤	Heraklion		-	1600	4.15
BY727B		1710	-	Heraklion	➤	Newcastle	2125	4.15
BY717A	Newcastle	2330	➤	Palma		-	0200	2.30
Wednesday								
BY717B	-	0320	-	Palma	➤	Newcastle	0550	2.30
BY104A	Newcastle	0920	➤	Athens		-	1320	4.00
BY104B	-	1405	-	Athens	➤	Newcastle	1805	4.00
BY634A	Newcastle	2055	➤	Rhodes		-	0115	4.20
Thursday								
BY634B	-	0230	-	Rhodes	➤	Newcastle	0650	4.20
BY217A	Newcastle	0825	➤	Corfu		-	1155	3.30
BY217B	-	1310	-	Corfu	➤	Newcastle	1640	3.30
BY258A	Newcastle	1825	➤	Tenerife South		-	2315	4.50
Friday								
BY258B	-	0330	-	Tenerife South	➤	Newcastle	0820	4.50
BY715A	Newcastle	0920	➤	Tenerife South		-	1410	4.50
BY715B	-	1450	-	Tenerife South	➤	Glasgow	1935	4.45
BY595A	Glasgow	2015	➤	Rimini		-	2255	2.40
Saturday								
BY575B	-	0100	-	Rimini	➤	Glasgow	0340	2.40
BY170A	Glasgow	0730	➤	Palma		-	1030	3.00
BY170B	-	1105		Palma	➤	Leeds/Bradford	1350	2.45
BY160A	Leeds/Bradford	1510	➤	Palma	-	-	1755	2.45
BY170B	-	1830	-	Palma	➤	Glasgow	2130	3.00
BY028A	Glasgow	2330	➤	Gerona		-	0215	2.45
Sunday								
BY028B	-	2.45	-	Gerona	➤	Glasgow	0530	2.45
BY062A	Glasgow	0730	➤	Alicante	-	-	1040	3.10
BY055B	-	1125	-	Alicante	➤	Leeds/Bradford	1420	2.55
BY055A	Leeds/Bradford	1520	➤	Alicante	-	-	1815	2.55
BY062B		1910		Alicante	➤	Glasgow	2155	2.45
BY671A	Glasgow	2340	➤	Larnica			4.50	5.10
Monday								
BY671B	-	0810		Larnica	➤	Glasgow	1320	5.10

The above table is representative of just one Britannia Airways 737 flying 'plan' during the peak season 'sometime in the mid-1980s'. This plan, multiplied by the number of aircraft in the fleet shows just how complex the Ops and Crewing Department's task were. The times shown are all in GMT and are 'standard'; that is as planned, not what actually happened. At peak, an aircraft could be airborne around eighteen hours a day with turnarounds overseas kept to an absolute minimum - in some cases as little as thirty minutes.

The answer is to build in 'buffer' slots to take up the slack when trouble comes; otherwise, a 'snowball' situation can quickly develop - bringing with it chaos to the airline's schedule.

Aircrew, Ops and Crewing all talk the language of the patterns of Inclusive Tour flights, something that was very different to short-haul scheduled service flights that almost repeated themselves daily. 'Back-to-Backs', 'Two One Ways', 'W-Patterns' and 'Split Loads' all were part of the jargon of charter airline operations.

One aspect of the layout of the operations centre at Luton owed its origins to the earliest days of Euravia. In that first wooden building which served as the complete administrative facility, the only way non-operations staff could gain access to the operations team was through a small hatch. Even after 'Ops' moved to a much bigger operations centre, none of the pilots or crew was allowed into it. The reasoning for this is that the controllers were responsible for the whole of the Britannia flying schedule including Gatwick, Manchester and the other UK departure points. Therefore, just because a crew was flying from Luton, it was thought unfair that they should have direct access, whereas those based at other airports cannot.

Flight operations were responsible for the day to day running of the fleet. Each aircraft was allocated a board which listedthe day's activities, consisting of

Right: An explanation of the patterns flown by Britannia on their charter operations

Below: G-AXNA starts to run down the hill from the runway to the passenger terminal at Luton in July 1972. This was the second Britannia colour scheme worn by their 737s in two years. (*author*)

the departure airport, arrival airports, aircraft registration, crew names, estimated departure and arrival timings and the number of passengers on board. Telexes monitored the actual departure and arrival times, and these were entered on the boards in green if within one hour of the estimated timing or red if outside this time.

Delays can and did occur from time to time, the reasons being varied and diverse. An airport may be closed due to adverse weather, forcing the pilot to fly to an alternate. It would result in passengers being taken by coach from the first airport to the substitute thus adding to the delay.

By no means, all of Dave Cox's work - or that of the thirty people working in the department - centred around the arrival or departure of aircraft.

'Golf Alpha X-Ray November Charlie, line up and hold...' G-AXNC
'Isambard Kingdom Brunel' at London Gatwick. *(Richard Vandervoord)*

Operations were also concerned with the detailed planning of the airline's schedule. It entailed the department working closely with Commercial and with the tour operators using the airline's services.

In addition to tour firms such as Thomson Holidays and Horizon Midland, Britannia also worked closely with the Ministry of Defence. The Ministry chartered about fifteen flights a week from Britannia to transport Army and RAF personnel and their families to units in West Germany

The department worked to very tight time scales. In many cases it had to plan its flight programme more than twelve months ahead of the departure date- and this called for close cooperation between all parties. For example, in the case of the summer 1975 holiday brochures, the department was working to a deadline of May 1974.

Dave Cox: 'It's a big and costly process. The difficulty for us is getting the right mix. The tour operators are keen to get the maximum allocation in the beginning, but sometimes they cut back flights - known as consolidation - as the departure date draws near. leaving us with gaps in the programme."

Other factors have included Air Traffic Control disputes, flow control restrictions to ease and avoid congestion on an airway, or an aircraft developing a technical problem - luckily, this was a rare occurrence. As well as these factors night closures and restrictions had to taken into account. It could be due to airfield maintenance or runway extension work or simply, as in the case of several UK airports, a night-time curfew on flying to consider residents who resided close to an airport.

Crew rosters were also affected in the case of delays as maximum flying hours per day were laid down by the Civil Aviation Authority. A delay could result in a crew being out of hours before the flight took off, so a fresh crew had to be found for the flight.

Given these factors, it is a credit to Britannia that while in its the twenty-fifth year of operation, eighty-five per cent of its flights departed within thirty minutes of scheduled departure time. In its first year of operations, with the 767, Britannia claimed a ninety-eight per cent dispatch reliability.

Although the airline would not operate from all these airports over one season, it did hold licences to operate from them and has done so in the past. The airports were as follows: Aberdeen, Belfast, Birmingham, Blackpool, Bournemouth, Bristol, Cambridge, Cardiff, East Midlands, Edinburgh, Exeter, Glasgow, Humberside, Inverness, Isle of Man, Jersey, Leeds/Bradford, Liverpool, London (Gatwick), Luton, Manchester, Newcastle, Norwich, Prestwick, Southend, Stansted, Stornoway and Teeside.

By the turn of the century, 'Ops' evolved into a organisation employing around one hundred and twenty people, divided into numerous departments, not only responsible for the UK business but that of Germany and Scandanavia as well.

Crew Planning: Jenny Crinnion, as Crew Planning Manager, headed up the planning area of Ops which covered everything up to 21 days before the flight. This area had seen several changes designed to improve the level of service and support for cabin crew and pilots.

Crew Support Team: The main task of the Crew Support Team (previously known as Ops Admin) was to update the database of personal details of well over 2000 cabin crew and pilots. They ensured that all passports and visas were up to date, reminded pilots when they are due for a medical or to renew their licences and made sure that every pilot had the current Airfield Clearances

Ops Planning - 1994 style!

Even though things have changed from the 1970s. today it all looks very dated with the size and shape of the VDUs - properly known back then as Visual Display Units, not monitors - very noticable.

The displays themselves (below) now look incredibly old-fashioned.

(Brittannia Airways via Simon Peters Collection).

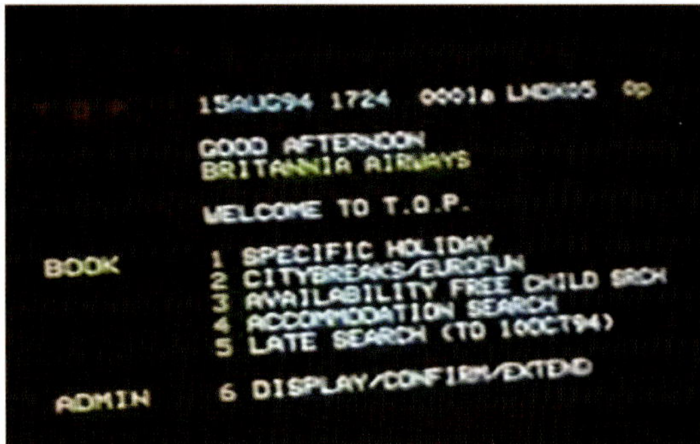

for every airport into which they flew.

The team used the same IOS computer system (Integrated Operational System) used by everyone in the department which managed all aircraft and crew. They actioned all crew requests for leave, and from the Journey, Log filled in by the Captain on each flight, updated each crew members flying and ground duty hours, which was vital information for the Rostering Team later on. There was a constant supply of Journey Logs landing at this department, and it was easy to let a backlog accumulate. However, with the help of a 'Mums Army' working in the evening, the team managed to input around 2000 a month during peak times!

Crew training Unit: The Crew Training Unit was established in response to the increased training programme which, to meet JAR Ops requirements to cover Germany and Scandanavia. Mike Duxbury led the team which planned and scheduled all new and recurrent training courses for pilots and cabin crews, including supernumerary flights, SEPS and simulator training. With a dedicated team covering all areas, all trainees and trainers were allocated to courses before the rosters were prepared.

Rostering Team: Once all leave dates, crew duty hours and training requirements were in the system, it was down to the Rostering Team to plan the rest of the working lives of crews. Over twenty staff of the team were able to build the rosters for both cabin crew, and flight deck were allocated individual bases and up to 250 crew to the roster, usually covering two weeks at a time. Once the rosters were planned, it was back to Crew Support to publish and distribute them, usually three weeks in advance.

Eileen Naughton-Harris managed the second main area of Ops as Ops Control Manager. This area covers everything from twenty-one days ahead of the flight to the point of departure of the flight itself.

HotAc and Travel Team: Once the rosters have

The Crew Support Team taking a break from entering Journey Log details - standing left to right Sharon Boxall, Margaret Warner, Joella Dench - Supervisor, Margaret Paisley, ylea McGovern; sitting l-r Nicola Wigger, Valerie Blackman, Rachel Lane.

been published it is time for the HotAc and Travel team, led by Andrea Evans to book all hotel accommodation and travel arrangements to ensure the crew were in the right place at the right time. The team also co-ordinated hotel bookings for the rest of the company and HotAc and Travel for the engineers when operationally required.

Crewing Team: The Crewing Team had the unenviable task of dealing with all changes to rosters following initial publication - the reasons could be many and varied, ranging from crew needing days off, sickness and changes due to aircraft being delayed resulting in crews going 'out of hours' (exceeding the legal amount of flying hours as laid down by the Civil Aviation Authority). This department included the Crew Information Desk, established to deal with all crew

enquiries including hotel details, roster swaps and all general questions regarding the roster. They received, on average, three hundred calls a day. A subsidiary Crew Information Desk was established in Berlin as a contact point for all German crew. Neil Doherty (Ops Central Superintendent) trained the Germans in this aspect.

Ops Control: Ops Control was the 'sharp end' of Britannia Airways. It was manned twenty-four hours a day, seven days a week, three hundred and sixty-five days a year. This area included Flight Watch, the ATC Cell, the CSO Desk and the Ops

A beaming sea of faces from the Rostering Team: back row left to right Mark Seymour - Superintendent, Pete Fraser, Juliette Hall; middle row Anita Grant, Sandra Theodore, Anne Plancherel, Elaine Martin, Andrea Lawrence, Olivia Hunt, Sue Cooper, Heather Richardson, Jenny Crinnion; sitting Sharon Jackson, Julie Remon, Sue Rovai - Superintendent.

Control SUperintendent, who managed all of the departments within the Ops Control area. 'Flight Watch' and the ATC Cell were primarily concerned with that particular day's flying programme. Ownership of the Aircraft programme passed from (Advanced Planning (later part of the Commerical Division) to Ops three days before the flight. 'Flight Watch' then took responsibility for the programme, making any changes required due to disruptions caused by ATC delays, weather or any technical problems. They also provided Ops and ATC Services to Britannia Germany and Britannia Scandanavia.

There was always a Customer Service Officer (CSO) on duty, playing the critical function of dealing with any passenger-orientated problems that could arise due to any operational issues.

By liaising with the relevant base stations,

From left to right are the Crew Training Unit namely Ken Greenaway, Linda Humphries, Sheila Duffy, Mike Duxbury and Lynn Cooke.

Some of the Hotac and Travel Team from left to right Kirsty Ball, Andrea Evans, Charlotte Millard, Marcia Newman and Carra Fensome.

lessons were carried out in highly realistic mock-ups of the 737 and 767 cabins with working galleys. The mock-ups were equipped with smoke generators for use in emergency training. Although the industry was very cyclic and cabin crew training had its ups and downs, overall there was a steady increase in cabin staff recruiting.

It was not always like that - in the early days recruit training lasted all of one week and took place in a cramped spare room in a wooden hut. The only aid to practical work then was a fire extinguisher!

Things changed rapidly. By the mid-1980s the Britannia training centre was in a new purpose-built building with offices, five classrooms and the benefit of aircraft mock-ups. The training matched these facilities in its professionalism.

Recruits were usually taken on in the spring for a short contract covering the busy summer months - at the end of that period, the best of them might be offered a permanent career, subject to the operational needs at the time. Some of the summer intakes could consist either of staff previously engaged by the airline or recruited from other airlines, but the majority would be young people new to the airline industry.

Those wishing to join the company received not only an application form but also a two-page sheet that explained in what today would be seen as somewhat blunt terms what the job was about and the requirements that needed to be met.

'Britannia Airways is one of the leading independent airlines in this country and is part of the International Thomson Organisation. Britannia celebrated its 25th anniversary in 1987.

Our fleet is made up of Boeing 737 and 767 aircraft. Britannia's route network encompasses more than 20 departure points in the UK to more than 70 airports overseas. Principal destinations are the major European holiday' resorts - the Spanish Costas and Balearic Islands, the Canaries, Greece

keeping them up to date with the progress of any delay and co-ordinating meal vouchers, transport requirements and accommodation for the passengers, the CSO left the rest of the team free to deal with other arrangements, such as sub-chartering an aircraft, liaising with Engineering and co-ordinating ATC slots etc to get the programme back on time as quickly as possible.

Cabin Staff

Cabin staff went through a comprehensive course at Luton in Britannia's Cabin Training School. Here recruits learned the all-important tasks of looking after passengers safety and comfort. Many of the

Despite the brutally honest information package that accompanied the Cabin Crew Application form, Britannia Airways still promoted the glamorous aspect to the job with this picture. *(Britannia Airways)*

and the eastern Mediterranean. But the network is more widespread, serving destinations as far apart as Banjul in the Gambia and Moscow in the USSR.

In 1986 we carried 5.5 million passengers. The airline operates a large proportion of Thomson and Portland Holidays' charter flying. Contracts are held with many other leading tour operators. A scheduled service is operated between Gatwick and Gibraltar for GB Airways, and Britannia operates Ministry of Defence trooping flights between UK, Germany and Gibraltar. In   May 1985, Britannia began scheduled services in its own right.

If you are prepared for hard work, coupled with irregular hours and enjoy meeting people, you may be the person we are looking for. If, however, you prefer a regular social life and working from 9 to 5, Monday to Friday, do not read further - this is not the life for you.

We are looking for Cabin Crew Members to join us on a Temporary Contract for our summer season. As this is our busiest time, we are unable to honour holiday commitments.

Successful applicants will have to undertake an intensive training programme at Luton lasting four weeks. The course will include instruction on all aspects associated with the position of a Cabin Crew Staff Member, i.e. Emergency Training, First Aid, Passenger Handling, In-flight Duties, Duty-Free Sales Training, Grooming etc. Examinations have to be taken as a regular part of the course.

As a Cabin Crew Member you could well be flying to anywhere in Europe, but be prepared to see nothing but the airport as there are very few night stops abroad. However, you may be required to night stop in the UK.

If you meet the basic requirements and fulfil all the qualifications listed overleaf, then we look forward to hearing from you.

Basic qualifications:

Age:	19 - 27
Height:	Minimum of 5 feet 2 inches (157.5 cm) without shoes.
Weight:	Must be proportional to height. Applicants who are invited to attend an interview will be weighed and measured (without footwear).
Appearance:	Neat, presentable appearance; the ability to wear the company uniform is essential.
	Well cared hands and nails are important.
	Hair - clean natural style (no high fashions or very exaggerated styles).
	Complexion - good.
	Tattoos are not acceptable
	Stewardesses: Make-up: - subtle and effective.
	Stewards - A small moustache is acceptable, but not beards.
Health:	Excellent health and hearing. Good eyesight is required. No dentures, or visible birthmarks or scars.
Education:	Three 'O' levels or equivalent. Nursing, First Aid and a knowledge of Italian/Spanish would be useful, but not essential. Clear diction is essential. Academic certificates MUST be

presented when attending an interview.

Nationality: You must be in possession of a full, valid passport and there must be no restriction on your employment in this country.

Work Experience: A minimum of one year in full-time employment in direct contact with the general public. Selling experience is an advantage.

Residential Requirements: Successful applicants 'for bases other than Luton will be accommodated in a hotel for the duration of the course. (The finding of accommodation before the course is the trainees own responsibility.) Luton based Cabin Crew have to find their own accommodation for the duration of the course and thereafter. Successful candidates must live within 45 minutes travelling distance from their base airport and must be able to proceed to and from home without assistance from the company.

Personality: We look for friendly, approachable people, with a mature outlook who will care for our passengers. A sense of humour and a willingness to work hard as part of a team and the ability to accept the unpredictable is essential.

Applicants who do not meet all requirements WILL NOT be considered.

Once interviewed, and then selected, the recruits were placed on training courses which lasted four weeks. Before that, they were handed a cabin staff information booklet which welcomed them to the company and provided a potted background about the airline, the training, airline jargon, abbreviations and codes, the 24-hour clock, and foreign currencies.

The booklet included details of personal appearance - from the wearing of earrings' only one in each ear, please!' - to the requirement that the length of hair-drop at the nape of the neck must be 'ten inches maximum and four inches minimum'.

They were tested on the book at the end of their first day. How much they knew after study was a good indication of their future enthusiasm and application.

An example of this could be seen with the 1985 intake. Since courses began in January, more than 400 temporary cabin staff were recruited and trained. To meet this demand, the school worked three shifts, the first starting at 7.00 am and the last finishing at 11.00 pm. The intensive four-week course trained students to work in both the 737 and 767 and were conducted by the Cabin Staff Training Managers and fifteen line trainers, all experienced cabin staff.

The courses covered both safety training and cabin services. Safety was tackled first because it was recognised to be an intense subject, and should a pupil not able to cope, with that, then there would be little point in continuing to other aspects. Cabin services teaching included practical classroom tuition such as fire-fighting, smoke training, and then passenger work, using the mock-ups, including serving drinks, meals, and duty frees, advice on special meals, meeting medical needs, as well as quickly gaining rapport with passengers - and dealing with difficult ones.

Gavin Scott remembers his days of training in the nineteen-eighties: 'After being accepted, we were told to report to Britannia Flight Training Centre, Luton Airport, at 09.00 Monday morning to commence our three-week training course. The centre was basically three classrooms and a mock-

Guidance Notes for Applicants

TEMPORARY/JUNIOR CABIN CREW MEMBER

Britannia Airways is one of the leading
independent airlines in this country, and

If you are prepared for hard work, coupled
with irregular hours and enjoy meeting people

Above: '... a facemask will drop...' New recuits - complete with training manuals before them were taught the finer details on flight safety.

Left: Regular cabin staff acted as passengers in the cabin mock-up as trainees did meal, drinks and duty free services, while instructors watched their performance. *(both Britannia Airways)*

up of a Boeing 737 cabin, we were introduced to our immediate superiors called Co-ordinators.

After the usual blah-blah about how selective we all were, and what a great company Britannia was, we were asked for our bank details, then had our passports checked. We were off to uniform stores - actually a high-end shop - to get measured and fitted out with the uniform. The next day my colleague Bernie Quinn and I were given the day off as we were the only two males with thirty females and they were to attend a course on how to apply mascara, makeup, lipstick and God knows what else. The rest of the first

two weeks was taken up with cabin services, bar service, meals, selling of duty-free goods etc. being given homework and an exam every day, an absolute doddle!

Week Three was a bit more exciting and to stand us in good stead for the rest of our lives, learning First Aid, Fire-Fighting and cabin evacuation, opening doors in an emergency and deploying chutes. It was great fun sliding down the chute, after training we were given a must pass examination set by the CAA, Civil Aviation Authority. Yes, we all passed and looked forward to our supernumerary flights and summer of undiluted pleasure. On occasion some of us had to go through our pockets the following morning to check what currency we had, to remind us which country we were in, as we were flying all over the place. After the first year the job got boring very quickly and the novelty soon wore off, I don't think many of us had to use our SEP (safety and emergency procedure) skills. When

198

Cabin Crew undergo training in a full-scale working mock-up of a 767 aft galley at the Luton Training School.

The 'new look; 737 interior.
(all images Britannia Airways via authors collection)

Cabin staff had to face the daunting escape slide. No one has ever been able to explain to me why the 'victims' have black knees on their coveralls, but I love the little bootees! *(both authors collection via Britannia Airways)*

the rosters were given out one month in advance we very seldom flew with a colleague we had flown with before. Of course, it was a very sociable job, Too friendly some would say.

The success of Britannia's cabin crew philosophy was based on attitude and teamwork. It meant, for instance, that in an emergency, the crew knew what was going to happen and felt confident about dealing with it and knowing what colleagues are also doing. Reaction to a given set of circumstances became intuitive.

Britannia drew cabin crew members from line duty to become trainers themselves. And it is actual crew members who became the 'stars' of video training films which were now used extensively on courses. Several of these dealt with the incidents which are considered most likely to occur on flights as a result of analysing reports regularly submitted by cabin staff.

Before Britannia commissioned their own videos that were more suitable for their requirements, use was made of a more generic film, which happened to be of American origin. The trainees became convulsed with laughter when, in an emergency, a stewardess with a pronounced Brooklyn accent drawled' Grabe your ayncles' and another, when there was an attempted suicide on board, demurely murmured:' Please sir, don't worry about the mess. We'll clear it up!'

It became increasingly important in training - as has been proved by international hijack cases - that there should be complete understanding between the flight deck and cabin crew. The Britannia courses not only included an emphasis on clarity and quickness of communication, but a line captain was introduced to the class so that they could cross-question him and gain a direct appreciation of what was required in a crisis.

Things Medical

More work for the airline meant more pressure on staff and Britannia Airways had become the UK and world leader in the study of the therapeutic effects of flying on Flight Deck and Cabin Crew, mainly through the work of Dr Alan H Roscoe, who joined the airline in 1983 as its Chief Medical Officer. After internationally acclaimed reports on pilot workload, he turned his attention to the effects of flying on cabin crew health and

The 767 simulator was, in theory available for 'Flying with Confidence' courses, but in the main the 737 sim was used. *(Britannia Airways)*

performance, particularly the so-called 'flight attendant burnout' syndrome. His report, presented at the 5th Annual International Aircraft Cabin Safety Symposium in Oakland, California, explained: 'Examination of the case histories of 100 (97 female) consecutive consultations for recurring minor illnesses - mainly upper respiratory tract infections - seen over the previous five years at Britannia Airways revealed that a disproportionate number had been flying for between four and six years at the time of consultation and, importantly, most had previously been quite healthy. This epidemiological evidence suggests that many of these individuals were suffering from the cumulative effects of flying — the flight attendant' burnout' syndrome. Further support for this diagnosis was obtained on re-examining several of these patients, when almost two-thirds admitted to symptoms which included lethargy,

forgetfulness, loss of concentration, recurring headaches and irritability; and, in some cases, to a lack of motivation to fly'.

Britannia continued in its ground-breaking medical research, mainly through the efforts of Dr Roscoe. More than a decade of research into the workload of commercial pilots, using volunteer pilots like Captains Stu Grieve and Paul Watson as guinea pigs, provided data which could be of value to the design and ergonomics of future-generation flight decks. The result was 'Flight Deck Automation and Pilot Workload' presented to AGARD, the Advisory Group for Aviation Research and Development for NATO, the North Atlantic Treaty Organisation.

The paper was an in-depth discussion of the introduction of 'new technology' automation into the flight decks of modern jet transport aircraft hadhad a

Boxer Nigel Benn - in the Captains seat - along with Captain Steve Billet - in a Britannia Simulator before his 'Flying with Confidence' flight to Belfast. *(Britannia Airways)*

significant impact on pilot workload. This paper presented several examples of workload assessment involving automatic flight performed during research and development flight trials and routine airline operations in Europe. Subjective evaluation by pilots, augmented by recording their heart rates, was used to compare the workload experienced during various degrees of automatic flight with that experienced during non-automatic flight. The examples selected are used to illustrate some of the implications of increasing automation; the possibility of too much automation leading to a decrement in piloting performance was of particular concern. This report was later used by Boeing, NASA and the United States Air Force.

Dr Roscoe also produced 'Cosmic radiation and the frequent flyer', a study that demonstrated that there might be a cancer risk associated with exposure of airline crews to cosmic radiation. He also wrote papers on emergency onboard medical kits, in-flight medical emergencies, medical fitness to travel by air and much more.

On the airliner cabin environment, Dr Roscoe commented: 'Many passengers are under the impression that the cabins of modern jet airliners are not as healthy as they should be. Passengers believe they suffer health problems when they fly because of the recirculated air in modern airliner cabins.

In fact, the aircraft cabin is much healthier than most public rooms and ground-based transport, and air quality compare favourably with hospital burns units and operating theatres.

For some passengers, the biggest problem with a holiday package is the basic fear of flying. In the early 1990s, Britannia launched a 'flying with confidence' course at the airline's training centre at Castle Donington.

The course was initially started as a commercial decision. Britannia's customer relations department was taking calls from people who were afraid of flying. The only airline running a course was British Airways, and Britannia was referring their passengers to them. The Department Manager at the time, Tina Barbour, decided that perhaps there was an opening for the airline, not only to help people to fly but because these were potential Britannia and Thomson, customers.

The main fear was claustrophobia, followed by people feeling they were not in control and fear of heights. Also, people who had been in severe turbulence were often very concerned. The whole point of the course was for participants to achieve an hour's flying at the end of the day. There are usually between seventy-five and eighty-five people on the course, and a lot of Britannia staff from all levels and departments came along to help out on a volunteer basis.

The early 1980s saw another change in inflight magazines with a change of titles and some interesting articles, including one piece by Jack Moss, Manager, In-flight services: 'Weight is a limiting factor in these days of soaring oil prices. The cost of additional fuel to carry even a few kilos of catering equipment is prohibitively expensive. We calculated recently that if we were to add a large orange to the meal of every passenger, our fuel bill this year would be increased by no less than £50,000'.

Between the volunteers and course staff, it was quite reasonable to persuade more than ninety-five per cent to take the hours flight. The course did not cure people; it was the people who cured themselves. It was very much their strength of character that got them through and helped them confront their demons.

In 1997 Britannia published a book called 'Flying with Confidence' written by Dr Roscoe, in which he explained: 'Fear of flying is not confined to any particular type of personality - the timid or anxious person, or what might be termed the 'nervous individual' - but also affects the internationally famous entertainer, the successful business executive and the leading politician. Several people who are well known for their risk-taking activities, such as mountaineers, professional boxers and explorers, suffer greatly when they fly, and many avoid flying altogether when other modes of travel are available'.

Dr Alan Roscoe had plenty of praise for the course. 'It is without doubt one of the best of its type, and it is an essential element of the course that people fly and that they fly in an airliner, which is the way they will travel. Around twenty per cent of the population of the developed world is frightened of flying, and some ten per cent avoid going by air because of that fear.

Engineering

From inception, engineering support for its aircraft was a feature of Euravia's operations. As we havew seen, Constellation maintenance was undertaken in the airline's somewhat cramped hangar shared with Vauxhall Motors. Britannia and Boeing 737 maintenance was also undertaken in this hangar, which by the second half of the 1960s was reaching its maximum capacity.

A new hangar which was opened in 1970 was able to handle four 737s at a time, thus easing the strain considerably. With the airline becoming the first in the UK to operate the 737, it could not turn to any other company for support, or advice and

Up, up and away soar the service bills for a jet

THE next time you take your car in to be serviced and moan about the bill, pause for a while and think what it costs in men and skill to keep a modern jet flying high.

For example, if your car gets hit by a stone it may dent some chrome or, if you are unlucky, shatter the windscreen. Recently one of Britannia's Boeing 737 jets picked up a stone in one of its engines — the cost, £50,000, or five Rolls-Royces.

A modern jet is checked after every 100 flying hours, has a more thorough service after every 400, and a complete service after 12 and 24 months.

At the end of a year 15,000 man hours have been spent on each jet at a cost of around £40,000.

Swarming

At a car service something would be seriously amiss if the engine had to be hoisted out but at a two-year jet overhaul most of the 50,000 parts are checked and the plane is almost dismantled and put together again.

While two or three mechanics may be working on your motor there will be around 50 men swarming over an aircraft when it is given a thorough going over.

Modern-day motor mechanics do a five-year apprenticeship to qualify them for work on your car. Aeroplane craftsmen also do an apprenticeship and some go to America for courses in aircraft maintenance. When they qualify their work is subject to Government as well as company inspections.

Fault

Most motorists leave parts of their cars until they go wrong and then replace them but this would hardly do with jets carrying hundreds of people. Each part is computerised and replaced well before it wears out.

It is inconvenient breaking down on the motorway but rather frightening to imagine what could happen if an assistance. Fortunately, airlines which purchase Boeing aircraft are allowed the services of a Boeing representative and with guidance from Boeing, maintenance and inspection procedures were devised to allow the maximum amount of flying while maintaining a high standard of maintenance.

Bernard Newton worked for the airline in many roles. 'During my period with Britannia, these included Duty Engineer, Station Engineer, Deputy Maintenance Manager, Deputy Support Services Manager, Chief Engineer, Engineering Director, and finally Technical Director and board member, which, I held for seventeen years before my appointment to TUI in Hanover.

'I rejoined as a Duty Engineer. Having worked for Euravia and Britannia previously from 1962 to 1964, it was attractive for me to come back to a company and people that I knew. I came from Donaldson Airlines at Gatwick, where I was a Licensed Aircraft Engineer on the Boeing 707. I gained my 737 licences at Luton and as I was still living in the Gatwick area and commuting to Luton, I welcomed the opportunity given to me by Geoff Parkins, the then Technical Director (after whom Hangar 61 was officially named in March 1990 by the Minister for Aviation) to set up a base at Gatwick to look after the airline's three 737 aircraft based there. I was a one-man-band; I didn't have a vehicle or spares,

Above: Looking suspiciously 'posed', a Pratt & Witney JT8D receives attention.

Right: Britannia Engineering not only did work on their own fleet, but also worked under contract for other airlines. Here an Air Tanzania 737 - complete with giraffe on the vertical - undergoes maintenance.
both Britannia Airways)

Above: A Britannia 737-200 undergoes a stripdown and major check at Luton.

Left: one of over 1500 tyres inspected in the wheel bay annually.
both Britannia Airways)

minimum deferred defects.'

'I used to be on 24-hour call, seven days a week. I relished the responsibility and knew that when the telephone rang, I had to go and 'fix' the problem, whether it was engine, airframe, avionics or radio. As I had all the required approvals on the 737s, I was sometimes called out as many as three times in one night. I loved it, just loved it.'

'It was sometime in 1978 that I was approached by Roy Phillips who, along with some others, was in the process of setting up a new airline to operate out of Gatwick and Manchester. I knew Roy very well, who had previously worked for Dan-Air, BEA and Court Line. Roy's new airline was planning on operating 737s and so he, on behalf of Air Europe, signed a Maintenance contract with Britannia. I was Station Engineer at Gatwick at the time, and as such tasked by my boss' Geoff Parkins' to set up a complete support infrastructure, which provided me with the opportunity to employ people, get them trained, set up the stores, the technical library, establish shift patterns and work ethics. It did not take us long to get Air Europe off to a brilliant start, and they did not

but I had enthusiasm and determination that Gatwick would be a great success.'

'I started from scratch at Gatwick in 1976 and eventually got a vehicle, a few manuals and spares. I began to set what I considered to be the Britannia standards, i.e. the cleanliness of the aircraft and the experience their first technical delay for twelve weeks, and that was only for ten minutes.'

'So I established an Air Europe Line Organisation, albeit on behalf of Britannia. After a couple of years, Roy decided he would develop his organisation which, I always thought would be the case. As a result, all the groundwork had been done for him by Britannia.'

No matter who the airliners fly for, aircraft were serviced with a series of checks, the first, and the lowest level of which was called an 'A' check. This is a basic pre-flight daily inspection of the aircraft which ensures that the aircraft is fit for flight. It covers essential items such as ensuring that the engine covers were removed, no damage was apparent, all lights are intact, tyres were inflated correctly and other issues which required checking before each flight. At the airline's engineering stations this check was carried out by the airline's engineering staff and at other stations in the UK and abroad this check is carried out by the flight deck crew.

A 'B' check is a more elaborate 'A' check and was always carried out by the airline's engineering staff.

Right: The £4 million hangar, Parkins House, was built at Luton by Britannia to house their wide-bodied 767s, and named after their late technical director, Geoff Parkins. The then Aviation Minister, David Mitchell, unveiled the commemorative plaque at the opening of the hangar, watched by Mrs Elizabeth Parkins and Britannia chairman Derek Davison.

Below: A company 767 is rolled into the new hangar for the first time. *(both Britannia Airways)*

The interior of a 737 is gutted during a major overhaul, making it almost unrecognisable.
(Britannia Airways)

Ideally, this should be done every twenty-four hours; however, the operation of aircraft away from bases did not always allow this and the airline ensures that this check was completed within every thirty-six hours. This check did not require hangar facilities, and it was done on the ramp at Luton or Gatwick, Birmingham, Manchester, Newcastle or Glasgow.

All aircraft which were on a based operation at any other stations must, therefore, pass through a Britannia engineering station during their normal process thus saving the airline the time and expense of positioning flights to an engineering station. After three hundred hours flying time, each aircraft must undergo a 'C' check which was carried out at Luton. This check was a detailed inspection of the aircraft and any parts which need replacing were replaced during this check.

These checks were an ongoing process, and during the three hundred hours, the aircraft would have undergone many 'A' and 'B' checks. The aircraft then underwent a series of 'P' checks which took place every three hundred hours commencing at six hundred hours. The 'P' checks ranged from P1 to P6 and were carried out in the hangars at Luton. P7 to P12 are repeats of the P1 to P6, but they again were more intensive than any previous checks. A P6 involved the aircraft being stripped of its interior: seats, galleys, toilets, stowage bins and panelling. The engines were removed for inspection; the flaps are removed, the avionics suite was taken out for review and the airframe thoroughly inspected for cracks, corrosion or defects.

Consequently, the engines and avionics were tested in several workshops for any defects. On any visit to Luton, a visitor was likely to see at least two aircraft undergoing P6 checks, and another being stripped of the colour scheme in readiness for a repaint. It was essential that the aircraft be kept clean not only for the public image of the airline but also since dirt and grime added extra weight to an aircraft, thus increasing its

Technical Director Bernard Newton,
(Britannia Airways)

fuel consumption.

In addition to its hangar facilities at Luton, the airline also had a modern avionics workshop in which the aircraft systems were tested: these items included flight deck instruments and flight data recorders. With the increase of more and more sophisticated methods being employed in aircraft, the avionics shop was kept well used.

The spares shop, located behind the hangar, was capable of kitting out a complete aircraft, such was its variety of holdings. Britannia had to balance its spares supply between cost-effectiveness and need since to hold large volumes of spares which were infrequently used cost not only cash but could result in spares becoming time expired if they lay on shelves unused within their lifetime.

It is fair to say that within Britannia Airways, Building 100, tucked away off Provost Way, was often forgotten. Yet the building fulfilled a vital role in the maintenance not only of Britannia's 737 fleets but also those of other UK and international operators.

Around twenty-five staff were employed there, allowing an enormous amount of component work to be done in the component workshops where mechanical, hydraulic and pneumatic components were worked on., with bench space for eleven fitters.

Among those who could be found in and around Building 100 was Dave Bull, Wheel Bay Supervisor, Jeremy Reed, Wheel and Tyre Bay Improver, John Wainright, Workshop Fitter, Dave Cummings, Component Bay Supervisor and Dave Miles, Component Workshop Supervisor.

Almost 2000 components passed through the component shop annually, some 500 of them being third party work either from aircraft being worked on in Britannia's hangars or those of several different client airlines.

In addition, Building 100 had a non-destructive test lab for a range of steels and light alloy components. Also housed there were rigs for the full functional testing of hydraulic and pneumatic components from aircraft flight control and undercarriage systems.

Each wheel and tyre on Britannia's aircraft visited Building 100 every five weeks in the peak summer months. In the Wheel and Tyre Bay, tyre changes were carried out, and each wheel was inspected for fatigue cracks using an eddy current test system. Brakes and undercarriage components were also examined and overhauled. More than 1500 wheel and brake units came through annually, either for tyre changes or overhaul. Another busy area of the building handled overhauls on thrust reverser units.

Left: Some of the workers! Ernie Brooks, Jock Roberts, Terry Searles, Joe Chamberlain, John Weedon, Jim Cushen, and Bill Bowden are among those in this picture.

Below: PP-SRW of VASP in partial Britannia colours.

Above: Ray Goddard (left) and Kaz Ale.

A skin change on the aft fuselage of a Boeing 737-200 is done sometime in the mid-1980s. The engineers are Tony Barber (left) and Tony Berti. *(Britannia Airways)*

Britannia's metalwork shop, along with the fibreglass and composites workshop offered different skills and techniques for the repair of airframes and components. At the heart of the metalwork shop were the traditional skills of the sheet metal worker, able to fashion the most complex shapes out of a single sheet of metal.

In the fibreglass workshops, new methods were applied to the shaping of materials that gradually replaced traditional metal in many parts of the aircraft.

Twenty-three staff were employed in the metalwork shop, including two sheet metal workers and a welder. Only three staff were used in the fibreglass workshop adjacent to the 767 hangar, but Workshop Superintendent Dave Roll, who supervised both shops envisaged that the number employed in each would balance out as the new technology materials find increasing use.

Work carried out in the metalwork shop included repair work from the most straightforward battery tray to complex flying control repair schemes which had to be approved by the manufacturer. A wide range of materials were used, some requiring particular care to handle, as well as repairs. The shop was often called upon to work up one-off specials for use in other workshops or elsewhere in the airline. There was seemingly nothing that could not have been fashioned out of sheet metal by the workshop engineers.

The repair and maintenance of the hundreds of miles of line pipework used throughout aircraft were also carried out by the metalwork shop which employed two coppersmiths, skilled at handling this often intricate work. One winter these skills were called upon for a significant pipework modification on four of the Boeing 737 fleet, two of which had to be worked on overnight.

Sheet metal shops, composite material work and sub-assembly repair and inspection. All such work was possible. *(all Britannia Airways)*

The metalwork shop also included an area for the maintenance and repair of Boeing 737 airstairs. As well as work on Britannia's airstair units a number came from other 737 operators for third party maintenance work. Britannia had two full rigs which allowed the operation of the airstairs to be tested before the airstairs are returned to an aircraft.

In the fibreglass workshop, repairs were mostly to control surfaces, fuselage fittings and fairings. Handling the new materials called for extreme precision. Many people will have seen fibreglass used in the repair of boats or even cars, but the work carried out in the fibreglass shop demanded far more care and experience. Until the end of 1986, the fibreglass workshop was, as Dave Roll put it '...a bench in the corner of the plant maintenance shop but eventually boasted its own shop with all the specialised equipment required'.

The increasing use of new technology materials placed increasing importance on this workshop. Meanwhile, the metalwork shop with its longer-established skills and techniques continued its vital role in the engineering and maintenance division.

Steve Prescott was team leader, materials control (engineering division). He started with Britannia almost straight from school in 1982 as a despatch clerk, shipping spares worldwide. He then worked in the Stores and Goods Inwards. From 1998 onwards Steve headed up a team of seven who co-ordinated requests for aircraft spares that could not be provided from standard stock. The group, based at Hangar 89, Luton had all spares requests and communications passed through them, including working with client airlines such as Hapag-Lloyd who put eleven aircraft through maintenance at Luton. This entailed the team visiting Germany, establishing communication links between Britannia and Hapag-Lloyd and writing procedures.

On the other side of the Luton apron, the airline's engine cell and thrust reverser bays were located. It was there that all engines and thrust reversers were overhauled and maintained. The airline undertook engine maintenance up to the 'hot end' stage. It was this part of the engine that the air and fuel are mixed and support beyond this stage is carried out by Caledonian Airmotive at their Prestwick headquarters, the engines ferried from Luton by road.

In addition to maintaining the existing fleet, the airline received its Boeing aircraft without seats, galleys and other items since it had the facilities at Luton to install these items: thus a new 737 delivered to the airline would spend a few days after delivery in the hangar being fitted out.

At the time of delivery of the 767, there was an upgrade to existing 737s, the aircraft being fitted with a new type of seat designed by Avio Interiors. The 767s already carried this type of seating together with the modern look interior consisting of several shades of blue. This style of interior was retrofitted to the 737 fleet as they underwent overhaul and repaint into the new colour scheme.

As well as maintaining its fleet the airline undertook regular maintenance for Air Belgium, Air Europe, Orion Airways and various private operators. The airline was fully licenced by UK and US authorities to undertake Boeing 707, 727, 720B and McDonnell Douglas DC-8 maintenance in addition to the Boeing 737 and 767. They also did VC-10 work for the Royal Air Force.

Chapter 8

Tales from 'Down The Back'

In the Inclusive Tour Industry, the 'Tour Rep' was the holidaymakers' primary point of contact with the tour company, just as the Air Hostess was the passengers' central point of contact with the airline. They were both individuals whose job was to look after the welfare of the clients.

With Britannia Airways, this connection was especially noticeable, for both staff members were working for the same group; passengers - known by all in the industry by the abbreviation of 'pax' - were flying with a holiday airline and they saw it as if all the staff were part of the same 'deal'.

Just as the public's perception of the cabin staffs job was to meet, greet, serve meals and duty-frees and look after the passengers every need, so it was that a Tour Reps job was equally straightforward: arranging excursions, car hire, and doing the occasional piece of interpreting. In reality, however, it was never that simple. Aircraft could run late; coaches would break down; employees go on strike; air traffic control would cause chaos;

rooms can be changed at the last minute, and clients either fell ill, got drunk, or died. Crises were part and parcel of a holiday rep's life - and the efficient way in which he or she dealt with them was the measure of the man or woman concerned.

That was the image holiday companies wanted to present. Reps would never use hard-sell techniques to push excursions, or to steer clients deliberately into individual shops in case, heaven forbid, it was thought they had an 'understanding' with that shop's proprietor. They were to be around only if wanted by the client, and they were to be helpful, cheerful and amusing at all times.

Yeah, sure, right. The reality, right from the very early days, tended to be very different.

Though the vast majority were well behaved, there were incidents of drunken or troublesome passengers causing problems for cabin staff and other passengers. It was not unknown for Britannia to exercise its rights under the Air Navigation Order and turn an aircraft back from

Something of an oddball was A40-BG, dry-leased from Gulf Air. It was later to become G-BGFS. The aircraft is seen here during turnaround at Manchester. *(Richard Vandervord)*

taxying out for take-off, to remove passengers who were causing offence to other passengers and interrupting the safety demonstration. Even more extreme, but necessary would be an unplanned landing while en-route to remove unruly passengers causing disruption and therefore endanger aircraft safety. Fellow pupils acted as 'guinea pig' passengers in the cabin mock-ups, and it was well known that these could be some of the worst 'passengers' in the world.

I would like to make it very clear; in all my experience with Britannia, and I flew with them a good number of times over the years, I never saw anything but the highest professional standards of customer care and service - it's just that cabin crew humour, born under the stress of adversity, could be well, shall we say 'quirky'?

Vicky Craner worked as a contract hostess for Britannia in the 1980s, and also as a tour rep for Thomson Holidays: 'The typical Brit abroad took great comfort in being able to return to the same hotels in the same resorts year after year to try to create that holiday dream, a home from home. You could hear the returning conquerors as they made their way back to their favourite resorts aboard the rep-guided coaches fresh from the airport. 'They've changed the road since last year, love. It seems wider than it was.' This was the start of a typical conversation we often heard, spoken loudly aboard the coach as the seasoned visitors found themselves arriving into growingly familiar surroundings.

The newcomers - and there always were newcomers onboard - looked out of the windows of the coach at the surroundings and must have thought to themselves what on earth they had let themselves in for; If it was a busy resort like Benidorm they would be wondering about the continual building work; if it were a remote Greek island, they would be wondering just where the hell they were - especially if it was at night! 'When does paradise begin?' they must have thought. We tried to reassure them 'Soon, very soon'.

Before long, the coach began to discharge its human cargo at their respective destinations. The front of these hotels invariably looked very different from the manufactured sea-view vistas in the brochures, and this had the effect of filling new visitors to the area with suspicion. As the first people new to the area were discharged to retrieve their cases and make their way inside their homes for the next two weeks, you could almost hear the people left on board thinking, 'I'm glad we're not staying there.' One by one, the families were despatched, and the race to check in at reception began.

Mr and Mrs Been-There-Before anxiously and loudly sought out 'Pedro', 'Pepé' or 'Yani' or whatever they thought their barman's remembered name was in the hotel bar to renew their lifelong friendship, so powerfully struck up during a previous visit. 'Pedro, it's us. Pete and Susan. We were here last year when you had that rowdy group in.'

Pedro, who was really Miguel, and has only

Another poor quality, but historic newspaper cutting shows 23-year old Sheila Miller, from Milton Road, Harpenden sitting inside the engine intake of a new company 737. Sheila is wearing the new bluegrass blue uniform designed by Chief Stewardess Elizabeth Harrison and Assistant Chief Stewardess Meryl Craven.

Above: G-AXNA *'Robert Clive of India'* with everything down and out, coming in to land at London Gatwick. *(Richard Vandervord)*

Right: The Magazine of Britannia Airways - Britannia Inflight, No.2

worked there for the last six weeks, was far too professional to look confused, just smiled politely and reciprocated the hugs, kisses and handshakes. If he was worth his salt he would also flash a faux look of recognition to his long lost 'friends' - and if he was outstanding, he would already be visualising his tip at the end of every drunken day with these returning conquerors.

The humour was not only observational. Cabin Crew had to deal with the passengers, no matter what the request: 'My name is Gavin Scott - BY ID 1175, I joined Britannia in April 1981 as cabin crew, my first flight as a supernumerary crew member was aborted a split second before V_1 by Captain Graeme Freeman, What a start! I have many stories and anecdotes that you may find interesting.

For example; an early morning flight departing Heraklion, Crete at 4 a.m. One steward was serving breakfast, and one pax asked him 'can my wife have a fried egg?' The steward replied not missing a beat; 'Sir if your wife can lay the egg I will fry it'.

'Then there was the time we had a three-hour delay at Tenerife around 20.00 (estimated time of departure - ETD - 17.00) going to Glasgow I was sent over to the terminal to reassure the pax we would be leaving shortly. Escorting the pax out to the aircraft I asked the well dressed young-to-middle-aged suntanned lady if she had an enjoyable holiday? After a three hour delay, the slightly dishevelled looking Glaswegian replied, How dae I luk?' I replied 'you look like a fresh egg madam', trying to cheer her up, 'oh dae-ah' was the reply that came back. 'Yes madam, you look like you have just been laid! She turned to her husband, Ya hear what he jist said? Her husband roared with laughter. Standing at the top of the stairs was the number1 stewardess waiting for all three of us to board ready to close the door, whispering in my ear, what did you say to them?'

Linda Taylor recalls her days in aviation, and with Britannia in particular. 'In June 1964, I joined a company called Autair International as a ground Receptionist (they later became Court

Line). During the winter months, I transferred to the offices in the hangar and worked as a secretary in their technical records department.'

'In Spring 1965, I saw a job advertised with a Gatwick Handling Agency called Airborne Aviation. They handled various airlines, including Caledonian Airways. All ground staff were issued with two uniforms - to meet a Caledonian aircraft you had to wear tartan, and for all other carriers, a navy/white uniform was provided. The idea of being a 'quick-change artist' appealed to me. I was pleased to get the job with them, but it wasn't to be as the company folded before I joined.'

'Britannia was advertising for ground staff, so

Left: Linda Taylor worked for Britannia from 1965 until 1985 as both ground and cabin crew.

Below: Fix beer, Metaxa brandy and empty Ouzo bottles - it could only be Greece, and off the beaten track!
(author)

I applied and was taken on as a temporary ground receptionist. In the winter, I was made permanent. In those days, we were very, very quiet during the winter months, and those of us working on the ground sometimes helped out in other departments. I worked on the switchboard, helped out in the Navigation Department and even worked in the Thomson booking office in Luton.'

'The Luton Airport Terminal Building was located alongside the Airport Control Tower and resembled a Nissen hut. During that year Britannia was taken over by the Thomson Organisation, as was our sister Company. Universal Sky Tours (now Thomson Holidays). Apart from having a new owner, nothing seemed any different.'

'In 1966 the Luton Corporation opened a new Terminal Building. I can distinctly remember the staff getting excited about this new building.

'In March 1967, I transferred to Cabin Crew as a temporary 3/4. I had absolutely no illusions that the job would be glamorous; nevertheless, I was sure I would enjoy it. I was right on both counts! Flying as a stewardess was right up my street, and the Bristol Britannias were excellent aircraft to work on.'

'In 1968 came the introduction of the Boeing 737s. We were all so worried about how we would cope as a Palma flight on the Britannia was three hours, yet on a 737 it was two! Of course, we managed, and once we got used to operating on

Gavin Scott and Jenny Dagley.

Air Traffic Control delays and strikes - often involving the French and the Spanish - were a common thing in the 1970s and early 1980s caused overcrowded passenger terminals and grumpy passengers that in turn gave the cabin staff hell. It was something that Britannia Airways strived long and hard to overcome. *(author)*

the 737s, I enjoyed the flights.'

'In 1971 came the 707's and this meant both long haul and short-haul routes. The crews felt they had the best of both worlds.'

'When the 707s went in 1973, we thought it was the 'end of an era 'for crews going overseas - but along came the Yemen Airways contract. Most of the crews enjoyed their Yemen visits. As ground engineers and Operations/Traffic staff were also based out there, it meant that crews got to know their colleagues from these departments, which in turn meant better rapport.'

'1977 saw stewards joining the ranks of Cabin Crew. We were apprehensive how they would 'fit in' and were delighted how well they all did.'

'1978 brought lots of Air Traffic Control delays, numerous problems and many epic flights. Many may recall the situations we all had to deal with. I was a Flight Stewardess and helped out in twenty-four-hour crewing, as well as being shipped off to places like Palma. Gerona and Ibiza to try and keep the passengers informed. On the whole, the passengers were very tolerant and understanding.'

'1979 stands out as a year of change. A lot of lessons had been learned during 1978 and changes were necessary to overcome problems encountered. The changes were particularly significant within Cabin Services, the Management Team was restructured entirely, and the roles of Co-ordinators were introduced. They were introduced to give Cabin Staff more support and keep Cabin Staff in smaller groups so that they felt some sense of identity and not just a number.'

'In 1980 the company decided to evaluate which type of aircraft to purchase and the Boeing 767 was chosen. A lot of work was done behind the scenes, and several Cabin Staff members were selected to be on the 767 committees. Galleys were designed with the help of the committee, unlike many things' done by committee', they did a splendid job!'

'31 July 1985 marked the end of my life in aviation. I enjoyed my twenty years with Britannia, not only because I liked working for the company, but also because of the people I've worked with'.

The success of Britannia's cabin crew philosophy was based on attitude and teamwork. It meant, for instance, that in an emergency, the crew know what is going to happen and felt confident about dealing with it and knowing what colleagues are also doing. Reaction to a given set of circumstances became intuitive.

Britannia drew cabin crew members off from

line duty to become trainers themselves. And it is actual crew members who became the 'stars' of video training films which were now used extensively on courses. Several of these deal with the incidents which are considered most likely to occur on flights as a result of analysing reports regularly submitted by cabin staff.

Before Britannia commissioned their videos that were more suitable for their requirements, use was made of a more generic film, which happened to be of American origin. The trainees became convulsed with laughter when, in an emergency, a stewardess with a pronounced Brooklyn accent drawled 'Grabe your ayncles' and another, when there was an attempted suicide on board, demurely murmured: 'Please sir, don't worry about the mess. We'll clear it up!'

Passengers did the strangest things - another occurrence from Gavin Scott: 'Although I was Luton based we flew out of every CAA Airport in the UK night stopping in all of them, whereas local crews only flew out of their designated base such as NCL-NCL, MAN-MAN etc. Yes, I loved flying in and out of Glasgow. During the World Cup of 1982 in Spain we were flying from Glasgow to Malaga where Scotland was playing a game in Seville, although Britannia was mainly a holiday, inclusive tour operator we did carry a few passengers going to such worldwide events as part of their holiday. Whilst boarding we noticed a few Scotsmen wearing kilts, nothing new to me I think it was a first for my colleagues, the flight was going smoothly, and the talk amongst all the passengers was what are we going to do with the World Cup when the team returned home, the Team was managed by the late John 'Jock' Stein CBE, a true legend.

About thirty minutes from landing I started the first clearing up of empty glasses, believe me, there were quite a few. About halfway down the cabin I attempted to take away an empty glass from a gentleman wearing a kilt. Could you please leave the glass where it is I am not finished with it. It's empty sir and we will be landing shortly. The gentleman then raised his kilt and pointed to his catheter bag which was full of urine, thinking he needed to empty his catheter I turned away, about thirty seconds later I turned round to witness

A photograph thought to have been taken during a press shoot. Supposedly it shows Britannia Air Hostess Sue Knight tidying up the interior of a 737 after a flight. It is thought to have been taken sometime in 1980.
Simon Peters Collection)

Food menu's on holiday airlines were not that common. This one, coded TFHM4 is thought to be from the early days of long-haul 767. (Britannia Airways).

Britannia

Malachite Kingfisher
Alcedo cristate

Photo, Ardea London

Bar Service

Black Lion Liebfraumilch
Cuvee Borie Red Bordeaux

Henkel Trocken
German Sparkling Wine

Spirit and Liqueur
Miniatures

Fruit Juices and Soft Drinks

Menu

Artichoke and Palm Heart
Salad

Fillet Steak with
Madagascar Sauce
Broccoli
Carrot Puree
Chateau Potatoes

Fresh Fruit Salad

Cheese and Biscuits
Roll and Butter
Tea or Coffee

TFHM4

Menu

the gentleman drinking his now filled glass of urine, literally speechless. His mate quietly said in my ear, 'it's awright he thought whisky wis awfy expensive oan the plane, theres nowt wrang wi his willie!'

Tour reps invariably held introductory of 'welcome' meetings the first morning after guests arrived at the resort. The reasons were two-fold, yes, it was to tell the clients about the delights of where they were staying. but it was also because they wanted their money. or what was left of it. for trips - or more importantly, for their commissions.

Over the years the reps became more and more cunning - or was that skilful? - So that they had become more than just a hard sell. Guests secretly loved these little get-togethers, because it gave them their first chance to have a good moan at the rep. They liked to have a go about the state of their accommodation or the quality of the flight or any number of a hundred and one other things they could think of. It also allowed them to see their very own rep for the first time. Many would have seen lots of other reps before on their travels, especially those who came back to the same resort year after year. They would ask their current rep if they knew the reps they had met before on their travels. The chances of this for a new rep to the company were very remote, but none the less, the conversations took place. 'We were here two years ago, so you can't tell us anything about this place. Our rep then was a fella called Gary. A tall lad with dark hair. Do you know him? Come on, you must know him! Tall, dark, I think he might have been one of those 'nice boys', you know, but he was a great rep.'

Vicky Craner again: 'I did a couple of years as contract cabin crew with Britannia, then caught the Greek bug and decided to transfer across to Thomson Holidays as a Tour Rep, getting a posting to Corfu and later to Santorini.

'Out in Greece, most of us noticed that the season, running roughly from May to October, could be divided into segments according to the type of people who came at particular times. It mirrored what I had already noticed on the Britannia flights but was much more noticeable at the resort than on the flights. In May and June it walkers and birdwatchers. They were nice if rather over-active, and they all went to bed at 10 p.m. much to the disgruntlement of the taverna owners who did not get many sales. The tourists then used

Becoming Number One Charter Airline - as stickered by the entrance door (right) was only achieved by practising delivery of the right service to the pax. *(Britannia Airways)*.

to get up before dawn to eat hearty breakfasts of their preparation before striding off across the landscape bristling with kit to terrorise the local wildlife!

In July and August, the teachers arrived. Back home, they did a great job under challenging circumstances - on holiday, they just seemed mad. They asked many questions, and never waited for the answer before starting the next one. They addressed everyone as if they were schoolchildren. They wore bizarre clothes, and spoke slowly and patiently to their offspring, explaining everything reasonably and usually twice. In the evening they played Scrabble on their balconies while the children drank beer in the bars.

The last two months brought a more relaxed class of holidaymaker. They didn't annoy the local wildlife or confuse the waiters with bad Greek. They were there to get a nice end-of-season tan and drink. They were mostly retired, their children had left home, and they wanted a reasonable time after years of struggle, often sporting T-shirts with the motto: 'Sod The Grandchildren. I'm Spending It!' They didn't need much medication. And they usually remembered to bring what they needed.

Talking of medication, it always baffled many reps how normally intelligent, well-organised people, the kind who ran successful businesses at home, could go on holiday unable to even tie their shoelaces.

Demonstrations - variance on a theme...

Doing the demonstration of what to do in an emergency was something that all Britannia Cabin Crew were more than capable of doing - the problem was getting the passengers to pay attention to the routine. Gavin Scott recalls some of the schemes he had for dealing with it. 'After a couple of months on the line I met up with a colleague Bernard Quinn, who attended the same interview as me, and we began with Britannia on the same day Needless to say we became good friends. I remember one time while socialising we were talking about the safety demo and how we both disliked doing it, Bernard told me that by placing the oxygen mask over his right ear instead of his mouth always got them laughing, meaning they were paying attention, I was to follow suit, and that was just the beginning of a new routine'.

'As the summer wore on, I worked up this safety demo; the oxygen mask over-ear, when indicating the exits. I copied John Travolta's dance 'finger and point' routine from 'Saturday Night Fever'. For the life jacket demo, I imitated a Scottish bagpipe player, moving my fingers as if I was playing an instrument - after that, I was struggling to tie the tape that secured the jacket to my body, and eventually blew the whistle in a naval quartermaster blast!

I still had not found a different way to present the safety card. I would have liked to have held up a girlie magazine; indeed I went as far as to buy a *Playboy,* an excellent piece of literature as it turned out but, being a stickler for company policy I asked the fun-loving Number One what she thought. 'Excellent...' she replied '...but only one thing - on holiday flights there are always children aboard, and they pay attention to everything!'

Judy Pirie was another contract Cabin Crew who moved across to Thomson Holidays: 'Clients would cheerfully approach us fresh off the aircraft and blithely tell us that they had left their life-saving medication at home. One such incident that sticks in my mind involved one rather nervous-looking lady in her mid-thirties, who approached me at Alicante as just as I was trying to deal with someone using a wheelchair, two sets of lost luggage and a baby without nappies. 'Are you my rep?' the woman demanded of me. 'Yes, I think so' I replied, looking up from the task in hand. 'But is it very urgent, because I'm a bit tied up at the moment. 'It is, I'm afraid. I'm a manic depressive, and I've left my medicine at home. If I don't take it within an hour, I'm liable to self-harm'.

It was amazing how quick the reps learnt the names and phone numbers of the local pharmacy, the doctors and even the police!

Gavin Scott again: 'I cannot remember the details of this particular flight, but I was halfway down the cabin doing a bar service when a rather impatient passenger tugged at my cabin jacket by the hem. Now one thing none of us can stand is being touched, never mind being lightly grabbed by the hem of a jacket! 'Can I have a drink please?' Drinks service can be pretty frantic, and it's often possible to 'run out of hands' - He got the sharp reply 'Sir I was born with Testicles, not Tentacles!'

Over the years, I have met many reps, of just about every mental persuasion. Probably the best, and certainly the most memorable was a guy called Paul, who was working for the legendary Sunmed Holidays on the Greek island of Santorini.

He had everything down to a fine art. His idea of a welcome meeting was handing out a single photocopied sheet: 'These are the trips available. The Sunmed office is there...' his hand swept around, taking in one half of the black volcanic sand beach at Kamari'. 'Look for my beanie hat and a bottle of Metaxa. If the hat is on a stick, the office is open'.

He did very little apparent 'work' - a trick he carried off supremely well because everything he arranged - like a three-day 'beach barbeque' at the Villa White House - was very organised. Paul claimed to have a different 'girlfriend' flown out every week, bringing him two pounds of English smoked bacon and a carton of 200 cigarettes. I never did find out if the former was right, but in

Above: 767 G-BNYS at London
Gatwick
(Emma Dayle Collection).

Left: The drinks service could be
hectic, especially on the widebodies.
(Britannia Airways).

the three weeks I was there, he certainly had three different girls staying with him!

Some passengers carried loyalty to the airline to extreme levels. In 1998 Peter Bailey, who regularly flew with Britannia out of East Midlands Airport marked his 90th flight with the airline, by presenting them with a silver salver. As Peter told *Britannia AirWaves:* I have been flying with Britannia for the last twenty-five years, travelling abroad at least twice a year, often to my favourite resort of Malaga. I always chose Britannia and Thomson. Many of the crews at EMA and BHX know me as the Toblerone Man, as I always give them a pack at the end of the flight. I appreciate just how hard they work to deliver the top quality service that is synonymous with Britannia'.

The stresses and strains of Cabin Crew are occasionally not helped by the antics of passengers. On one notorious occasion - possibly archetypal - the senior Britannia Cabin Crew member's post-flight report for a 737 flight out of Palma to Birmingham achieved a much wider circulation than usual. It concerned an unmarried couple who were sitting next to each other on the flight. At some point, the couple disappeared into a lavatory together but omitted to bolt the door. A little old lady waiting outside the toilet realised that the couple was intent on joining the Mile High Club. She was horrified by this and reported it to the Cabin Crew who, one suspects, wanted just to let nature take its course, but eventually the Number One succumbed to the old ladies protestations and went to the Captain, explaining the problem.

The Captain was a man of action; he knew exactly what to do - he immediately told his First

Temperatures below zero with snow on the ground and aircraft made the sun and swimming pools look all the more enticing. *(Britannia Airways).*

Officer to go back and sort it out! By the time the First Officer headed back to the lavatory, the couple were in their seats and fast asleep with big smiles on their faces, and the First Officer didn't have the heart to do anything about it!

'Troublesome Pax' was something that Gavin Scott was well aware of. ''Again meeting up with Bernard, who was an ex-policeman, we were discussing rowdy passengers, agreeing they never travel alone, always in a group - I asked how he dealt with them.

He told me - look for the biggest of the group and have a quiet word in his ear. Tell that idiot if he doesn't start behaving the lot of you will be met on the ground by the local police and your holiday will begin in a Spanish Jail - even drunken idiots listen to the big man!

' I was glad Bernard told me what to do as I had reasons to do it a couple of times down the route. It may not have been in the Britannia Handbook, but it certainly saved the company a lot of money by not diverting into an unscheduled airport and upsetting all the rest of the passengers'

The airline took pride in its standards of service and comfort for passengers and was continually seeking to improve its facilities. A £700,000 galley up-date programme was announced for completion by the summer of 1987 which introduced to the 737 fleet a serving cart system similar to that on the 767. Previously Britannia launched new plastic meal trays with a specially developed front slot which allowed easy insertion of hot meals into the trays after heating in the oven and before serving to passengers. This seemingly minor detail actually resulted in a considerable time saving for cabin staff who previously had to remove the covers from each meal tray to add the hot entreé.

Passengers enjoyed a high standard of comfort on the 767. With free video and audio entertainment, Britannia is currently the only charter airline in Europe to provide this standard of in-flight entertainment to its passengers. Video also provides the pre-flight safety drill, previously several members of the cabin staff would demonstrate emergency procedures and life jacket use; it has been found that the video presentation provided a more effective means of getting the safety message across, while freeing the cabin staff to prepare refreshments and meals for serving once the aircraft is airborne.

Passengers heading back to Britain from abroad could view a fifteen-minute news roundup of events and stories of the previous fortnight. Also fitted across both fleets was what was then a unique passenger information system. Small electronic displays located throughout the cabin regularly indicate the aeroplane's altitude and ground speed.

The mid-1990s saw the start of a unique relationship between Britannia Airways and one of the world's leading animal charities. The Born Free Foundation, founded as Zoo Check in 1984, was renamed in 1990 and officially established a year later. Its history went back to 1966 when Bill Travers and Virginia McKenna starred in the film Born Free, which told the true story of George and Joy Adamson who returned Elsa the lioness to the wild and devoted their lives to the protection of lions and other species.

It all started in 1995 when the lion and lioness Raffi and Anthea were rescued from Tenerife. They, and Rikki, a leopard, had been kept in cages on the roof of a bar. The Foundation had been

Above: Britannia cabin staff with one of two seven-year old Siberian tigers, Tara and King, brought back on one flight. The big cats had been rescued from tiny cages in a circus trailer in Northern Italy. *(Britannia Airways)*

trying almost five years trying to get them, and it was only when the *Mail on Sunday* carried a major expose of their pitiful existence that they succeeded.

Britannia carried the big cats in their crates back to the UK in one of their aircraft and, after two years at the Big Cat Sanctuary in Kent, flew them to Shamwari, a private game reserve in South Africa as their new home in a vast bush enclosure.

In 1996 Britannia flew Rikki the leopard from Tenerife back to the UK. The next year five tigers were rescued from an Italian circus trailer and flown back, and in 2000 two lions were rescued from a run-down zoo in Greece. That same year the airline started the 'Spare Coins Save Lives' in-flight appeal, which by the end of 2001 bad raised more than £1 million.

As Virginia McKenna said at the time: 'I can't speak too highly of the airline. Britannia goes to great lengths, over and above what is required, to ensure the cats' journey is smooth and trouble-free. Extra staff are laid on to guide us through unfamiliar countries and their regulations, and to liaise with officials at the various airports en route. There have never been any problems with transporting animals. I am sure they don't much like being kept in a crate in the belly of the aircraft, but they invariably seem calm and unstressed. We always have our vet with them and Britannia very kindly allow him to access the hold via an internal chute.

From time to time, the Captain will announce to the passengers that they have a lion, tiger or leopard on board, and everyone is delighted and excited when they hear about their unusual travelling companions!

We will always ask Britannia for help if they have any flights available. They are our first choice for these rescue flights, and we are incredibly grateful for their continued support and generosity'.

Other celebrities were heavily involved in Born Free and Britannia. The efforts of the airline staff and passengers helped rescue fifteen chimpanzees and relocate them on a jungle island in the middle of Lake Victoria. The project was filmed by BBC Television and starred Nicholas Lyndhurst of *'Only Fools and Horses'* fame. Joanna Lumley of *'Absolutely Fabulous'* was also a keen supporter of Born Free and has helped

Joanna Lumley with acress and aminal rights activist Virginia McKenna at the naming ceremony of 767 'Bill Travers' *(Britannia Airways)*

promote the Britannia Airways onboard appeal, as did Martin Clunes of *'Men Behaving Badly'*.

Sometimes passenger behaviour was darkly determined. On a flight from Manchester, not long after take-off, a male passenger had a heart attack and unfortunately passed away by the time the aircraft had diverted to Bristol. The ambulance crew took the body off, and the Britannia crew explained to the widow that they could not get their baggage off before the aircraft arrived at Palma, where it would be offloaded and flown back to the UK. She was most upset. 'What do you mean, take it off? I have paid for this holiday, and I am going to Palma,' she said. And that's precisely what she did.

Bearing in mind that Brittania carried ten million passengers a year, there were very few deaths on board, and the crew and the airline did everything they could to ease the pain for the bereaved. There was, however, one occasion when the crew were surprised by a widow who was flying back from Spain with her husband's body in the hold. She was buying double quantities of duty-free whisky and cigarettes, and the crew pointed out the right amount that she could take back into the UK. 'Oh,' she said, 'that's alright, there's always the entitlement for him in the hold.'

Chapter 9

A new MD, Rivals, External Consultants - and the 757

There were management changes in 1989, with Dave Hopkins moving to Chairman and the arrival in November of Roger Burnell, who became the company's new Managing Director. He had previously been Managing Director at Thomson's Lunn Poly operation.

Burnell was the first Managing Director of Britannia not to have been a pilot. He felt this placed him at an immediate disadvantage in that he knew little about flying and so he decided to learn to fly, which is very convenient at Luton because Britannia has its own flying club on the airfield. At the very least then he would know what was going on from an operational point of view and would also know the terminology.

One of his early tasks was to take a good look at the business, employing external consultants to help with the process. What was discovered from this review was that although everyone in the airline thought Britannia provided the best customer services, and were the best in the business, the reality was that it was no longer true.

In the early 1980s, a number of new holiday airlines had been created in the UK - Horizon started Orion, Harry Goodman's International Leisure Group started Air Europe and the former Dan-Air and Air Europe executive Errol Cossey had formed Air 2000 and later Flying Colours. Thomson Holidays, as a tour operator, did most of its flying with Britannia but it also contracted the other airlines. Britannia soon discovered that the quality score with airlines like Air 2000 was better than their own product. On every Thomson holiday, there was a questionnaire to fill in on the way back; it included questions on the resort and the hotels, and there were around six questions about the flight.

From that, the company discovered there were airlines out there doing better than Britannia, and that the travelling public did not have that high a regard for their aircraft. When the 737s were brought in some twenty years earlier, they were way ahead of their time, but by 1989, this was no longer the case. The Boeing 757 was becoming the workhorse of the charter airlines in the UK; it was more efficient, more reliable and comfortable.

Britannia was facing growing competition from a number of other airlines. Apart from Air Europe and Air 2000, - companies like Airtours, JMC and Flying Colours all began to aggressively operate in what was a very crowded market. Even Richard Branson's Virgin group began to operate a small fleet of A320s under the brand-name Virgin Sun. Lancastrian David Crossland founded the Airtours tour operating company and quickly established its in-house airline, Airtours International Airways, on 1 October 1990. It started operations on 11 March 1991 flying McDonnell Douglas MD-80 aircraft to destinations throughout Europe.

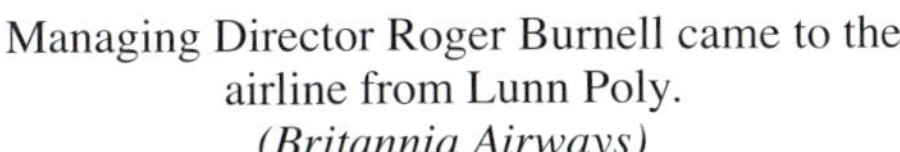

Managing Director Roger Burnell came to the airline from Lunn Poly.
(Britannia Airways)

Britannia experienced great rivalry from the newcomers to the business in the late 1980s through to to turn of the century. Air 2000 - seen represented above by Boeing 757 G-OOOV with the First Choice brand by the front door was one. *(Air 2000)*

Flying Colours - also started by Errol Cossey was another, as was David Crossland's Airtours.

Cardiff-based Aspro Holidays and their inhouse airline, Inter European Airways were acquired by Airtours and integrated in November 1993 adding new aircraft types such as the Boeing 757 and Airbus A320 to the fleet. The MD83's were replaced in 1995-1996 with more Airbus A320s. In 1996 the parent company also acquired Danish charter airline Premiair. Airtours also had operations in Germany with airline FlyFTi, operating Airbus A320s until this was merged back into the UK fleet during 2003.

Flying Colours was Errol Cossey's third foray into the charter airline business and began operations in the summer of 1996 with a fleet of Boeing 757-200, Airbus A320 and A321 airliners.

A320 G-VKIS *'Sundance Kid'* was part of the Virgin Sun fleet, another rival - albiet a small one - to the Britannia operation. *(Kirk Smeeton Collection).*

Flying Colours had several operational bases outside of its Manchester Airport headquarters, including London Gatwick Airport and Glasgow International Airport. The airline quickly established a positive reputation in the charter industry, with a fleet of newly built aircraft and new features; Flying Colours were the first airline in the UK to have liquid crystal display TV screens in the cabins of their 757s.

In 1998 the tour operator Thomas Cook Group acquired Flying Colours Leisure Group. Subsequently, the in-house charter airline of Thomas Cook, Airworld, adopted the Flying Colours Airlines brand. JMC Airlines Limited - also known as JMC Air, JMC Airlines or simply JMC and stylised as jmc - was formed by the merger of Caledonian Airways and Flying Colours Airlines, following the purchase of Thomas Cook & Son by the Carlson Leisure Group. JMC Air was named after the initials of the son of Thomas Cook, John Mason Cook.

The situation was not all Britannia's fault. Within Thomson Holidays a view had evolved and stabilised around getting their flying in 130-seater 'chunks' was the ideal. Even the 767s exactly doubled that number of passengers, and so it was perfectly acceptable to fit two 'chunks' into one aircraft.

Britannia found itself in a position where the service to the travelling public was not as good as it should have been and the fleet was becoming tired looking. Finally, the costs of running the airline were too high.

A good example of this was the way the pilot workforce was employed. Because the base was at Luton, the pilots had been employed at Luton, and that meant that fifty per cent of the pilots were based at there, although it only represented a small percentage of the flying. At least fifty-five per cent of the flying was out of Gatwick or

Airtours - also known as Airtours International was later to evolve into MyTravel, was another Britannia rival, as seen here with A320 G-TICL. *(Emma Dayle Collection).*

Manchester, with the result that the airline had pilots in taxis being ferried around or in hotel beds, which resulted in a vast and expensive inefficiency. The result was a strategic review that in turn brought forth a scheme which was called *'Flight Plan for the 1990s'*.

This was a very public statement, making it clear that things were going to change. The airline management sent a video to every member of staff, explaining what was going to happen, to show that they were serious about the plan. The net result was that Britannia had around 220 redundancies and about 170 moves around the company.

The most obvious change was that the airline started to introduce Boeing 757s and lose some of the 737s. At the time many would not admit it, but in truth everybody in the company realised that the changes were overdue and so there was not a huge backlash from the staff or the unions when the changes were introduced.

The objective was that everyone was in place by the summer of 1991, with the pilots based at different airports. The company also started a study of replacement aircraft for the 737s, and after a lot of investigation, including looking at a possible Airbus A320, the airline made the decision to stick with 757s and 767s. By 1992 they had sold all the 737-300 series that were inherited from Orion during the takeover (see later chapter) and were looking to sell off the 737-200s.

There was a lot of standardisation between the 757 and the 767 in terms of components, but more important was the flight-deck and crew commonality.

Many people have always thought that Britannia was an all-Boeing airline, but enough documents have survived that show that it was certainly not the case. There was strong evidence that Britannia took what was most suitable for their needs. If, for instance, the Airbus A321 had been around in the early 1990s, that could have been the ideal choice.

Below: 767 G-BKPW comes in to land at London Gatwick. *(Kirk Smeeton Collection)*.

Right: Britannia Airways inflight magazines has changed again by the 1990s, with barely any reference to the airline on its cover.

Above: 757 G-BYAD climbs out for another return trip to the UK. *(Richard Vandervord)*

Left: One of Roger Burnell's 'questionaires' waits to be completed by the passengers to show their views on the airline.

Whatever the aircraft in the Britannia fleet, they worked hard for the airline. 737 utlization was about 4500 hours a year, and perhaps 6000 hours a year with the 767. Certainly, as the 737s got older, they required a great deal of maintenance, but the 757 and 767 were more sophisticated and required a lot less maintenance. In fact, in 1993-94 when Britannia rolled over the whole fleet and got rid of the last of the 737s, the maintenance requirements halved overnight.

The way to make money with a charter airline is with certainty, and it was with that basic thinking and determination that Britannia Airways set about confirming its role during the early-to-mid 1990s.

Britannia's Managing Director Roger Burnell insisted that despite the United Kingdom's economic problems - particularly the debacle of 'Black Wednesday' in September 1992 when Britain suspended its membership of the Exchange Rate Mechanism (ERM) - the airline stuck to its plan and knew how its business should be run.

It appears that there was a common thought within the organisation that Britannia was an independent airline - it was not. No matter how the staffs saw themselves, Britannia was part of an integrated travel group. Part of this came from the fact that the airline held eighteen scheduled service licences. Burnell arranged for the airline to voluntarily to give them up to concentrate solely on charter operations.

The airline then focused the need on serving Thomson tour operations and quite quickly moved the percentage of flying for Thomson to over ninety per cent. The planning became much more of a dual activity, with both companies actively involved.

The management team set up the operation internally, so it was in the interest of the

757 G-BYAH with an early example of www.brittania.com on the side of the fuselage departs on another charter flight. *(Kirk Smeeton Collection)*.

Thomson Travel Group to fly the aircraft as intensively as possible; they enjoyed cheaper and cheaper seat rates the more they flew the aircraft. That meant the aircraft utilisation moved up dramatically.

Certainty was the key so that if the organisation planned to fly a certain programme and all the resources were geared up to service that programme, it was possible to make a great deal of money. Disrupt either the flying or the schedule, and it becomes costly. An excellent example of this was Britannia's long-haul business, which grew dramatically from 1994 to 1998. The airline obtained bigger 767 aircraft to handle the workload, and in one year it increased to twenty-five per cent of the company's business.

Part of this increase came from Britannia's long-haul business from Gatwick to Australia, which celebrated ten years in November 1998. The airline's staff newspaper Airwaves, reported the event.

Passengers on the first Perth/Adelaide flight of the winter season were treated to a Buck's Fizz reception and a slice of the 24-inch cake. The first charter airline to start flying down under with fortnightly flights from Luton to Perth and Cairns, Britannia also had three flights a week to

Below: Another holiday charter over! 767 B-BLKW comes in to land at London Gatwick.
(Richard Vandervoord)

Right: The core of the 'Royal Service' branding, introduced in the early 1990s.

Brisbane, Melbourne, Perth and Adelaide, plus a weekly service to Auckland, New Zealand.

Consultants and re-branding

The early 1990s was a time when just about every British airline indulged in a massive series of almost pointless but very expensive 'branding' exercises. Britannia was no exception when it launched its in-flight 'Royal Service'. This meant that for the first time, the airline was putting branding on their in-flight service. The meal tray had 'Royal Service' written on it; all the items were dark blue. The carpets were dark blue, the seats were dark blue, and the headrest was red and blue.

'Royal Service' existed for three or four years. Clearly, it was an attempt to make the in-flight service appear more upmarket. However, it was quickly realised that the whole concept was more than a little pretentious and that the airline was trying to be something that it was not. By all internal documents located, it had come about with the best of intentions, but in truth, it looked as though Britannia were trying to copy scheduled service operators such as British Airways or even Dan-Air and Air Europe who were both venturing into the scheduled service market.

When news of the change of in-flight service style reached the media, a somewhat strange reaction occurred. Under headlines such as 'Britannia Waives the Royals' newspapers went on to describe how 'Holiday giant Britannia is dropping the word 'Royal' from its flights. In an embarrassing blow for the Royal Family, Britains biggest charter firm says that the title no longer has positive associations'.

The firm's PR chief, Richard Hedges, was quoted as saying 'We have done some market research and have found that the name 'royal' no longer has the kudos it did when we introduced it'. Although tagged on to Hedges comment, I suspect the following came from the journalist 'Since the airline's one-class royal service (sic) was launched four years ago, the House of Windsor has been rocked by scandal and divorce. Both Charles and Diana have made public confessions of adultery'. A Buckingham Palace spokesman is supposed to have said 'This is a matter for the company and is not something we would comment on'.

A new in-flight service brand seemed to be in order, apparently no matter what the cost. This took two years and involved consultation with several professional branding companies. The result was '360', the new brand name for' Britannia's in-flight service. The interiors of the aircraft were re-furnished using a basic lilac colour, which was thought by the designers to be bright and cheerful and had an enjoyable holiday feel about it. The same consultants branded all the meal trays, the in-flight entertainment and even the cocktail sticks. It was also time to change the uniforms.

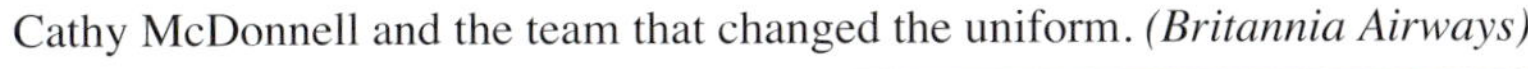

Cathy McDonnell and the team that changed the uniform. *(Britannia Airways)*

Cathy McDonnell, Cabin Crew Regional Manager North, was given the task of replacing the Royal Service Uniform. She knew that satisfying the tastes and requirements of crews, the company and the passengers was not going to be easy. The uniform needed to be practical, comfortable and enjoyable to wear. It needed to contrast with the then-current uniform that was popular with the passengers but regarded as unflattering by the cabin crew. Said Cathy: 'We approached the crews to see what they wanted. They asked why couldn't they have a proper fashion designer?'

'We sent out briefs to a number of big names in the fashion world, and Elizabeth's preliminary sketches proved the most exciting'. 'Elizabeth' was Elizabeth Florence Emanuel (née Weiner, born 5 July 1953) is a British fashion designer who is best known for designing, with her former husband David Emanuel, the wedding dress worn by Diana, Princess of Wales, in 1981. Since then she developed her own label, worked in costume

Two cabin crew pose sitting inside the intake of a 767 engine, showing off their new Elizabeth Emanuel uniforms. *(Britannia Airways)*

Cabin crew pose with fashion designer Elizabeth Emanuel at the launch of the new '360' uniform. *(Britannia Airways)*

design for airlines, cinema, pop video and television productions, as well as providing a couture service to some of the world's most famous women.

So, where next? Cathy pulled together a project team, whose views and opinions were paramount in developing the new uniform. Wensum Corporate Clothing was chosen to manufacture the uniforms and worked closely with both Elizabeth Emanual and the Britannia team throughout the project. Cathy again: 'Above all, the crews had to like it. If they like what they are wearing, they are going to be happier at their jobs'. With the final designs in place, a new challenge arose. 360 was emerging as the new on-board service and Cathy and her team had to find a way of incorporating the concept and colours into the uniforms, for 360 had not even been conceived at the start of the uniform project.

Eventually, the solution was relatively simple. All it took was a change to the tie and scarf and a tabard and name-badge that featured the highlight colours of 360. There were now two looks to the uniform - a smart corporate outdoor look and a bright and colourful on-board 360 look.

360, OBK and Market-speak

In case anyone was wondering about how the name was chosen, it was explained in *Britannia Briefing'*: 'We chose 360 because it has no meaning, but is memorable'. It must have struck the right note with some people, for the design recieved a Certificate of Excellence in the European Design Annual Awards in 1999.

The branding was launched to the managers in March I997, when the new uniforms - commissioned and designed by Elizabeth Emanuel to a brief for a more informal uniform - away from the formal military 'Royal Service' look - were also displayed.

During the next month, 1450 Cabin Crew visited the Hilton Hotel at Gatwick, where they were fitted for their new blue and red uniforms and trained in the new service.

The 'Royal Service' had been very traditional, not just in its name but in the look of the cabins, which was thought of by many as being very austere and old fashioned. The 360 service not only modernised the cabins but it gave the Cabin Crew the chance to become real people. The airline management wanted them to let their personalities come through and deliver a service that was fresher and more contemporary. It was suggested by some that perhaps the idea of the 360 logo was that it was all-encompassing, a complete service.

There were substantial changes in catering. Britannia introduced things like afternoon tea, sausage and mash, roast beef on inbound flights on Sundays, and, in something almost directly taken from the 1994 BBC Two comedy series *'The High Life'*.the idea of themed menus for destinations, just as appeared in one episode. Not all the ideas were successful. Passengers didn't like afternoon tea - they preferred a hot meal.

At the same time, passenger meals were enhanced. Complimentary audio and video entertainment were offered, and an award-winning 'OBK' programme (On-Board Kids) is in place to make flying fun for the younger passengers who make up a large percentage of holiday charter customers. As the promotional material said: 'With our children's service, OBK, we have captured children's imaginations by listening to what they want, not what we think they want. OBK is their own club with plenty of fun-packed features and activities to keep them occupied and amused such as activity-packed OBK magazines and their own OBK Television and Radio programmes. They also have their own meals and drinks selection catering for younger tastes'.

Left: 'Jet Cadets'.

Below: 757 G-BYAR seen taxing at Kephalonia.
(Richard Vandervord)

To the surprise of many of the branding and image-consultants - but not the cabin staff - , many of the passengers did not like the '360' branding; they thought that the airline was dropping the 'Britishness' of the airline.

Passenger surveys revealed the strangest of things as a press release from the company revealed in 1999: men took fewer changes of underwear on holiday than women. The survey conducted on flights out of Manchester and Gatwick airports asked holidaymakers on their way to Spanish resorts questions about their habits and plans. Asked how many changes of underwear they had brought with them, the average number for men was 0.89 per night, compared with 1.2 pairs for women.

The holidaymakers, however, did take with them stocks of teabags, photos of loved ones and jars of Marmite and Bovril. They often forgot to take a toothbrush, cameras and film, batteries, electric razors and plug adaptors. They also missed their pets more than their family.

One customer caused chaos at the security area when he was discovered in possession of his pet goldfish, safely travelling in a Tupperware box that he wanted to take with him on holiday. It seems he was concerned that it would have to go through the X-Ray machine. Needless to say, Britannia staff took the finned traveller back to their office until the human holidaymaker returned to collect it!

Using 'Sexy Words' with Customer Relations.

With, on average, 13,000 telephone calls received by customer relations in the the peak summer months, Britannia urgently needed assistance to help work through the additional 400 customer letters received over the same period.

Procter and Procter, a consultancy group from Fulham, specialising in marketing services, were engaged and given the task of helping the airline to change its working practices to make their workload more manageable.

The first step was a two-day course at the East Midlands Training Centre on how to reply to passengers by telephone instead of in writing, enabling the airline to speed things up and surprise the customers by dealing with their queries immediately.

It was not an easy task, as the Britannia staff were used to replying by letter. In itself, it seemed a very plausible and benifical task, but of course, this being the 1990s - the typical buzz-words and management-speak crept in. As Kate Varley and Doreen Slack from Customer Relations said at the time: 'With the consultants help we were taught how to control our telephone conversations and show that we care and are listening to our customers by the types and words we use and how we said them. For instance, 'we will be delighted to do that for you' or 'we would like to be able to help, however'… and it works at home too!

'Putting these new telephone techniques into action back at the office was difficult at first and we were all nervous, but after a few dozen calls, we became confident and we found to our amazement that our 'sexy words' as Procter and Procter call them it worked - even with our older customers.'

'Of course, not everyone is available to speak to on the telephone, so follow-up course 'Be Passionate with your Pen' was arranged. The course title was guaranteed to worry our partners!.

'The training, like the telephone course, taught us to reply positively and provide a better service. By using the same 'sexy words', we were taught many ways of explaining different situations to our passengers that showed our concern for their welfare. Having been used to

Being Passionate with their Pens are from bottom left clockwise Customer Relations manager Tina Barbour, Customer Relations Officers Krysia Wood and Suzanne Harley, Senior Customer Relations Officer Ros de Visscher, Customer Relations Officers Kay Varley and Doreen Slack and Customer and Trade Communications Manager Deborah Clark.

'Name tags to be worn on tabards when working in the galley or doing meal services'. Sue Catton and Chrissy Clarke working hard in the galley of BY312, a 767 flight. *(Simon Peters Collection)*

explaining at length to our passengers of the reasons for delays, different services and the like, we found this new style of writing to be more efficient. So much so that we were able to catch up on our backlog of correspondence quickly'.

Incident at Gerona...
Britannia Airways Flight BY226A was an international charter flight from Cardiff, which crashed on landing at Girona Airport, Spain, on 14 September 1999 and broke apart. Of the 236 passengers and nine crew on board, two received severe injuries and forty-one sustained minor ones. One of the passengers who had sustained only minor injuries died five days later of unsuspected internal injuries. The Boeing 757–204, registration G-BYAG, was damaged beyond economical repair and scrapped.

The flight was landing at night, through thunderstorms with heavy rain at 21:47 UTC (23:47 local). Several preceding flights had diverted to Barcelona which was also planned as BY226A's alternate. The weather prior to the landing approach had been reported as 'Surface wind 350/6 kt, visibility 4 km, thunderstorm with heavy rain, cloud 3-4 octas at 1,500 feet, 1–2 octas cumulonimbus at 3,000 feet, 5-7 octas at 4,000 feet, temperature 20 °C/ dewpoint 20 °C, QNH 1010 mb, with recent rain.'

The crew initially executed the VOR/DME non-precision instrument approach procedure to runway 02. Upon becoming visual, the crew determined that the aircraft was not adequately aligned with the runway and initiated a missed approach. A change in wind direction now favoured the opposite runway, so the crew repositioned for an ILS (Instrument Landing System) approach to runway 20. The aircraft descended below the cloud and became visual with the runway at around 500 feet above ground level. At a late stage in the final approach, the airfield lighting failed for a few seconds. The aircraft touched down hard, bounced, and made a second heavier touchdown causing substantial damage to the nosewheel and its supports. This caused further damage to the aircraft systems, including loss of electrical power, interference with controls and an uncommanded increase in thrust.

The 757 left the runway at high speed, approximately 3,300 feet from the second touchdown point. It then ran 1,125 feet across flat grassland beside the runway, before going diagonally over a substantial earth mound adjacent to the airport boundary, becoming semi-airborne as a result. Beyond the mound, it hit several medium-sized trees, and the right engine struck the boundary fence. The aircraft then passed through the fence, re-landed in a field and both main landing gears collapsed. It finally stopped after an 800-foot slide across the field, 6,200 feet from the second touchdown.

The damage was substantial: the fuselage fractured in two places, and the landing gear and both engines detached. Despite considerable damage to the cabin, the crew evacuated the aircraft efficiently. However, three of the eight emergency exits would not open, and several escape slides did not inflate.

The tower controller, aware that something was amiss, activated the emergency alarm. However, the emergency bell did not ring. Fire crews were alerted by a dedicated telephone line and went to the threshold of runway 20 and drove along the runway looking for the aircraft, without success. The search spread to the sides of the runway and the overshoot area. The wreckage was eventually located eighteen minutes after the accident. There was a further fourteen-minute delay while the fire crews tried

The ill-fated G-BYAG takes off on another charter - it was to meet its demise at Gerona on 14 September 1999. *(Kirk Smeeton Collection)*.

to gain access to the site.

There were no immediate fatalities, and the injuries were few: two serious and forty-two minor. However, one passenger, who had been admitted to hospital with apparently minor injuries and discharged the following day, died five days later from unsuspected internal injuries. Criticism was aimed at the Airport authorities after the accident, particularly for the fact it took rescue crews more than an hour to reach and evacuate the scene. Indeed, at least one passenger walked across the airfield to the terminal to seek help.

Staff from both the airline and tour company were quickly assembled and were sent to Gerona to give whatever assistance they could. Most passengers were not hurt, and most of those who were only had minor injuries, so the vast amount of passengers elected to stay in Spain and continue their holiday. However, as all personal belongings were trapped on the aircraft for several days, a great deal of assistance had to be given both financially and practically to ensure all passengers had the basic necessities of life. After about three or four days, the accident investigation team cleared the Britannia team to go onboard and collect the suitcases, handbags and items like spectacles, of which they found sixty pairs alone.

One memorable event involved a lady passenger who said that she had lost a gold bracelet in the mud, worth some £35,000. She described to the searchers exactly where it was; who went there and found it immediately!

The support operation lasted two weeks and was understandably emotionally draining for all the staff involved.

The inquiry into the accident started immediately, but as in all air accidents proved to be quite complex. A brief interim report was published in early 2000, but the detailed final report was not published until 10 December 2014!

The accident was investigated by the Spanish Civil Aviation Accident and Incident Investigation Commission. In its final report, the finding was: It is considered that the most probable cause of the accident was the destabilisation of the approach below decision height with loss of external visual references and automatic height callouts immediately before landing, resulting in a touchdown with excessive descent rate in a nose-down attitude. The resulting displacement of the nose landing gear support structure caused disruption to aircraft systems that led to uncommanded forward thrust increase and other effects that severely aggravated the consequences of the initial event.

The following contributing factors were also determined:

• Impairment of the runway visual environment as a result of darkness and torrential rain and the extinguishing of runway lights immediately before landing.

• Suppression of some automatic height callouts by the GPWS 'SINK RATE' audio caution.

• The effect of shock or mental incapacitation on the pilot flying at the failure of the runway lights which may have inhibited him from making a decision to go around.

• The absence of specific flight crew training in flight simulators to initiate a go-around when below landing decision height.

• Insufficient evaluation of the weather conditions, particularly the movement and severity of the storm affecting the destination airport.

Chapter 10

Sports, Social and Families

The staff leisure side of things was well catered for over the years, with some regular groups and events and innumerable 'one-offs'.

From sports matches to charity events, from days out to helping others, the list is almost endless and it would be impossible to mention them all. However, here are just some of the things that went on.

On Christmas Day 1985, Comic Relief was launched live on BBC One from the Safawa refugee camp in Sudan during Noel Edmonds' Late Late Breakfast Show. The telethon idea happened for the first time in 1988, and many Britannia employees participated over the years. Kingsley Punnet, Paint Workshop Supervisor, put on his overalls for charity and raised £1,400 by painting a Britannia Flying Club Piper Warrior; two teams from Engineering met to play a little known version of football, which involved wigs and wellies being worn by the players - the Vauxhall Brache Arena waived charges for the use of the pitch and C&A fashion chain provided the natty T-shirts worn by the teams. The final score was 3-3 and over £700 raised. Other events included John Russell, Commercial Route Planning Officer, shaving off his beard and raising over £200 much to the delight and amusement of his colleagues while Richard Hedges, General Manager Communications raised an impromptu £10 for suffering the loss of blood supply to his nose by keeping the red nose on all day!

Staff at Luton, Manchester and East Midlands all organised events. Everything from champagne days out to Ascot, Boozy Barge Cruises and even a day out t'Blackpool finishing off with a Harry Ramsden Fish Supper.

There was also a cycling team which not only entered races, but also participated in charity fundraising events such as the London to Brighton Bike Ride, one year raising £7,000 for the British Heart Foundation. 'The fifty-eight-mile route is chosen for practicality and safety and runs through some of the most picturesque English villages. You need to be moderately fit' said Captain Jon Pepper, one of that year's team when talking about the event. 'It is not a race, and there is plenty of time to practice. It's great fun with a brilliant atmosphere. Also, you don't have to cycle back at the end of it - there are trains organised for the return journey'.

Individually, Dave Creese from Britannia's Wheel and Tyre Bay was a keen club time triallist

High fliers and speeders!
Above: left to right: Captain Jon Pepper, Captain Mark Stephens and Jayne Pepper at the end of the London to Brighton cycle ride.

Left: Bruce Moore and Mick Neil getting ready for 'The Island'
(*both Britannia Airways*)

Above: 'The Britannia Bombers' may seem an inappropriate name to describe a gentle netball team, but this was what these ladies insist on calling themselves. At the time this picture was taken, the team was on the lookout for more recruits (the female variety) and anyone interested in joining 'The Bombers' was to contact the team's secretary, Connie Smith, in the Publicity Department. The line-up from left to right: Maureen Franklin, Lynn Glendenning, Christine Baker, Janet Smith, Connie Smith, Wilma Maclean, Joan Kelsall, Susan Townley, Marilyn Goodchild. *(Kaz Ale Collection]*

Left: Dave Creese 'on his bike'. *(Britannia Airways)*

and cycling fifteen to twenty miles each way to work managing to double-up commuting with training. David Mallard from Tech Records participated in the London marathon along with systems analysis Stuart Parkes and several others. Bruce Moore from engineering and Mick Neil, another Britannia employee, participated in the Isle of Man Tourist Trophy motorcycle race, entering into the sidecar event, finishing a very incredible twelfth out of eighty-one competitors from twenty-one countries.

There was also a series of very strong Pools Teams - especially during the 1980s - when they won innumerable awards and trophies.

Britannia also took to the water in the form of

Above: One of the many Britannia Airways football teams. Kaz Ale as 'Coach/Manager' is on the extreme right.

Right: One of the football Cup Final tickets that has survived.
(*Kaz Ale Collection*)

A & B SPORTS
NORTH HOME COUNTIES SUNDAY FOOTBALL LEAGUE
present

THE LUTON NEWS
CUP FINAL

LEWSEY RESERVES v BRITANNIA AIRWAYS

KENTS ATHLETIC GROUND
TENBY DRIVE

SUNDAY 14th MAY 1995   KICK OFF 10.30am
ADMISSION BY TICKET £1.00

the Britannia Small Sails club who apart from their own sailing, assisted the 2nd Ampthill and Woburn Scout Troop under supervision of Don Searson, Steve Parker and Jeff Parsons of the engineering department to experience the joys of sailing with the Britannia Dinghy Club, based on Willen Lake, Milton Keynes for their scouts proficiency in sailing award. There was also an Offshore Sailing Club based at Northney Marina on Hayling Island.

Over the years many different football teams were playing under the Britannia name, including competing in and winning several cup finals.

Kaz Ale was involved a lot with the social side of the airline, being a member of both the Flying club and involved in running the football teams, which played in the North Home Counties League and practised at the Brache Training Ground in Luton.

'If one thing Britannia was - it was a family airline for the staff and they encouraged staff to get into all sorts of activities and Britannia helped as much as they could. There was the footie team which the then MD Martin Vatter allowed you to play for the club while on duty for both the Saturday and Sunday teams. He would be there whatever the weather to support the team. I used to go home off nights, had a couple of hours kip, play for the team, home some more sleep and back in that night for twelve hours and he recognised that by letting us go to play on day shift'.

Britannia Airways Flying Club

Membership of the Britannia Airways Flying Club was open to all employees of the Thomson Travel Group, whether qualified pilots or complete novices.

Andy McNeile, the Chief Flying Instructor explains the advantages of joining the Britannia Flying Club. 'You can then enjoy the privileges flying anywhere in the European Community without hindrance. For instance, you could enjoy

Some members of the 1984/5 Britannia Airways 'A' Pools team. They won the Luton Central Club Pool League Watney Cup. They are, left to right: Adrian Morgan Tony Berti, Mick Rogers, Terry Smailes, Dave Kay and Tony Barber. *(Britannia Airways)*

a meal at a classic French restaurant within an hour and a half od leaving Luton. The cost of flying there, taxes and an excellent meal amounts to under fifty pounds a head'.

There were six aircraft in the Britannia flying club, Three at Luton, one at Redhill near Gatwick, one at Wellesbourne Mountford near Birmingham and one at Manchester, operated by local flying instructors at each base 'did the business'!

Captain Andrew McNeile	STN
Captain Ray Newell	LTN
F/O Allan Cooper	LGW
F/O Joe McLaughlin	BHX
Captain Chris Entwistle	MAN
F/O Adrian Reed	STN
F/O Mike Hadlow	CWL
Captain Malcolm Hagan	BRS
F/O Keith Davis	NCL

Much of the major servicing was done in the 757 hangar at Luton under the auspices of the club's dedicated engineer, John Walton, who kept all the aircraft in immaculate condition. The club treasurer was flight crew admin manager Charles Alyott, who was the first member of the club on its inception. Technical Director Bernard Newton was the director responsible the club and is a keen pilot. Managing Director Roger Burnell obtained his Private flying license through the club.

The company generously funded the acquisition of the clubs fleet, which from their point of view was a good thing, for it allowed rapid engineering support to be dispatched to any of the Boeing fleet that was grounded.

Kaz Ale again: 'The flying club was also represented by senior Pilots at the time. I started in 1991 and had my licence in 1992 which I enjoyed for 22 years, a great club it was too. I was social secretary for both clubs and wrote about

A formation line-up of the Britannia Airways Flying Club fleet. *(Britannia Airways)*

Above: Creating patterns in the Apron at Luton.

Right: Delivery of Piper Warrior G-BNMD to the Manchester section of the flying club. Right to left: Club Treasurer Charles Alyott, First Officer Mike Dyson, Captain Chris Entwistle, and Technical Director Bernard Newton. *(Britannia Airways)*

our Fly-ins and taking part in the well- known Young Eagles started in the USA to introduce kids to flying. The Footie team which I was in took part in an Inter Airline tournament in Malta where we sent two teams.'

There was also the opportunity for employees to discover for themselves the joys of flight - as the Chief Flying instructor put it, there was also the chance that anyone could progress to the point where they could join Britannia as a pilot!

Two 'fledged' pilots, Stuart Brooks and Chris Jarvis, recount their experiences of the Flying Club.

Stuart Brooks, Media Relations Executive, LTN: 'I had never flown a light aircraft before I experienced a flight in one of the company's Piper Warriors - and I was hooked. Learning to fly had never been a particular ambition of mine (I wanted to be a chef when I grew up), but I had always been interested in transport, particularly the flying variety. The convenience of having an aircraft readily available on-site and at the far cheaper costs involved when compared to a private flying school made the opportunity all that more attractive.'

'Having embarked on the journey to attaining a Private Pilots Licence, not only was it a great deal of reading and study but a continuity of flying was all-important. I lost count of the number of cancellations due to poor weather, but you soon become an expert weather forecaster!'

'The course itself was very rewarding and enjoyable, and I was expertly coached by Luton-based Captain Ray Newell. The feeling of driving a car having just passed your test does not remotely compare to that of taking off on your inaugural flight as a qualified pilot - I can thoroughly recommend it! '

Air Steward Chris Jarvis, BHX: A year after I started work at BHX as a steward in 1994 our own flying club aircraft arrived, and I could not wait to have a go. On my first lesson, I was amazed that I actually took off and was amazed to have control for virtually all of the flight. When my instructor Andy Hawkins (a fellow steward at BHX) took control he made it look so easy but to me even flying straight and level was difficult, however I was hooked. After between ten and fifteen flying hours and having passed the Air Law exam, you're ready for the first solo which is usually a circuit of the airfield. The daunting flight rushes on to you so quickly there's no time to get nervous, and it's only afterwards that the enormity of the achievement dawns on

South East Derby band was created by Conductor Stephen Shimwell in the 1980s, which eventually became Orion Airways Brass, and later Britannia Airways Brass. *(Britannia Airways)*

you. Flight training continues with more exams, and navigation flight test, A solo cross-country flight and the general flight test to complete the course. Now I have my Private Pilots Licence thanks to the hard-working dedication of Andy and chief instructor First Officer Joe McLaughlin that lifelong ambition to be a pilot might not seem quite as unobtainable as I first thought.

Brass Band

After the takeover of Orion Airways, Britannia agreed to continue with the sponsorship of the top quality Midlands-based band. Formerly known as Orion Airways Brass, it was re-named Britannia Airways Brass and, with the financial backing that sponsorship provided, the future tor the band looked as bright as the brass instruments its members played!

The thirty=strong band has already played at several prestigious concerts under the guidance of its Musical Director. Stephen Shimwell and Honorary Chairman, John Gee. All the players have been supplied with a Britannia uniform and stand banners for concert occasions.

Their tenth anniversary was marked by a special concert at the Alfreton Leisure Centre, Derby, attended by well over one thousand music lovers. Participating guests included veteran bandleader Harry Mortimer, TV entertainer Roy Castle and the Tideswell Male Voice Choir.

Chapter 11

Mergers and Subsidiaries

To see the way towards the eventual disappearance of Britannia Airways as both an airline and a brand, once again, we have to go back.

The late 1980s and early 1990s saw a period of airline collapses, take-overs and mergers all interspersed with aggressive corporate raiding. The story of the UK's holiday air travel business became so convoluted over the years that for a long time it was almost impossible to know who owned what. Both holiday companies and in-house holiday airlines were 're-badged' or 're-branded', merged, taken over or just disappeared. All of this was to have an eventual impact on Britannia Airways and the Thomson Travel Group.

Orion Airways

As far as Britannia was concerned, this took the form of taking over Orion Airways. Horizon Travel created Orion on 28 November 1978 to support Horizon's package holiday business at a time when there was a shortage in capacity provided by charter airlines. Orion began operation with three Boeing 737-200s on 28 March 1980.

Court Line bought the ailing Horizon Group in early 1974; it was, of course not the original company formed by Vladimir Raitz, but the former Horizon Midland that had been floated off by him in 1972. It was not destined to be a long relationship because in August that year Court itself collapsed.

After being rescued from the ruins by a consortium led by Bruce Tanner, Horizon Midlands began a new era based in Birmingham, and it was this company which grew into Orion Airways.

As its the first step, Horizon sought out an expert in the form of Bob Muckleston, a very knowledgeable executive working for Britannia. His brief was to conduct a feasibility study, and, on the assumption that there could be the right sort of opportunity to exploit, to recommend the right kind of aircraft and arrange their purchase.

After evaluating suitable aircraft, Orion decided that the Boeing 737-200 would meet its requirements. Two were ordered from the manufacturer in late 1978 while leases were arranged for a further pair to enable operations to commence. All went according to plan, the first aircraft touching down at East Midlands on 12 February. Following its official welcome, G-BGTW departed to Luton, where the cabin seats were installed, a task completed in time for it to return to its headquarters six days later.

Captain Ray Johnson, also from Britannia, was recruited as Chief Pilot and Operations Director and later became deputy Managing Director. From there, the task of selecting 120 cabin staff from 1,500 applications and 62 pilots from the 600 interviews was a significant undertaking. The job took two months of concentrated effort to complete

Orion Airways (known simply as 'Orion') had its head office on the grounds of East Midlands Airport in Castle Donington, North West Leicestershire. Here G-BGTV is seen about to depart on another service from EMA. *(Kirk Smeeton Collection)*.

Journey	Flight No.	Date	Latest Check-in-time	Departure Time	Meals	BAGGAGE ALLOWANCE 20 Kgs (44 lbs) None for Infants
Outward	BY 242	01/10/82	15.45	16.45	COLD PLATE	
Return	BY 243	15/10/82	10.55	12.25	COLD PLATE	

A Horizon flight ticket from October 1982, showing that despite having their own airline, Orion, were still using Britannia Airways. *(John Hamlin Collection)*

and then began the matter of training the crews to the standards that Orion had set themselves. Most of the pilots went to the Boeing facility at Seattle while cabin staff were involved in a rigorous schedule at East Midlands. The task was completed within 18 months after Bob Muckleston had been asked to prepare his preliminary brief on the founding of the airline.

Orion Airways' livery was a traditional white body with a grey underbelly separated by a triple cheatline in an unusual combination of gold, orange and chocolate-brown. The distinctive chocolate-brown tail bore a large stylised orange 'O.'

An inaugural flight took place to Pisa on 26 March, but it was two days later when Orion's first commercial sorties were flown, all three 737s being used for a similar number of IT trips. Until the fourth 737 came on strength, the airline sub-chartered some of its work to Britannia, but from 3 May it was no longer necessary because G-BHCL entered service on lease from the Belgian company, Trans European Airways.

During its first year, Horizon provided almost all Orion's passengers. In early 1981 the first of three more 737s was delivered, its arrival allowing TEA's aircraft to return to its owner. One of the newcomers opened up Horizon's programme from Gatwick on 11 April 1981; the additional capacity made it possible to undertake more ad hoc charter work. Orion's livery was to be seen at smaller airports such as Blackpool, from where a short series of ITs was originated later in the year, although due to runway length restrictions the Tenerife-bound aircraft had to call at East Midlands to pick up more fuel. Extra 737s were acquired during each of 1982, 1983 and 1984 to bring the total number of the series 200 in service to eleven for the summer season. As the peak passed, so the leased specimens were gradually returned, not only in anticipation of a market decline in 1985 but because a year or so earlier a decision had been taken as to which type would meet the future requirements of the airline and this would be available to take over some of the duties in the New Year.

Several designs were evaluated, but when Boeing announced the go-ahead for the 737-300 in March 1982, Orion chose this derivative, a firm order for four being placed with the American manufacturer. Although capable of accommodating 149 seats in its lengthened fuselage, the UK carrier decided to limit the number installed to 144, using some of the extra space to provide a third toilet.

Five years to the day that Orion Airways had its first inaugural flight to Pisa, the company added to its rapidly expanding prestige in the inclusive tour market by having another inaugural flight, this time for the introduction of the first Boeing 737-

300 in Europe. Not only that but they had installed, at their newly-built East Midlands Airport headquarters, the first Boeing 737-300 simulator to enter service in the world.

Orion's new airliners began to arrive in February 1985 when G-BLKB was delivered to the company's base, the remainder of the four-strong batch joining it by the end of March.

By this time, the source of the business had changed a little. Whereas in the early days Orion relied upon Horizon to provide the passengers, from 1984 the tour operator intentionally reduced its overall dependence upon its subsidiary by contracting some of its work to outside carriers.

About two-thirds of the capacity was taken up by the parent company, the remainder going to independent tour operators and scheduled services. The latter was introduced in the autumn of 1986 after licences were won to enable the airline to operate from Birmingham to Palma, East Midlands to Palma and Malaga, Gatwick to Almeria and Manchester to Alicante. British authority was also received later to cover the routes from Manchester to Ibiza and Mahon and Birmingham to Ibiza and Alicante.

Also based at East Midlands was Orion Aircraft Support and Inspection Services which was set up in 1986, and Orion Flight Training (OFT), a company jointly owned by the carrier and Singer-Link-Miles.

By becoming the lead European customer for the 737-300, it meant that there would be no existing training facility for the type. An order was therefore placed with Rediffusion for a flight simulator to be delivered before the first aircraft's

Below: three of the first four 737-300s delivered to Orion, with G-ABLKD closest to the camera.

Inset: Orion's 737 flight simulator could be adapted for either -200 or -300 series aircraft and cost £5 million to install. *(both Orion Airways)*

Captain Ray Johnson - formerly of Britannia - the deputy Managing Director of Orion Airways, kept his hand in by flying some of the services of the airline himself. He is seen here in the cockpit of one of the then-new Boeing 737-300s, four of which were delivered in time for the 1985 holiday season. A fifth was delivered in 1986. *(Orion Airways)*

arrival. At the time Boeing was advising airlines that because of the variant's commonality with the series 200, there would be no need to invest in a complete training device. However, Orion considered that while the flying characteristics of the two models were similar, the automated flight deck was undoubtedly different. Accordingly, the airline decided to acquire a full simulator, not only for its use but to sell training time to other operators of the aircraft.

Delivered in November 1984, the new equipment was installed in purpose-built accommodation for the commissioning stage to begin, a task completed in February 1985. Since it was the only one of its kind in the world, there was no shortage of customers from among the growing number of carriers due to introduce the variant. Operational twenty-four hours per day, the allocation of the actual slots depended entirely on the availability when booked. Orion was no exception and bought time along with all other customers, the only concession being that it had the first choice of the bookings.

Gatwick began to account for some forty per cent of Orion's activities, the remainder of the effort shared principally between East Midlands, Manchester and Birmingham with appearances at several other airports made on a smaller scale. With the growing volume of traffic at Luton, slot availability began to have an even more significant effect in 1986. So as combat this problem and the increasing loads at the southern airport, it was decided to introduce larger capacity airliners into service.

Negotiations were completed in early September for the lease/purchase of a pair of Airbus A300B4s from Lufthansa for which the registrations G-BMZK and ZL were reserved. Released by the German flag carrier, 'Zulu Kilo' was overhauled by Hapag-Lloyd at Hamburg and its cabin fitted with 324 Rumbold- manufactured seats in an all-tourist layout.

Resplendent in Orion's familiar livery, the machine duly arrived at East Midlands on 21 April 1987, positioning to Gatwick two days later in readiness for its first revenue-earning departure to Corfu at 07.40 hrs on 24 April. With the operational programme for both aircraft already organised, it was necessary for the pair of A300s to be on station by 15 May, which left insufficient time for the same refurbishment to be carried out on the second airframe. However, internally it was reconfigured to the same standard as its companion but spent the summer season on its previous owner's colours, albeit with new titles applied. As the workload reduced towards the end of the year, it became possible to release 'Zulu Lima' for its delayed overhaul. This time a long journey was necessary before work commenced because the Hong Kong-based company HAECO had been entrusted with the task of carrying out the D check and repaint. When completed in January 1988 the aircraft rejoined its colleague at Gatwick to maintain the airline's commitments during the winter.

In 1987 Horizon bought the tour company Wings from the Rank Organisation and then, during the spring of that year, the Horizon Travel Group was acquired by Bass PLC, the brewing, hotels and leisure group, for £94 million. As a successful holiday tour operator and integrated airline, it was an appealing, tidy, and importantly, a 'no-strings' package ripe for sale to a competitor. It was a deal which placed the considerable resources of the large organisation behind the airline, but at the same time did not interfere with the day-to-day running of the affairs under the direction of the existing management. It naturally embraced all of Orion's activities which were not confined to the movement of passengers to holiday resorts in Europe.

The airline quickly won a reputation for its quality of service, punctuality and distinctive look. Competition was fierce, but Horizon's destinations continued to increase, correlating with Orion's increased route-network and fleet growth.

At that time Thomson, mainly in the form of Britannia Airways, carried around 3.5 million passengers a year, meaning that it controlled some thirty per cent of the market. Horizon's one million, mostly flown by Orion, represented ten per cent. Together they would be roughly double the size of their nearest rival, Harry Goodman's International Leisure Group, mostly services by the Air Europe group of companies.

The matter had been discussed in advance with Thomson and Britannia's attitude was that it should not be done from the point of view of Britannia growing. The airline would instead prefer to grow organically than take over Orion, which would mean inheriting some of their problems. Lord Young, the Trade Secretary, referred the takeover to

Airbus G-BMZL departing Hong Kong after its check and repaint.

Inset: the Orion 737-300 SQ sticker the letters 'SQ' standing for Super Quiet, a reference to its CFM-56-3 engines. *(both Orion Airways)*

the Monopolies and Mergers Commission, which gave its blessing the following January.

However, it went ahead and inevitably they did inherit some problems. It was hard to walk into another airline and tll then that they were under new ownership, but it had to do that with Orion, and it took a lot of effort to go through the period of change and integration. One interesting aspect was that the new owners soon discovered that they had always overestimated how good Orion was and the deals they had. When Britannia administrators entered Orions headquarters and saw the other side, they realised that they had given them a lot of credit they didn't deserve. The only exception discovered was that the rates they had negotiated with their handling agents in Greece were better than theirs.

When the news was released that Orion was to be integrated into Britannia during 1989, it came as a surprise to the industry and public alike. Not all Orion staff were happy with the speed of the take-over, or the attitude of those moving into their East Midlands facility.

The last flight took place on 26 January 1989, and it was not long before the familiar livery and titles disappeared from aircraft and buildings at East Midlands Airport because the new owner understandably intended to concentrate its activities at its Luton Airport base. Naturally, the scheduled licenses were transferred to Britannia without interruption, but at the end of the 1990 summer season, the airline decided to withdraw from this market in favour of its charter work.

A Feeding Frenzy of Consolidation.
The big tour operators had grown larger through acquisition and also moved into foreign markets. Consolidation raised new fears among small companies, whose campaign for what they saw as fairer competition, supported by consumer lobbyists, finally prompted a reference to the British Monopolies and Mergers Commission in November 1996. The cause was vertical integration, the ownership of travel agencies, charter airlines and tour operations by the same group. The Office of Fair Trading had already looked at this issue in 1993 and decided a reference was not justified. But power wielded by the dominant groups had intensified. Five companies found themselves under the scrutiny: Thomson, which had some twenty-five per cent of the foreign package market in 1996; Airtours, which had sisteen per cent; First Choice, with ten per cent; Sunworld, which had just been bought by Thomas Cook; and Inspirations, which had two per cent and was also destined to be swallowed up by Cook's. Of these, only First Choice did not then own a chain of agencies, though Thomas Cook held a stake in it.

The Commission's report was made public in December 1997. To the dismay of many, it concluded there was still plenty of competition in the industry and that there was no need to sharpen it by forcing the big groups to shed any of their component parts. Players came, the report said, and players went. There was no significant barrier to entry either as a tour operator or retailer.

However, there were some minor items to be put right. The Commission stated that the practice among agents of tying high priced compulsory travel insurance to bargains was likely to mislead customers into thinking they were receiving a bigger price cut than was really the case. It also criticised 'most favoured customer clauses' in agreements between operator and agent. These obliged the retailer to cut the price of that operator's packages in line with discounts from other tour firms. The Commission decided they could discourage agents from discounts which they would otherwise be prepared to offer. And it urged that the big groups should make more apparent to consumers exactly which operators were linked with which agents. The Government said it would take action on all three, but while the first two practices were quickly outlawed, the third, ensuring greater transparency of ownership, proved stubbornly difficult to achieve.

The report caused a few minor difficulties, but it blew open the doors for a rush of takeovers. Cook's linked up with the Carlson Leisure Group, with over a thousand owned or affiliated agencies, tour operations including Inspirations and its airline, Caledonian. Airtours bought Panorama and two other operators. Thomson's shopping spree included the Simply Travel and Magic groups, Headwater and ski operator Crystal Holidays. First Choice acquired long-haul operator Hayes and Jarvis and wintersports firm, Flexiski.

Foreign ownership was nothing new to the industry. Thomsons had a Canadian parenthood. Inghams and Cosmos were Swiss owned. However, when the Midland Bank sold Thomas Cook for £200 million to LTU in June 1992, it seemed a turning point. LTU was Germany's third biggest tour operator with seventeen per cent of that country's package market. Thomas Cook was a symbol of all things British. It was not long before UK companies were operating in other European countries. Airtours moved into the German market, then Scandinavia, Belgium,

Holland and France, with a large slice of the organisations owned by the American Carnival Cruise Lines. First Choice bought the Spanish company, Barcelo, then announced it would target markets so far left untapped by its rivals, such as those in Greece and Italy.

Thomson launched operations in seven other countries - Germany, Ireland, Sweden, Norway, Denmark, Finland and Poland. Its move abroad helped to make it, like Thomas Cook, a target of German interest. Still Britain's largest tour operator, it had been through difficult times since its flotation on the London Stock Exchange in May 1998 with a valuation of £1.7 billion. In April 2000, German travel company C&N Touristik, jointly owned by Lufthansa and the stores chain Karstadt Quelle, approached the Thomson Travel Group with an offer of 130 pence per share. The UK firm, twenty-three per cent owned by the Canadian Thomson family through its Woodbridge holding company and roughly twenty per cent owned by small shareholders, many of which were employees and others lured in by the prospect of cut-price holidays through membership in the 'Thomson Founders' Club', which offered a ten per cent discount on Thomson holidays. Membership was conditional on retaining a minimum of 294 shares. Shareholders rejected the C&N Touristik approach, but it left the door ajar for C&N should the Germans come back with a better bid. C&N eventually raised its offer to l60p, valuing Thomson at £1.6 billion.

Its management thought it had sealed the deal, but it was beaten to the post by German rival Preussag, the former industrial conglomerate which owned TUI, Europe's biggest tour operation, and which had acquired a controlling stake in Thomas Cook. Preussag agreed to pay £1.8 billion for TTG.

The deal created a giant. Between them they operated 106 aircraft and over four thousand city centre travel agencies. Preussag had to agree to sell its sisty per cent stake in Thomas Cook in order to secure approval from the European Commission. Westdeutsche Bank, owner of one-third of Preussag, was also obliged to sell its stake in Thomas Cook's.

There then followed a massive re-naming and re-branding exercise. In 2000, TTG was acquired by Preussag AG, an industrial and transport conglomerate. Preussag was renamed TUI AG on 1 July 2002 and Thomson Travel became TUI UK. Britannia Airways was rebranded Thomsonfly, then

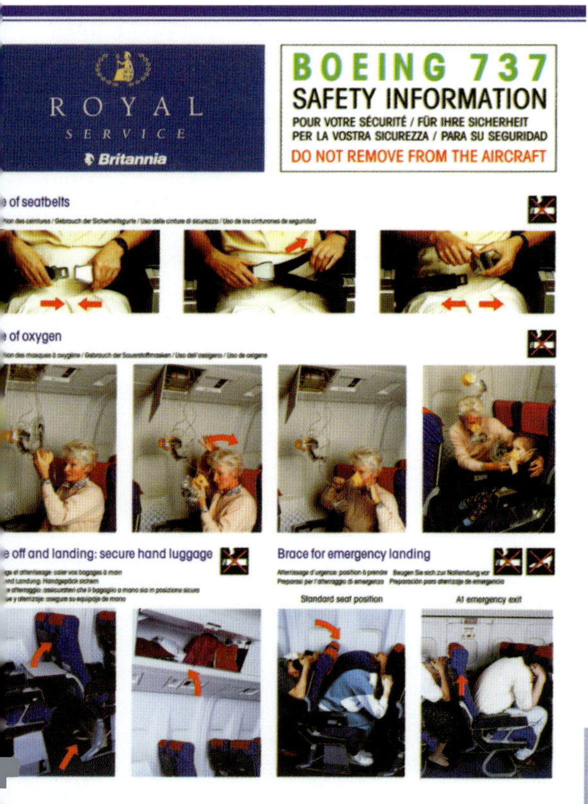

Below: G-BLKE, one of the former Orion 737-300-3T5s In full Britannia colours. *(Kaz Ale Collection)*

Inset: The Royal Service style safety card for the 737.

G-BYNB was a 737-800 and is seen at London Gatwick. *(Kaz Ale Collection)*

Thomson Airways after the merger with First Choice Airways, and now TUI Airways became subsidiaries of TUI AG.

First Choice started operations on 11 April 1987, launched by the Owners Abroad Group under the name Air 2000 with two Boeing 757 aircraft and a flight from Manchester to Málaga. The fleet doubled a year later, with one aircraft being based at Glasgow International Airport.

Long haul services to Mombasa in Kenya were introduced during the 1988/89 season. The 757s were re-equipped for extended range and flights to the United States began in 1989. The airline was granted a licence for scheduled operations by the CAA in 1992, which commenced in 1993, initially between London-Gatwick and Paphos, Cyprus.

Expansion saw new bases in the UK established, with Dublin becoming the airline's first overseas hub in 1996. Leisure International Airways was fully integrated after the acquisition by First Choice of Unijet in June 1998. This included the entire fleet of aircraft, and an order for four Airbus A330-200 aircraft, which First Choice immediately cancelled in favour of the rival Boeing 767-300 aircraft. Air 2000 received a new colour scheme - however in March 2004 the Air 2000 branding was removed and First Choice Airways branding added.

The airline carried 6.5 million passengers during 2002. The 2005 total was 6.0 million - fifth highest passenger figures of any UK airline. In 2004 it announced plans to refurbish another six Boeing 767-300 aircraft to expand its long haul operations. The airline was the first in the UK to use the Boeing 777-style interior on their 767 fleet. The company had six aircraft flying long haul in 2007, in a two class layouts. All seats featured Panasonic seat back entertainment and mood lighting in Star Class Premier.

On 23 April 2007, First Choice confirmed it was to close its bases at London Luton Airport and Cardiff from 1 November 2007 however, due to the merger with Thomsonfly, who also operated from these bases, the combined airline operated from these airports.

Thomsonfly and First Choice Airways merged following the merger of the travel division of TUI AG and First Choice Holidays PLC in September 2007. Thomsonfly Limited changed its name to Thomson Airways Limited on 1 November 2008 and the Thomsonfly operating certificate was changed to Thomson Airways on the same day. On that date, Thomsonfly and First Choice Airways both rebranded their operations to Thomson Airways, merging with a fleet of 75 aircraft. with a number of new Boeing 787 aircraft on order.

The new brand retained the Thomsonfly colour scheme, and aircraft in the fleet were gradually repainted. Several First Choice Airways aircraft remained in the First Choice livery as they were due to be phased out of service. A new livery, named 'Dynamic Wave' was introduced in May 2012.

When Preussag took over TTG, membership of the Founders' Club was made permanent and unconditional. However, ten years later, on 31 January 2008, the Club was abolished without notice or compensation.

Britannia GmbH.

In early 1998 - and backed by their tour operators - Britannia Airways made a massive expansion into the German market, providing intercontinental services out of Germany, pushing prices down and disturbing what was, up until then, a cosy status quo. It caused alarm bells to ring amongst some of the other carriers.

Britannia was thus the first foreign charter carrier to compete in a market dominated by tour operators TUI, C&N, Condor, Neckermann, Touristik and LTU, and their respective charter airlines Hapag-Lloyd, Condor and LTU International Airways - and drastically undercut its German rivals.

Despite pulling out all the stops, the German tourist industry failed to prevent Britannia, Europe's largest charter airline, from providing long-haul services to the Dominican Republic out of Berlin-Schonefeld.

Attracted by higher growth rates and the opportunity of exploiting its lower cost base, Britannia had already tried in 1996 to operate direct flights from Germany to the central American state. But the move was blocked by the German authorities because Britannia's parent, Thomson, was Canadian owned. The only option open to the airline was to reroute the service via Manchester.

A year later Britannia tried again, this time by setting up a German subsidiary. But once more it ran into problems because of its Canadian parentage when the German CAA argued it was not enough for Britannia to be based in the UK, the subsidiary had to be ultimately owned by EU capital. Britannia was forced to hand over majority ownership of fifty-five per cent in Britannia Airways Germany to European investors. Most of that was held by a German bank with a small portion controlled by Britannia's German partner, tour operator Forsch Touristik International (FTI), with which the carrier had a five-year deal.

Local travel industry sources reported that, despite wrecking advertising campaigns by the rival German tour operators implying German passengers were going to get poor levels of service and safety, Britannia filled its aircraft.

By March 1998 Britannia was operating a two-week revolving flight schedule to the Dominican Republic with a Boeing 767-300 from Berlin, Munich, Frankfurt, Cologne, Hamburg and Stuttgart. A further two 767-300s were due to enter service and flights to Cuba, Jamaica, Majorca and Malta were to be added for the European summer season.

Industry analysts thought that Britannia was in Germany to stay. Although undercutting local carriers by twenty to thirty per cent, Britannia Airways Germany was expected to be profitable in its first full year. They thought that if Britannia's low price concept caught on in Germany, the potential could be enormous - especially as it had been reported that nineteen million Germans flew with tour operators in 1997 and long-term market prospects looked good.

Britannia's ability to offer lower prices swung on its higher seating densities, fleet efficiencies, higher load factors and low distribution costs. Britannia's standard fleet allowed for cross-crewing

767-304ER D-AGYC of Britannia GmbH. Note the tiny German flag on the top of the fin, just under the 'last two' letters of the aircraft registration. *(Kaz Ale Collection)*

and brought about tremendous economies of scale.

German charter flights typically had lower load factors than their UK competitors. Britannia was quickly achieving ninety-five per cent in Germany, at least ten per cent higher than its German rivals. The Germans also incurred higher costs from selling tickets, an exercise which required a marketing and distribution network whereas Britannia relied mostly on tour operators.

Of course, Britannia was restricted as much as the native charter operators by Germany's higher labour costs and restrictions on night flying. Fewer cycles per day meant lower profits and therefore Britannia could not hope to match the returns in the UK. Nevertheless, the threat to local players was real enough for some charter airlines to have already begun cutting prices and reducing seat pitch.

The German charter airlines publically stated that there would be no changes to their services; however, Condor, which carried 7.1 million passengers the previous year, revealed that it did have plans on file to modify prices should Britannia's restricted lower priced services take off in Germany. A spokesman from LTU, while recognising a growing market for low-cost air travel in Germany, said that it was standing by to see how the new entrant performed before it made any changes.

However, one senior industry source said that Condor had also set up a 'Lite' subsidiary operating four or five A320s out of Schonefeld airport and was putting more seats on its flights to the Dominican Republic with a view to doing the same on other routes. It also provided a business class on this service, aiming at both a higher and lower price bracket than before. Senior German travel industry sources stated that LTU had already introduced a lower-priced service on a trial basis on some transatlantic routes. Clearly, the German charter carriers were attempting to improve their cost base by taking more pages out of the UK charter industry's book.

1997 saw a shakeup in the complex web of cross-shareholdings in the German travel industry. In September logistics group Preussag Aktiengesellschaft, known simply as Preussag took over Hapag Lloyd, the tourism and shipping group which included the third largest charter airline in Germany. This transaction gave Preussag's main shareholder, the state bank Westdeutsche LB, control of TUI, the number one German tour operator. Hapag Lloyd owned thirty per cent of TUI, while West LB directly owned another thirty per cent. Preussag was believed to want complete control of TUI to combine Hapag's charter airline with TUI's tour operating and retail interests. Lufthansa's own subsidiary, Condor, which claimed to be the leading German charter airline with a twenty-five per cent market share, formed a DM7 billion (US$3.8 billion at 1997 values) 50:50 joint venture called C&N Condor Neckermann Touristik, with Neckermann, the country's second-largest tour operator. This was believed to allow them to obtain the kind of cost efficiencies associated with the UK model.

Although it was still not clear what the German carriers were going to do, Britannia was still confronted with the basic problem of accessing the German market. Although described by Britannia as the 'fastest growing tour operator in Germany', Forsch Touristik International, then rated as the fifth biggest in the country, was dwarfed by its larger rivals.

What Britannia really wanted was Thomson backing it up on German ground. Thomson Travel group was to float on the stock market that May and

Boeing 767 D-AGYC of Britannia GmbH comes in to land wearing *'Duty Free Muss Bleiben!'* titles which translates as *'Duty Free Must Stay!'*. *(Emma Dayle Collection)*.

made it clear it was looking for a way into the German market. With UK rival Airtours, it was in talks to buy the tour operating arm of LTU, in which West LB bank was being forced to relinquish its thirty-four per cent stake due to the acquisition of the TUI shareholding.

It was unclear whether LTU International Airways was to have been included in a deal. However, the German cartel office allowed all of LTU to be put in a blind trust, to be kept at at arms length from West LB, for a period of three years. LTU International Airways said that political pressures on its two main shareholders, West LB bank and the Konler family, meant that foreign ownership was ruled out for the time being. National elections due later that year could clear the way for a fresh look at ownership. Until then Britannia's only option was to grow with FTI. Nevertheless, the plan was in place for an eight-aircraft operation to be flown out of Germany by the end of the century.

At its peak, Britannia Airways GmbH employed roughly 200 people and operated a pair of Boeing 767-300s. However, this division was relatively unsuccessful and ultimately closed down during March 2001.

The German market was by no means the only one targeted by the expansionist UK tour operators and their charter carriers. Britannia had been flying the Hadj for many years, and 2000 was the fourth

Delivered new to the UK's Britannia Airways in April 2000 as G-BYNB, it was wet leased to Britannia AB (Sweden) on delivery for one month before returning to Britannia UK. It was again leased to Britannia AB, this time on a dry lease as SE-DZM in January 2002. It operated with them until April 2005 when it was transferred within the TUI Group to Hapagfly (Hapag-Lloyd) as D-ATUB. It returned to Thomsonfly (later Thomson Airways) in November 2005, now as G-CDZM, and served with them until it was returned to the lessor in May 2012. *(Matt Black Collection)*

Right: 737-800 safety card.

Boeing 737-8Q8 OY-SEA, seen on take-off. *(author)*

year in succession that they had been operating flights from Indonesia to Mecca on behalf of Garuda. This year Britannia was to operate six aircraft on 'damp' lease - that is Britannia flight deck crew and Garuda cabin staff. As Britannia Briefing reported: 'It is a group operation as one of the aircraft will be D-YF from Germany, and eighteen pilots from Germany will join ninety pilots from the UK who along with with a team of engineers and Ops staff will be based on the Indonesian island of Sulawesi'. The flying programme was to run from 14 February to 17 April.

Britannia AB

Britannia's move into Germany was quickly followed, in December 1997, by Thomson's US $427 million acquisition of Swedish tour operator Fritidsresor and its charter airline Blue Scandinavia, now named Britannia AB. The airline was originally formed in 1985 as Transwede Airways operating both charter and scheduled flights to destinations around Europe. The airline, which flew 1.3 million passengers the previous year, and began operating under its new identity in February, employed 450 staff and operated five leased 757s from Norwegian and Swedish airports to destinations in the Canaries, Israel and the Mediterranean on behalf of Fritidsresor.

Britannia AB's intentions was to provide all of Fritedsresor's seats - at the time of the take-over, only one-third were supplied in-house. Long-haul destinations such as Thailand and the USA were primarily served by Premiair, a Danish charter carrier whose parent organisation, Simon Spies Holdings, was owned by Thomson UK's rival, Airtours International Airways through its ownership of Scandinavia's largest tour operator, Scandinavian Leisure group. Thomson, and

therefore Britannia AB, saw considerable potential in developing the long-haul market using its own fleet of airliners.

Blue Scandinavia's back story was equally convoluted. It was formed in 1996 following the acquisition by Fritidsresor of the charter arm of Transwede. Airline president Jan Carlzon, the former head of SAS, resigned as a result of the take-over. Britannia aimed to make the service on its Swedish subsidiary indistinguishable from its UK operation by the European summer, and the use of a clear corporate stamp - the Britannia livery was on the aircraft from day one of the launch in February - marked a clear move away from cooperation with Airtours.

Britannia Nordic - as the concern was later termed - took delivery of the first of the new generation 737-800 aircraft on 16 January 2000 and marked a special flight of guests, business partners and journalists from Boeing in Seattle to Arlanda. As Britannia Briefing said, 'SE-DZH will be followed by SE-DZI, and SE-DZK before the end of April, and during March the two British registered aircraft, G-BYNB and G-BYNC will be delivered to the UK. They will be stationed at Leeds Bradford and Glasgow airports respectively.

The same edition went on to say that Britannia Nordic was about to open a new base at Trondheim in Norway for the summer of 2000. Cabin crew recruitment was complete and training was under way in Oslo. One of the new 737/800s was based in Trondheim, flying mainly to Mediterranean destinations.

After Preussag (TUI) acquired the Thomson Group in 2000 the airline was rebranded as TUI Fly Nordic in 2005.

By now, things started to become really complicated.

Chapter 12

Responding to the Changing Habits of a Nation

The holidaymaking public in the United Kingdom always sought out new destinations that were usually further and further afield - and generally at the lowest possible price.

What started with 36-seat piston-engined airliners that took a day to reach Corsica in the 1950s had evolved into 120 seater jets in the 1960s. These machines could range further afield much more quickly, and while the western Mediterranean was a prime destination with the piston-engined aircraft, with the jets the eastern Mediterranean came within range.

The boom in leisure air travel brought forth demands to get more passengers on board and to keep the price low. Efficiencies of scale meant larger aircraft - so the short-range BAC 1-11s and early model Boeing 737s were replaced by Boeing 707s for the long haul and later by Boeing 757s, 767s and Lockheed TriStars.

The number of passengers carried per trip may have gone up dramatically - after all, a Britannia Airways 737-200 carried around 130 passengers whereas one of their 757s carried 260. However, the aerodynamics of the aircraft put weight restrictions on many of the smaller airports they could use.

It was not a problem for the UK operators, as the market was changing; there was less interest in the Mediterranean. The Red Sea area and further afield

The holiday starts here! Passengers check in for their Royal holiday flight at Luton International Airport. *(Britannia Airways)*

An example of a multi-sector service - Boeing 737-7K2 PH-XRE of Transavia departs Xios National Airport having arrived from Amsterdam and Mytiline Airport on Lesvos and now heading for Thessaloniki for fuel before flying back to Amsterdam. *(author)*

beckoned. Aircraft like the 757 and 767 were perfectly capable of flying that distance. With the use of ETOPS - an acronym used to describe Extended-range Twin-engine Operational Performance Standards, a certification that permitted twin-engine aircraft to fly routes which may, at the time, be sixty minutes flying time from the nearest airport that is suitable for an emergency landing - trans-Atlantic and trans-Pacific flights with twin-engined aircraft were allowed.

Improvements in aerodynamics and flight control computerisation - especially with the A320 family - saw a more significant number of passengers carried into the smaller airports. Indeed, Britannia did flirt with members of the Airbus family when in a temporary move away from its nearly 30-year Boeing tradition came when Britannia leased a small number of Airbus A320s from TransAer. The 180-seaters brought back a chance to compete for smaller-capacity charters that had been lost by the 737 fleet disposals.

It was here that UK operators began to diverge from some of their northern European neighbours. In the UK it tended to be 'get em out - get em back' - in other words, direct flight outbound, immediate flight return, known in the business as 'back to backs' with maybe a tech stop for fuel somewhere in the middle.

Some of the Dutch, Belgian and Scandanavian charter airlines had other ideas - they were prepared to fly multi-sector flights. For example, Transavia of Holland and Thomas Cook Belgium flew from Amsterdam and Brussels respectively into Omiros National Airport on the Greek island of Chios. From here they flew to either Samos, Lesvos, Karpathos or Thessaloniki before departing for their home airport.

The late 1990s was an intense period of change. In 1998 Britannia took part in the first series of a television series called 'Airline'; a British so-called fly on the wall television programme produced by London Weekend Television (LWT) that showcased the daily happenings of passengers, ground workers and flight crews of the airline at Manchester Airport.

The programme, in which Britannia ceased its involvement with at the end of the first series, followed some passengers and staff on what the production team called 'interesting journeys and during important moments in their lives'. Wedding proposals, marriages, illnesses, business trips, reunions and once-in-a-lifetime experiences were all been filmed, both happy and sad. One good - if definately futile - aspect was that the programme attempted to educate the airline's passengers concerning its rules and regulations. Some of the highlighted issues related to missed check-in, incorrect travel documentation, and the carriage of prohibited items.

Behind the scenes, as the Parent evolves...
From 1990 to 1992, Thomson saw its revenues and profits rise from $5.36 billion to $5.98 billion; its operating profits, however, stumbled from $726 million to $692 million, before partially rebounding to its 1992 figure of $714 million. Two straight years of double-digit profit declined for Thomson

Newspapers, caused by recession-influenced decreases in advertising, explained this trend. According to Thomson's 1992 annual report, however, US circulation increased slightly, and overall market share remained strong. Also, more than 400 new products were introduced, including the first corporation-generated project, an entertainment weekly entitled *CoverSTORY,* whose circulation, primarily through Thomson newspapers, approached one million. Consequently, the division faced the future optimistically and expected to renew its growth track with economic recovery.

In 1984, it was claimed that '...The Thomson empire has been in the vanguard among media empires in branching into nonpublishing ventures, but it is a member of the pack, not the leader, in today's mecca for the press lords - information services.'

By 1992, Thomson had gone far toward quelling such criticism, for it could by then boast ownership of 190 online services, 161 CD-ROM products, and a large number of other software offerings, all part of The Thomson Information/Publishing Group (TIPG). Thomsons were slowly but inevitably at an ever-accelerating pace, moving away from the travel trade and airline business. In April 1992 Thomson accelerated its entry into information services with the $210 million purchase of New York-based JPT Publishing; according to Publishers Weekly and Thomson's chief financial officer, the deal was struck primarily to acquire data provider Institute for Scientific Information (ISI). ISI enjoyed over 300,000 customers worldwide and was believed to be generating healthy annual profits estimated at $15 million.

During the mid-1990s Thomson completed several more acquisitions, three of which were particularly important. In 1994 the company paid about US$465 million for Foster City, California-based Information Access Company (IAC), a former division of Ziff-Davis Communications Co. IAC was a leading provider of reference and database services for academic and public libraries, corporations, hospitals, and schools. Also in 1994 Thomson added to its

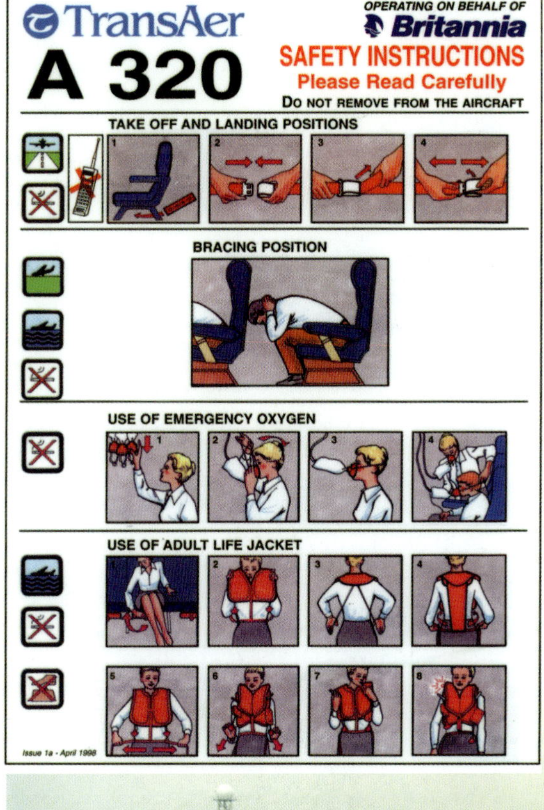

In something of an attempt to get back charters into the smaller holiday destination airports, Britannia leased a small number of A320s from the Irish airline TransAer. The safety cards (left) bore the legend 'Operating on behalf of Britannia'.
(Matt Black Collection)

Airbus A320 EI-TLJ on lease from TransAer in basic Britannia colours, complete with the 'Keep Duty Free' campaigning slogan. *(Hugh Jampton Collection)*

healthcare information portfolio with the US$339 million purchase of the Medstat Group but lost out to rival Reed Elsevier plc in the bidding for a leading information database, Lexis-Nexis. Two years later Thomson completed the largest acquisition in its history when it paid US$3.4 billion for Eagan, Minnesota-based legal publisher West Publishing Co., maintainer of more than 6,000 electronic databases on law, medicine, and insurance. Thomson and West were the two largest US legal publishers, which prompted close antitrust scrutiny and objections from competitors in the field, most notably Reed Elsevier plc. To gain antitrust approval, Thomson and West had to sell off more than fifty legal publications, while resolution of a lawsuit filed by Reed Elsevier was reached when Thomson agreed to sell some of these legal publications, Meanwhile, Thomson's newspaper holdings grew smaller still through the 1995 divestment of its remaining UK newspaper holdings and the 1996 disposal of 43 daily newspapers in the United States and Canada.

Michael Brown was named deputy chairman in 1998, replacing longtime adviser to Kenneth Thomson, John Tory; Brown was in turn replaced as president and CEO by Richard Harrington. The early 1998 acquisition of Computer Language Research Inc. for about US$325 million bolstered Thomson's existing tax and accounting information operations, which centred on its Research Institute of America Group. By this time, Thomson's information services operations were the core of the company, with overall information revenue increasing by more than seventy-five per cent over five years, to US$4.8 billion.

The Thomson group was floated on the Stock Market in May 1998, and all the management efforts were being directed towards that event. In 1997 the airline hit their targets, and they had to achieve the same thing again in 1998 so severe actions had to be taken, like selling a flight simulator and outsourcing some work.

In 1999 things were proving very difficult. With the floatation, there was no financial cushion left. Britannia was struggling with operations and losing out on their on-time performance record. There was also a pilot shortage. By 2000 things had improved. The airline had acted firmly in getting costs down, the pilot shortage had been sorted out, and the operational side was developing fast. The passengers, of course, had no idea of any of the problems.

July 2000, saw the European Commission approve the takeover of the Thomson Travel Group by German group Preussag in a £1.8 billion deal. Preussag was the world leader in tourism. The group covered more than eighty per cent of the European market and included 3658 travel agencies, seventy-five tour operators and brands, ninety aircraft and around 270 hotels. Its customer base was about 22 million holidaymakers. Its global brand for tourism is the 'World of TUI'. At the time of the EU approval for the takeover, Dr Michael Frenzel, Chairman of the Preussag management board, said: 'Like the TUI Group, Thomson has a strong market presence, a balanced brand portfolio and a high degree of integration across all links of the value-added tourism chain. With TUI Group and Thomson, we have achieved a quantum leap towards the formation of the leading integrated tourism group'.

Passengers who were 'Going Places' disembark into the sun from a Britannia 767. It was rumoured - I have never been able to confirm or deny it - that Britannia once tried to get a 767 into Skiathos Airport' Alexandros Papadiamantis', but after landing 'Captain Speaking got it wrong again Hoskins' and managed to get the huge aircraft stuck. It took a lot of ground manoeuvring to get it clear, and they never repeated the experiment!
(Britannia Airways)

The changing face of Technology

In the past, the Inclusive Tour passenger had been, by and large, indifferent to the airline on which they flew, having bought the package for its price and destination. Even so, the image of the airline had been essential in helping to achieve repeat custom for the tour operator and thus, indirectly, for the airline itself. With opportunities now beginning to appear for airlines such as Britannia to sell 'seats only' and to provide scheduled flights to holiday destinations, the image became progressively more important.

By the turn of the century - 6 January 2000 in fact - Britannia Briefing announced that the Group Development department of Thomson Travel Group had launched Britannia Direct, a new initiative selling Britannia Airways flights on a seat-only basis. Bookings could now be made online at the Britannia Direct website and also by telephone through Manchester Flights as advertised on Teletext.

Britannia Direct offered greater flexibility to passengers who only required a flight, and was initially only available from Manchester, Birmingham and Gatwick to Tenerife and Alicante. Passengers could book one way or return, and there was no minimum stay.

At the same time, a new cross-divisional team was formed to look at the development of an internal 'intranet' for use by all members of staff. Plans also included a massive expansion of the Britannia website.

Britannia Briefing also announced that the airline had three new non-TTG tour operators featuring in the summer 2000 programme. Greek specialist Kosmar Holidays were flying from East Midlands Airport to Corfu, and Libra Holidays would fly by BY from Manchester to Larnica. The third operator, Avrom would fly from regional airports to Malaga.

With all these changes and the introduction of e-commerce on the internet, the holiday companies including the Thomson Travel Group and therefore Britannia Airways , foisted a whole raft of subtle 'revisions' on to the travelling public. Printed, hard-copy holiday brochures were drastically phased out, to the point where they almost become a thing of the past, and they are all now websites - as were the High Street Travel Agents.

By all accounts, the traditional 'Inclusive Tour' holiday was heading for the emergency exits to become a thing of the past - it evolved into the 'All Inclusive' deal.

But isn't 'All Inclusive' the same as 'Inclusive

767 G-BYAL in TUI colours comes in to land at Leeds/Bradford Airport. *(Richard Vandervord)*

Tour'? No, not at all. An 'Inclusive Tour' got you out to your destination, and made things easier for the traveller by providing 'reps' who knew the local area, and provided transport to and from the accommodation from your destination airport. Once there, you were free to do as little or as much additional 'arranged' activities as you wished. 'All-Inclusive' on the other hand, is totally different.

As a typical e-brochure described: 'With an All-Inclusive holiday, all of your food and drink is included in the price, so you won't have to fork out to enjoy dinner. You'll also find that most hotel activities and entertainment are included too. So from the day you arrive to the time of your flight home, you can indulge in as much or as little as you like. Some of the activities available include windsurfing, kayaking, cycling, and tennis. For those quieter days, you can enjoy the likes of movies, dance shows and cookery demonstrations. And the best bit? It's all included in the price.

Our All-Inclusive holidays are ideal for anyone looking for a break from their wallets, especially if you're travelling as a group or family. And with top destinations across the globe to choose from, you'll soon see why...

For full details of what's included in your all inclusive holiday, check the hotel description.
Why choose an all-inclusive holiday package?

- Unlimited local alcoholic drinks
- All meals
- Snacks, soft drinks, tea and coffee
- Activities and entertainment'

As the UK travel tour industry said, they are just responding to the demands of the tourist market - everything the holidaymaker could need was arranged for and provided within the price. But think about it - they say you can do as little or as much as you please - and that includes drinking and eating, so the 'price' must be set at least some form of average. Drink, eat and use the facilities lower than this mythical average, and you are paying over the odds.

On the face of it, 'All Inclusives' are just an extension of the vertical integration concept Tom Gullick of Clarksons pioneered back in the early 1970s taken to the extreme. Clarksons and Court Line owned the airline that took holidaymakers out to the Spain and Carribean where they stayed in group-owned hotels, eating food provided by group owned farms in group owned restaurants and carried around on group owned coaches!

There is market demand for all inclusives: we all want holidays, and in the current difficult economic times - which always seems to be happening - all-inclusives offer the opportunity to feel assured that we can afford such a holiday. When evaluated from the customers' perspective, the guarantee of a fixed travel budget is understandable. By choosing all-inclusive travel packages, tourists know they are in safe hands, and there will be a quality product for a manageable price. Operators can enhance their control over the quality of the end product, and hotels can increase their efficiency and predictability of demand.

Indeed, tour operator First Choice, part of TUI, switched all its holidays to all-inclusive. Thomas Cook reportedly increased the number of all-inclusive holidays it offered by ten per cent. But what does the emergence of the all-inclusive model, where tourists are invited to '...leave their wallets at home', mean for the destinations we visit?

The words of the marketing men' leaving your wallet at home' did not sit well with many local economies. The phrase allegedly coined by Johan Lundgren, the UK and Ireland managing director of TUI, but has now been disowned. 'It was a PR phrase that we used. We don't advertise on that basis. If that's a phrase that we've used before then perhaps that doesn't help with the local area, and we need to be mindful of that,' said Christian Cull, director of communications for TUI UK and Ireland. First Choice began to trade under the banner of 'Home of All Inclusive'. But they are by no means the only tour company operating in this manner.

The effect of the all-inclusives has been felt in many holiday destinations. In Majorica, Spain all-inclusive holidays were blamed for the loss of local businesses. On some Greek islands open to direct flights from the UK, many local communities claimed that the all-inclusives have not only wrecked the local holiday economy, they decimated the local island economy! Many prefectures and hotel associations reported an ever-increasing groundswell of local anger at how not only were the all-inclusives actively discouraging tourists from leaving their gated resorts by keeping the gates closed at all times, they were also shipping in staff – that is waiters and waitresses, cleaners, maids and the like – for the season from eastern Europe, at lower than local wages, thus depriving the local economies of income. There were also indications that bulk buying of food and drink was being made on the mainland and then being trucked over instead of being purchased locally.

In Turkey, there were many reports conveying anger, frustration and distress from mayors and hotel associations describing how they had to succumb to pressure from UK operators to transform their hotels into all-inclusives. Analysis of an all-inclusive Holiday Village in Fethiye, Turkey, found that just ten per cent of the tourist spend reached the regional economy, with economic benefits to the neighbouring Sarigerme village put at even less. For example, the estimated average guest spend in the village shops was put at just one Euro per guest per day according to the BBCs *Fast Track* programme.

Further afield, in Mombasa, Kenya, the World Bank stated all-inclusive beach holidays contributed the least economic benefit. In Jamaica – all-inclusive hotels attracted tourists in the short term but blocked the development of other types of tourism. In the Dominican Republic there were numerous reports that all-inclusive holidays were blamed for restaurant closures and increased negative attitude towards tourists. In Goa, India there were reports of 'enclave tourism', where local taxis and guides were losing business to all-inclusive resorts.

There was a whole raft of hidden dangers where

The era of the 'World of TUI' that featured the Britannia name. Boeing 757 G-BYAD, photographed turning onto the main drag at London Gatwick, along with the associated safety card. (*Richard Vandervord*)

767-300 G-OBYB 'Bobby Moore OBE' in TUI colours at Birmingham . *(Richard Vandervord)*

local economies could suffer. For example, tipping is an essential source of revenue for people working in the hospitality business but the all-inclusive model results in fewer tips and therefore reduced income for many workers.

Other local businesses, such as restaurants, shops, taxi drivers and small guest houses, all lose out to the all-inclusive model, as guests are deterred from leaving the hotel or complex grounds. In some destinations, countless businesses have been forced to close, which in turn deters other tourists holidaying on bed and breakfast packages, as the destination has less to offer. Local entrepreneurs from Spain, Greece and Cyprus, from The Gambia to Kenya, and from St. Lucia to Jamaica have all complained of being unable to run their businesses any longer because the footfall of tourists coming out of the all-inclusives is so low.

All-inclusives can alienate tourists from the destination they are visiting and the people who live there. This can hamper positive cultural exchange, while allowing resentment to build amongst local people who are blocked from being able to benefit from the tourism economy. This can lead to a vicious circle, in which tourism harassment levels increase - itself an issue that is frequently capitalised upon by the hotels themselves - which in turn further deters people from leaving the hotels.

Thomsons took another significant step that furthered its focus on information in May 1998, when it spun off Thomson Travel through a public offering that generated net proceeds of US$2 billion. As a result, more than eighty-three per cent of 1998 revenues were derived from

Managing Director Peter Buckingham. *(Britannia Airways)*

Thomson's information businesses.

Perhaps even more dramatically, given the company's historical roots, Thomson announced in mid-February 2000 that it intended to sell off all its remaining newspaper interests, with the exception of the flagship *Globe and Mail*. Thomson Newspapers included fifty-five daily newspapers and more than seventy-five non-daily newspapers and generated US $810 million in 1999 revenues. Proceeds from the sale--perhaps as much as US $2.5 billion - were expected to be used to bolster Thomson's growing portfolio of electronic databases further. Acquisitions remained a key company strategy, as evidenced by the March 2000 purchase of the Prometric business of Sylvan Learning Systems Inc. for US $775 million. Prometric, which became part of Thomson Learning, was a global leader in computer-based testing and assessment services. Prometric was a prime example of the type of company Thomson intended to pursue: one that was electronic and global - not print and local.

The future of Thomson - that of an electronic information powerhouse - seemed clear at the beginning of the 21st century. By 2005 the company aimed to generate eighty per cent of its revenue from the electronic distribution of information (compared to the fifty per cent figure of early 2000) and, more specifically, between thirty-five and fifty per cent from the delivery of data and services over the Internet. Only seven per cent of overall revenues were Internet-based in early 2000. The company was spending US $600 million per year on technology and the creation of Web platforms for Internet delivery. To achieve its ambitious Internet growth, however, Thomson would need to rely on increased penetration of high-speed Internet hookups in businesses and homes-- mainly because the company's databases were typically on the broad side. Another issue for Thomson in the new century was the preparation for a leadership transition. That issue was at least partially resolved in May 2000, when Chairman Kenneth R. Thomson announced his decision to retire within two years. The septuagenarian leader requested of the board that they consider his son David Thomson and a fellow director, to be his replacement. Another Thomson heir, David's brother Peter was also being groomed for executive office in the coming years.

In 1998 Britannia Airways was the world's leading holiday airline; from 1999 to 2001 it maintained position as number one airline for on-time departures. During the summer season, it operated more than thirty thousand flights from the UK and the Nordic region to eighteen different countries, carrying millions of passengers to the sun. In 2000 the number exceeded ten million for the first time.

It became a challenge for the airline that regularly received awards and praise to see that every passenger felt that his or her holiday really did start at the departure airport, and ended in a relaxed style on return to the UK. The 'comfort factor' was achieved by hard work, intelligence and common sense, and the need constantly to look ahead to ways of improving matters. A passenger charter announced in January 2002 by the Vice-President of the European Commission (EC) Loyola de Palacio, intended to improve air passenger rights, came as no surprise to Britannia, which had long championed those rights and, genuinely, puts the passenger first

Charles Gurassa, at the time Executive Chairman TUI Northern Europe and Preussage Airlines, promoting the 'World of TUI' image. *(Britannia Airways)*

Michael Frenzel was the Chief Executive Officer of TUI AG from 1994 to 2013.

in its policies.

As Madame de Palacio told the media at the time 'Too many Europeans experienced a bad surprise when checking in for their flight. We want to cut the number of passengers who suffer from denied boarding; our proposals will make this practice much less common. We want to protect passengers against cancellations of flights for which operators are responsible, particularly when unexpected and made at a late stage. Strengthening the rights of passengers will help restore their confidence in air travel'.

At that time, non-scheduled flights, including package holiday flights, were excluded from the air passenger rights but Loyola de Palacio, who was in charge of energy and transport, wanted to see these airlines included in the new reinforced regulations.

Madame de Palacio was looking to be the consumers' champion for air travel. She meant all modes of air travel, whether it be scheduled, chartered, domestic or international. Her plan included being able to deliver the right prices, the proper fare structure, the right information ahead of travelling, dealing with delays and a whole variety of matters affecting the passenger.

Many of the EC proposals were already in place with Britannia, who regarded their 'complaint ratio' as being minimal. After all, they were carrying over eight million passengers, and there was inevitably the chance of upsetting them either outbound or inbound flight. Including the minor problems, Britannia stated that their complaint ratio was better than one in seven hundred.

Part of this was due to the fact that there were integrated customer services with Thomson and Lunn Poly to become a seamless group operation, which meant communication was much better, particularly as far as the customer is concerned. If, for instance, there had been a problem in the shop with selling the holiday, Lunn Poly could ask Britannia to add a little touch with a bottle of champagne on board or some other service which would show the customer that the group recognised there had been a difficulty. If there was a problem on the post-departure side, a policy was in place to deal with each complaint as an individual matter. Customers became more discerning and knew what to expect, and they did not want to be brushed off.

In 2000, Thomson Travel Group, and thereby Britannia Airways, were acquired by Preussag AG (TUI Group) of Germany. As part of a wider reorganisation of TUI's UK operations in September 2004, it was announced that Britannia would be rebranded as Thomsonfly. The aircraft of this airline carried the Thomson colours and logo while Thomsonfly became the trading name of Britannia Airways. On 1 November 2005, the legal name of the company was changed from Britannia Airways Limited to Thomsonfly Limited. Thomsonfly later merged with First Choice Airways and was renamed Thomson Airways, retaining the previous logo and colours.

Kevin Hatton, then 55, had just retired from British Airways Cargo, moving to Florida with his wife. Shortly before retirement, he was called by Charles Gurassa, Executive Chairman TUI Northern Europe and Preussag Airlines, who mentioned the possibility of some potential opportunities at his group, but Hatton declined any offer. Gurassa did not give up, and contacted Hatton again, telling him that Thomson was now owned by Preussag and there would be a vacancy at Britannia Airways and was he interested? Hatton consulted his family, then returned to Europe and met with Gurassa and Dr Frenzel, the Chairman of Preussag and eventually joined the airline in January 2001 and took over as Managing Director from Peter Buckingham, who had taken over from Roger Burnell as Britannia's Managing Director in July 1998. He moved to the Thomson headquarters, where he became Head of Group Integration. Kevin Hatton knew Britannia well from his work in BA and other airlines.

Dr Michael Frenzel was born in Leipzig, at the time in Russian-occupied Germany, on 2 March 1947. When aged nine, he escaped to West Germany with his father and lived in a refugee camp for three years. He studied law at the Ruhr University Bochum, and worked at the university as a scientific assistant, and graduated with a doctoral degree in law.

He joined Westdeutsche Landesbank in 1981, in Düsseldorf. He was promoted to manager of the Industrial Holdings Department in 1983 then the Equity Holdings Division in 1985. There he managed holdings in banking and real estate. In 1988 Frenzel joined Preussag AG as an executive responsible for trading and logistics. He was promoted to the position

Sometimes the requirements of maintenance and spare-part availablility resulted in some strange colour-scheme combinations. Here a 757, in the full Thomsonfly scheme but also the legend 'Operated by Britannia Airways' wears an 'old' nosecone. *(Matt Black Collection)*

Below 767-300 G-OBYD in TUI at Manchester. *(Richard Vandervord)*

Britannia staff meet Her Royal Highness Queen Elizabeth during the opening ceremony for the new terminal at Luton. *(Britannia Airways)*

of chief executive officer in January 1994. During his time as chief executive, Frenzel transformed the company from an industrial conglomerate into a travel services company. He oversaw Preussag's acquisition of Hapag-Lloyd in 1997 then, in 2000, he oversaw Preussag's £1.8 billion takeover of Thomson Travel. The company also acquired the German tourism operator TUI in 1998 and the French firm Nouvelles Frontières. After these acquisitions, Preussag was Europe's leading tourism operator. In July 2002, Preussag was rebranded as TUI, short for Touristik Union International, the name of a subsidiary it had bought previously.

Frenzel retired from TUI in February 2013, and was succeeded by Friedrich Joussen. He became a World Travel and Tourism Council ambassador in 2018.

Amongst its peer group Britannia had an outstanding reputation, but Kevin Hatton noticed the differences between charter and scheduled operations in terms of operational and professional abilities.

Britannia had to make best use of the assets, having three rotations a day on short-haul operations and items like that, but Britannia did not cut corners. In the hangars, on the flight deck, or with the Cabin Crew, it was obvious that the standards were very high indeed.

The major challenge was how Britannia reacted in times of disruption. Unlike scheduled airlines in adversity, they could not cancel flights; Britannia had an obligation to bring customers back.

That reality hit home in June and July 2001, when there was a coach drivers' strike in the Balearic Islands. Some of the scheduled airlines just cancelled their flights, but unlike them, Britannia could not just give the tickets back to their passengers and tell them

to sort their own problems out. Some passengers decided not to fly out in the first place and needed information and help in dealing with their insurance matters. There had to be liaison with Lunn-Poly, the resorts, via an incident room at Thomson and the incident room at Britannia.

Britannia put as many staff as they could out to airports in the UK to deal with passengers. Britannia people abandoned their normal jobs to help out. Compared with the competitors, the airline went that bit further to help and although the passengers were upset by delays caused by the strike, they did appreciate that the staff were there and did not merely rely on handling agents at the airports to sort out the problems.

A new 'pocket rocket' - and more changes
A temporary move away from its nearly 30-year Boeing tradition came when Britannia leased three Airbus A320s from TransAer. The 180-seaters brought back a chance to compete for smaller-capacity charters that had been lost by the 737 fleet disposals. Any hopes in Toulouse for further Airbus orders from Britannia were dashed when the airline instead placed a $270-million order for five Boeing 737-800s.

The Boeing 737 Next Generation, commonly abbreviated as 737NG, or 737 NextGen, is the -600/-700/-800/-900 series of the 737 airliner. It was the third generation derivative of the basic design and follows the 737 concept that can be traced back to the mid-1960s. They are short-to-medium-range narrow-body jet airliners powered by two engines. Produced since 1996 by Boeing Commercial Airplanes, the 737NG series included four variants and could seat between 110 and 210 passengers.

737-800 SE-DZN at Luton just on the point of transfer to Britannia AB. *(Kaz Ale Collection)*

The Boeing 737-800 was a stretched version of the 737-700. It replaced the 737-400. The Boeing 737-800 competes with the Airbus A320. It seats 162 passengers in a two-class layout or 189 passengers in a one-class layout. The 737–800 was launched by Hapag-Lloyd Flug (laterTUIfly) in 1994 and entered service in 1998.

Following Boeing's merger with McDonnell Douglas, the 737-800 also filled the gap left by Boeing's decision to discontinue the McDonnell Douglas MD-80 and MD-90 aircraft.

Britannia already had experience of the next generation 737-800, for its Scandinavian subsidiary Britannia AB had been flying one that had been leased from Sterling European Airways in 1998.

In October 2004 Britannia Airways' parent, TUI UK announced that it was to shed 800 jobs across its businesses under a reorganisation that would see its Thomsonfly low-cost carrier brand applied to the entire UK-based fleet.

The Thomsonfly brand had been launched in 2004 with four Boeing 737-500s at Coventry airport as a spin-off from in-house charter carrier Britannia. TUI began the process of dropping the Britannia name from its UK charter fleet and replacing it with Thomson and then began rebranding it as Thomsonfly in November 2004.

TUI claimed it already had seat-only customers on its charter flights and the move to roll out the Thomsonfly name across its whole fleet was designed to make it easier for customers to see the entire flight network available.

TUI said that it would invest in its fleet, through a refurbishment programme and new aircraft, but did not give details - Thomsonfly management had previously outlined plans to grow the carrier's 737 fleet quickly. However, consolidation across the business saw about 800 jobs - around eight per cent of its UK-based workforce - eliminated.

'This is about reshaping the business so we can compete in a much more competitive environment,' said TUI UK managing director Peter Rothwell. 'We want to grow and take advantage of new distribution channels, particularly the internet, which is growing fast for TUI UK.'

By this point Britannia was part of the TUI airline group, which included significant partner Hapag-Lloyd and Hapag-Lloyd Express in Germany, as well as Corsair in France, Britannia Airways Sweden and TUI Airlines Belgium.

A coming together.

So it was that the diverse fleets started to merge under the TUI name. TUI Airways became the first UK airline to take delivery of Boeing 787s, receiving the first aircraft in May 2013. Passenger services with the aircraft began on 21 June 2013 with a flight between London Gatwick and Menorca. Also in 2013, the parent group TUI Travel, now known as TUI Group, ordered seventy Boeing 737 MAX for delivery to group airlines.

On 13 May 2015, it was announced by the TUI Group that all five of TUI's airline subsidiaries would be named TUI while keeping their separate Air Operators Certificates, a process taking over three years to complete. TUI Airways was the last airline to be completed in late 2017. The rebrand began in mid-2016, with the addition of the new 'TUI' titles to its fleet.

The 'old lady in a wheelchair' is long gone as is the famous shepherds pie. The flight code 'BY' still survives, but that's about all that is left - all good things, it seems, come to an end!

Chapter 13

Memories...

The story does not quite end there however. The Britannia Airways Retired Staff Association (BARSA), 'The 'Real' Britannia Airways 1964-2005' Facebook page and a number of other groups and organisations are doing all they can to keep the memory of the airline alive.

This small chapters shows memories, events and contacts that help to keep the airline alive, along with some of the stories..

Hello

I was a Luton based member of the cabin crew, March 1986-September 1993, flying on the 737-200, 767 and 757. Many happy memories of places, people, happenings.

I always felt there was something different and unique about Britannia. For starters, I've yet to see a more aesthetically pleasing livery. But there was such a warm atmosphere amongst flight crew (and ground staff), that it did feel like a family. However, having never worked for any other charter airline, I have no different experience to

compare it with! I did, however, spend six months or so working for debonair at Luton, as cabin staff interviewer and trainer, starting well before the airline took delivery of its first aeroplane. There certainly wasn't the same dynamic there, and if ever a business model was bound to fail, it was the cut-price with frills model employed at debonair. Flying around Europe all but empty tells its own story, but hidden in the background was a cabin services department which suffered from autocratic and demotivating management. I locked horns with the demonic cabin services manager... and she won. I was sacked!

Much happier stories from Britannia. Wonderful times, beautiful people, wonderful travels worldwide.
John Lapwood

Hi

I was with Britannia from March 1976 to March 1979 from memory. I was based at Luton but, in

The 2019 get-together. *(Kas Ale)*

general, I flew out of Gatwick, East Midlands, Cardiff, Manchester, Glasgow, etc.
Tina Theodorou.

Hi
I joined Britannia in May 1987 as a 737-200 First Officer and went through the ranks, becoming 757/767 F/O, Training First Officer, Technical First Officer, Technical Development Pilot, Captain, Training Captain, Pilot Manager and finally Fleet Manager 757/767. I retired after converting onto the 737-800, in 2015. I was based at Luton, Birmingham and Cardiff over the years.

As Technical Development Pilot in the 1990's I was heavily involved in the introduction of the 767-300 into service, TCAS and RVSM along with other technical issues. Then the Haj operation when I was a First Officer in 1999, going on to operate as a Captain then Lead Pilot on a number of occasions. As Fleet Manager 757/767 I was heavily involved in fuel saving measures, alignment of our procedures with our German, Scandinavian and Dutch sister airlines, integration with First Choice Airlines and many other issues.
John McMillan

Hello
I was a dual licensed engineer Airframes and Engines for Brits at Luton from 1983 to 1999 working almost entirely in heavy maintenance.

I was also the convener for the AEU for 3 or 4 years.
Chris Goodwin

Chapter 14

Fleet List

What appears here is the known fleet list of Euravia, Britannia Airways, Britannia Airways Gmbh, Britannia Airways AB and Orion Airways.

Please note, from the mid-1990s onwards, due to the movement of aircraft around the different companies within the Thomson Group and later the organisations that made up the TUI conglomerate, it has not been possible to guarantee with any degree of accuracy those movements and dates. They have, however, been included here for completeness.

Lockheed Constellation

Regn	C/N	Reg Date	Variant Remarks
G-AHEL	1977	L-049E	Previously with Trans-European Airways from 25.08.61. To Euravia Ltd 02.05.63. To Britannia Airways 16.08.64. To Britair East Africa 11.64. Scrapped at Shannon, Ireland 05.66.
G-AHEN	1980	L-049D	Previously registered to Universal Sky Tours from 13.02.62. To Euravia Ltd 02.05.63. To Britannia Airways 16.08.64. Scrapped at Luton 04.65.
G-ALAK	2548	L-749A	Previously registered to Skyways Ltd from 06.59. To Euravia 01.09.62. To Britannia Airways 16.08.64. To ACE Freighters 06.08.65. To Aviation Charter Enterprises, Crawley 14.09.65. To USA 8.08.67
G-ALAL	2549	L-749A	Previously registered to Skyways Ltd from 07.59. To Euravia 01.09.62. To Britannia Airways 16.08.64. To Aviation Charter Enterprises, Crawley 14.02.65. To USA 28.08.67
G-AMUP	2051	L-049E	Previously with Trans-European Airways. To Euravia Ltd 02.05.63. To Britannia Airways 16.08.64. Scrapped at Luton 08.65.
G-AMUR	2565	L-749A	Previously registered to Skyways Ltd from 07.59. To Euravia 01.09.62. To Britannia Airways 16.08.64. Leased to ACE Freighters 07.65 to 14.09.66. To Nelson C Puente as N1949 28.02.67.
G-ARVP	1967	L-149D	Previously registered to Universal Sky Tours from 13.02.62. To Euravia Ltd 02.05.63. To Britannia Airways 16.08.64. Scrapped at Luton 04.65.
G-ARXE	1965	L-149	Previously registered to Universal Sky Tours from 13.02.62. To Euravia Ltd 02.05.63. Leased to Skyways Ltd. To Britannia Airways 16.08.64 Scrapped at Luton 05.65.

One of Euravia's Constellations, thought to have been photographed at Heathrow. *(Kaz Ale Collection)*

Britannia G-ANBA taxies in from another trip. *(Kaz Ale Collection)*

Bristol Britannia

Regn	C/N	Variant	Remarks
G-ANBA	12902	102	Leased by Britannia Airways from BOAC from 25.03.65. Withdrawn from use at Luton and scrapped 11.69.
G-ANBB	12903	102	Leased by Britannia Airways from BOAC from 18.11.64. Crashed Ljublijana 01.09.66.
G-ANBD	12905	102	Leased by Britannia Airways from BKS Air Transport 1968. Returned.
G-ANBE	12906	102	Leased by Britannia Airways from BOAC from 01.02.66. Withdrawn from use at Luton 12.70. Scrapped 07.72.
G-ANBF	12907	102	Leased by Britannia Airways from BOAC from 12.02.65. Withdrawn from use at Luton 10.69 and scrapped 04.70.
G-ANBI	12910	102	Leased by Britannia Airways from BOAC from 03.02.66. Withdrawn from use at Luton and scrapped 10.69.
G-ANBJ	12911	102	To Britannia Airways from BOAC 29.10.70. Withdrawn from use at Luton 10.70 and scrapped 02.71.
G-ANBL	12913	102	To Britannia Airways from BOAC from 29.07.70. Withdrawn from use at Luton 12.70 and scrapped 07.72.
G-ANBN	12915	102	Leased by Britannia Airways from Laker Airways 1968. Returned.
G-ANBO	12916	102	To Britannia Airways from BOAC from 16.03.70. Withdrawn from use at Luton 10.70 and scrapped 05.71.

Boeing 707

Regn	C/N	Variant	Remarks
G-AYEX	19417	-355C	From British Caledonian Airways. Ret 16.3.73
G-AYSI	18707	-373C	Leased from GATX 1971-1973

Boeing 720

Regn	C/N	Variant	Remarks
TF-VLC	18820	049B	Leased from Eagle Air during 1979.

Not the best of pictures, but interesting to say the least! the apron at Luton in the mid-1960s. *(Kaz Ale Collection)*

The leased Boeing 720 TF-VLC at Luton during 1979. *(Kaz Ale Collection)*

Boeing 737-200 series

Regn	C/N	Variant	Remarks
G-AVRL	19709	-204	Obtained new 07.07.68. Named *Sir Earnest Shackleton*. To Aerolineas Argentinas 24.1.70, returned 28.4.1970. To Yemen Airways 11.12.73, returned 01.74. To Presidential Airways 3.4.86 as N311XV.
G-AVRM	19710	-204	Obtained new 09.08.68. Named *James Watt*. To Far Eastern Air Transport as B-2605 26.11.76, returned 15.4.77. To Far Eastern Air Transport as B-2605 03.11.77, returned 24.04.78. To Presidential Airways 01.05.86 as N313XV.
G-AVRN	19711	-204	Obtained new 08.04.69. Named *Captain James Cook*. To Transavia Holland 01.12.74 as PH-TVG, returned 25.03.75. To First Security Bank of Utah 27.10.93 as N172PL.
G-AVRO	19712	-204	Obtained new 28.04.69. Named *Sir Francis Drake*. To Far Eastern Air Transport 21.11.76 as B2605, returned 15.04.77. To Far Eastern Air Transport 03.11.77, returned 24.04.78. To Presidential Airways 01.05.86 as N313XV.
G-AWSY	20236	-204	Obtained new 12.05.69. Named *General James Wolfe*. Leased to Yemen Airways 11.75, returned 01.76. To Polaris Aircraft Leasing Corp as N173PL 08.10.93.
G-AXNA	20282	-204C	Obtained new 17.03.70. Named *Robert Clive of India*. Leased to Transavia as PH-TVF 31.09.74, returned 08.05.75. To TAT as F-GGPC 04.10.90.

Caught in a rainbow, with a thunderstorm backdrop are these two Britannia 737-200s. *(Kaz Ale Collection)*

G-AVRL arrives from Seattle in July 1968. *(Kaz Ale Collection)*

G-AXNB	20389	-204C	Obtained new 17.04.70. Named *Charles Darwin*, previously *City of Birminham*. To TAT 01.02.90.
G-AXNC	20417	-204	Obtained new 14.05.70. Named *Isambard Kingdom Brunel*, also reported *Sir Frederick Handley Page*. To Altanata
G-AZNZ	19074	-222	Obtained from United Airlines 01.03.72. Named *Henry Hudson*, previously *City of Nottingham*. To GPA/America West 01.04.85
G-BADP	20632	-204Adv	Obtained new 04.01.73. Named *Sir Arthur Whitten Brown*. Leased to Air New Zealand 03.04.90, to Aloha Airlines 23.10.90, returned 28.03.91. Returned to Boeing 2.92.
G-BADR	20633	-204Adv	Obtained new 1.02.72. Named *Captain Robert Falcon Scott*. Leased to Aloha Airlines 15.11.89, leased to COPA Panama 01.10.91 returned 10.91. Returned to Boeing 12.91
G-BAZG	20806	-204Adv	Obtained new 15.01.74. Named *Florence Nightingale*. Leased to Yemen Airways 1974, returned 26.02.75. Leased to Yemen Airways 11.75, returned 02.76. To COPA Panama as HP1195CM 28.09.91
G-BAZH	20807	-204Adv	Obtained new 08.02.74. Named *Sir Frederick Handley Page* also reported *Isambard Kingdom Brunel*. To Polaris Aircraft Leasing Corp 12.11.88, returned 12.11.93. To Ambassador Airways 27.03.94. To Sabre Airways as G-BSEB 15.12.94.

November Alpha, *Robert Clive of India*, with a mountainous backdrop. *(Kaz Ale Collection)*

G-BAZI	20808	-204Adv	Obtained new 14.02.74. Named *Sir Walter Raleigh*. To Guiness Peat Aviation 28.03.85.
G-BECG	21335	-204Adv	Obtained new 13.04.77. Named *Amy Johnson*. To Polaris Aircraft Leasing Corp 29.06.88, withdrawn from use 04.11.93. To GB Leisure.
G-BECG	21335	204	Obtained new 31.03.77. Withdrawn from use 04.11.94. To GB Leisure 14.02.94.
G-BECH	21336	-204Adv	Obtained new 27.04.77. Named *Viscount Montgomery of Alamein*. To Polaris Aircraft Leasing Corp 29.06.88. Withdrawn from use 04.11.94. To GB Leisure 14.02.94.
G-BFVA	21693	204Adv	Obtained new 20.11.78. Named *Sir John Alcock*. Leased to COPA 02.11.89, returned 08.05.90. To COPA as HP-1163CN 02.08.90.
G-BFVB	21694	204Adv	Obtained new 28.11.78. Named *Sir Thomas Sopwith*. Leased to Nordair 01.05.85, returned 30.04.86. To Polaris Aircraft Leasing Corp 29.06.88. To Ambassador Airways 28.03.94.
G-BGFS	21359	-2P6	Leased in aircraft from Gulf Air 13.09.77 registered A40-BG, returned 01.80.
G-BGNW	21131	-219	Leased in aircraft from TEA (ex-OO-TEJ) 04.79, Named *George Stephenson*. Returned to International Lease and Finance Corp 11.06.90
G-BGYJ	22057	204	Obtained new 07.01.80. Named *Sir Barnes Wallis*. Leased to Royal Brunei Airways 11.81. Leased to Midway Express. Leased to Transmed 10.12.89, returned 30.04.90. To Ryanair 30.03.94.
G-BGYK	22058	204	Obtained new 14.01.80. Named *R J Mitchell*. Leased to Transmed 10.12.89, leased to Aloha Airlines 09.02.90. Leased to VASP as PP-SRW 08.12.90, returned to Britannia 29.02.92. To Ryanair as EI-CJG 25.03.94.
G-BGYL	22059	204	Obtained new 18.02.80, Named *Jean Batten*. Leased to COPA Panama 17.04.92. W/O 07.06.92 when crashed during a thunderstrom.
G-BHWE	22364	204	Obtained new 09.09.80. Namwed *Sir Sydney Camm*. Leased to British Airtours 01.04.85, returned 25.03.87 To ILFC/Air New Zealand 10.02.94.
G-BHWF	22365	204	Obtained new 01.12.80. Named *Lord Brabazon of Tara*. Leased to Air New Zealand 19.01.88. Returned 30.04.88. To Air New Zealand 14.12.93.
G-BJBJ	22632	2T5	Originally delivered to Orion Airways 22.03.82. Leased to America West Airlines 11.11.86, returned 04.04.87. To Guiness Peat Aviation/Britannia Airways 15.04.87, returned to GPA 31.10.87.
G-BJCT	22638	204	Obtained new 06.04.82. Named *Hon C S Rolls*. Named Leased to Spantax 01.07.85 as EC-DXK, returned 31.03.86. Leased to Midway Airlines 11.88,then to Euralair 20.10.89 returned 26.04.90. To International Lease and Finance Corp/Air New Zealand 05.11.93
G-BJCU	22639	204	Obtained new 20.04.82. Named *Sir Henry Royce*. Leased to Spantax 01.11.84 as EC-DVE, returned 30.11.85. To Ryanair 17.03.94.
G-BJCV	22640	204.	Obtained new 30.04.82. Named *Viscount Trenchard*. Leased to CP Air 01.11.85 as C-GXCP, returned 30.04.86. Leased to Canadian Airlines as C-GCAU 26.10.87, returned 03.04.88. Leased to Air Sul 31.01.89 as CS-TMA, returned 09.04.90. To Ryanair 21.04.94.
G-BJXJ	22657	219	Obtained from ILFC 01.11.87, returned 14.09.92.

G-BTZF, *Sir Alliott Verdon Roe. (Kaz Ale Collection)*

G-BJZW	22277	296	Leased from Quebecair 01.05.82, returned 5.11.82.
G-BJZW	22516	296	Leased from Quebecair 10.05.82, returned 05.11.82
G-BKBT	20943	SK2C	Leased-in aircraft from Transavia 04.82, previously PH-TVD, returned 30.10.82 Leased in 01.05.84, returned 01.05.85.
G-BKHE	22966	204	Obtained new 11.02.83. Named *Sir Francis Chichester*. Withdrawn from use 09.02.94. To Ryanair.
G-BKHF	22967	204	Obtained new 15.03.83. Re-registered G-BTZF 29.04.91 Named *Sir Alliott Verdon Roe*. To Ryanair 30.03.94.
G-BMMZ	20544	2D6	Leased in aircraft from UAS/Aerolineas Argentinas 27.03.86, returned 18.09.92.
G-BNIA	22737		Obtained on lease from PLUNA 13.04.87, returned 04.11.87.
G-BNYT	21114	275	Leased-in aircraft from GPA 12.04.87, returned 19.03.88.
G-BONM	22738		Obtained on lease from PLUNA 03.05.88, returned 08.11.88.
G-BOSL	22161	2U4	Obtained new on lease from ILFC 17.04.80. Returned off lease 31.10.83. To Dan-Air.
G-BPLA	22906	2K2	Obtained on lease from Transavia 01.05.89, returned 30.03.94.
G-OSLA	22576	2U4	Obtained new 08.05.81. Named *Sir Geoffrey de Havilland*. To International Lease and Finance Corp 1.11.83. To America West Airlines same day.
OO-PLH	20128	-247	Leased-in aircraft from IBL/Air Belgium 01.05.86, returned 28.10.86
PH-TVR	22025	2K2	Leased in aircraft from Transavia 06.81, returned 1892.
TF-VLK	22453	2Q8	Leased from Eagle 21.04.81. Returned 11.81.
TF-VLM	21715	248	Leased-in aircraft from Aer Lingus/Eagle 02.04.82, returnned 10.82. Leased again 22.12.82, returned 31.03.83.

Boeing 737-300 to 800 series

Regn	C/N	Variant	Remarks
G-BLKB	23060	3T5	Obtained new by Orion Airways, 21.12.84. Listed as managed by Britannia Airways 26.01.89. To Morris Internatiional Air 11.04.93 as N753MA.
G-BLKC	23061	3T5	Obtained new by Orion Airways, 04.02.85. Listed as managed by Britannia Airways 26.01.89. To Morris Internatiional Air 14.12.92 as N744MA.
G-BKLD	23062	3T5	Obtained new by Orion Airways, 01.03.85. Listed as managed by Britannia Airways 26.01.89. Leased to Aloha Airlines 13.12.90, returned 30.03.91. To ILFC 13.04.92.

The maintenance area at Luton was always busy. *(Kaz Ale Collection)*

G-BYAW on finals. *(Kaz Ale Collection)*

G-BKLD	23062	3T5	Obtained new by Orion Airways, 01.03.85. Listed as managed by Britannia Airways 26.01.89. Leased to Aloha Airlines 13.12.90, returned 30.03.91. To ILFC 13.04.92.
G-BNRT	23064	3T5	Obtained new by Orion Airways, 14.03.88. Leased to Hispania as EC-213 09.11.88, returned 01.89. Listed as managed by Britannia Airways 26.01.89. Leased to Australian Airlines 26.10.89, returned 29.04.90. To ILFC 7.11.92.
G-BOWR	23401	3Q8	Leased by Orion Airways from Air Belgium 31.10.88. Listed as managed by Britannia Airways 26.01.89. To ILFC 15.01.92.
LN-NOS	23830	33A	Leased from Norway Airlines 28.05.88, returned 11.88.
G-BOLM	23942	3T0	Leased by Orion Airways from Polaris Aircraft Leasing Corp 20.04.88. Listed as managed by Britannia Airways 26.01.89. Sub-leased to Australian Airlines 04.11.89, returned 29.04.90. Returned to Polaris Aircraft Leasing Corp 27.10.90.
G-THOC	24694	59D	Leased from Guiness Peat Aviation 22.04.04. Operated in ThomsonFly colours. To Argentina 29.05.08.
G-THOD	24695	59D	Leased from Guiness Peat Aviation 30.06.04. Operated in ThomsonFly colours. To Aeroflot 18.07.08
OO-TUM	24750	4B3	TUI Belgium 26.04.06. Listed as owned by Britannia Airways AB. To Jet4You.com 27.04.07.
G-THOA	24859	59D	Leased 03.03.04. Operated in ThomsonFly colours. To SkyExpress 11.04.07.
G-THOB	24928	59B	Leased 17.03.04. Operated in ThomsonFly colours. To SkyExpress 17.05.07.
G-THOE	26313	8Q8	Leased 09.12.04. Operated in ThomsonFly colours. To Air New Zealand 03.11.07
G-THOF	26314	8Q8	Leased 09.12.04. Operated in ThomsonFly colours. To AVE 08.06.09.
D-AHFH	27983	8K5(W)	Leased from Hapag-Lloyd 09.03.99. Returned 01.05.02
OY-SEA	28213	8Q8	Leased 10.06.98 Britannia Airways AB. To Sterling European 30.04.00.
OY-SEB	28214	8Q8	Leased from Sterling European 01.11.99. Returned 30.04.00
SE-DZH	28227	804	Leased from ILFC 15.01.00 by Britannia Airways AB to Britannia Nordic 05.05 to ThomsonFly 17.02.06.
G-CDZH	28227	804	Leased 17.02.06. To Thomson Airways 01.11.08. To Corendon Dutch Airlines 02.05.12.
SE-DZI	28229	804	Leased from ILFC 09.02.00 by Britannia Airways AB. To Britannia Nordic 05.05
G-CDZI	28229	804	To ThomsonFly 26.02.06 to Thomson Airways 01.11.08 to Jet2 25.01.12
SE-DZK	28231	804	Leased from ILFC 18.05.00 by Britannia Airways AB. To Britannia Nordic 05.05. To TUIfly Nordic 04.06.
G-BYNC	30465	804	Britannia Airways. Leased out as PH-AAV, returned 06.11.01. To Britannia Airways AB 07.11.01.
G-BYNB	30466	804	Obtained new 08.04.00.Leased to Britannia Airways AB as PH-ABE

757 G-BYAY lands at Bristol Lulsgate. *(Kaz Ale Collection)*

			08.01.02 later SE-DZM 09.01.02 to HapagFly 02.02.05 as D-ATUB. To ThomsonFly as G-CDZM 23.11.05 to Thomson Airways 01.11.08. To El Al 16.05.12
D-AHFR	30593	8K5(W)	Leased from Hapag-Lloyd 13.12.02. Returned 04.03.
SE-DZN	32903	804	Obtained new by Britannia Airways/Britannia Airways AB 09.05.02. To Britannia Airways ThomsonFly 29.04.05, as G-CDZN. Registered PH-AAW 13.02.06. To Britannia Nordic as SE-DZN 16.02.06. To TUIfly Nordic 04.06.
SE-DZV	32904	804	Obtained new Britannia Airways/Britannia Airways AB 31.03.03. To Britannia Nordic 05.05. To TUIfly Nordic 04.06.To TUIfly as D-ADZV. To TUIfly Nordic 27.10.16. To Jet Time.

Boeing 757

Regn	C/N	Variant	Remarks
G-BTEJ	25085	208	Delivered new to Britannia Airways 23.05.91. To Iceland Air 09.05.93.
G-BXOL	24528	23A	Leased from Sunways Airlines 26.11.97 to Air Holland 09.04.99.
G-BYAC	26962	204	Obtained new 10.04.92. To Istanbul Airlines 10.04.97.
G-BYAD	26963	204	Obtained new 06.02.92. To ThomsomFly 31.10.05 to Thomson Airways 01.11.08. To WFBN 07.12.09.
G-BYAE	26964	204	Obtained new 12.05.92 leased to Iceland Air from 02.11.94 until 21.04.95. To ThomsonFly 31.10.05. To Thomson Airways 01.01.08 to WFBN 03.07.09.
G-BYAF	26266	204	Leased from ILFC new 13.10.93. To Air New Zealand from 02.12.95 until 22.04.96. To ThomsonFly 31.10.05. To FedEx 08.04.08.
G-BYAG	26965	204	Obtained new 22.01.93. Cashed Gerona, Spain 15.09.99.
G-BYAH	26966	204	Obrained new 05.02.93. Leased to Air New Zealand from 25.02.95 until 29.03.95. To ThomsonFly 31.10.05. To Thomson Airways 01.11.08. To Jet2 29.03.11.
G-BYAI	26967	204	Obtained new 01.03.93. To ThomsonFly 31.10.05. To Thomson Airways 01.11.08. To Jet2 11.02.11.
G-BYAJ	25623	28A	Leased new from ILFC 04.03.93. To ThomsonFly 31.10.05. To TUIfly Nordic 29.01.08 as SE-RFO. To Air Finland 31.01.12.
G-BYAK	26267	204	Leased new from ILFC 06.04.93. To ThomsonFly 31.10 .05. To FedEx 08.04.08.
G-BYAL	25626	28A	Leased from new from ILFC 12.05.93. To ThomsonFly 31.10.05. To Thomson Airways 01.11.08. To FedEx 24.05.12.
G-BYAM	23895	2T7	Leased from ILFC 01.03.94. Returned 16.08.99.

G-BYAN	27219	204	Leased new from ILFC 26.01.94. To ThomsonFly 31.10.05. Leased to TUIfly Nordic as SE-RFP from 26.11.07 until 16.05.11. To ThomsonFly as G-OOBR 16.05.11. To PrivatAir 07.06.13.
G-BYAO	27235	204	Obtained new 03.02.94. To ThomsonFly 31.10.05. To Thomson Airways 01.11.08. To Allegiant Air. 14.03.12.
G-BYAP	27236	204	Obtained new 15.02.94. To ThomsonFly 31.10.05. To Thomson Airways 01.11.08. To Allegiant Air 02.04.12.
G-BYAR	27237	204	Obtained new 01.03.94. Leased to Air Holland from 18.07.02 until 05.06.03. To ThomsonFly 31.10.05. To Lithuanian Airlines 28.03.08.
G-BYAS	27238	204	Obtained new 09.03.94. To ThomsonFly 31.10.05. To Thomson Airways 01.11.08. To FedEx 15.06.09.
G-BYAT	27208	204	Leased new from ILFC 21.03.94. Named *Eric Morecambe OBE*. To ThomsonFly 31.10.05. To Thomson Airways 01.11.08. To La Compagnie 04.05.15.
G-BYAU	27220	204	Obtained new 18.05.94. To ThomsonFly 31.10.05. To Thomson Airways 01.11.08.To FedEx18.05.12.
G-BYAW	27234	204	Obtained new 03.04.95. To ThomsonFly 31.10.05. To Thomson Airways 01.11.08. To TUI Airways 02.10.17.
G-BYAX	28834	204	Leased new from ILFC 24.02.99. To ThomsonFly 31.10.05. To Thomson Airways 01.11.08. To Abakan Avia 23.04.14.
G-BYAY	28836	204	Leased new from ILFC 13.04.99. To ThomsonFly 31.10.0. To Thomson Airways 01.11.08. To TUI Airways 02.10.17
G-OAHF	24136	27B	Leased from Air Holland 10.05.91 returned 15.05.96.
G-OAHI	24137	27B	Leased from Air Holland 05.11.90 returned 01.11.91.
G-OAHK	24291	23A	Leased from Air Holland 07.11.90 returned 01.05.92.
SE-DUK	25054	236	Leased Britannia Airways AB 04.98. To Air 2000 09.01.02.
SE-DUL	26151	2YO	Leased by Britannia Airways AB 04.04.98 To Britannia Airways 15.04.00 until 31.10.00. To Arkia 27.04.01.
SE-DUN	22612	225	Leased by Britannia AirwaysAB from Air 2000 04.98. Sub-leased to Britannia Airways 31.07.98 returned 04.99.
SE-DUO	24792	236ER	Leased Britannia AirwaysAB 04.98. To Britannia Airways 20.02.02 as G-CDUO. To ThomsonFly 09.05.05. To Britannia Nordic as SE-DUO 11.10.05. To TUIfly Nordic 01.05.06
SE-DUP	24793	236	To Britannia Airways AB 24.03.98. To Britannia Airways as G-CDUP 30.04.02. To ThomsonFly 01.11.04. To Britannia Airways AB 23.03.05 as SE-DUP. To Britannia Nordic 01.06.05. To TUIfly Nordic 17.03.08. To Jet2.

Boeing 767

Regn	C/N	Variant	Remarks
G-BKPW	22980	204	Obtained new 27.02.84. Named *Earl Mountbatten of Burma*. To Ansett Australia 01.11.95.

Boeing 767 G-OBYJ comes in to London Gatwick *(author's Collection)*

G-BKVZ	22981	204	Obtained new 06.02.84. Named *Sir Winston Churchill*. To Ansett Australia 01.11.95.
G-BLKV	23072	204	Obtained new 11.02.85. To Air New Zeland 21.05.90.
G-BLKW	23250	204ER	Obtained new 25.03.85. To Air New Zealand 21.09.90.
G-BNCW	23807	204	Leased new from ILFC 25.08.87. To Ansett Australia 19.05.96.
G-BNYS	24013	204ER	Obtained new 29.03.88. Leased to AirNew Zealand from 01.01.94 to 27.04.94. To Air Atlanta Icelandic 30.04.01.
G-BOPD	24239	204ER	Obtained new 01.11.88. To Air Atlanta Icelandic/Exel Airways 10.05.01.
G-BPFV	24457	204ER	Obtained new 27.03.89. Leased to TACA from 06.12.94 until 24.01.95. To Air Europa 18.04.96.
G-BRIF	24736	204ER	Obtained new 10.03.90. Leased to Air Holland from 28.10.90 until 08.10.91. Leased to Dinar 31.12.94 until09.03.95. To ThomsonFly 31.10.05. To Silverjet 14.09.07.
G-BRIG	24757	204ER	Obtained new 10.04.90. Leased to TACA 05.11.92 until 28.10.95, then leased to Air New Zealand until returned to Britannia 20.12.95. To ThomsonFly31.10.05. To Silverjet 08.05.07.
G-BXOP	25221	3S1ER	Leased 19.02.98 until 23.03.99. Leased again for Britannia Airways AB 25.10.99 until 01.06.00.
G-BYAA	25058	204ER	Obtained new 23.04.91. Leased to Aruba 01.05.91 to 10.10.91then 19.11.91 to 27.04.92. To ThomsonFly 31.10.05. To Thomson Airways 01.11.08. To WFBN 16.01.09.
G-BYAB	25139	204ER	Obtained new 11.06.91. Named *Brian Johnston CBE MC*. To ThomsonFly 31.10.05. Leased to Garuda Indonesian Airways 01.11.08 until 17.01.09. To WFBN 21.01.09.
G-OBYA	28039	304ER	Obtained new 15.05.96. To Britannia Airways GmbH from 02.11.97 until 11.06.98 as D-AGYA. To Britannia Airways GmbH again 28.10.99 until 25.03.00. To Aeris 01.07.02.
G-OBYB	28040	304ER	Obtained new 17.05.96. Leased to Garuda Indonesian Airways from 05.01.03 to 17.03.03, then leased to Corsair until 08.09.03. Leased again to Garuda Indonesian Airways from 27.12.03 until 05.03.04. To ThomsonFly 01.11.04. To Garuda Indonesian Airways from 12.05 to 17.02.06. To ThomsonFly 10.02.07.To TUIfly Nordic 21.10.13. To Kalitta Air 26.01.16.
G-OBYC	28041	304ER	Obtained new 21.05.96. To Britannia Airways GmbH 17.04.98. as D-AGYC until 14.04.99. To Britannia Airways GmbH again 16.03.00 until 02.11.00. To Garuda Indonesian Airways 06.01.03 until 17.03.03 then Dutchbird 02.12.03 until 27.12.03. To Garuda Indonesian Airways 27.12.03 until 05.03.04 when returned to Britannia Airways. To ThomsonFly 11.04. Leased to Garuda Indonesian Airways 15.12.04 until 26.12.05. Leased again to Garuda Indonesian Airways 23.12.05 until 15.02.06. To Air Italy.
G-OBYD	28042	304ER	Obtained new 04.03.97. Leased to Britannia Airways AB as SE-DZG from 01.05.00 until 24.04.01. To ThomsonFly 31.10.05. Leased to Garuda Indonesian Airways 17.11.05 until 26.01.08. To Thomson Airways 01.11.08. Leased to Garuda Indonesian Airways from 06.11.08 until 20.10.09. To Nordwind Airlines
G-OBYE	28979	304ER	Obtained new 26.02.98. Leaed to Britannia Airways GmbH 30.10.98 until 29.10.99 as D-AGYE. Leased to Garuda Indonesian Airways 02.01.03 until 17.03.03. Leased again to Garuda Indonesian Airways 23.12.03 to 07.03.04. To ThomsonFly 11.04. Leased to Garuda Indonesian Airways 13.12.04 until 27.02.05. Leased again to Garuda Indonesian Airways 11.11.06 until 30.12.09. Leased again to Garuda Indonesian Airways 09.10.10. To Arkefly.
G-OBYF	28208	304ER	Leased new from ILFC 06.06.98. Leased to Britannia Airways GmbH 10.06.98 until 29.04.01 as D-AGYF. Leased to Garuda Indonesian Airways 04.01.03 until 16.03.03. Leased again to Garuda Indonesian Airways 14.12.03 until 06.03.04. To ThomsonFly 11.04. Leased to Garuda Indonesian Airways 11.12.04 until 25.02.05. Leased again to Garuda Indonesian Airways 06.12.05 until 16.02.06. Leased again to Garuda Indonesian Airways 18.11.06 until 03.03.07. Leased again to Garuda

Regn	C/N	Variant	Remarks
			Indonesian Airways 17.11.07 until 09.02.08. To Thomson Airways 01.11.08. To TUIfly 07.11.14.
G-OBYH	28883	304ER	Leased new from ILFC 04.02.99.To Britannia Airways GmbH 22.03.99 as D-AGYH. To Britannia Airways AB 27.04.01 as SE-DZO until returned to Britannia Airways 25.04.02. Leased to Garuda Indonesian Airways 22.12.03 until 08.03.04. To ThomsonFly 31.10.05. Leased to Garuda Indonesian Airways 19.11.05 until 14.02.06. To Thomson Airways 01.11.08. To TUI Airways 02.10.17.
G-OBYI	29138	304ER	Obtained new 01.02.00. Leased to Garuda Indonesian Airways 05.01.03 until 17.03.03. To ThomsonFly 31.10.05. To Thomson Airways 01.11.08. To Arkefly 06.10.10.
GOBYG	29137	304ER	Leased from ILFC 13.01.99. Leased to Garuda Indonesian Airways 28.12.03 returned 08.03.04. To ThomsonFly 11.04 until 30.11.05 when leased to Garuda Indonesian Airways until 28.02.05. Leased again to Garuda Indonesian Airways 12.05 until 13.02.06. To Thomson Airways 01.11.08. To TUI 07.11.15.
GOBYJ	29384	304ER	Obtained new 19.02.00. Leased to Garuda Indonesian Airways 06.01.03 until 16.03.03. To ThomsonFly 31.10.05. To Thomson Airways 01.11.08. To Arkefly 04.04.11.
VH-NOE	25535	33AER	Used by Britannia Airways GmbH from 02.00 until 07.05.00.
ZK-NBJ	23250	200	Leased from Air New Zealand 28.04.97 until 3.11.97.

Airbus A320

Regn	C/N	Variant	Remarks
EI-TLE	429	231	Leased from TransAer 30.04.99 to 08.12.99
EI-TLF	476	231	Leased from TransAer 01.05.88 to 30.11.88, then again from 30.04.99 to 05.11.99
EI-TLH	427	231	Leased from TransAer 28.04.98 to 12.11.98.
EI-TLJ	257	231	Leased from TransAer 01.05.98 to 22.11.98
EI-TLO	728	232	Leased from TransAer 30.04.99 to 05.11.99, then again 01.05.00 to 12.12.00.
EI-TLR	414	231	Leased from TransAer 27.04.99 to 03.10.99

Cessna 421 Golden Eagle

Regn	C/N	Variant	Remarks
G-BRIT	421C-0046		Obtained from Rogers Aviation, Bedford 13.07.78. To Chaseside Holding Ltd Exeter 01.07.1987.

Britannia Airways Flying Club

Regn	Serial No.	Maker - Type
G-BTNT	28-7615401	PIPER PA-28-151
G-ATHR	28-2343	PIPER PA-28-180
G-OBAL	24-1601	MOONEY M20J
G-OIBO	28-3794	PIPER PA-28-180
G-BNMB	28-7615369	PIPER PA-28-151
G-CBAL	28-8116087	PIPER PA-28-161

Bibliography

Britannia Airways had a myriad of in-flight magazines and staff newspapers, many of which have been called upon to gather information for this book. Most of the known in-flights have been located and used from a period 1965 to 2001. Likewise, SkyTours and Thomson Travel Group holiday brochures have been consulted and used where appropriate. There are far too many to list individually.

Staff magazines and newspapers include *Britannia Off Chocks, the magazine for Britannia Airways Cabin Staff* - editions 1-42.
Britannia News - assorted
Britannia Briefing - editions 1 through 150

Britannia Airways Fact Sheet - assorted
Britannia Airwaves: the newsmagazine for Britannia Employees.
Either as internal documents or corporately sponsored publications, there have been several titles:
Flying to the Sun by Geoffrey Cuthbert.
A Chartered Success by Ian Ormes.
Flying with Confidence by Dr Alan H Roscoe.
Flight Plan for the 1990s. - internal document.

Numerous articles have appeared in the specialist aviation media over the years, including:
Aircraft Illustrated, Airliners, Air International, Flight International and *Aviation News.*

Kas Ale's view of Luton from a Britannia Airways Flying Club' Piper. *(Kaz Ale)*

Index